PASIFIKA BLACK

T0326945

BLACK POWER SERIES

General Editors: Ibram X. Kendi and Ashley D. Farmer

Fight the Power: African Americans and the Long History of Police Brutality in New York City
Clarence Taylor

Pasifika Black: Oceania, Anti-colonialism, and the African World
Quito Swan

Pasifika Black

Oceania, Anti-colonialism, and the African World

Quito Swan

NEW YORK UNIVERSITY PRESS

New York

NEW YORK UNIVERSITY PRESS
New York
www.nyupress.org

References to Internet websites (URLs) were accurate at the time of writing. Neither the author nor New York University Press is responsible for URLs that may have expired or changed since the manuscript was prepared.

Library of Congress Cataloging-in-Publication Data
Names: Swan, Quito, author.
Title: Pasifika Black : Oceania, anti-colonialism, and the African world / Quito Swan.
Other titles: Oceania, anti-colonialism, and the African world Description: New York : New York University Press, [2022] | Series: Black power series | Includes bibliographical references and index.
Identifiers: LCCN 2021031267 | ISBN 9781479885084 (hardback) | ISBN 9781479835263 (paperback) |ISBN 9781479867929 (ebook) | ISBN 9781479889334 (ebook other)
Subjects: LCSH: Melanesia—Politics and government—20th century. | Decolonization—Melanesia—History. | Black nationalism—Melanesia. | Black power—Melanesia. | Blacks—Melanesia—Social conditions. | African diaspora—History—20th century. | Pan-Africanism.
Classification: LCC DU29 .S93 2022 | DDC 995—dc23/eng/20211214
LC record available at https://lccn.loc.gov/2021031267

New York University Press books are printed on acid-free paper, and their binding materials are chosen for strength and durability. We strive to use environmentally responsible suppliers and materials to the greatest extent possible in publishing our books.

Manufactured in the United States of America

10 9 8 7 6 5 4 3

Also available as an ebook

Dedicated to the freedom struggles of Oceania

Members of Aboriginal and Torres Strait Islander communities are advised that this book contains names and images of deceased people.

CONTENTS

ILLUSTRATIONS

Introduction

Robert Nestor Marley's October 1979 album *Survival* is a pulsating anthem of pan-Africanism that commemorates global Africa's survival of slavery, colonialism, and racism. Its cover art features quotes from Marcus Garvey, photographs of Ethiopia's Haile Selassie, and the troubling image of a slave ship ruthlessly packed with Black human cargo. Designed by Jamaican graphic artist Neville Garrick, the front cover features the national flags of forty-eight African nations and only one country from outside the geographic continent of Africa—Papua New Guinea. In April 1979 Garrick traveled with the Wailers to Australia and Aotearoa (New Zealand) on their *Survival* tour. In Aotearoa, the group grounded with indigenous Rastafari leaders Miriama Rauhihi-Ness and Tigilau Ness, who had been cornerstone members of the Polynesian Panther Party. Perhaps these exchanges led Garrick to perceive Papua New Guinea, the largest country in Melanesia, as being a nation of Black survival. Regardless, this is a powerful signifier of how the modern African Diaspora—through travel, grassroots organizing, print media, and berths of politics and culture—has historically engaged Oceania as a Black Pacific.[1]

This marks the essence of this book, *Pasifika Black*, which explores the relationships between Black internationalism, Oceania, and decolonization. It charts how Pacific movements in their diverse fights for self-determination from French, British, US, Indonesian, and Australian colonialisms embraced Africana freedom struggles. The book's protagonists include playwrights, visual artists, environmental activists, martyrs, religious leaders, musicians, revolutionaries, students, political prisoners, and poets who carried the banners, books, and bibles of Black Power, Negritude, the Nuclear Free and Independent Pacific movement, Black liberation theology, pan-Africanism, and the Pacific Women's Conference across the Black world. *Pasifika Black* maps the Black internationalist imaginations, radical cartographies, and gendered geographies of these women and men across the universities, water-ways, reservations, nakamals, plantations, villages, harbors, churches, and concrete jungles of the European-imposed boundaries of Melanesia, Polynesia, and Micronesia. In doing so, it shows how their efforts linked Black metropoles across Suva, Brisbane, Harlem, Paris, Lagos, Tripoli, and Dakar.

The book is primarily focused on Melanesia, which etymologically means "islands of Black people." At the time of writing, Melanesia today refers to some 11 million people, 2,000 islands, 1,300 languages, and 386,000 square miles of land across the waters of Vanuatu, Papua New Guinea, the Solomon Islands, West Papua, Fiji, and New Caledonia. Excluding Australia and its 750,000 individuals of Aboriginal descent, who make up 3 percent of the country's population of 25.5 million, Melanesia is demographically the largest subregion of the rest of Oceania's 17.2 million inhabitants. Home to over 70 percent of persons in the subregion, Papua New Guinea's population of 9 million stands in stark contrast to New Zealand's 4.8 million (of which some 900,000 are Māori), Polynesia's total population of some 685,000, Micronesia's 550,000, Hawai'i's 150,000 indigenous persons, and the rest of Melanesia's 2.1 million. *Numbers don't lie, but misrepresentations do*—Europe's racist, sexist, and scientific framings of race, gender, and phenotype have globally projected indigenous Oceania as being principally Polynesian while only peripherally Melanesian. As such, Melanesia's historic centrality to the region from an ethnic, ecological, cultural, and geopolitical perspective is often unrecognized. But in today's world of racial modernity, where the sun never sets on the blazing banner of Black Lives Matter, when countries like Australia have a shameful record on Black deaths while in police custody, is it possible to map Oceania *without* engaging a Black Pacific?[2]

The Black Pacific, the Black Atlantic, and the Black Diaspora

In 1976 Australian Aboriginal poet Oodgeroo Noonuccal (Kath Walker) gave the keynote lecture at the First Independent Papua New Guinea Writers' Conference, where she asked, "Is it too much to hope that before long, the Black artists of the Pacific, will meet yearly to celebrate in a Black Pacific Festival of Arts? Where we can learn from each other?"[3] Noonuccal's piercing query reflects this book's use of the Black Pacific in relation to the political experiences of indigenous communities of Oceania that have been racially colonized as being Black and Brown. However, the Black Pacific conceptually holds currency for a wide range of other themes, including Afro-Asian political and cultural relationships; Black populations who reside on the Pacific coasts of the North, Central, and South Americas; Black internationalism in the Pacific; and Africa's engagements with Oceania via the Indian Ocean. While it is a phrase loaded with tension, the analytical importance of a Black Pacific is reflected in the intensity of Black Lives Matter protests in Oceania as well as the growing number of academic full-length studies, dissertations, articles, book chapters, and conference panels that are raising crucial questions about the significance of the Pacific in relation to the Black Atlantic.[4]

Given all this, *Pasifika Black* is less concerned about challenging the limitations of a Black Atlantic framework as it is about approaching the Pacific via the lens of African Diaspora studies and Black intellectual history. It is written in concert with critical studies on race and decolonization in twentieth-century Oceania. This includes a canon of Pacific scholarship focused on Melanesian politics that emerged in the 1970s and 1980s. Journalist David Robie's sweeping *Blood on Their Banner* explores nationalist movements in Oceania. John Maynard's *Fight for Liberty and Freedom* discusses the Universal Negro Improvement Association (UNIA) in Australia. Gerald Horne's *White Pacific* documents "blackbirding," US imperialism, and African Americans in the Pacific, largely in the nineteenth century. David Chappell's *Kanak Awakening* shows how anti-colonial movements in the French colony of New Caledonia politically engaged the Black Francophone world. The late Tracey Banivanua Mar's *Decolonisation and the Pacific* details how decolonization in the Pacific was both an indigenous and international phenomenon that transcended the region's colonial and national borders. Robbie Shilliam's *Black Pacific* is centered on the Polynesian Panthers, Rastafari, and Black Power in Aotearoa, but also explores centuries of Māori anti-colonialism. My own *Pauulu's Diaspora* explores Afro-Caribbean relationships in Oceania through the lenses of Black Power, pan-Africanism, and environmental justice.[5]

Pasifika Black takes its name from the Bislama word for Pacific— *Pasifik*. Bislama is a both a creole and official language of Vanuatu.

The word *Pasifika* also has clear roots in Aotearoa, where it has been used by non-indigenous government officials to refer to Polynesian migrants to the country. It is also used across Oceania as a display of ethnic solidarity. This book's use of *Pasifika Black* is a nod to Pacific Islander communities who were defined and largely self-identified as being Black, namely, Melanesia. As such, it prioritizes Melanesia's own engagements, identifications, understandings, and radical imaginations of Blackness as being part of a global Black Diaspora.

Take for example the words of the former permanent secretary for education and cultural affairs of the Solomon Islands, Francis Bugotu, who in 1968 informed the University of Papua New Guinea's (UPNG) Waigani Seminar on the History of Melanesia that it was "a big disadvantage in this world to be Black. The trouble with us Solomon Islanders is that we are too Black."[6] Bugotu's compelling notion of being *too Black for the world* is striking when we consider the oft-cited colloquially academic claims that Oceanic peoples are not really a part of the Black Diaspora because they are not *Black enough*.

But African Diaspora studies as a formal academic discipline has always been concerned about the global dimensions of the Africana world both west *and* east of Africa across the Atlantic, Indian, and Pacific Ocean worlds. At UNESCO's First International Congress of African Historians (Tanzania, 1965), historians Joseph E. Harris and George Shepperson participated on a panel entitled "The African Diaspora or the African Abroad." Questions about African-descended communities in the Middle East prompted Harris to write his first book, *The African Presence in Asia* (1971). Harris, who taught at Howard University from 1975 to 2003, founded the discipline with these global questions in mind. He convened African Diaspora Studies Institutes at Howard (1979) and in Kenya (1981) and published papers from those meetings in *Global Dimensions of the African Diaspora* (Howard University Press, 1982). Major themes from that text include voluntary and involuntary migration, slavery and freedom, pan-Africanism, colonialism, dispersal myths, identity, return movements, and Africa as homeland. Harris argued that the worldwide slave trade (conducted primarily by Arabs, Europeans, and Americans), enslavement, and colonialism created a "global socioeconomic condition which linked Africans and their descendants abroad," and the majority of the Black Diaspora lived in the margins of their societies while Europeans and their descendants benefitted from "entrenched privileged positions."[7]

In his 2003 *Radical History Review* article "Expanding the Scope of African Diaspora Studies: The Middle East and India," Harris wrote that "pre-Islamic Arabs conducted a trade in Africans from northern and eastern Africa to parts of Europe, across Turkey, the Middle East, India, and as far as China centuries before the Atlantic slave trade peaked in the nineteenth century." These routes spanned the Mediterranean and Red Seas and the Indian and Atlantic Oceans, creating African-descended communities throughout Asia. Since the fifteenth century, he continued, "the Portuguese took shipments of captive Africans to the Persian Gulf region, India, China, and Japan; the Dutch transported them to India and Indonesia; the French shipped them to India and the Mascarene Islands . . . ; the British took them to India, Mauritius, and China; and of course, all of them and the Danes shipped captive Africans to Europe and the Americas. The Euro–North Americans brought them to the Americas as well."[8]

However, Harris argued that it would be a mistake to attempt to understand the Diaspora only through the "prism of the slave trade," as African communities migrated outside Africa voluntarily since "ancient times." They were involved in Islam's eighth-century expansion from the Middle East into southern Asia and encountered non-Muslim Africans who had long lived in the region. Harris called for focus on the African Diaspora in southeastern and "far eastern" Asia, and the settlement of these communities in the Pacific islands, an area that beckoned "to become the next frontier for global African diaspora research."[9]

Harris's articulation of a global African Diaspora was not a mere accident. He obtained both his BA (1952) and MA (1956) in history from Howard, where he studied under the likes of Rayford Logan, John Hope Franklin, E. Franklin Frazier, and Merze Tate. As a professor, he shared an office with Leo Hansberry and Tate, who inspired him as "a scholar who had written on colonialism in the Pacific."[10] This was an understatement. Tate, an esteemed professor of diplomatic history, likely wrote more about Oceania than any other African American scholar. This included her 1965 article on blackbirding, "Slavery and Racism in South Pacific Annexations," published in the *Journal of Negro History*. Tate's 1943 article "The War Aims of World War I and World War II" argued that the darker people of the world included millions of Black communities in the United States, the Caribbean, and South America, but also African people south of the Sahara and Islamic peoples of the Mediterranean littoral, the 400 million people of India and Burma, the people of Malaysia and the former Netherlands East Indies, Chinese, Japanese, and "Polynesians of Oceania and the Melanesians, those Negroid inhabitants of the islands of the Central and Western Pacific, including the Solomon Islands." For Tate, these darker people were "no longer willing to accept the White man's exalted view of trusteeship." Instead, they no longer quaked

> at the teachings of the White man's missionaries, who bring them the White man's God but a God in whom the White man does not believe; no longer are glass beads and trinkets marvelous to them; they are much more interested in the marvels of the White man's guns. Once the colored races feared the White man; today that fear has turned to secret contempt. Once they were filled with terror at the White man's power; today they know that they themselves are power. Their past weakness has not been due to their lack of numbers nor to inferior physical stamina but to the fact that the white man had guns, cared little for God and much for his guns. Today the Yellow, Brown, Black peoples know that the Whites are in a minority with no special "capacities" which mean "innate superiority"; moreover, that minority is divided and is slaughtering itself.

Furthermore, through participation in wars and revolutions, the "man of color" had been initiated into the "former dark mysteries of their armaments" and now questioned the reality of the White man's superiority while contemplating their own "possibilities of attack."[11]

How Black internationalism offered Oceanic movements for self-determination "possibilities of attack" is what this book is about. By intentionally embracing Black internationalism, Melanesia became part of a radical Black Diaspora of anti-colonialism. *Pasifika Black* shows how Melanesian women and men "forged Diaspora" with not only global Africana political struggles but also ethnic and nationalist movements *within* the Pacific. It adds to a critical body of scholarship on Black internationalism, which has paid relatively little attention to Melanesia in the era of decolonization. Intentionality is a deep undercurrent of this work, which, drawing on Michael West, William Martin, and Fanon Che Wilkins's *From Toussaint to Tupac*, frames Black internationalism as a deliberate struggle against slavery, colonialism, and racism. Black movements in the Pacific applied these international experiences to their local and regional contexts. While *Pasifika Black* is not just about Black women's internationalism in Oceania, it demonstrates that these architects of anti-colonial movements were often Black, indigenous, grassroots, and working-class women. This discussion includes the ways the Black world experienced, engaged, and consumed Oceania.[12]

The text is threaded by a number of key themes related to Black internationalism: the creation of political and cultural berths, travel, grassroots organizing, the circulation of print media, and state surveillance. Lea Kinikini Kauvaka's 2016 article "Berths and Anchorages: Pacific Cultural Studies from Oceania" describes berths as being "real spaces influenced and constrained by geography, holding real memory of journeys, departures, homecomings, and crossings." For Kauvaka, berths are not equivalent to roots or routes; rather, they are "spaces of reciprocal exchanges that signify, create, and maintain relationships over distance and across time."[13] *Pasifika Black* uses berths to describe how indigenous leaders in Oceania built Black internationalist relationships via temporary but potentially transformative spaces (mobile metropoles) such as political, academic, cultural, and religious conferences and meetings across the Black world.

Traveling to international berths posed a number of challenges for these organizers. In the context of colonial Oceania, travel was both an economic and political matter, based on imperialist boundaries and restrictive immigration policies regarding indigenous people. Still, travel was critical, but not *everything*. Here, historian Keisha Blain's notion of "grassroots internationalism" is important, as it describes the experiences of working-class Black women who often did not have the material means to travel but still found ways to advance Black internationalism through "their writings, community work, and local collaborations with men and women from various parts of the globe." To be certain, these activists worked at the state and international level when possible. But in lieu of state support, activists in Oceania organized and communicated at the grassroots levels to circumnavigate the difficulties of travel. The circulation of print media also allowed the ideas, radical imaginations, and "insurgent political cultures" of decolonization to globally spread. This activity resulted in intense state surveillance, harassment, and police repression of Black internationalist organizations.[14]

Pasifika Black embraces Linda Tuhiwai Smith's overlapping framework of "self-determination, decolonization, and social justice" as a research methodology. Its approach is contextualized within the broader historical, political, and cultural context of decolonization in Oceania and the continued struggles of the Black Pacific for social and environmental justice.[15] In addition, it uses research methodologies drawn from Africana, African Diaspora, and Pacific studies. In 2014, while I was conducting research in Oceania, a botched attempt to sail from Fiji to Vanuatu landed me at a marina (Vuda Point) and resort off the western coast of Fiji named First Landing. The insistence by a member of this community that First Landing was where their ancestors from Tanganyika (Tanzania) first landed in Fiji sparked my curiosity about Melanesia's consciousness of Africa. My interest in Melanesia's engagements with the African world deepened during my nearly three-month sojourn across Fiji, Papua New Guinea, Vanuatu, and Australia. As such, *Pasifika Black* is based on extensive interviews and groundings that I had with Melanesian political leaders, community activists, students, village leaders, artists, scholars, athletes, and musicians across sites like Sydney's Aboriginal Tent Embassy in Redfern, Melbourne's Aboriginal Advancement League, the University of the South Pacific in Laucala and Emalus, and Vanuatu's Melanesian Institute, Pentecost Island, and Mele village. It also is based on print media, anthropological accounts, conference proceedings, photographs, state surveillance, and government documents from across Oceania's labyrinth of universities, libraries, and archives.

Chapter 1 explores how twentieth-century architects of Black critical thought, such as Marcus Garvey, Anna Julia Cooper, and W. E. B. Du Bois, referenced Oceania in their global discourses on race. Their views on ethnicity in the Pacific were influenced by Europe's racialized and gendered imaginations of the region. The work of acclaimed photographer Eliot Elisofon reveals how these problematic racist and sexist notions of the region persisted through World War II via print media such as *Life* magazine.

Chapter 2 explores West Papua's ongoing struggle against Indonesian imperialism. In the 1960s West Papuan organizers self-identified as being African "Negroids of the Pacific." With the backing of Senegalese President Léopold Senghor, in 1975 they established an office in Dakar, Senegal. Senghor defended his support as being an act of Negritude.

Chapter 3 explores the Black internationalism of Australian Aboriginal poet Oodgeroo Noonuccal (Kath Walker). Born in 1920, Noonuccal's art and activism on behalf of Aboriginal peoples took her across Oceania, Africa, Europe, and the United States. The Australian government placed Noonuccal under intense surveillance due to her affiliations with the Australian Communist Party and her leadership in the Federal Council for the Advancement of Aborigines and Torres Strait Islanders (FCAATSI). Her son Denis Walker founded Australia's Black Panther Party in 1971.

Chapter 4 is centered on the Niugini Black Power Group (NBPG), which was formed by students at UPNG in 1970. Influenced by Melanesian nationalism, Negritude, global Black Power discourses, and Africana literature, the NBPG focused on the issues of Australian colonialism, segregation, and environmental justice. As playwrights, novelists, poets, and visual artists, they produced a tremendous canon of Melanesian art, literature, and theatre. Chapter 5 describes how this Melanesian arts movement drew Black Power activists, artists, educators, and scholars from across the Global South to the halls of UPNG.

Chapter 6 charts the dramatic experiences of the Australian and Papua New Guinean delegation to the 1977 Second World Black and African Festival of Arts and Culture (FESTAC) in Lagos, Nigeria. Noonuccal and members of the NBPG found themselves on the festival's steering committee. Full of contradictions and challenges, this trip reflected both the pitfalls and potential of Black internationalism in Oceania.

Chapter 7 details Black women's internationalism in Fiji through the activism of organizers Claire Slatter, Vanessa Griffen, and Amelia Rokotuivuna, who transformed the country's Young Women's Christian Association into a space of radical feminism and political praxis. These women hosted both the Nuclear Free Pacific (NFP) Conference and the Pacific Women's Conference in 1975. They launched the Pacific People's

Action Front and its revolutionary newsletter *Povai*, which brilliantly detailed Oceania's anti-colonial struggles.

Chapter 8 unpacks the Kanak struggle against French colonialism in New Caledonia through the efforts of activists Déwé Gorodey and Nidoïsh Naisseline and revolutionary groups like Groupe 1878 and the Foulards Rouges. In the 1960s Kanak students based in Paris returned to New Caledonia armed with the ideas of Negritude and Black Power and the theories of Frantz Fanon. Battling severe police repression and White violence, the ongoing movement remains a powerful symbol of Melanesian nationalism. Chapter 9 reveals how Kanaky leaders like Yann Uregei controversially received support from Libya's Mu'ammar Qaddafi and joined over sixty liberation organizations from across Oceania and Asia at Tripoli's 1987 anti-imperialist Pacific Peace Conference.

The final chapter discusses the New Hebrides National Party's intense struggle against British and French colonialism in Vanuatu. The party sent delegates to Tanzania's 1974 Sixth Pan-African Congress. Led by Anglican priest Father Walter Lini, this movement embraced Black liberation theology and worked extensively within the global religious network of the World Council of Churches. Upon achieving independence in 1980, Vanuatu became the first nation to open a permanent United Nations mission in Harlem, New York.

We Are the Ocean: Race, Gender, and Ethnicity in Oceania

Recent scholarship asserts that indigenous peoples reached Oceania some 30,000–50,000 years ago. DNA studies argue that Aboriginal Australians are direct descendants of Africa's first Diaspora from some 72,000 years ago. These communities traversed Papua New Guinea, Australia, and the Solomon Islands. Archeological unearthing of Lapita pottery—distinct for its comb-toothed designs—has marked a second major migratory wave into the region via Southeast Asia some 3,000 years ago. Lapita communities navigated the Pacific across Melanesia and Polynesia, sailing across Vanuatu, as far south as New Zealand, as far west as Tahiti, and as far north as Hawai'i (and west to Madagascar), creating an Oceanic diaspora based on the Lapita cultural complex.[16]

Tonga's pioneering scholar of Pacific studies, Epeli Hau'ofa, has written wonderfully about the world of Oceania. His *We Are the Ocean* epically describes how its indigenous "myths, legends, oral traditions and cosmologies" reflected diverse worldviews, cosmologies, systems of governance, kinship networks, and ecological systems that stretched across and linked the region. Oceanic communities saw themselves as being a part of the ocean first, and the land second. Their world was an interconnected "sea of islands," rather than isolated "islands in the sea" dislocated far from the metropoles of power. Hau'ofa called for the use of *Oceania* as opposed to the *Pacific* when referring to the region.[17]

Indeed, there is inherent hegemony implied in the word "Pacific"—it is a geopolitical construct that marks Europe's violent assault on Oceania through genocide, blackbirding, forced labor, sexual abuse, displacement, colonial borders, ecological destruction, and imperialism. After all, it was European colonialists, explorers, monarchs, conquerors, kidnappers, and traders who "drew imaginary lines across the sea, making the colonial boundaries that, for the first time, confined ocean peoples to tiny spaces." This is today's Pacific, where islanders "are in danger of being confined to mental reservations if not already physical ones."[18]

For the Pacific to be created, a part of Oceania had to die. As Tate details, one of the first colonial strikes against indigenous sovereignty was Europe's renaming of the region. Some scholarship suggests that *papua* was a Malay word meaning "frizzly-haired." Islamic Sultan Al-Mansur of Tidore (1475–1526) possibly enslaved Papuans in what is now West Papua, leading to the archipelago of "Papua" becoming a reference to a "nation of slaves."[19] In 1545 Spanish explorer Yñigo Ortiz de Retez reached Papua. He called it Nueva Guinea, asserting that its inhabitants phenotypically resembled people from Africa's Guinea coast. In the 1640s Dutch explorers called "Australia" New Holland and its distant neighbor New Zealand. Tasmania carries the name of Dutchman Abel Tasman. The Torres Straits reflect the travels of Spain's Luis Váez de Torres. Spain's Álvaro de Mendaña de Neira spotted the "Solomon Islands" in 1568. Having found signs of gold, he imagined that this was the source of the biblical King Solomon's wealth. Britain's James Cook named New Caledonia and New Hebrides so because they "reminded him of the Scottish Highlands."[20]

Prior to the mid-nineteenth century, European observers alleged that two races inhabited Oceania. The first was described as a race of noble savages who were phenotypically yellowish, with a complexion ranging from "coppery" to near-white, closer in culture to Europe civilization, surrounded by boundless natural resources, straight-haired, athletic and well-proportioned, more amicable to Whites, of benevolent temper, formed nations and monarchies, and comprised of beautiful, free, and sexually available women. The other was a race of unredeemable savages who were phenotypically dark brown, sooty, with skin "almost as black as that of the Kaffirs," cannibalistic, devoid of government structures or resources, strongly averse to Europeans, warlike, with curly, wooly, crisp, and frizzy hair, ugly, mistrustful and tempersome, unpleasant, frail and with disproportionate limbs and noses pressed backwards, and barbaric, with small tribes as opposed to nations; the women of this race were perceived as ugly and inaccessible.[21] These views were circulated and refashioned across the Western world.

Portugal's Pedro Fernandes de Quirós reached Vanuatu in 1606, calling one island Australia del Espiritu Santo, which still bears this name. His instructions in dealing with indigenous communities were, "Learn from the natives whether there are other . . . lands near, if they are inhabited, of what color are the natives, whether they eat human flesh, whether they are friendly or carry on war. Enquire whether they have gold in dust, or in small lumps, or in ornament, silver worked or to be worked, metals, all kinds of pearls, spices and salt."[22]

English explorer William Dampier's 1697 *Voyage round the World* placed Aboriginal peoples in Australia on the lowest rung of the Pacific's racial scale. In his mind, they were the world's "miserabilist people." Monomatapa's "nasty" Khoi Khoi were "gentlemen" compared to New Holland's brutish, "poor winking inhabitants," whose eyes were "always half closed to keep the flies out." These "poor winkers" could not see far unless they held their heads very high. They had "great bottle-noses, pretty full lips and wide mouths." Lacking two upper front teeth, they did not have one "graceful feature in their faces." Their hair was "black, short, and curled like that of the Negroes," and their skin was "coal-black like that of the Negroes of Guinea."[23]

In 1756 French writer Charles de Brosses invented the idea of Polynesia, meaning many islands. He was certain that the Pacific contained an "old race with black skin" that was "black like the Negroes of Nigritia" (a reference to an imagined Negroland in West Africa), with "thick lips, frizzy woolly hair," and "in every respect like African Negroes." In 1778

J. R. Forster wrote that the first race lived in the east, toward Tahiti and beyond. The second race occupied New Caledonia, Fiji, Tanna, and Malakula, where Blacks lived like "a tribe of monkeys."[24]

French naturalist Jean Baptiste Bory de Saint-Vincent argued that the Blacks of the Pacific were quite different from the "Negroes of Africa." His 1827 *Zoological Essay on the Human Species* described them as "Mélaniens" (from the Greek word *melas*, for dark) and racially distinct from "Australian and Neptunian" (Polynesian) races. By the 1830s, France's Jules Dumont d'Urville refined these views, dividing Oceania into Polynesia, Micronesia, Malaysia, and Melanesia. He described the lighter-skinned race as occupying Polynesia and Micronesia, and Melanesia became "the home of the Black race of Oceania." This included Australia. Melanesians were described as being "largely inferior to those of the copper-skinned" Polynesian race. According to Serge Tcherkézoff, these framings had little to do with geography, but were more about contributing to "racial theories of human variation."[25]

Almost thirty years prior to his 1859 *Origin of Species*, Charles Darwin's five-year expedition on the *Beagle* took him across South America, the Pacific, and Africa. Darwin attributed his formulation of the theory of natural selection to this trip. He claimed that South America's "Fuegians" were bested only by the South Sea Islanders in savagery. Tahitian men, with "ornamented curved bodies," were the finest he had beheld. Yet he disavowed their "unbecoming hairstyles" and their comfort in their skins. After observing an abundance of fruit, tubers, fresh rivers, fish, and the shade of the "dark green knotted" stems of kava, he reckoned that "savage man, with his reasoning powers only partly developed, [was] a child of the Tropics."[26]

Darwin wrote that New Zealand's Māoris lacked the elegance of Tahitians, possessed no government, and were the world's most "war-like race of inhabitants." The "twinkling in their eyes" indicated "cunning and ferocity." Both their persons and houses were "filthily dirty and offensive" and "the idea of washing . . . persons or clothes" never "entered their heads." He also claimed that Australia's "Aboriginal blacks" would not cultivate the ground. He found it "curious thus to see in the midst of a civilized people . . . harmless savages wandering about without knowing where they will sleep and gaining their livelihood by hunting." White men seemed "predestined to inherit" their country, as Aborigines were "delighted" at and "blinded" by their gifts of dogs, offal, and milk. In Tasmania, "Aboriginal blacks" had been "all removed" or imprisoned. This cruelty was necessary, "although without doubt the misconduct of the Whites first led to the necessity."[27]

Darwin found the Blacks of Western Australia to be "very ugly," "abominably filthy," and "true savages." At a corroboree where he witnessed their emu and kangaroo dances, Darwin abhorred their "heavy footsteps, grunting, marching," beating of clubs and weapons, wild cries, and "gesticulations." For him, this "barbarous scene" lacked meaning, and "the group of nearly naked figures, . . . all moving in hideous harmony," was a "festival amongst the lowest barbarians." He imagined that this was akin to what he would see "amongst the same-colored people" of Southern Africa.[28]

The sexual imaginations of European men about gender, women, and Tahiti played a crucial role in the contrasts they perceived between Polynesia and Melanesia. Though he was in Tahiti for only ten days, French navigator Louis de Bougainville's 1771 *Voyage autour du monde* had a tremendous impact on European Enlightenment writers like Jean-Jacques Rousseau, notions of the Noble Savage, and the idea that Polynesian women were prone to offer sexual favors to European men.[29] Bougainville claimed that after spending only one night in Tahiti, his disease-ridden men were cured of scurvy. "The very air which the people breathe," he wrote, "their songs, their dances, almost constantly attended with indecent postures, all conspire to call to mind the sweets of love, all engage to give themselves up to them." Tahiti was his "Garden of Eden" and Nouvelle-Cythère, the mythical land of Aphrodite. In spite of his crew's "precautions, a young girl boarded their ship." She allegedly "positioned herself" in front of the men, carelessly dropping the cloth that covered her. Now naked, she "appeared to the eyes of all beholders, such as Venus showed herself to the Phrygian shepherd, having . . . the celestial form of that goddess."[30]

Cook's first Pacific expedition was in 1768. On board his ship was botanist Joseph Banks, who subsequently advised the British government on Australian affairs. On his suggestion, Britain established Botany Bay as a penal colony. Both men shared Bougainville's views on Tahiti as being "the truest picture of an Arcadia of which [they] were going to be kings." Yet Banks found the wife of a chief to be "ugly in conscience," as she had sat close to him "without little invitation." But it seems her real infraction was that she intervened in his advances toward a "pretty girl with a fire in her eyes," whom he had "loaded . . . with beads and every present" to please her. But the chief's wife "showed much disgust" and continued to give him fish and coconut milk.[31]

European writers used Tahiti to imagine Polynesia as a paradise of ageless innocence, sexually available women, and weaponless men. In contrast, they claimed, in Melanesia the men were armed and the unavailable women unattractive. For Foster, the women of Tahiti and the Polynesian race were soft, unreserved, and beautiful. They enjoyed love and from an early age abandoned "themselves to the most libidinous scenes." Their arms, hands, and fingers were so delicate that they "would do honor to a Venus dé Medici." However, in "Melanesia," the ugly and deformed women were "packhorses" who labored for their "indolent husbands."[32]

Surveying New Hebrides, Boyle Somerville claimed that Christianity had reversed its "once, dirty, naked, licentious, polygamous cannibals." Yet, with "fertile savage imagination," they still worshipped ancestors, stones, and volcanoes. Their "worship stones" bore representations of the sun and moon, pointing to an "earlier civilization" that they had degraded from. He watched about eighty "savages" dance and chant in the rain of the night. Moving to the drums, their "black wet bodies [glistened] in the torchlight as they madly whirled." To his disappointment, he and his crew were not allowed to watch the women dance.[33]

Somerville claimed that these women were "degraded to the level of brute beasts, doing all the hard field work," and "made to carry loads . . . disproportionate to their ugly-shaped bodies and thin legs." They disliked bearing children, because they "got in the way." Twins were "neglected and starved." Girls suffered the same fate if the population became too large. Women learned only what they needed to know to be slaves to men. They were sold into marriage at fifteen years of age, "already showing signs of toil, though passably good looking." Yet "four or five years later, having borne perhaps two children, they [were] little short of hags, with stooped frame and pendulous breasts; and so [they remained], getting more and more wrinkled and grey, until old age and probably living burial [fell] on them." Husbands beat, thrashed, kicked, and killed their wives without fear of reprisal. Ironically, Somerville was annoyed that these indigenes referred to their uncles, aunts, and cousins as father, mother, brother, and sister. But his most "ridiculous sight" was of a man calling a small girl much younger than him "mother."[34]

The reality is that Europe transformed Oceania into the Pacific through violence. Being imagined as a space of "noble savages" did not "save" Polynesia from White imperialism any more than did being referred to as "unattractive cannibals" prevent Melanesian women from being the targets of European sexual violence. These gendered and violent imaginations were about legitimizing White patriarchal power. As such, any women could be targets for abuse and all the lands could be for the taking.

The White Pacific

In 1788 British captain Arthur Philip invaded Australia with what has become infamously known as the "First Fleet." Although it was inhabited by almost a million indigenous people, Philip claimed the land and all of its adjacent islands for the British crown under the concept of *terra nullius*—that the land was unoccupied. Essentially, this Pacific version of "Manifest Destiny" claimed that no human beings were present before the British arrived. Having lost its American colonies, Britain turned Australia's New South Wales into its new "dumping ground" for its convicts.

Oceania faced the day and fought back. In 1790 Pemulwuy of the Bidjigal led a legendary twelve-year guerilla war against the First Fleet. Born with a "turned eye," he was "spiritually gifted." His band fought with spears, stones, and boomerangs. After an attack on a work camp, his skull was cracked in battle with "Black Caesar." Born perhaps in Madagascar or the West Indies, Caesar was Australia's first bushranger (escaped convict). After Pemulwuy was killed in 1802, his head was preserved in alcohol and sent to England.[35]

After successive murders of his people, Yagan of southwest Australia warned that "one White life would be taken for every Noongar killed by a White." In 1832 he led food raids and "payback" killings of White settlers. Eventually he was killed, and his nation markings were skinned from his back. His decapitated head was smoked over eucalyptus wood for three months and then taken to England. In the 1950s Noongar leader Ken Colbung found Yagan's body in an unmarked grave in Liverpool. In 1997 his remains were brought home, "wrapped in a kangaroo skin cloak."[36]

According to Tate, Australia had its own "Monroe Doctrine." In 1840 the British government signed the Treaty of Waitangi with the Māori of Aotearoa. In contrast to the government's colonial relationship with indigenous Australia, this recognized (on paper) Māori sovereignty over their lands while certifying Britain's presence in the region. Tate writes that "New Zealand seemed fit for a mission of manifest destiny in the Pacific due to its proximity to the islands and wind currents." New Zealand governor George Gray asserted, "Any attempt to confine the Anglo-Saxon race within the limits of New Zealand . . . must pose a failure. It might well be attempted to confine the birds of the ocean within the same land. They will navigate the Pacific in every direction."[37]

Violent clashes with indigenous communities were inevitable. In the Black War alone (1820–1832), the British killed about nine hundred indigenous people in Tasmania. In 1829 Truganini of Tasmania's Kulin was violently raped by White timber-cutters and her fiancé brutally killed. Sailors murdered her mother, soldiers shot her uncle, and sealers kidnapped her sister. After the war, she was moved to Flinders Island with the remaining one hundred Tasmanians. She joined a group of outlaws who killed two White whalers. Truganini survived a gunshot to the head, but her allies were tried and hanged in 1842 in front of a crowd of five thousand. She married "King Billy" and died in 1876. The Royal Society of Tasmania later exhumed her skeleton and placed it on display. In 2002 pieces of her hair and skin were found in England's Royal College of Surgeons. These were returned to Tasmania.[38]

In the 1820s British traders and French bêche-de-mer sailors raided New Hebrides for sandalwood. These assaults developed into a system of slavery, kidnapping, and forced labor known as blackbirding. European traders took Melanesian men and women to work primarily on sugar and cotton plantations in Australia, Fiji, and New Caledonia. In Fiji, laborers were referred to as "black ivory." Between 1863 and 1904, over 62,000 Melanesians were taken to Australia's Queensland as agricultural laborers. Horne writes, "As in North America where the indigenes were massacred and Africans brought in to labor, Queensland

Figure 1.1. Australian South Sea Islander women laborers on a sugarcane plantation near Cairns, Queensland, ca. 1895. John Oxley Library, State Library of Queensland, Australia.

witnessed the massacre of the Aboriginals just as South Sea Islanders were blackbirded."[39]

Between 1862 and 1863, at least 3,600 individuals from Polynesian communities across the Easter Islands, Niue, and eastern Pacific atolls were blackbirded to Peru (others were taken to the mines of the Andes) with devastating effect. In Peru the abolition of African slavery drove the search for new labor sources to exploit; laborers were sold—men for $200, $150 for women, and $100 for children. The American Civil War's impact on cotton production created a lucrative opportunity for the expansion of cotton across Peru's *haciendas*. Intended to target "dangerous Melanesians," the first ships were designed like armed slaving vessels. Some ships were rumored to have been involved in the Atlantic slave trade.[40]

After the Haitian Revolution overthrew slavery in Saint-Domingue, France increased its production of sugar in the Indian Ocean colony of Reunion. In 1858 the Australian ship *Sutton* kidnapped sixty-five Pacific Islanders from Kiribati and the Solomon Islands. Some five months and nine thousand miles later, they arrived in Reunion, where they were sold as indentured sugar laborers for £40 each.[41]

Blackbirders were notorious. They abused people through unfair labor contracts and false impressions about the nature of the work they were being hired for. Villages were ambushed at night. Many were placed in chains. Some were enticed to board ships with promises that crews wanted to barter or go on short cruises. South Sea Islander Faith Bandler's father told her that he was shackled in irons onboard a ship in Tanna and sold in Australia, where overseers forced him to work with "guns and whips." In 1847, by bribing local chiefs, John Kirsopp blackbirded eighty islanders from Vanuatu. In 1871 James Patrick Murray and his crew impersonated missionaries to lure unsuspecting victims. Once gathered, they were forced onto boats at gunpoint. Locked in the hold of his ship *Carl*, these captives revolted. Murray and his men fired into the hold and killed over sixty people. The dead and seriously injured, some bound by their hands and feet, were thrown overboard. Horne writes that the blackbirding carried out by American captain William Hayes was "inextricably linked to his promiscuous sexual exploitation of girls and women."[42]

British laws regarding the abolition of the Atlantic slave trade were applied to the Pacific, and some blackbirders were charged for "slaving." This included Henry Ross Lewin, who was prosecuted unsuccessfully for the rape of a thirteen-year-old Tannese girl. In the 1871 case of the *Jason*, its Captain Coath argued that it was "no offence to go to islands inhabited by" savages "and to bring these people into the protection of English." To land "naturally unfree natives" on British soil was an act of liberation, as they became "free men." Coath cited the monumental 1854 *Dred Scott* case, suggesting that savages had no right to representation in British court. Convicted but pardoned, Coath died by poisoned arrow. Queensland supporters of the trade claimed that "irrespective of how Melanesians were brought to the colony, the civilizing influence of the more advanced European world could . . . only improve them."[43]

Blackbirding was transnational. Prior to the American Civil War, British merchants felt that Queensland cotton could make them "independent of American slave grown cotton." In response to the ending of the War, American Confederates rapidly developed blackbirding in Fiji. At least fifty vessels sailed under French, British, and American flags.

Figure 1.2. South Sea Islanders working in the canefields, North Queensland, n.d. Digitized copy print from APO-32 Queensland Views Photograph Album. John Oxley Library, State Library of Queensland, Australia.

Figure 1.3. South Sea Islander woman, Farnborough, Queensland, ca. 1895. John Oxley Library, State Library of Queensland, Australia.

Since Fiji cotton was considered highly valuable, commercial operations connected the trade to American cities like San Francisco.[44]

According to Tate, such "incessant cruelty, violence, and rape perpetrated by sandalwood traders fomented hatred among New Hebrideans against all foreigners, whose motives were generally regarded with suspicion." This included missionaries like John Williams, the so-called Apostle of Polynesia. In 1839 he was allegedly "attacked by cannibals, clubbed to death, and eaten."[45] In 1870 some 180 Solomon Islanders en route to Fiji killed all but one of their captors and attempted to sail home. In 1871 John Patterson, the Anglican bishop of Melanesia, was killed in Nukapu, Solomon Islands. Just days before his death, blackbirders kidnapped five men from Nukapu. When the *Southern Cross* approached their community, villagers in canoes attacked the ship with arrows, shouting the names of the kidnapped. Shortly afterwards, a group of women paddled out to the waters and set a canoe adrift with Patterson's body wrapped in a coconut mat. His skull was crushed, and four other wounds had been inflicted after death. A "branch of coconut palm with five knots in its fronds had been stuck in the mat." According to the *Fiji Times*, the knots symbolized the five captured. This was a "payback" killing.[46] The deaths of missionaries prompted the British government to pass laws regulating the labor trade. This included the 1868 Polynesian Laborers Act and the 1872 Kidnapping Act.

Just as Europe fraudulently utilized the suppression of the Atlantic slave trade as an excuse for its imperialism in Africa, Europe used the subduing of blackbirding as a rationale for the colonization of Oceania. Germany's first overseas colony was German New Guinea (Kaiser-Wilhelmsland), which it "claimed by flag" in 1884. This would come to include northeast Papua, Bougainville, the Solomons, Samoa, Micronesia, and the Marshall Islands. Weeks later, when Bismarck convened the Berlin Conference, the Pacific geopolitics were on the agenda; he was expressly concerned that Britain was impeding his interests in Africa and Oceania. Germany administered New Guinea with machine guns and violently punitive expeditions. After their 1904 massacre of the Herero in German South West Africa, German officials considered exiling survivors to New Guinea. Britain held more than eight flag-raising ceremonies, claiming "southern" New Guinea (Papua) with the same violence used by its colonial competitor.[47]

At an 1887 First Imperial Conference, Britain and France's Anglo-French agreement created a joint Pacific naval commission to "protect the life and property of British subjects and French citizens in New Hebrides." This "citizenship included the Compagnié Caledonienne des Nouvelles-Hebrides, which exported copra, coffee, and maize. Britain gave up claims to all islands located leeward of Tahiti and France conceded to her Egypt and the Suez Canal. In 1906 they created a joint colonial administration in New Hebrides.[48]

Australia became a Commonwealth nation in 1901. In an attempt to define Australia as a White state, government officials created a constitution based on *terra nullius*. Australia's immigration policies reflected racist modern myths of White supremacy and policy formation around "whitening." A 1901 Immigration Restriction Act extended its 1888 Chinese Restriction Act, which prohibited the entry of "all persons of any colored race" from Asia, Africa, and the Indian and Pacific Oceans. The British government strongly suggested that this law should not, "in print," exclude any races. Australia circumvented this by using South Africa's diction exam, which required immigrants to write out fifty words recited by an immigration officer. The officer chose which European language the test would be administered in. According to Alfred Deaken, second prime minister of Australia, the ostensibly "colorless" act was "designed and used only to exclude the colored races." It drew a "deep color line of demarcation between Caucasians and all other races," and immigration officers stopped only people of color.[49]

Similar rules applied to British New Guinea, which was annexed to Australia in 1902 to "give civilization to the natives, make wealth for Australia, and encourage development under European auspices, foreign capital, and native labor until the island was under total control." The 1905 Papua Act stated that Commonwealth laws did not apply to indigenous peoples. Furthermore, the governor of Papua could not introduce into New Guinea the immigration of "aboriginal natives of Australia, Africa, Asia, or any island of the Pacific."[50]

Laws were also created to deport South Sea Islanders from Australia. The Pacific Island Laborers Act of 1901 stated that Pacific Islanders could not enter Australia beyond 1904.[51] In 1894 South Sea Islanders formed the Mackay Kanaka Farmers Association. In 1901 the Pacific Islanders Association (PIA) staged protests against these deportations. In 1903

Figure 1.4. Map of Oceania. US Central Intelligence Agency, 1982, Library of Congress, Washington, DC.

Figure 1.5. Map of Melanesia. Saylor Academy, 2012.

seventy-five Australian-born Islanders petitioned the governor to not break up their families. PIA chairman Henry Diamuir Tongoa argued that if they had to leave Australia, "the White men [would] have to leave the islands." In 1906 Tongoa and thousands of others were deported.[52]

Europe used these laws, guns, racist imaginations, and colonial violence to create a "White Pacific" that would legalize, legitimize, and protect White power in the region well into the twentieth century. In this context, it should be reiterated that *Pasifika Black* is not written as a challenge to the academic framework of the *Black Atlantic*. Rather, it is really centered on describing how Oceania resisted a *White Pacific*, one that continues to exploit indigenous communities in Oceania. New Caledonia, West Papua, Micronesia, and Tahiti are still colonized, indigenous persons in Australia and Aotearoa do not have sovereignty, and Hawai'i is not free.

1

Garvey's Caveat

Pan-Africanism and the Black Pacific

In 1893 a brazenly racist article about supposed "South Sea savages" at Chicago's World Fair circulated widely in the American press. Written by sensationalist journalist J. M. Scanland, the piece claimed that an indigenous group of "tattooed cannibals" from Australia was being taken to the fair by R. A. Cunningham, an affiliate of P. T. Barnum's traveling circus. The article referred to members of this group as the lowest specimens of humanity on earth. Cunningham claimed that they were from the jungles of Queensland, Australia, where they were embroiled in a "bushwhacking war" with Chinese laborers. There, they "relished the dead body of a Chinaman much better than that of a Caucasian because the Celestial has not so much salt in his composition. . . . They [could] stomach opium laded meat, but abhorred salt." He claimed that members of the group begged civilized English and American settlers for tobacco and whisky, and they carried only boomerangs, spears, and shields. Driven by hunger, they possessed incredible physical attributes— highly observant "little black eyes" and the ability to stay underwater for three hours at a time while breathing through the stems of water lilies. They used this latter technique to steal the wives of rival tribes while their husbands slept, with lassos made of native grass; incredibly, the women rarely made a sound while they were abducted from their male "masters." Aborigines were a "distinct race of people, black as the Negro," but without the Negro's receding forehead or "kinky hair." Their cannibal feasts were celebrated with corroborees, where their "black bodies, striped with white paint gave a sepulchral effect, where they contorted their disfigured bodies as opposed to dancing to what they called music." They had no "language of their own, only a gibberish," and were "the most illiterate of all peoples"; with no conception of time or dates, they could not count to ten.[1]

The Aboriginal delegation was not the only Pacific group at the exposition, which also featured Samoans, Māoris, and Hawaiʻians. That being said, it was through racist print media such as this article, self-study, travel to Oceania, and actual encounters at ethnographic displays like Chicago's fair that the Black world engaged and consumed Oceania. The turn of the twentieth century was an intense era of global Black self-rediscovery. This chapter explores how the icons of Black radical thought in this moment referenced Oceania in their analyses of race. In doing so, these writers, poets, and architects of Black nationalism, Ethiopianism, and Pan-Africanism framed their views within the troubling context of scientific racism and European colonial imaginations about race in the Pacific. They found the phenotypical similarities *and* histories of oppression that linked the peoples of Oceania and the Africana world to be more than enough to legitimize a political cartography around Blackness and a common struggle against racism, colonialism, and White supremacy. This would be particularly significant in the post–World War II era, when Black and Brown bodies were surveilled via photographers like Eliot Elisofon, anthropologists like Margaret Mead, and the US military. As Western popular culture, academia, and military institutions collectively "downpressed" Oceania's pushes for self-determination, the Black Pacific turned to the Black world for international support.

Born in 1819, pan-Africanist Alexander Crummell was one of the nineteenth century's most vocal advocates of African American emigration to Liberia. He was a close friend of E. W. Blyden, and his masculinist views on pan-Africanism, African redemption, and Christianity were also informed by his perception of indigenous communities across the world. In 1853 he gave a sermon to the Brixton Ladies' Negro Education Society about how the strong vital power possessed by the Negro distinguished him from other races. Wherever European civilization went, he claimed, the "natives vanished as the morning mist before the rising of the sun." This included indigenous peoples of the Americas and Tasmanians. Crummell wrote, "The Aborigines of the South Sea Islands, of New Zealand, of Australia, are departing, like the shadow before the rising sun of the Anglo-Saxon emigrant." He found something "exceedingly sorrowful in this funeral procession of the weak portions of mankind, before the advancing of civilization and enlightenment." However, the American Negro was the exception, as his vitality and "strong moral character" had allowed him to survive slavery—"Ethiopia *shall* stretch forth her hands unto God."[2]

Crummell would oft repeat this theme. In 1895 he argued that enslaved Africans had arrived in America as naked and ignorant pagans. However, slavery brought African people into contact with Europe's enlightened civilization. At the same moment, he argued, nations and tribes in Africa and in the Pacific and Atlantic Oceans were in the same "semi-barbarous condition as the Negro." These included American Indians, New Zealand's Māoris, and Aboriginal groups in Australia. European colonization allowed them all to be "touched for the first time by the rising rays of civilization." However, it was only the Negro who survived and thrived out of slavery, largely because of his "moral and spiritual perception."[3]

Others raised similar questions. In 1862 William Lloyd Garrison's abolitionist paper *Liberator* argued that the Anglo-Saxon race did not tolerate "any inferior races," such as "the American Indian, the Negro, the Aborigines of Australia and Van Dieman's Land, the New Zealander, and the Kaffir." In 1879 pan-Africanist Martin Delany asserted that indigenous peoples in Australia, Tasmania, New Zealand, and Papua New Guinea were descendants of a mixed Malay race. "Who can doubt," asked Delany, "the fact that the African once preponderated and was the resolvent race among them?" In 1900 the Los Angeles *Evening Express* repeated Crummell's "vitality" thesis. In an article titled "Negro Progress in Jamaica," it argued that "the Negro would not go under the march of civilization like the Carib, the Kanaka, American Indian and the Australian Aborigine"—he had "too much vitality" and throve on civilization.[4]

W. E. B. Du Bois was also a part of this tradition. His classic 1903 *Souls of Black Folk* prophetically reads, "The problem of the twentieth century is the problem of the color-line—the relation of the darker to the lighter races of men in Asia and Africa, in America and *the islands of the sea*" (italics added). In 1921 Du Bois was forwarded a letter from a Jamaican doctor who had been told by the island's high commissioner that the feeling in Australia was very strong "against a colored person no matter how well" he was educated, and that he should not emigrate to that country. In response, Du Bois referenced the Australian immigration diction tests that were designed to keep out "all colored immigration" and particularly "Chinese, Japanese, Indians and Negroes."

Anna Julia Cooper's 1925 "Equality of Race and the Democratic Movement" also decried Australia's "White only policy."[5]

In 1925 Du Bois wrote to the Australian Labor Party, asking for the NAACP to be represented at its planned Pan-Pacific Conference in Honolulu, Hawai'i. He informed the party that Black people in the United States had the impression that organized labor in Australia was their "global enemy" and suggested that "no real Congress of the Pacific" could "take place in which . . . Colored people's labor was not represented." Years later, Du Bois would remark that one could "trace the African black from the Great Lakes of Africa to the islands of Melanesia."[6]

In 1920 Carter G. Woodson received a letter from A. Goldsmith, a "Negro Exile" in Melbourne. Goldsmith informed Woodson that he read several Black newspapers and magazines from the United States. This included the NAACP's *Crisis*, the African Blood Brotherhood's *Crusader*, the Universal Negro Improvement Association's (UNIA) *Negro World*, the *Emancipator* (the socialist weekly edited by W. A. Domingo and A. Philip Randolph) and Woodson's *Journal of Negro History*.[7] John Maynard details the activities of Sydney's Colored Progressive Association (CPA), which was formed in 1903. Comprised of Black sailors who faced racism and immigration discrimination, it included African Americans, West Indians, and Aboriginal peoples. Aborigine activist Fred Maynard, who helped to found Sydney's chapter of the UNIA in 1920, was also a member.[8]

The CPA organized social events for heavyweight boxing champion Jack Johnson during his fights in Sydney. This included his 1908 world championship victory over Tommy Burns. Australian newspapers denounced these affairs "of the colored cult of the city," attended by a "few white men," "full black, half and quarter caste beauties," "negresses, quadroons and octoroons."[9]

During his fight with Burns, the sight of a "colored man sitting on a fence" gave Johnson strength. After visiting a museum, Johnson told newspapers that archeology was his first hobby. He remarked, "The Australian natives must have been geniuses" to invent "ancient art, boomerangs, stone axes and other examples of Paleolithic and Neolithic man's skill." Such comments by the African American boxing legend flew in the face of White Australia's racist policies toward indigenous peoples and self proclaimed anthropologists like Daisy Bates. Johnson emerged from his victories in Australia as a global Black sports icon. Black Pacific Islanders received news of his success with "great delight." One Solomon Islander who was present at the Burns fight described it as the "greatest day" of his life. British officials in the Solomon Islands suppressed the news of Johnson's victory to prevent the "natives" from taking "an inappropriate message from it."[10]

The Sydney branch of the UNIA was formed in 1920. Maynard asserts that the UNIA's "call for a return to Africa meant nothing in Australia to the Aboriginal people, but the call for recognizing cultural significance and the importance of their own homeland, struck a chord with the Aboriginal leaders."[11] It might also be fruitful to consider how South Sea Islanders may have made sense of Garveyism and the question of returning home to the islands.

Representatives from Australia attended the UNIA's 1920 First International Convention of the Negro Peoples of the World in New York. Garvey and the *Negro World* would poignantly reference the genocide of Black Australians in their call for African unity. "Over the world," Garvey told an audience at Liberty Hall, "in some parts of Asia, the islands of the sea, Europe and Australia, Blacks had been regarded as less than human." Whether it was in Europe, Canada, or Australia, he was told the same, "This is White man's country."[12]

Garvey also asked, "Do they think that they are going to exterminate four hundred million of Blacks as they have exterminated . . . the North American Indians . . . and the Aborigines of [New Zealand] and Australia?" In 1922 the UNIA petition to the League of Nations charged, "If Black men have no right in America, Australia, Canada [or Europe] then White men should have no right in Africa."[13] In 1928 he informed an audience in Jamaica's St. Andrew's Liberty Hall that

North American Indians . . . have been buried by the white race. . . . Today there are but a few of them left out on the reservations. . . . What is true of America, is true of Australia. A couple of decades ago Australia was populated by a Black type of people—the Australian Bushman. The White man . . . [has] gone into Africa with the same purpose as when they went into Australia and North America. If you sleep on your intelligence, in our ability, in another twenty five years Africa will be lost to the Black man, and instead of Black men living on top of the earth they will be buried under the earth as the North American Indian, as the Australian Bushman.[14]

Communications between Amy Jacques Garvey and the Sydney branch were published in the *Negro World*. In 1923 Sydney secretary Robert Usher reported that his branch was "filled with the spirit of the UNIA," whose "far reaching effects" reached throughout Australia. Usher hoped that Marcus Garvey could visit on his upcoming world tour. In fact, Garvey and UNIA leaders such as Henrietta Vinton Davis planned to visit Africa and spend a month in Australia.[15]

In 1924 Black Australia "sent greetings" to the UNIA's Fourth International Convention. In a letter to Jacques Garvey, Sydney branch leader Tom Lacey offered the UNIA the support of "60,000 Aboriginal people nationally." However, the government Aboriginal protection boards and missions had "doped the minds" of Aboriginal people so much that they believed that they could "never become a people." Lacey also hoped that "God would hasten the day we will be back in our mother country." He also stated that "Mrs. Hassen," his sister and treasurer of the UNIA branch, would send more news material from Australia.[16]

Perhaps due to Hassen's efforts, over the next few months the *Negro World* reprinted stories about race from Australian newspapers. During Marcus Garvey's incarceration, the *Negro World* continued a distinctly gendered focus on its coverage of Oceania. Now under the editorship of Jacques Garvey, in September 1924 it reported that Blacks in Australia and New Guinea were being "enslaved, exploited and raped by White Europeans." It reprinted reports by Sydney's *Labor Daily* and *Worker's Weekly*, applauding the "Labor and Communist organizations" for highlighting these concerns. The *Labor Daily*, paper of the historically racist Australian Labor Party, stated that indigenes from New Guinea's Sepik region charged a colonial officer with ordering their chief to send him a young woman at night for an "immoral purpose." The community refused to do so, charging the officer with being consistently drunk and forcing natives to work for him personally. Furthermore, natives were "sold like bags of chaff." The Communist Party of Australia's (CPA) *Worker's Weekly* claimed that there was a "slave trade in New Guinea. Under the British flag men and women were worked to death," "women and children" were starved, "women were treated as drunken men treat dogs," and the millions who slaved their "lives for their masters" were robbed of all they produced.[17]

A week later, the *Negro World* revealed that "Black women in New Guinea" were "victims of White rule." Citing the *Labor Daily*, it described how the police flogged "natives" on the orders of White officials. Beaten badly with *kundas*, some victims needed morphine to deal with the pain. One colonial official had "carted a native woman with a two month's old child at breast from village to village" and forced her to sleep with him. After handing the woman over to a patrol officer, the officer's troops raided a village and handcuffed eighteen hostages. When released, their hands and feet were "swollen up like footballs." They were imprisoned for six months. The *Negro World* felt that these "vile horrors" were far worse than those of South Africa. Australia was "conniving the enslavement and torture of native Blacks [and] the seizure of Black wives to be concubines for White men." The UNIA pledged to fight against the "common practice of White men living with Black women as a convenience" and "casting them off with bastard children."[18]

At an October 1925 meeting, the UNIA discussed a public plan in Australia that suggested building a "Black State" to "save the Blacks" from "dying out." Citizenship of this Australian Zion State or Black State was to be restricted to "full blooded blacks, half castes, quadroons or octoroons." In 1926 the UNIA reported that White people were "killing off the Black Australians." The paper found it "hardly believable that the White rulers of Australia . . . had dealt with the Black natives in a spirit of exterminating them root and branch, without regard." Citing a *New York World* article, it felt that Whites were "hastening the destruction" of Aborigines "by means of poison and gun." It compared these outrages to "lynchings in America."[19]

In 1924 members of Sydney's UNIA formed the Australian Aboriginal Progressive Association (AAPA). Led by the aforementioned Fred Maynard, its platform focused on Aboriginal land rights, "citizenship, stopping the government practice of removing Aboriginal children from their parents, and defending a distinct Aboriginal cultural identity." Its motto was the popular UNIA phrase, "One God, One Aim, One Destiny." The group's emblem was an indigene circled by the phrase "Australia for Australians," suggesting that Aboriginal peoples were *true*

Australians. The AAPA aimed to protect Aborigine communities from the "sinister" protection board, whose policies Maynard lambasted as "deliberately [stinking] of the Belgian Congo."[20]

Other US-based Black organizations took an interest in Australia's racial politics. In the 1930s Father Divine claimed to have established a Peace Mission kingdom there. In 1922 the NAACP's *Crisis* declared that Australia was "being held for white settlers . . . while colored people are being kept out." In 1928 the *Pittsburgh Courier* declared that a race war was emerging in Southern Australia. Seventeen "natives" were killed after Aborigines murdered a rancher in an uprising.[21]

Minkah Makalani demonstrates how the Communist International (COMINTERN) created a space of Black internationalism from which African and Asian revolutionaries built political community. The COMINTERN also raised questions of race and imperialism in Oceania and the French colonial world. For example, in 1922 Ho Chi Minh questioned the global scope of France's colonies: "Between Annam and the Congo, Martinique, and New Caledonia, there is absolutely nothing in common, except poverty." In 1924 he argued that "the question of Indochina and the Pacific seemed to be of no concern to European workers." Most islands in the French Pacific had been yielded to companies "that robbed the natives of their land and made them work as slaves."[22]

Sponsored by the COMINTERN, the International Trade Union Committee of Negro Workers (ITUCNW) was founded in 1930 to "organize Negro workers in Africa, the West Indies and other colonies." In 1932 its journal *Negro Worker* (edited by the likes of George Padmore, Cyril Briggs, O. E. Huiswood, and Garan Kouyaté) published an article by H.I.M., "Native Peoples under the Union Jack," which asserted that Australia's Aborigines had "no political, social, or economic rights" and were "among the most exploited subject peoples in the world." They suffered from inhuman exploitation, forced labor, slavery, and a "campaign of mass physical extermination." They were arrested and forced to work with chains around their necks, and Aboriginal women were "subjected to terrifying experiences."[23]

Discourse on Colonialism, published in 1950 by Aimé Césaire, was a Third World manifesto. In this magnificent poetics of anti-colonialism, Martinique's architect of Negritude also references the struggles of Oceania: "I see clearly the civilizations, condemned to perish at a future date, into which [Europe] introduced a principle of ruin: the South Sea Islands, Nigeria, Nyasaland."[24] In 1928 Paris-based Jane Nardal, also from Martinique, chastised Josephine Baker for playing in to White fantasies. Writing in *La Revue Negre*, she argued that Baker seemed "happy to sing 'Bake that Chicken Pie' despite its racial slurs; to accept a gift of a monkey and . . . a leopard as her pet companions; and to present herself as a Tahitian" if that was what her public desired.[25]

Cameras, Soldiers, and Sexual Surveillance

World War II brought increased visibility to Melanesia to the African Diaspora through the African American press and African American soldiers who served in Pacific campaigns across Papua New Guinea, Vanuatu, and the Solomon Islands. Cleveland's *Call and Post* reported that African American soldiers stationed in Papua New Guinea "found colored men there already." Atlanta's *Daily World* reported that Melanesian "Fuzzy Wuzzies" of the "malaria infested jungles of New Guinea were becoming legendary fighters."[26]

The all-Black 24th Infantry Regiment served in Vanuatu and numbered some 3,450 men. During the US occupation in 1941, 50 percent of American military personnel were Black; this increased to 70 percent the next year. The labor of African American soldiers included housekeeping duties on base, stevedoring, truck driving, handling ammunition storage, malaria control, and "working in base laundries, hospitals, officers' clubs, galleys and mess halls." According to Lamont Lindstrom, the presence of "several thousand uniformed and armed Black soldiers" had "lasting social and political consequences in Vanuatu, particularly for its dark-skinned indigenous inhabitants." Their presence influenced the spread of the John Frum movement, which has been problematically referred to as a "cargo cult." Frum was a spiritual figure who appeared in Tanna in the late 1930s, before the outbreak of World War II. The movement's message was that Americans would return to New Hebrides to help liberate them from British and French colonial rule and bestow upon them the material goods and wealth that the US military possessed. Lindstrom documented much of this via a major oral history project in which he interviewed Ni-Vans about their experiences in the occupation; these interviews

Figure 1.1. Three US Naval personnel, bartering with local traders, Nggela (Florida), Solomon Islands, September 1943. The original caption from the National Archives indicates that two of the personnel are Black Americans. University of Hawai'i at Mānoa Library Digital Image Collections, https://digital.library.manoa.hawaii.edu/items/show/6636, accessed January 6, 2021. US National Archives.

Figure 1.2. Solomon Islanders performing a dance for US military personnel, Halavo Seaplane Base, December 26, 1943. UHM Library Digital Image Collections, https://digital.library.manoa.hawaii.edu/items/show/6791, accessed January 6, 2021. US National Archives.

revealed a number of atrocities that the US military records did not document, including a number of well-known rape cases, such as the Maevo incident of Luganville.[27]

In 1945 *Life* magazine assigned iconic photographer Eliot Elisofon to Pearl Harbor to photograph "racial mixtures of Hawaiian people." Having taken over eleven trips to Africa, Elisofon has been heralded as awakening Westerners "to the true humanity of Africa," despising the "image of Africa" that was derived from "Tarzan films and racist books" and "eradicating myths" of Africa. He donated his art and over 80,000 photographs to the National Museum of African Art in Washington, DC. However, his canon of work in Africa overshadowed his decades of racist and sexist work in Oceania. This is troubling. As Raoul Granqvist writes, "The problem is that Elisofon myths are still uncritically repeated," anchoring his legacy in "a false dream world of misrepresentation."[28]

Figure 1.3. Solomon Island laborer receiving wages from an Australian officer, Guadalcanal, January 28, 1943. The original caption refers to the laborer as "a blue-black"; he earned five shillings a week as a stevedore. UHM Library Digital Image Collections, https://digital.library.manoa.hawaii.edu/items/show/6667, accessed January 5, 2021. US Marine Corps.

Elisofon's work smacked of White patriarchy, sexual surveillance, and colonial misrepresentations of Oceania. By 1963, he had made five trips across Polynesia, Melanesia, and Micronesia. These trips were professionally lucrative for Elisofon. He gave lectures, gained fellowships, and was widely touted for his photographs. This included a 1963 talk entitled "The South Seas: Its People, Its Art" at the May Company of Wilshire, where 1,100 pieces of "New Guinea Primitive art"—ancestry tablets, figures, masks, drums, spears, bark painting, totem poles, and shields—sold for up to $11,000.[29]

In 1949 he traveled across the region, including to the mountainous ranges and central highlands of New Guinea, where he spent time among "unfriendly natives" like the Wahgi. Here he was hosted by a "fabulous" Swedish-Australian named Edward Hallstrom, who owned a livestock station and a zoological garden. Hallstrom had been given permission by the Australian government to build the station supposedly "for the benefit of the highland natives." This involved teaching these communities to shear sheep for wool, prepare mutton, and use simple weaving to "produce body covering" and bedding. He rented the 340 acres of land from the Australian government for ten shillings per acre. He employed forty Wahgi laborers, who dragged two logs to the station each day.[30]

Elisofon described the Wahgi as being a completely "unspoiled" Stone Age people, as they had only been exposed to "the White man" some fifteen years prior. Like Africa's Nilotes and Maasai, the Wahgi braided their bleached hair with red ochre and animal fat. The Papuans in the South of New Guinea, he claimed, were "a different race with browner skins, frizzy high standing mops of hair, and women with elaborate body tattoos." Primarily agriculturalists, Wahgi women worked the land and grew sweet potatoes, bananas, papayas, and peanuts. The men hunted for birds and marsupials. Kangaroos, once a part of their diet, were now sold to the station. Elisofon claimed that the Wahgi yodeled their voices over far distances like Tarzan. They wore small loincloths and elaborately decorated themselves with birds of paradise feathers, yellow, green, and red face paints, and artfully decorated shells. They once exchanged these shells with coastal peoples for their stone axes; now, they received them from White men in exchange for their labor. His report of the station largely noted Wahgi women. He claimed to have had seen one woman simultaneously suckling a piglet on one breast and a little child on the other. He remarked that the polygamous community's chief had six ugly wives and eleven children.[31]

He also described the racist activities of Hallstrom's Irish manager, Captain Neptune Blood. Blood's daughter was cared for by a "native house boy," who happened to be in the doghouse because he had let her feet get sunburned. This community was allegedly excited by her blond hair and blue eyes. However, they were not encouraged to handle the child because they "were not too clean." Blood stressed that they were so afraid of water that a European missionary used a water pistol to keep them away from "restricted areas." He further professed that they had a considerable body odor that his wife was "having great trouble getting used to."[32]

In Australia, Elisofon lamented that a torrential rainfall prevented "local belles" from appearing on a beach that he visited. As he was only there to find women, he admitted that he was quite the bitter character. He noted that Australians had "elementary political and social viewpoints" and were "the most adolescent" people that he had met. He decried the country's deportation of non-Whites and the forced removal of "half-castes" from New South Wales.[33]

He found the people of Port Moresby, Papua New Guinea, to be beautiful. Here, he claimed, the young girls in their long grass skirts and dark blue tattoos over their dark skins were only describable by photographs. He associated their features with women from Bali, while the older women were "tremendously pendulous" and pejoratively called "razor straps" by Australians. At the village of Koki, his notes showed that he made sure to take plenty of pictures of the attractive Papuan girls. One he found to be particularly striking—she had "absolutely cylindrical breasts," which he had only seen in Africa. He continued, "It actually resembles a bottle sticking straight out of the chest and the nipple is always large and extends well back on the greater part of the organ." He also found time to purchase shields and bowls and take photos of homes decorated with "weird shields and human skulls."[34]

In Northern Australia he passed through Darwin, where he stayed with an Australian farmer some few miles from Delissaville, an Aboriginal reservation. Here he met with one of "the great characters of Australia," Bill Harney. An early caricature of "Crocodile Dundee," Harney fashioned himself as an expert of the Australian bush. He entertained Elisofon with racist and sexist stories about Aboriginal peoples—about groups that supposedly regurgitated and reconsumed their food, and how all Aboriginal women knew how to shoot out sperm ejaculated into their reproductive parts by a muscular action called backfiring.[35]

In January 1955 *Life* magazine published Elisofon's photographic essay "Storied Isles of Romance in the South Seas," based on his unpublished manuscript, "The Literary South Seas." One of his photos graced the cover of the issue. Captioned "Tahitian Girl Bathing," it was a picture of a young naked girl with a crown of flowers in her hair. "Storied Isles of Romance" featured Elisofon's photographs next to quotations from White writers like Herman Melville, Paul Gauguin, and Robert Louis Stevenson. To produce the piece, Elisofon sailed across the Pacific to take pictures that would capture the words that these men wrote decades and centuries before.[36]

Oversexualized images of indigenous women and girls were central to his racist and sexist piece. For instance, one staged photograph depicted a long-haired woman wearing a wet and white brassiere standing in the ocean, holding fish that she appears to have just caught. Next to this photo was a quote from Frederick O'Brien: "It was a picture of an artist's dream, the naked girl laughing in the torrents of transparent water, the wet crimson blossoms washing from her drowned hair." This was followed by a quote from Stevenson, "She had been fishing; all she wore was a chemise, and it was wetted through." Underneath this image was a scene of "natives" bathing and washing clothes and a naked woman placing a flower in her hair while she sits in water, images that W. Somerset Maugham found to be a passionate "scented languor." Other themes and captions included Melville's quotes about "pagan worship," idolatrous "altars of savages," and the "mischievous evolutions" of Marquesan girls who danced by moonlight.[37]

Life magazine considered the essay to be a scientific and artistic success. Elisofon's photojournalism across the Pacific and Africa boosted his career not only as a photographer but also as a pseudo-anthropologist of primitive art. In 1958 he became a research fellow of primitive art at Salem's Peabody Museum. In that same year, he organized an exhibit of primitive art at the Boston Museum of Fine Arts.[38]

In 1956 he was a key member of a Peabody-sponsored expedition across Oceania. Representing *Life*, Elisofon was joined by William Robinson, a White American who ran a French medical research institute in Tahiti, and parasitologist David Bonnet. The purpose of the trip was ostensibly to study the artifacts, sailing technologies, and canoe manufacturing in the outer islands of Melanesia, in an effort to chart Polynesian migration in Oceania via its seafarers. This was based on a racist assumption that Polynesian communities were technologically superior to their Melanesian counterparts. They hoped to test "natives" twice daily for filariasis, claiming that Polynesians and Melanesians had different variants of the condition.[39] Robinson sensationally referred to this process as "bloodletting." While *Life*'s editors did not envision the trip as a "pleasure junket," their plans were less "scientific." The magazine hoped to give Elisofon the chance to do an adventure essay on Melanesia along the lines of what he had done with Polynesia in "The Literary South Seas."[40]

Robinson aimed to sail his brigantine, the *Varua*, across Pape'ete, Tahiti, Fiji, New Guinea, Bali, and Siam. Writing in January 1956 from Honolulu, he sent one of many cables to Elisofon in preparation for the trip. He asked him about Komodo dragons, whether the "Big Nambas" from Vanuatu's Malekula island still wore phallus baskets, whether "Balinese breasts" were still bare, and whether the Indonesian government shot *Life* photographers on sight or after trials.[41]

Elisofon combined this trip with travel to Tokyo to shoot a story that *Life* published in 1962, "Japan's Dazzle after Dark." He wrote back to officials at *Time*, referencing that this would include "Geishas, tea houses, strip teasers, cabarets, whorehouse baths, everything anyone dreams about."[42] *Time* particularly wanted his trip to pass through Wallace and Futuna, as it was a place where a mission had "locked up all girls at sunset for years" due to their "Polynesian tendencies." Of major concern was a warning from the British consul, who stressed that the US military was about to "launch hydrogen bomb tests of such a magnitude that all navigation in the Pacific [would] cease for an indefinite time."[43]

The magazine's editors also hoped that the trip across Bangkok, Samoa, the Solomon Islands, the Admiralty Islands, and Borneo would also pass through Rennell Island, regionally known as Mugaba. This would be a challenge, as Rennell was a part of the Solomon Islands; the

British colonial administrators tried to keep ships away from the island, as its indigenous people were "so susceptible to alien diseases." The editors claimed that while the island was geographically in Melanesia, its indigenous peoples were "physically and linguistically more Polynesian than Melanesian." They alleged that during World War II US military brass marked it as "off-limits" when American soldiers "discovered that the women on the island were good-looking Polynesian types" instead of "ugly Melanesians." The local chief, however, "with very little else to sell," did all right with his "womenfolk." They also noted interest in other things, like clan relics, canoes, weaving, and artifacts. At the suggestion of Harvard professor Douglas Oliver, *Life* sought the support of Charles van den Broke d'Obrenau of the Department d'Oceania at Paris's Musée de l'Homme, who had taken recent photos of the island.[44]

British, Indonesian, and Dutch colonial administrations approved of the scientific trip, which also had the support of commercial interests. For example, the Apia, Western Samoa, branch of Burns Philp South Sea Company transmitted very telling instructions to Elisofon. These included notes for him to partake in Kava ceremonies, to visit Rotuma, whose peoples were perhaps "mixed with Negro," and to document suckling pig–sacrificing cults in New Hebrides. The instructions remarked that Rennell would be fascinating to visit since it was isolated from traders, missionaries, colds, and gonorrhea, was led by a chief who traded his women's services for iron, possessed chunky, ultra-friendly women, and had handsome men who looked "partly Caucasian, partly Polynesian."[45]

Robinson's letters to Elisofon reveal that the intentions for the trip were laced with troubling interpersonal issues. He intended the crew to include his two daughters and a "photogenic" Tahitian girl to take care of them, his adopted fifteen-year-old girl from Tahiti's Tuamoto, and two Tahitian entertainers. All of them sang, danced, and played the guitar and ukulele.[46] With admitted pessimism, Elisofon lamented to *Life* about these and other "misgivings." Robinson's wife had a nervous breakdown before the trip, and he brought all three of his daughters, aged four, two, and one. He also brought a "handsome Tahitian girl"— who had now become "his wife or what have you"—and her personal maid. The boat had become a circus, and Elisofon decided to make the yacht the central protagonist in his story.[47] But with three children, including a crawling baby, and one nurse who left the ship while another was almost sent home twice, detailing activities on board the ship would be a "risky" prospect.[48]

Elisofon's editors at *Life* found all this to be amusing at best. They were not concerned about "women passenger problems" but wanted him to capture the feeling of a personal adventure so that *Life* readers would say, "That's what I always wanted to do." Aiming for "forty percent" coverage of "natives and native ceremonies" and sixty percent of life on the board the ship, *Life*'s editors wanted more shots of Robinson "talking or eating with islanders."[49]

The trip would eventually be published by *Life* in February 1957, titled "Romantic Voyage of the Varua." The article was replete with pictures of bare-breasted and tattooed "Polynesian" girls and women of the Solomon Islands, who were described as having honey-colored skin and being linguistically different from other "darker skinned natives" of the region. In contrast, in the Melanesian New Hebrides, the group trekked through the territory of a "savage" tribe.[50]

Robinson's report of the trip stressed that the travelers were on a scientific mission. Unsurprisingly, it was full of sensational references to skin complexion, blackness, and savagery. For example, among the Tikopea community of the Solomon Islands, he recalled meeting the "most startlingly theatrical group that they had ever seen," "with bush lime-bleached hair, incredible painted makeup and tattooing, bloody looking mouths with black teeth from betel chewing." The chief, Ariki Tifua, had the "wildest head of bleached hair of all, and the widest smile with possibly the blackest teeth and bloodiest looking mouth." This meeting was followed by a "bartering orgy." On Fatuna, they claimed to have met definitively Polynesian peoples who curiously had an "un-Polynesian rancid smell." In Vanuatu, they crossed the remnants of ex-American bases, and Santo's "Million Dollar Point," where tons of American military equipment were bulldozed into the ocean after the war. This included the shipwrecked luxury liner SS *President Coolidge*, Nissen and Quonset huts, rotting docks, and cranes. In Malekula, the group witnessed dancers who drummed to "blood stirring rhythms," a "well-formed" girl of about fourteen years old who was as "wild and shy as a forest animal," old men in phallus wrappers who retained "their savage dignity," and Kali, leader of the "Big Nambas" language group

(V'ənen Taut). Robinson described Kali as being tall and beautifully proportioned and walking with the "grace and assurance of a forest animal and a king." Here, he noted, Bonnet conducted his experiments on "the most primitive people in the Pacific."[51]

In the island of Aoba, they ran into a group of thirty schoolgirls at a mission hospital, one who was supposedly "so Polynesian in appearance that she would have been lost in Tahiti." Robinson watched attentively while the older girls, dressed in little grass skirts and "with their torsos and firm youthful breasts glistening with perspiration," cleared a field. He was hypnotized by witnessing centuries-old dancing rituals that were unbelievably violent, and included women who moved in strange, hunched postures, and chanting small children. Robinson consistently distinguished supposed Polynesian peoples from "black Solomon Islanders."[52]

Elisofon represented *Life* on the ill-fated Harvard 1961 expedition to West Papua, which was led by Robert Gardner of the university's Peabody Museum. Elisofon claimed that the expedition aimed to "study the behavior patterns" of "the world's rarest anthropological treasure," West Papua's "Stone Age natives." Yet it also sought to manufacture such perspectives. It was perhaps an open secret that the group paid an indigenous group to start a battle that it would document and later depict as being legitimate. Elisofon described this fight as "hundreds of stark-naked savages" brandishing spears, with "their faces made even blacker with war paint organized in fighting squads like Zulu Impis." The party apparently witnessed these "savages" celebrating the killing of one of their enemies. The trip included Michael Rockefeller, whose mysterious disappearance two months later only added to the notion that New Guinea was a land of Stone Age peoples.[53]

In September 1962 *Life* published Elisofon's article on Papua as "Survivors from the Stone Age: A Savage People That Love War." It included photographs taken by Rockefeller. Describing the region as a "twin dinosaur," Elisofon claimed that in these unexplored highlands of New Guinea, people had "never seen a foreigner" or a piece of metal. Left to themselves, they thrived on sweet potatoes, pigs, wooden tools, and stone implements.[54]

These notions in the realm of Western popular culture mattered, particularly in the international debates surrounding Indonesian impe-

GARVEY'S CAVEAT | 43

rialism, West Papuan sovereignty, and post–World War II Melanesian movements for self-determination. They would also influence policy at the state level. In 1947 the US State Department produced a confidential summary about "trouble spots" in Oceania. It spanned French, British, Dutch, New Zealand, and Australian colonies. This included "native unrest" in the Solomon Islands in the form of the Maasina Ruru (Marching Rule), a movement against the "political and economic supremacy of the White man." According to the State Department, this religious and emotional movement was based on intense envy and hatred of the White man. Officials further claimed that Western influences stimulated other characteristics that emerged out of the "dislocation" of native social systems, namely, the blind following of a "native prophet" and his "fantastic promises," local patriotism, religious fervor, and anti-Whiteness.[55]

In 1963 the Central Intelligence Agency compiled a secret report entitled "Security Problems in the Pacific Islands Area." It anticipated that movements toward self-government and semi-independence in Oceania would emerge in the coming decades. It asserted that the problem for the Western powers was how to "handle this transition with minimum damage to their military and political interests in the Pacific and elsewhere." For the US government, these interests lay within Oceania's military strategic value and its potential for space and nuclear missile testing programs. It was likely that frictions would "arise between Western Powers and the native leadership and peoples," and "if not resolved satisfactorily, these frictions could be exploited by Communist and other anti-Western elements to encourage local sentiment for complete political independence." This included French plans for nuclear testing on Mururoa in French Polynesia, which was already drawing heavy criticism.[56]

The Agency's perspectives on the peoples of Oceania were based on the racist attitudes and pseudo-anthropological accounts outlined earlier in this book. This is unsurprising. In preparation for its occupation of New Hebrides in World War II, the US military officially studied *Among the Cannibal Isles of the South Pacific* and *Cannibals of the South Seas*, both films by explorer and vaudeville showman Martin Johnson, for background information on Melanesian cultures and social conditions.[57] "Security Problems in the Pacific Island Area" surmised that twenty-five thousand years ago, Stone Age humans who walked and sailed on crude rafts from Asia into the archipelagos of Oceania included both "dark-skinned, short Negritoid people, and taller, heavy-browed Australoids." Despite thousands of generations of interbreeding, it argued, such peoples still formed the mass of indigenous people in New Guinea and Australia. However, they were joined fifteen thousand years later by "tall, brown-skinned people" with "racial characteristics like those of the Caucasoid peoples of Europe, who brought with them new Stone Age cultures." These more sophisticated sea voyagers pushed earlier inferior peoples inland and to mountainous areas. Circa 1000 BCE, Asians of "Mongoloid character" penetrated the region, interbreeding with communities there to produce the ethnic populations of modern Malaya, Indonesia, and the Philippines. This pushed communities further into the forests of New Guinea and eastward into the Pacific Ocean, creating the distinguishable cultural and racial groups of Melanesia, Micronesia, and Polynesia. As such, when Europeans arrived in Melanesia, they found a variety of "dark-skinned folk, tall and short, wavy-haired and frizzy," with dominant "Negrotoid or Australoid" features. In opposition, the Polynesians spread out through the Eastern Pacific through "prodigious feats of seamanship and navigation," before Mongoloids (with "lighter or more yellowy skin") reached the West, leading to their major Caucasoid and minor Negrotoid characteristics. These notions certainly impacted how US military officials perceived the political demands for self-determination made by indigenous Pacific Islanders. In a moment when there were bound to be political frictions between Western powers and indigenous communities, the report tended to frame the political movements of Melanesia (Solomon Islands) as "backward" as opposed to the sophistication of Polynesia (French Tahiti).[58]

A 1975 conversation between US secretary of state Henry Kissinger and deputy secretary of state Robert Ingersoll speaks to this issue. In talks with the deputy prime minister of Fiji, who was six foot five and weighed three hundred pounds, Ingersoll asked him about his weight. The deputy minister retorted that the ancestors of Fijians "were cannibals and had a good diet." The conversation then turned to "the Papuan," Papua New Guinea's ambassador to the United States, who was noted as being much shorter than the Fijian minister. Kissinger sarcastically referred to "the Papuan" as "having a high intellectual level," and that he had a "real winner of a conversation" with him. He was particularly amused that "the Papuan" had told him that he had not made up his mind about what he was going to say in the General Assembly. Also present was Philip Habib, US assistant secretary of state for East Asian and Pacific affairs, who considered "the Papuan" to not be very sophisticated in international affairs, although his pending speech to the UN General Assembly was written by his aide, "a sharp cookie."[59]

Angela Gilliam, Susanna Ounei, and Black Women's Pacifics

To be clear, US military officials did not casually make such assessments. The Boston-born Black feminist anthropologist Angela Gilliam writes how the US armed forces drew on Margaret Mead's ill-informed and racist perspectives on Pacific Islanders as a rationale to deny them self-determination. In 1954 Mead published an article, "Melanesia, Black Islands of the Pacific," in UNESCO's *Courier*, arguing that Melanesians had a far less developed culture than Polynesians, lacked the political ideas necessary for developing kingdoms, and lacked "any developed historical sense."[60] In 1971 she reiterated these ideas in a conversation with James Baldwin. Mead's relationships with the US military in the Pacific began in 1925. The latter found use in Mead's "cross-cultural surveys" that concentrated on areas of probable combat operations in the Pacific. Her "social science discourse and terminology often masked the military potential of studies that were often labeled cross-cultural, intercultural, transcultural, and concerned with group or human relations." Mead argued that "the study of national character by anthropological methods" could "throw much light upon problems of immediate military importance in both direct and psychological warfare, contribute to the establishment of smoother cooperation with allied nations, and prepare personnel for problems of relief, reconstruction and world reorganization after the war." Part of the military effort was about how the work of anthropologists like Mead could "produce short case studies on how best to get Polynesians to cooperate with the military on, for example, building an airfield on an atoll."[61]

In their *Confronting the Margaret Mead Legacy*, Gilliam and Lenora Foerstel argue that "Mead's focus on the South Pacific islands and their use as experiments in understanding social change" became militarized. In conceptualizing Pacific peoples as her laboratories, Mead established a paradigm for an analysis of Pacific peoples that was adopted by the US military "in order to control and manipulate leadership toward a specific and desired direction." The military suggested themes for research, such as political development in West Papua. It recommended the study of cult movements as "an expression of Western desire to mold indigenous movements that defied colonial rule." These movements were a "threat to colonialism because they comprised a unique cultural pattern for protest, not easily decoded and therefore more difficult to control." Mead's work on psychological warfare during World War II was later transferred for application during the Cold War.[62]

Gilliam consistently used her positionality as a Black anthropologist to create gendered *Black Pacific* networks and spaces across the Black Diaspora from which the *White Pacific* could be collectively challenged. For example, as a visiting lecturer at the University of Papua New Guinea from 1978 to 1980, she organized international and African film festivals. *Confronting the Margaret Mead Legacy* emerged out of a session at the 1986 meeting of the American Anthropological Association, which brought together US and Pacific intellectuals to use anthropology to address issues of "nuclear sovereignty" in the region. The session included Melanesian activists like Vanuatu's Hilda Lini and New Caledonia's Susanna Ounei, founder and former president of the women's organization within the Kanak Socialist Liberation Front (FLNKS), and the Kanak and Exploited Women Syndicate (GFKEL).[63]

In July 1985 Gilliam chaired an iconic session with Ounei, "The Impact of Racism and Class Oppression on the Scholarship about Women," at Kenya's World Conference to Review the United Nations Decade for Women. This panel of Black Diasporic women included South Africa's Lindiwe Mabuza (chief representative of the African National Congress in the United States), Mamphela Ramphele (formerly of South Africa's Black Consciousness Movement), Afro-Brazilian anthropologist Lélia Gonzalez (of Brazil's Movimento Negro Unificado Contra a Discriminação Racial), and Rose Catchings (executive secretary of the United Methodist Church's Ministry of Women and Children).[64]

Ounei's paper, "For an Independent Kanaky," described the history of Kanak struggle against French colonialism's apartheid-like, racist, and violent policies. The idea for GFKEL emerged while Ounei had been incarcerated for her participation in an anti-colonial demonstration.

Ounei recognized the story of New Caledonia in the words of her "Black sisters in Brazil and South Africa." FLNKS needed international help in its movement.[65]

In 1984 and 1985 Ounei spent fifteen months studying English in Aotearoa. In June 1985 she gave a talk about the Kanak, "the Black, indigenous people of the French South Pacific colony" of New Caledonia, at Toronto's St. Paul's Center. In July she spoke at the Women's Alternatives for Negotiating Peace Conference in Halifax, Canada. In the aftermath of the conference, she conducted a two-month tour across twenty cities in the United States, including Atlanta, Miami, Philadelphia, Houston, San Francisco, Oakland, Chicago, New Orleans, Birmingham, and Greensboro. Her trip was initially sponsored by the National Black United Front's (NBUF) Conrad Worrill and Adeyemi Bendele, Elombe Brath of the Patrice Lumumba Coalition, Vernon Bellecourt of the American Indian Movement, the Young Socialist Alliance (YSA), and the US-Vietnam Friendship Society.[66]

She gave talks at Detroit's Central United Methodist Church, St. Louis's Berea Presbyterian Church, St. John's Episcopal Church in Los Angeles, and Rutgers University's Robeson Center, sponsored by its Afro-American and African Studies Department. In Berkeley, California, she spoke at the newly established La Peña Cultural Center. Printed in both English and Spanish, the event's flyer noted that Ounei's speech was about apartheid, the Nuclear Free Pacific movement, and her aims to use the tour to raise funds for FLNKS to establish a Kanak radio station and newspaper.[67]

In New York she recorded an interview with the *New York Times*, stating that if the French did not keep their promises, the Kanak had no other way but to fight. "We haven't arms. We have only stones. But I think we have done a lot with our stones."[68] According to the Socialist Workers Party's *Militant*, she "received an especially warm welcome from opponents of racism in South Africa. She spoke at a 2,000-strong anti-apartheid rally organized by the Free South Africa Movement in Chicago." She was also "a featured guest at a conference of Indian women" in Washington State, which included indigenous peoples from Hawai'i and Australia.[69]

In Washington, DC, Ounei conducted interviews with the *Washington Post*, National Public Radio, and Pacifica Radio. On September 10

Figure 1.4. Flyer (in both English and Spanish) advertising a talk
on Kanak independence by Susanna Ounei, Berkeley, 1985.
La Peña Cultural Center.

she gave a talk at Howard University's Undergraduate Library that was
sponsored by NBUF, the Howard University Student Association, the
YSA, and DC's Republic of New Africa. Howard's student newspaper,
the *Hilltop*, noted Ounei's concern about the presence of "all the traitors,
the supporters of French imperialism from Algeria, all the traitors from
Vanuatu, all the traitors from Vietnam . . . the rubbish of the world," who
were against their movement.[70]

While Ounei was visiting Howard, iconic Black feminist writer Audre
Lorde was a special guest at a Writers Week in Melbourne, Australia, organized by Women 150. During her keynote address to the Black Woman

Writer and the Diaspora Conference, held at Michigan State University in October 1985, Lorde informed her global audience how she had met "Pacific Island women, the Kanak women in struggle in New Caledonia, [and] Māori women of Aotearoa." On September 9, she participated in a land rights march in Melbourne alongside Black Koorie women and sisters from Angola and South Africa, who were "out of their countries, and still in battle." It was clear to her that "besides the particular differences of our struggles, the origin of our oppression was the same." This stimulated her "thoughts on what it [meant] to be indigenous," and what "her relationship as a Black woman was to the land struggles of indigenous peoples."[71]

For African American poet Lucille Clifton, this question of land was also a question of waterways. Her 1987 poem "Atlantic Is a Sea of Bones" was also about her fondness for the Pacific "as a nice ocean." This was because it was "difficult for a person of [her] complexion to be fond of the Atlantic" due to the legacy of the Atlantic slave trade. However, she was aware that Oceanic communities might not "be fond of the Pacific," perhaps due to its own troubled histories of violence.[72] These kinds of global and gendered networks of relational "sisterhood and survival" were part of a political and conceptual Black Pacific of decolonization.[73]

Negroids of the Pacific

West Papua, Senegal, and Negritude

In the summer of 2019, a blaze of protests torched the West Papuan cities of Wamena and Jayapura, denouncing racism and collectively calling for political independence from Indonesia. According to Radio New Zealand, dozens of Papuans were arrested and at least ten protestors killed in a security crackdown; the government shut down the Internet and maneuvered some 6,000 Indonesian soldiers to the 54,000 square mile region with a population of over 963,000. The government of Indonesia considers West Papua, which shares an island with Papua New Guinea, to be its second-largest province. In contrast, a critical mass of West Papuan communities, organizations, freedom fighters, artists, and political movements consider West Papua to be a nation ethnically, culturally, and politically distinct from but violently colonized by Indonesia. According to *Al Jazeera*, this includes the United Liberation Movement for West Papua, which was created in May 2019.[1] This is a centuries-old struggle.

Captured Land

Founded in 1971, the Provisional Government of West Papua New Guinea (RPG) dates the written history of Papua New Guinea to 724 CE. A document of its times, the RPG's political essay "Indonesian Colonialism vs the People of West Papua" argues that this was when their first contact with Indonesian peoples occurred in the context of the Indian Ocean slave trade. The document states that enslaved Papuans were the "chief merchandise" of Indonesian merchants, and "master-slave relations" defined the historical connections between "Asiatic Javanese," Black Papuans, and the Sultan of Tidore, Al-Mansur.[2]

The Netherlands expanded its influence over the region via the Dutch East Indies Company, including its eventual colonies of Indonesia and

West Papua. The 1824 Treaty of London divided New Guinea between Holland, Germany, and Britain "without the knowledge or consent of its Black population." In the 1920s the Dutch used West Papua as a place of "punitive exile" for leftist Indonesians from Java.[3]

Papua resisted Dutch colonialism. From 1938 to 1942, an indigenous priestess (Konor) named Angganeta Menufandu launched the Koreri anti-colonial spiritual movement. She encouraged mass noncooperation against Dutch orders to participate in forced labor gangs and to pay taxes, and laws and missionary bans on traditional dancing and singing. Her group inverted the Dutch tricolor flag (red, blue, and white) and added a morning star, a Biak cosmological symbol. Uprisings occurred when the Dutch arrested Angganeta and burned the homes of her community. She remained in captivity during Japan's occupation of West Papua during World War II. Stephen Simopjaref freed her and transformed members of the Koreri movement into an army of armed resistance. He declared, "Our time is coming, the masters will be the slaves and the slaves masters." Both Simopjaref and Angganeta were recaptured and beheaded by the Japanese, who killed between six hundred and two thousand people on Biak.[4]

Led by President Sukarno, Indonesia secured political independence from the Netherlands in 1949. A deal with Holland granted Indonesia its former Pacific colonies. Sukarno immediately claimed that Dutch New Guinea (West Papua) was ethnically and historically a part of Indonesia. It was not a given that he would take this position. In 1945 Indonesian vice president Mohammed Hatta expressed support for Papuan sovereignty, declaring, "Polynesia is for Polynesians, Micronesia is for Micronesians, Melanesia is just for Melanesians, as well as Indonesia is for Indonesians."[5] Intent on holding on to West Papua, the Dutch denied Indonesia's claims. Ironically, it was Dutch colonialism that had geopolitically oriented West Papua *west* toward the Dutch East Indies and the Indian Ocean, as opposed to *east* toward Melanesia and Oceania.[6]

In 1955 Sukarno hosted the historic Afro-Asian Bandung Conference, which he used as a platform to solidify Afro-Asian support of Indonesia's claims to West Papua. Melanesia's voices of dissent were silenced during the talks. Attended by twenty-nine countries, Bandung declared that "colonialism in all its manifestations" was evil, and that the "subjection of peoples to alien subjugation, domination, and exploitation" constituted a denial of human rights contrary to the UN Charter. The conference called for respect for the sovereignty and territorial integrity of all nations, and recognition of the equality of all races and nations large and small. It called on its members to refrain from the use of force against the political independence of any country. West Papua was the exception. Sukarno framed Indonesia's claims to the region as being part of a struggle against Dutch imperialism. As such, Bandung resolved to "support the position of Indonesia in the case of West [Papua] based on the relevant agreements between Indonesia and the Netherlands."[7]

West Papuan nationalists rejected Indonesia's position. As did the Dutch, they made clear distinctions between the racial and ethnic histories of Papua and Indonesia. As the conflict between Indonesia and the Netherlands intensified, they found themselves in a complicated situation. They repeatedly asserted that they were neither pro-Indonesian nor pro-Dutch and pushed for sovereignty. In response, Indonesia lambasted them as being puppets of the Dutch, defined them as Stone Age peoples unready for self-determination, and violently abused those who resisted.

In October 1961 West Papuans organized a National Congress at Hollandia. Through a free general election, a Papuan National Committee (PNC) was elected with the charge to lead West Papua to independence. Days later, it created a flag, arms, a national anthem, and names for the country and people, which it signed and distributed throughout the country. Sydney's *Morning Herald* stated that fifty Papuan representatives of New Guinea's 750,000 people declared "national unity." Representative Willem Inuri declared, "We want our own nation and to rename the territory West Papua."[8]

Dutch residents in Hollandia pondered whether West Papua was going to become a "New Congo." Perhaps to assuage these concerns, the Dutch passed an ordinance stating that the new flag could only be raised alongside a Dutch flag of greater height. Still, the Netherlands supported West Papuan nationalism in an effort to stave off Indonesia. Detractors claimed that the PNC was an extension of Dutch liberal politics, downplaying West Papuan nationalism.[9]

In December 1961 Sukarno vowed to "liberate the land" from the "grip of the Dutch." In dramatic fashion, he called for the "total mobilization of the Indonesian people" to invade West Papua. In a national broadcast to an audience of a million people, he ordered Indonesians to "wreck the Dutch efforts to set up a Papua puppet state" and instead hoist Indonesia's red and white flag over "West Irian." As reported in the African American newspaper *Atlanta Daily World*, he exclaimed, "There is no power in this world which can stop us—no fleet, no army . . . when we follow the path which is blessed and approved by Allah. We ask the Dutch what do you march with? At most, your cheese and butter."[10]

Sukarno framed the pending invasion as a "West Irian Liberation Command." His ambassador to Australia declared, "Historically and ethnically, we are entitled to Dutch West New Guinea . . . and certainly we would not allow the people of West [Papua]" to form an independent country with East New Guinea. In February 1962 the *Bermuda Recorder* reported that ten thousand Indonesian volunteers were ready to invade, reportedly "skilled in the type of jungle warfare required in the wilds of Dutch-held New Guinea."[11]

The PNC retorted that West Papuans were ready to defend themselves against an invasion. It remarked that there would be an "unending guerrilla war" if Indonesia attempted to occupy their mountains and jungles. Their warning was stark—only three hundred out of forty thousand Japanese who had tried to trek across New Guinea during World War II survived. Nicolaas Jouwe, second vice-president of the council, called for Papuans to resist Indonesia with arms if necessary. In January 1962 he informed Australia's *Age* that Indonesian propagandists had told Indonesians that Papuans would welcome them when they landed. "We will welcome them all right, but not with handshakes." Papuans would "resist Indonesian rule with everything in their power," including "flights of poisoned arrows." The PNC sought to form a People's Army, which, according to Herman Womsiwor, depended on finances from Holland. He wanted "warriors equipped with jungle carbines, grenades, and light machine guns." They hoped to bolster their Papuan Volunteer Corps via conscription. Six months were needed to train six thousand Papuans. In May 1962 Jouwe stated that his people's "volunteer battalion of jungle fighters" were urging the Dutch to arm them. "Because of our fighting prowess," he claimed, "I think we could fight against one hundred Indonesians with five soldiers."[12]

West Papua, Africa, and the United Nations

In 1962 the PNC began to seek direct support from Africa. At the PNC's insistence, the Dutch government invited African representatives to the United Nations to West Papua to investigate the situation. According to the PNC, a number of African ambassadors approved of the mission but declined the invitation "on account of Indonesian intimidation." Still, in 1962 Upper Volta's Frédéric Guirma and Maxime-Leopold Zollner of Dahomey visited West Papua for two weeks.[13]

Guirma held a press conference upon their return. In front of an audience of some fifty reporters and African diplomats, he concluded that Indonesia's claims to West Papua rested on "very weak" historical grounds that were as logical as if Indonesia were to claim Australia and the Philippines. Guirma felt that it was a "scandal that 700,000 New Guinea natives were living in the Stone Age" while the United States and Russia were "sending satellites to the Moon." The issue was not whether New Guinea should go to the Netherlands or Indonesia, but how to elevate "its people to the level of this century." He advocated that the UN administer the territory, and after West Papuans had "improved their way of life," a move should be made to complete self-determination.[14]

Guirma's comments were met with opposition. Guinea's ambassador stated explicitly, "I am in complete disagreement with my brother from Volta." Guirma was also chastised by African American journalist Charles Howard, who wrote, "Why do you, an African, come here and try to propagandize us, on behalf of a colonial power, while the UN and the Asian African group are doing all in their power to liquidate colonialism everywhere?"[15]

In Baltimore's *Afro-American*, Howard reported that Indonesia appealed to African delegates to the UN to help it restore West Papua to the republic. The appeal asked the peoples of Africa "to not heed to the poisonous babble of the Dutch puppets who [made] noises in the interests of their own pockets." Major J. Diamara, a leader of the Indonesia Defense Council, lodged the statement, "We, sons of West Irian and representative of West Irian independence fighters, hereby declare to all the peoples of Africa, wherever they may be, that West Irian is an integral part of Indonesia. We, the West Irian Community belong to Indonesia, and since olden times we have spoken Indonesian."[16]

The PNC launched an international campaign in response to Indonesia's pending invasion. It sent delegates to New York, Amsterdam, and cities across Africa. In May 1962 Jouwe took the case of West Papua to the UN in New York. Officially a part of a Netherlands delegation, he was very visible in the US media, declaring that Papuans wanted "freedom and justice" and refused to be the "victims of Indonesian blackmail." In July 1962 he asserted that Papuans "wanted the same thing the Americans wanted in 1776—freedom and independence." They refused to be handed down from "one colonial master to another."[17]

The PNC's thirty-six page booklet *Voice of the Negroids in the Pacific to the Negroids throughout the World* donned its red, white, and blue–striped starred flag, based upon Angganeta's design. Published in 1962, it began with a striking poem written by Tshaka Jomo Zekelkeyzulu, the Denver-based South African director of the New Africa League. Titled "Dutch New Guinea Is New Africa," it read, "Our Negroid people have increased, As those of African domain . . . The Netherlands will be our guide, Our friend for all the world to see, NEW AFRICA—we shall be free!" Including a map and geographic description of New Guinea, the booklet argued that the island belonged "geologically to another part of the earth than the Indonesian Archipelago." It argued that New Guinea was not a borderland of Indonesia, but of Oceania.[18]

It read, "BROTHERS AND SISTERS NEGROIDS! . . . You have heard about us from the Dutch and Indonesians, without having known us. Now we will take the floor ourselves. . . . We are living in the Pacific, our people are called Papuans, our ethnic origin is the Negro Race. . . . We do not want to be slaves anymore." The statement listed how Papuans had endured several colonizers—Dutch, British, Japanese, and now Indonesian. "Do you know this is a devious way to kill a people spiritually? Why does the world not give us Papuans, the opportunity to decide on our own destination?"[19]

Voice of the Negroids stated that the Nationalist Papuan Movement started in 1907, when Papuan students like Johan Ariks suffered racism at the hands of Indonesian students at a missionary school. This led Dutch missionaries to create a seminary at Miei just for Papuan students; Papuans began to elect leaders from here. In 1925 a Dutch missionary named Isaac Samuel Kijne composed a national anthem for Papuans, "Hai Tanahku Papua" (O My Land Papua). A number of his students became leaders in the nationalist movement. In 1949 the fifty-nine-year-old Ariks led a delegation that included Marcus Kaisiepo and Jouwe to the Hague's Round Table Conference between the Netherlands and Indonesia. It was here that they pushed for independence from the Netherlands East Indies.[20]

The booklet included the PNC's manifesto, which was signed by its forty members on October 19, 1961. Demanding independence, the group called for its flag to be hoisted next to the Dutch flag, that the national anthem be performed alongside the Dutch national anthem, that the country take the name Papua Barat (West Papua), and its people be called Papuan. It included a letter written to "all fellow-tribesmen of the Negroids throughout the world," reading, "We, the Papuan people of West Papua belonging to Negroids are calling all you fellow-tribesman to give us help!" Papuans were in a "dangerous position." If handed over to their Indonesian enemy, they would be forced to be slaves. This letter was signed by Dorcas Tokoro-Hanasbey—the only woman on the Legislative Council of West Papua, and the group's first and second vice presidents, Kaisiepo and Jouwe.[21]

Voice of the Negroids included a letter from the PNC to His Majesty, Emperor Haile Selassie of Ethiopia in Addis Ababa. Noting that Papuans were not trained in modern warfare, the letter beseeched Selassie not to abandon West Papua to Indonesian imperialism. It reiterated that Papuans were physically, racially, geographically, and religiously different from Indonesian Asians, and belonged "to the brotherhood of Melanesian people" and the Negroid race. It defined Selassie as a man of power, wisdom, and influence, and was concerned that he would be "misled by Indonesian propaganda" that sloganized "human values like freedom and anticolonialism" to further its imperialist goals. The PNC asked Selassie to send advisors to West Papua to see the state of the country, as it wanted freedom and self-determination—the same rights that His Majesty had been fighting for. It also asked him not to allow the sacred principles of the UN Charter and its Decolonization Resolutions to be sacrificed. Versions of this letter were sent to Liberia's William Tubman, Nigeria's Abubakar Balewa, Ghana's Kwame Nkrumah, the Congo's Joseph Kasavubu, Guinea's Sékou Touré, and Sierra Leone's Milton Margai.[22]

The booklet included a statement written to US president John F. Kennedy, in the aftermath of Robert Kennedy's visit to West Papua.

It argued that the latter had conducted a contemptuous television interview upon his return to the United States, particularly concerning "backwardness and lack of university training" of Papuans. The committee felt that this almost suggested that Indonesia eradicate Papuans. Yet, it claimed, the region boasted a higher literacy rate than Indonesia itself, had a representational council, free elections, and political parties. It read, "Independence and democracy can be understood and practiced by common people even if they have not seen Harvard."[23]

In fact, a 1960 Kennedy administration policy paper, "The Problem of West New Guinea (West Irian)," described West Papua as being the farthest from ready for self-determination of any other group in the world. It defined West Papuans as "semi-nomadic, stone-age headhunters" who spoke countless "unintelligible languages and dialects" and had no sense of government.[24] Furthermore, when questioned in 1963 by the foreign minister of the Netherlands about the United States' role in the conflict between Indonesia and Holland, Kennedy's response was that the United States and Europe had a "common civilization, common forms of government, and common color—*white*."[25]

The PNC popularized its struggle through the Black press. In April 1962 the *Pittsburgh Courier*'s two-page center spread read, "Papuans Seek Help from Negro Brothers and Sisters." Tokoro-Hanasbey, Jouwe, and Kaisiepo informed the paper that Papuans urgently needed help from their global "Negro brothers and sisters" against the "menace of Indonesian imperialism." This "clarion call" to the Black world argued that "African Papuans" were a sovereign Black people. They urged American Negroes and Africans to exert their influence to have them placed under UN supervision.[26]

Reprinted in the *Chicago Defender*, the article detailed the PNC's program around self-determination and freedom, ideals that Black people across the world fought for. Hence, it followed, Papua's quest for liberation was no different than that of the Africana world. The *Courier* pondered whether West Papuans would have a "right to make their own choice," or would "the other nations" allow a "dictator of Asian origin to keep them down?"[27]

The PNC's words were poignant, but the photographs that it circulated were arguably more impactful. *Negroids of the Pacific* included pictures of Guirma as he toured West Papua, Tokoro-Hanasbey being sworn in as representative, Papuans playing indigenous drums, PNC members dressed in shirts, ties, and pants returning from the Netherlands by plane, and Papuan women practicing traditional dances. Both the *Courier* and *Defender* published photographs of the October 1961 founding of the PNC. The images also included the PNC's red, white, and blue flag. One photograph of a PNC rally on Biak depicted West Papuan men, women, and children holding placards inscribed with the phrase "Pampampun—We Papuans reject Sukarno and his people."[28] The demonstrators' dress challenged mainstream misrepresentations of West Papuans as Stone Age primitives, headhunters, and cannibals.

This was critical, as depictions of Papuans as Stone Age people were widely perpetuated through the mass media. Leon Dennen, in an interview with Jouwe, claimed that it was "tough to be a free Papuan headhunter or the son of one in the age of anti-colonialism." The *Defender* found it "anybody's guess" why the Dutch or Indonesia wanted West Papua. A 1962 article in the *Amarillo Globe-Times* claimed that the "Stone Age habits" of Papuans were slowing their transformation to independence. West Papua's population of 700,000 was "just beginning to emerge from the Stone Age." The Dutch had repressed headhunting and cannibalism in few areas. Papuans had nothing in common, spoke two hundred "mutually unintelligible languages," and were mired in poverty and disease. The paper claimed that Indonesia needed West New Guinea like it needed "the holes Papuans used to drill in enemy skulls to remove the brains for eating."[29]

Acts of No Choice

Indonesia landed paratroopers in West Papua in April 1962. Without consulting West Papuans, Kennedy's administration brokered a deal between Indonesia and the Netherlands. This New York Agreement conceded West Papua to Indonesia. Sukarno recognized "internal self-determination" but not "external self-determination" of the Irian people. It was expected that Indonesia would hold a referendum in 1969 to determine whether Papuans wanted to be independent. The UN ratified this arrangement in September 1962.[30]

Now backed by the United States and the UN, Indonesia proceeded to colonize West Papua. Writing from New York in 1968, the Freedom

Committee of West Papua argued that Indonesia had become "more murderous." The committee was chaired by Jouwe and included Womsiwor and secretary general Ben Tanggahma.[31] It claimed that through violence, military occupation, intimidation, economic coercion, political incarceration, and propaganda, Indonesia sought to suppress West Papuan nationalism. West Papua was a "military fiefdom" that degraded Papuans because of their "darker skin" and supposed lack of civilization.[32]

In 1965 Lodewijk Mandadjan launched an armed resistance movement in the mountains of Manokwari with about a thousand fighters. After a clash in which an Indonesian police brigade was injured, the Indonesian military killed over a thousand people in a B-52 bomber air strike. While Papuans claimed that over two thousand had been killed, the Indonesian government initially stated that only forty people had died. Its "mopping up operations" netted a thousand World War II weapons and documents connecting the group to Operasi Papua Merdeka (Free Papua Movement, OPM).[33]

Supported by about 90 percent of the Papuan population, the OPM had become West Papua's core opposition to Indonesia. Yet the US State Department did not believe it to be an "all-pervasive revolutionary movement." The police had broken up its publishing ring in Jakarta. Loosely organized, it was hard to track down, not because it was security tight or unspoken of. Rather, it was because "everyone talked about it." Many Papuans claimed to be members of the OPM, which "had few secrets." Reflecting an "amorphous mass of anti-Indonesian sentiment," it had anywhere from 1,500 to 50,000 members.[34]

Papuan nationalists continued to coordinate their movement from outside the country. Jouwe led opposition to Indonesia from the Netherlands. By 1967, Kaisiepo had become "President in Exile of the Government of West Papua." In December of that year, he met with Francis Underhill, director of Indonesian affairs at the US Department of State. According to Kaisiepo, Indonesia had restricted free speech and free movement, and halted significant educational opportunities for Papuans. Papuans who referenced the pending 1969 referendum were imprisoned. Kaisiepo hoped that the US officials could use their influence to ensure that the referendum occurred fairly. Underhill suggested that he look to Holland for assistance. Ironically, he encouraged Kaisiepo to get the support of "Third World" countries, since the views of White nations about colonialism would be "arbitrarily dismissed." Kaisiepo responded that the Dutch could not assure that the referendum would be fairly administered. Furthermore, Papuan leaders had become "completely disillusioned" of any hope that the Afro-Asian bloc would be helpful, as it was "blinded by the 1955 meeting at Bandung" and would not challenge Indonesia.[35]

In January 1968 US political consul Thomas Reynders visited West Papua for a month. He reported that Indonesia focused its efforts on "suppressing political unrest," and that its presence in West Papua was primarily expressed via its ten thousand troops. Despite the presence of a West Papuan governor, whom Reynders insultingly referred to as a "sun-dazed frog," Indonesia's General Bintoro was "the government" of West Papua. He was also rector of its Tjenderawasih University, a "political indoctrination center" for West Papuan students. Most government officials were Indonesian, and worked hard to keep Papuans away from UN officials. The government also ran separate schools for Indonesians and West Papuans.[36]

Missionaries reported that almost everyone in West Papua's "developed areas" were anti-Indonesian. Westerners were certain that Indonesia would not win an open election. There were daily arrests of suspected rebels in Biak. Violence was inevitable, as nationalists would not accept union without a struggle, and Indonesia would not accept separation. The only question was how much violence. According to Reynders, the Indonesian government was developing ways to avoid an open election and set the stage for a "successful Act of Free Choice" in its favor.[37]

About a year before the referendum, Indonesian foreign secretary Adam Malik Batubara suggested that Indonesia use "careful groundwork" to win the support of some sixty "key tribal leaders." This included granting favors to them and their groups, scheduling personal visits with the governors, and bringing them substantial gifts flown in by C-130 military aircrafts—clothing, flashlights, tobacco, bead necklaces, tin goods, and sago. He also advocated giving amnesty to six leaders who had been arrested on charges of rebellion. At the time, Indonesia held about four hundred political prisoners.[38]

On August 9, 1968, the US Department of State summed up Indonesia's precarious task of "designing a form of self-determination that would ensure its retention of West [Papua] and yet not appear as a flagrant violation of its international obligations to the rights of the Papuans." Its current plan was to avoid universal adult suffrage and create a council with handpicked chiefs and "approved restricted voter lists." Meanwhile, the Dutch pledged not to sabotage Indonesia's plans. Serious opposition from the radical UN Afro-Asian bloc seemed improbable, given its support of Indonesia in 1962. Indonesia now had the backing of moderate African and Asian nations.[39]

If West Papuans did have some hope, it was that the UN had decided to send Bolivian ambassador Fernando Ortiz-Sanz to ensure that the referendum was fair. To the disdain of Indonesia, Ortiz-Sanz stated that he would preside over "a completely free election" in West Papua or resign. Ortiz-Sanz's team included two African Americans, James Lewis and Marshall Williams, who were also critical of Indonesia. They claimed that 95 percent of the country supported independence and that the Act of Free Choice was a mockery.[40]

According to the US State Department, Williams "made no secret of the fact that he identified with the Papuans because of his American Negro antecedents." He asserted that he was almost declared "persona non grata" because he openly criticized Indonesia. In one case, Indonesian soldiers removed him from a UN office during a demonstration because they thought that he was Papuan. The incident in question took place in April 1969, when the OPM organized a "one person, one vote" demonstration in front of Ortiz-Sanz's residence. Caught off guard, military troops fired on the crowd of around a thousand people.[41]

Upon his return to the United States, Ortiz-Sanz was certain that at least twenty-five African representatives to the UN would not accept the Act of Free Choice. In August 1969, as part of an effort to stave off this sentiment, Indonesia's Malik toured Europe and Africa to enlist the support of nations such as Congo-Brazzaville, Guinea, Senegal, Tanzania, Kenya, Congo, Liberia, Nigeria, Sierra Leone, Benin, Cameroon, Niger, and Madagascar. The State Department noted that OPM leaders abroad were mobilizing support by using "race—Brown Indonesia oppressing Black Irianese." Malik's Africa tour was "calculated to counter" these operations with its own propaganda. Indonesia hoped not to drop the ball after the "resounding wins" it had secured in Africa.[42]

Malik attended the UN's discussions on the Act of Free Choice. Supported by Gabon, Togo, Ghana, and Ecuador, Dahomey's ambassador to the UN objected to the short time allotted for the debate. Malik intriguingly argued that African states understood self-determination in ways that may have applied to Rhodesia; however, he claimed, they had "little understanding" of the 1962 New York Agreement. He asked US officials to convince the African nations to side with them—they were already discreetly but pervasively pressing them to do so. Of course, the US government had its own geopolitical interests in Oceania, Southeast Asia, and the Indian Ocean. It had supported Indonesia's push for political independence from the Dutch and saw the nation as a critical Cold War ally against communism.[43] The Act of Free Choice vote went in Indonesia's favor. Papuan nationalists derided the vote as an act of "no choice." They continued to press for self-determination on the international stage.

Negritude in Oceania

On July 1, 1971, the Revolutionary Provisional Government of West Papua (RPG) declared West Papua to be independent under President Brigadier-General Seth Rumkorem. The RPG stated that since 1963, Indonesia had killed over thirty thousand Papuan men, women, and children. Tens of thousands of others were fleeing the Indonesian army and joining the guerillas. The population's intellectual strata found themselves in concentration camps and prisons. Papuans were "slaves in their own country" and risked being placed on reservations like North American Indians and Aborigines in Australia. Rumkorem stressed that the Papuan people, their provisional government, and his National Army of Liberation would fight "until either their country was freed of the last Indonesian soldiers or [was] the graveyard of its own last child."[44]

By 1975, the RPG claimed to control a territory twice the size of the Netherlands. It operated schools and two hospitals and had excellent communication with its representatives in Holland and Papua New Guinea. Papuans also lived in exile—five thousand were in Australia (with five hundred under asylum), five hundred lived in the Netherlands, and others roamed its rainforests in fear. The RPG was represented abroad by Womsiwor, Filemon Jufuway, and Tanggahma.[45]

In 1971 Womsiwor met with Roy Wilkins of the National Association for the Advancement of Colored People (NAACP). He told Wilkins how, in 1969, the RPG had gone before the UN's 24th General Assembly and garnered the support of Gabon, Jamaica, Kenya, Sierra Leone, Tanzania, Dahomey, Central African Republic, Zambia, Barbados, Togo, Trinidad and Tobago, Uganda, Guyana, Zambia, and Israel. Yet it needed more support. Womsiwor asked whether the NAACP could take up the case of West Papua at its annual meeting. He gave Wilkins materials about the liberation struggle, including the essay "African Papuans Being Slaughtered by Indonesian Government." Sent to Holland from New Guinea in September 1970, the document claimed that between May and June 1970, Indonesian soldiers killed eighty-five villagers in Biak, including a pregnant teacher. In Meruake they executed fourteen Papuan men. In Bird's Head, freedom fighters who had returned to their villages under amnesty conditions were "rounded up and slaughtered on the beaches." From January to August 1970, 2,053 Papuans were arrested because they challenged the Free Act.[46]

Wilkins was convinced. In 1972 he released a charge to the UN from the NAACP. "Black Americans," he wrote, "know little or nothing about the situation of their ethnic cousins in West New Guinea, a former Dutch holding in the South Pacific. Papuans had resisted Dutch domination but found themselves under Indonesian control after WWII. A fraudulent plebiscite in 1969 was used as a pretext to further cement this unwanted control." In "accordance with its consistent stand against political domination of subject peoples," the NAACP urged the UN to grant West Papuans "a full and free hearing on their status with respect to Indonesia." At its 1971 convention, nearly two thousand delegates and over 1,700 local units voted unanimously to support West Papua. The same statement was printed in the NAACP's *Crisis* magazine. In the "interests of all Black people in the Pacific," in 1975 Womsiwor asked the NAACP to call on influential Black congresspersons to pressure the US government to intervene on their behalf.[47]

In December 1975 Rumkorem wrote to Wilkins from Hollandia, thanking his "dear brother" for his tireless efforts in supporting the "rights of the 2,000,000 Black people of West Papua New Guinea" who were victimized by racist suppression, genocide, and colonial subjugation. He found the NAACP's support to be critical "in the face of the utter failure" to "sensitize world opinion to their plight." The RPG had identified 1977 as the target year to resolve the conflict, and Rumkorem instructed Tanggahma to inform Wilkins about how to increase the public awareness of African Americans on the issue.[48]

The RPG toured Africa in search of allies, carrying literature and photographs depicting its struggle. This included images of Rumkorem and the National Army of Liberation. It argued that if São Tomé (with a population of 80,000) could be promised independence, why not West Papua with its population of 800,000? In 1974 it won the favor of the African and Mauritian Common Organization (OCM). Formerly known as the conservative Brazzaville Group, the OCM invited the RPG to attend its 1974 conference at Bangui, Central African Republic. Also attending Bangui was the iconic architect of Negritude, Senegalese president Léopold Sédar Senghor. Due to his political invitation and financial support, on July 1, 1975, Tanggahma opened an RPG coordinating and information office in Dakar, Senegal.[49]

Senghor ardently supported West Papua and its Melanesian "neighbor," East Timor. He attempted to have them seated at the 1976 Organization of African Unity's (OAU) Non-Aligned Coordinating Committee meeting. When the Parisian paper Le Monde questioned this interest, he retorted that Senegal supported Negritude, which was "the right of Blacks to work in an independent state" for the development of their own civilization. Senghor remarked that Papuans were Black and that Indonesians were "a mixture of Black and Yellow races," hence differing by race and culture. Senegal took the same approach with Palestine, which it had helped to create a national state; the Palestine Liberation Organization (PLO) also had an office in Dakar. In February 1978 Senghor told Australia's ambassador that he saluted the country's granting of independence to Papua New Guinea, as "the UN had made an enormous mistake in remaining deaf to the demands of Papuans," who stood on their Negritude and demanded independence.[50]

US officials found it striking that Senghor gave haven to groups such as the RPG, the PLO, the South West Africa People's Organization (SWAPO), and the South Moluccans, who were also pressing for independence from Indonesia and self-identified as being Black Dutchmen and Black Portuguese. They considered Senghor's association with "Indonesian separatists" more "adventurous radical chic" than his association with the PLO and SWAPO. Yet they felt that Senghor may have seen these relationships as bridges to Diasporic Black communities who identified with Negritude. Senghor's support for these groups was a closely controlled "vest pocket" operation. As an "African elder statesman with unparalleled access to, and respect in, western political and intellectual circles," he seemed "intent on also earning trust of radical movements" across the "Third World." Officials believed that Senghor, who had a reputation for being politically conservative, was hoping to internationally enhance his "progressive image" by supporting this group. He had in fact gotten "good political mileage out of being the first Black African state to have a PLO office." They argued that he was perhaps positioning himself to be a leading political power broker who could facilitate dialogue between opposing sides. Regardless, with the Dutch government also raising concerns, the State Department wondered whether the time was ripe for Indonesia to make overtures toward Senegal to wean it from its "flirtation with dissident elements."[51]

Senghor was sincere. Even Wole Soyinka, whose disagreements with Senghor were legendary, understood Senghor's solidarity with Melanesia to be a "logical extension of his pan-*Negritude*." Senghor's "obsession with the mapping of the geography of the Black race" took him beyond Atlantic African Diasporas to include the Pacific. Wanting more clarity about the region's political struggles, Senghor remarkably dispatched Afro-Cuban Carlos Moore—who lived in Senegal from 1975 to 1980 with his wife, Shawna Maglangbayan—to Melanesia. According to Soyinka, Moore somehow penetrated "through to the very earliest guerilla encampment of East Timor"; he returned to Senegal with a report and photographs of himself and a group of insurgents there.[52]

Moore's path took him through Fiji, where he was hosted by activists Claire Slatter and Vanessa Griffen. Both women were integral organizers in the Pacific Women's Movement, the Nuclear Free and Independent Pacific (NFIP) movement, and Fiji's Pacific People's Action Front (PPAF). They published the PPAF's newsletter *Povai*, which provided timely and reliable information about the "struggles of people in the Pacific." *Povai*'s March/April 1976 issue published an article on West Papua, which remarked at how little was known about its "protracted guerilla war against Indonesia since 1965." The article was based on information provided by Moore, who was covertly described as an "outside source in contact" with the freedom fighters. *Povai* also printed an excerpt of a speech made by the RPG's foreign minister Tanggahma at Colombo, Sri Lanka's 1976 Non-Aligned Conference.[53]

The pages of *Povai* demonstrate Oceania's solidarity with West Papua. In 1976 two hundred students at the University of Papua New Guinea (UPNG) staged a demonstration march to the Indonesian embassy in Port Moresby. They demanded that its government support West Papua and East Timor. These issues were also raised by organizations such as the Women's Action Group, which held a protest against Indonesian imperialism months before.[54]

Povai also discussed a February 1976 communiqué by Tanggahma that called for international support of West Papua and East Timor's fight against "Indonesian colonial aggression." He told the Senegalese paper *Le Soleil* that he had been informed by telephone that Indonesian bombings of villages had killed over 1,600 people. Nationalists responded by killing over 400 Indonesians, including two officers, and wounding more than 800 others. The communiqué denounced the "criminal action of the Indonesian junta and its neo-colonial satellite, Papua-New Guinea"; it revealed how Papua New Guinea's foreign minister, Albert Maori Kiki, stated that his government would cooperate with Indonesia and refuse sanctuary to the rebels.[55]

From Senegal, Tanggahma effectively popularized West Papua's struggle. A statement released during the establishment of the Dakar office informed media that Papuans were a Melanesian "sub-race of the Black Race." It argued that Indonesia wanted West Papua's gold, nickel, copper, oil, and other minerals. If left to the whims of Indonesia, West Papuans could be eliminated or forced to live on reservations like American Indians or Aborigines in Australia.[56]

He wrote to the NAACP's Wilkins and Mildred Bond Roxborough, asking to be invited to the association's 1976 national convention. This was due to the RPG's need to have the backing of "a strong movement of Black Americans on their behalf." In March 1976 he met with the foreign minister of Ivory Coast and sent a message from Rumkorem to its president, Félix Houphouët-Boigny.[57]

According to the US State Department, Tanggahma lived in a large house provided by the Senegalese government. His staff included a second officer from West Papua, and Tanggahma had recently told an informant that four more colleagues would arrive in the summer of 1976. The RPG's foreign minister maintained an exceptionally low profile, and US and Dutch officials found him to be "evasive." When US officers accidently encountered him in the SWAPO office, Tanggahma supposedly "withdrew in confusion," saying he should not be in contact with diplomats. The US embassy officials interpreted this to mean that he was "concerned about keeping within restrictions placed on his activities" by Senegal. Whether true or not, as his office was adjacent to the home of the embassy's communications assistant, the embassy believed that opportunities "for substantive contact with embassy personnel could arise."[58]

Tanggahma had his own reasons to meet with US officials. He had unsuccessfully attempted to speak with African American congressman Charles Diggs during the latter's visit to Dakar in 1976. In 1977 he toured Ghana, Liberia, Tanzania, and Mozambique. Upon his return, he visited the US embassy in Dakar. Stressing US official policy on human rights, he asked for moral and material support for the RPG. He shared with the US ambassador a memorandum, a letter for President Jimmy Carter, and a sixty-page document detailing the situation.[59]

Black Asian Diasporas

From February 4 to 6, 1976, Soyinka organized Dakar's seminar of Black writers, ENCOUNTER: African World Alternatives. A project of the African Union of Writers, the seminar aimed to be a "low-key" affair in an ongoing search to find "alternatives to existing world systems." Based at the University of Ghana's Institute of African Studies, Soyinka felt that 1976 was a "watershed in the liberated energies of the African world."[60] He convened a group of Black intellectuals, artists, activists, scholars, journalists, researchers, and scientists from across the Americas, Africa, and Australasia.[61]

Tanggahma also attended the talks, which resulted in a politically charged "Declaration of Black Intellectuals and Scholars in Support of the People's Struggle of West Papua New Guinea and East Timor against Indonesian Colonialism." The document was signed by some sixty-eight political and cultural luminaries, including Senegal's Cheikh Anta Diop, Trinidad and Tobago's C. L. R. James, Madagascar's Jacques

Rabemananjara, Brazil's Abdias do Nascimento, Ethiopia's Tsegaye Gabre-Medhin, Guinea's Camara Laye and Ibrahima Baba Kaké, Cape Verde's Onésimo Silveira, Haitian poet Gérard Chenet, Mauritius's Edouard Maunick, Nigeria's Soyinka, Sudan's Taban Lo Liyong, Venezuela's Joaquin Paez Diaz, and Haki Madhubuti, Harold Cruse, Shawna Maglangbayan, Jake Carruthers, Iva Carruthers, Anderson Thompson, and Calvin Hernton of the United States.[62] Soyinka's invitations to both Liyong, who taught creative writing and Negritude at the University of Papua New Guinea, and Australia-based African American dancer Carole Johnson reflected the global scope of the talks.[63] Linking the struggles of the Black Pacific to those of Africa, Asia, and the Americas, this roll call captured an incandescent yet largely invisible paragon of Black internationalism.

The declaration expressed indignation over Indonesia's "veritable campaign of extermination" against the "Melanesian (black) populations of West Papua New Guinea and East Timor." It was shocked that 165,000 West Papuan New Guinean Blacks had been "killed, imprisoned or herded into strategic hamlets" since 1965, and that 30,000 East Timorese were butchered by Indonesia since its annexation of East Timor in 1975. It denounced the racist and genocidal acts that Indonesia had carried out against the 2,700,000 Melanesians of both states, and its claims that these were savage or primitive peoples incapable of self-governance.[64]

It asserted that Melanesians were "distinct national communities" whose racial, historical, cultural, socioeconomic, and political affinities with Africa and the Black world were unquestionable. It found the armed struggles of West Papua and East Timor to be part of the struggles of "all oppressed peoples in Africa, North America, the Caribbean, South America, the Pacific, Asia, and the Middle East." It argued that by taking up arms against Indonesian oppression, the "20,000 guerilla fighters" who were "shedding their blood in a silent isolated struggle" were making a decisive and laudable contribution to the emancipation of the Black world.[65]

The seminar's group "of independent Black intellectuals, researchers, scholars and scientists from Africa, the Caribbean, North America and South America" expressed "unreserved fraternal solidarity" with their brothers, President Rumkorem of the RPG's National Liberation Army and President Francisco Xavier do Amaral of the Democratic Republic of East Timor's Revolutionary Armed Forces.[66] They attributed Indonesia's aggression to the greed and self-interest of Jakarta's Javanese ruling class, which had resulted in the deaths of Indonesian people and was supported by global transnational companies that sought to loot Melanesia's mineral resources. The seminar was convinced that "without the active mobilization" of the African Diaspora, the "fascist Javanese junta" would be encouraged to carry out further acts of genocide.[67]

As such, the declaration called on the Black nations of Africa, the Caribbean, South America, and the Pacific and other "justice seeking nations" to support West Papua and East Timor. It called on the terrorized 125 million people of Indonesia, "now crushed under the merciless boots of a right-wing fascist regime, to rise to their feet and contribute to their own national and social liberation" by aiding these states "against a common enemy." It called on the UN, the OAU, the Organization of Non-Aligned Nations, the Organization of Afro-Asian Unity, the Arab League, and the Organization of African, Caribbean and Pacific Nations to compel Indonesia to withdraw its armed forces from the region.[68] As one of its four resolutions, the seminar deplored Indonesia's atrocities against "the Black indigenes" in East Timor and West Papua.[69]

Interviewed by journalists Moore and Maglangbayan, Diop discussed the issue further. Asked about his opinion on the "role that Blacks in the United States, the Caribbean, and South Pacific should play" in "strengthening the development of the African world," Diop responded that the ties between "Black Africans and the Blacks of Asia, Oceania, the Caribbean, South America, and the United States" needed to be strengthened on a logical basis. Black Africans needed to entertain the closest cultural links with Blacks of the Americas, Oceania, and Asia. Out of the meeting an African Union of Writers and a World Black Researchers' Association (WBRA) was established. Elected president, Diop described the aim of the WBRA to be the establishment of a list of Black scholars from across Asia, Oceania, North and South America, the Caribbean, and Europe. The association placed particular focus on the inclusion of Blacks from Australia, Fiji, New Guinea, and the rest of Oceania, Asia, and parts of the world where Black populations were "scattered and isolated." This interview was published in English by Nigeria's *Afriscope* (1976) and the Institute of Positive Education's *Black Books Bulletin* (1977).[70]

Maglangbayan and Moore also interviewed Tanggahma, who allegedly had informed *Le Monde* that "the rebels needed to get rid of the guardianship of Indonesia," which was "favorable to yellow supremacy, racist, expansionist, colonialist, and fascist."[71] When asked by the couple about the relationship between Black communities in the Pacific and Africa, Tanggahma stated,

> Africa is our motherland. All of the Black populations which settled in Asia over the hundreds of thousands of years came undoubtedly from the African continent. . . . Hence, we the Blacks in Asia and the Pacific today descend from proto-African peoples. We were linked to Africa in the past. We are linked to Africa in the future. We are what you might call the Black Asian Diaspora.[72]

Tanggahma discussed the enslavement of Papuans in the Indian Ocean and Middle Eastern slave trade, enslaved "Black Philippinos" taken to Mexico by the Spanish, blackbirding, the migration of African people into the Pacific, and indigenous Black communities in China, Japan, and other parts of Asia. For Tanggahma, Melanesians were part of the African family, and shared a "common past and a single destiny" with the Black world. West Papua had received sympathy from Africa and the Caribbean, but it needed "active solidarity" in terms of "concrete material and humanitarian aid." Senegal and Senghor led the way in this regard.[73]

The RPG's ideology was "simply Melanesian nationalism—no less, no more." The Black peoples of Melanesia needed to "determine their own future and work together with . . . the rest of the Black world to redeem Black peoples from" servitude. How would they defeat Indonesia, with its military might and superiority of resources, while they had few weapons and little material backing? For Tanggahma, this was "a question that our ancestors in New Guinea, in Africa, the Caribbean and the Pacific must have asked themselves over and over again, in the face of the invading White man." The only answer was "reliance on the courage, awakening and determination of our people to be free" and the active support of the Black world.[74]

This question of ideology was critical. In 1978 the Dakar RPG office issued a press release regarding "recent splits" within its revolutionary ranks. Jacob Prai, president of the Revolutionary Provisional Senate, broke from the RPG and formed his own guerilla movement comprised of two hundred soldiers of his ethnic group, the Kerom. This had pushed Rumkorem's army deeper inland, which, having not received any supplies of weapons or medical assistance for over six years, was being hard pressed by Indonesia's forces. Prai had been impressed by the armed victories of Angola's People's Movement for the Liberation of Angola (MPLA) through military support from Cuba and the Soviet Union. As such, he urged the RPG to seek financial, military, and personnel assistance from the Eastern bloc. According to the RPG, Prai declared that Marxism-Leninism would make up the leading ideology of the West Papua struggle, and that, once established, an independent West Papuan state would be forged along the lines of socialism. He created a so-called "Revolutionary Provisional Government of West Papua" and named Holland-based Jouwe his vice-president. The press release also claimed that through Henk Joku and Bob Kubia—two Papuans who lived in Papua New Guinea—Prai established relationships with Australian Communist Party leaders such as Rex Mortimer and Denis Freney, and Julie Southwood of the British Communist Party. The brief claimed that Prai's Marxist allies had established offices in Australia, Holland, and Great Britain, staffed by European Marxists who asserted themselves as legitimate spokesmen of West Papua's national struggle. Further internal differences eventually split Prai's group. The communication stressed the RPG's ideological position as being a national liberation struggle as opposed to a class struggle: "Our ideology is Melanesian nationalism, not Marxism-Leninism." The RPG rejected "a doctrine or ideology inconsistent with the specific realities of West Papuan people, a Melanesian people ethnically and culturally linked to the people of Africa and the Caribbean, and quite dissimilar to those of Indonesia, Eastern or Western Europe." In essence, the RPG was non-aligned, and sided with neither "Capitalist nor Communist blocs."[75]

As to be expected, this created international complications. In February 1976 the NAACP'S Roxborough received a curious letter stating that Womsiwor was recalling Tanggahma from Dakar because the "fella that he was using from Jamaica, Charles Mandang or so-called General Awon" to communicate with the NAACP was claiming to be someone who had been killed in 1971. None of this is clear, but it was enough to give Roxborough some pause regarding a request from Tang-gahma to speak before the NAACP's 1976 convention.[76] Flanked by Van-uatu's Barak Sope and West Papuan singer and activist Andy Ayamiseba, in 1987 Rumkorem and Prai signed the Port Vila Declaration in Vanu-atu. The declaration pledged to safeguard the survival of the Melanesian race in West Papua and ended nine years of conflict between the two groups.[77]

The RPG was convinced that if not for Senghor's humanitarianism, they might have been "erased from the face of the planet." Indeed, the mere existence of an office in Dakar that was capable of denouncing "the crimes of Indonesia" had been "undoubtedly instrumental" in encour-aging Sweden to accept West Papuan refugees.[78] US State Department officials accurately accessed that the RPG's Senegal-based office strate-gically placed it in proximity to "Black organizers drawn to Dakar by *Negritude*."[79] Senegal's support for West Papua extended into the 1980s, when the RPG participated in Dakar's Solidarity Week, held from March 27 to April 2, 1980.[80] As reported in *Présence Africaine*, Dakar's 1980 First Pre-Colloquium of the Third World Festival of Negro Arts similarly ex-pressed that accounts of the historical dimensions of the Black world needed to include "the people of Oceania, Australia, and South-East Asia." This was because the history of Black Americans, West Indians, and Latin Americans was known through the lens of the slave trade. However, the pre-colloquium stressed that in an effort to understand the historic dimensions of *all* Black communities, scholars needed to carry out research in these former regions.[81]

In 2010 the Free West Papua Campaign participated in Dakar's World Festival of Black Arts. In opening the festival, Senegalese president Ab-doulaye Wade exclaimed that "West Papua is now an issue for all Black Africans." His comments welcomed to Senegal Benny Wenda of the Free West Papua Campaign.[82] When asked years later about the relevance of Black Lives Matter to West Papua, Wenda asserted that the killing of George Floyd was a reminder of the historic violence enacted against Papuans and Black people across the world. A former political prisoner, he continues to reach out to the broader Black world for international support.[83]

3

Oodgeroo Noonuccal

Black Women's Internationalism in Australia

On November 22, 1974, renowned Aboriginal activist poet Oodgeroo Noonuccal (Kath Walker) was awoken by the sudden sounds of rifle fire. She was among forty passengers on board British Airways Flight 870, which was being hijacked on the tarmac of Dubai's international airport. Yearning for more sleep, Noonuccal was on her way back to Australia from Nigeria, where she served on the steering committee for the Second World Black and African Festival of Arts and Culture (FESTAC, 1977).[1]

The VC10 aircraft was scheduled to stop briefly in the United Arab Emirates. Now, Noonuccal found her eyes focused on "a very tall, handsome black man" pointing his revolver at her. He was one of four Palestinian *fedayeen* of Martyr Ahmad 'Abd al-Ghafur, a militant organization based in Beirut, Lebanon. The group of hijackers demanded the freedom of thirteen *fedayeen* who had been captured and detained in Egypt after a similar attack in Rome, Italy. It also threatened to kill all Dutch and Belgian passengers if two Palestinians (Ahmad Nuri and Sami Ta'mimi), who had hijacked and blown up a British Airways aircraft in the Netherlands, were not let go. With the plane flown first to Tripoli, Libya, the releases of both the hostages and *fedayeen* were negotiated in Tunis, Tunisia; tragically, one passenger was killed. Driven off safely in a Black Maria vehicle, Noonuccal was reminded of how this same make of car was used by the Australian police force, which has a troubling history of persecuting Aborigines.[2]

This forty-six-hour ordeal had been a precarious test of Noonuccal's diplomatic prowess. Unsurprisingly, the seasoned fifty-four-year-old organizer rose to the occasion. As former Queensland secretary for Australia's Federal Council for the Advancement of Aborigines and Torres Strait Islanders (FCAATSI), Noonuccal had long since identified with

Palestine's indigenous struggle for sovereignty. But if a Black Maria is a Black Maria, then *a gun is a gun*. Remarkably, Noonuccal "built community" with her hijackers. Expressing sympathy for the "Arab cause," she poignantly told these *fedayeen* that hijackings were politically wrong and that they should join FESTAC instead, which they did not do. They were astounded that her "copper-hued" skin marked her not as Pakistani or East Indian but Aboriginal, and their two-way dialogue continued.[3]

The group's leader, Yussef, confessed to Noonuccal that he had given up a career as a pediatrician to join Palestine's armed struggle. This moved her to pen a striking poem on the sick bag found in the pocket of her seat, "Yussef (Hijacker)." "Yussef, my son," it asked, "what do you do here?" The poem described how Yussef's dreamy eyes reflected the sun and "the warm soft touch of a girl's embrace." It mused about his love for children, which poured from his heart, was easy to see because he wore it on his sleeve. The soft lines around his mouth told of endearments that he dared not speak. His tired eyes had seen bloodshed, tears, fear, and contempt. Still, Noonuccal saw him in the moonlight, contented in a girl's embrace. However, all of this was clouded by the reality of the repeating rifle that he caressed in his "desert-strong sunburned hands."[4] Noonuccal never published this complex piece, which expressed explicit admiration for Yussef's struggle but quiet disapproval of his means. This also evoked her mercurial relationship with her son Denis Walker, who founded Australia's Black Panther Party in 1972.

This chapter explores Black women's internationalism in Australia through the radical life of Noonuccal, whose activism bridged a post–World War II generation of indigenous civil rights and Black Power organizers such as Faith Bandler, Pearl Gibbs, Patricia Korowa, and Roberta "Bobbi" Sykes. Australia's Security Intelligence Organization (ASIO) placed Noonuccal under heavy surveillance during and after her stint in the Communist Party of Australia (CPA); literature based on these records strongly demonstrates her activism in FCAATSI. This chapter shows how she consistently sought to forge relationships with Global South liberation struggles. Her Black internationalism spanned her time at FESTAC, London's 1969 World Council of Churches (WCC) conference, and a 1978–1979 Fulbright Poet-in-Residency in the United States. But just like her poem "Yussef," this is not a narrative of simple solidarities. It is a compelling tale of Black internationalism in Oceania

Figure 3.1. Oodgeroo Noonuccal (Kath Walker), 1964.
National Archives of Australia.

brimming with ethnic and gendered tensions, personal mishaps, and political misadventures.

Noonuccal was born on Minjerribah (North Stradbroke Island) in 1920. Of the Noonuccal ethnic group, her family's totem was the carpet snake. Humbly raised as Kathleen Walker, she took the name Oodgeroo (paper bark tree) Noonuccal in the later years of her life. As a young girl she excelled at sports like cricket. During World War II, she joined Australia's Women's Army Service after her brothers were captured by Japanese forces. She met numbers of African American soldiers while serving as a signaler in Brisbane.[5]

Noonuccal came of age when public discourses about Aboriginal peoples were decidedly racist. For example, the 1936 report of Queensland's Chief Protector of Aboriginals—a most ironic name if there ever was one—used terms like "full-bloods," "half-castes," "quadroons," and "cross-breeds" to describe the indigenous population. It claimed that while the population of "half-castes" had increased in the past year, this was not due to miscegenation but from "the marriage of cross-breeds themselves to civilized Aboriginals or other colored races." One controversial suggestion to solving the "problem" of half-castes was the "absorption into the White race of the marriage of the young women to White men." However, this proposal—while suitable in cases of "quadroons and lighter types with definite European characteristics"—did not address the complexities of the "difficult problem." It continued, "not every half-caste is the product of European breeding—quite a large proportion are of alien blood more akin to the aboriginal race itself, such as Pacific Island, African, Malay, and others of Asiatic origin." Based on the "grave problem" of these groups steadily growing in northern cities, the Aboriginal Protection Acts of 1934 were amended to allow the government to consider the "establishment of a civilized half-caste colony" to provide opportunities of "superior types to raise themselves from the aboriginal environment." This was aimed to create a next generation that could be assimilated into European society. This apparently concerned some quadroons and others who had been previously exempted from the Protection Acts. The director also reported that a mission for "half-castes and quadroons" on Thursday Island and the Torres Strait was making satisfactory progress.[6]

In the 1950s Noonuccal joined the CPA. Drawn to its open critiques of Australia's exploitation of Aboriginal communities, she also left the party due to racism *within* it. The party had been markedly influenced by the Communist International (COMINTERN), which in the 1920s was decidedly focused on "the workers in the colonies." Afro-Caribbean communists Claude McKay and the African Blood Brotherhood's Otto Huiswood participated in the 1922 Fourth Congress, which addressed the "Negro question." For McKay the International stood for the "emancipation of all workers of the world, regardless of race or color." The meeting called on the Pacific's communist parties to unite the "proletariats in the races of the Pacific." In 1926 the COMINTERN aimed to "help the oppressed people of the Pacific to liberate themselves from imperialism and to fight against . . . racial borders that oppressed peoples and exploited classes."[7]

The CPA claimed to follow suit. In 1931 it published its "Fight for Aborigines Draft Program of Struggle against Slavery." This program argued that the "campaign of mass physical extermination" against the Aboriginal race included "Abo" shooting hunts, poisoning of desert water holes, police shooting parties, kidnapping children (particularly girls) and working them "hundreds of miles away from their race," killing off their game and starvation, arresting Aborigines without warrant and forcing them "to work with chains around their necks on Government roads and for station owners," and enslavement by the protection boards and mission stations. Aborigines had no political, social, economic, or property rights. Aborigine intellectuals were not allowed to practice their professions, and their tribal arts were stifled. Those who resisted or sought to expose these atrocities were "officially threatened with death and transported." Inquiries into "police murders of Aborigines" were few and police killings justified. Station owners and government officials raped Aboriginal women. White mobs destroyed the villages of those who fought back.[8]

The CPA stated that while conditions of the Aborigines had not been considered by "workers in the revolutionary movement," "no struggle of the White workers" was to "be permitted without demands for the Aborigines being championed." Speaking "in the name of White and Black workers," it demanded equal rights of all Aborigines with White races; removal of color restrictions on Aborigines and "half castes"; prohibition of forced labor; the unconditional release from prison of all Aborigines or half-castes until Aboriginal juries could decide cases; the removal of the protection boards; the prohibition of kidnapping of Aboriginal children by missions, prisons, and correction homes; and the right of Aboriginal parents to live with their children. Its final point called for the handing over to the Aborigines of "large tracts of watered and fertile country, with towns, seaports, railways, roads" to create "one or more independent aboriginal states or republics." These republics were to "be independent of Australia" and have "the right to make treaties with foreign powers, . . . establish their own army, governments, industries, and . . . be independent of imperialism."[9]

In 1951 the party argued that the "peoples of New Guinea and Papua, Fiji and other islands" faced "the same danger of ruthless exploitation and extermination" as Australian Aborigines. Its 1955 National Congress presented a plan for these islands, and also denounced US weapons testing in Western Australia and its impact on Aboriginal communities.

Black activists joined the CPA due to its positions on the "Aboriginal question." However, White party members were often paternalistic, opportunistic, and lacking in understanding of Aboriginal peoples. For example, until 1954 the party distinguished between "full bloods," "mixed bloods," and "half-castes." It defined mixed bloods as being an "oppressed minority" entitled to citizen rights and special concessions, and "full bloods" a separate race and an oppressed colonial people. After 1954 it classified all groups as an oppressed minority.[10]

According to ASIO, the CPA newspapers publicized "every incident involving" Aborigines. Concerned about the party's influence in Aboriginal affairs, it placed Aboriginal activists and organizations affiliated with the CPA under close watch. This included FCAATSI. Formed in 1958 by a number of Aborigine "welfare" groups, it was heavily driven by White liberals; at its initial conference of twenty-six attendees, only three representatives were of Aboriginal descent. Still, over the years FCAATSI's leadership featured indigenous organizers such as the Aborigines Advancement League's (AAL) Pastor Doug Nicholls, Joe McGuiness, Noonuccal, and Bandler.[11]

Noonuccal joined the council in 1961, and eventually became its national secretary of Queensland. The council had much to fight for and against. In 1964 campaign organizer Shirley Andrews published a revealing report, "The Australian Aborigines," which detailed how, according to Australia's constitution, indigenous people were not counted in the Commonwealth census and had no legal recognition. Constitutionally the federal government could make laws only for "people of any race other than the Aboriginal race in any state, for whom it [was] necessary to make special laws," as states and territories made their own laws regarding Aboriginal communities. For example, under various Aborigine "protection" and welfare acts, people defined as Aborigines could not travel freely across the country. In the Northern Territory, "wards" could be moved or held by the director at any time or anywhere. In Queensland, they could be moved on and off reservations on the order of the director but could not enter or leave them without permission. In Western Australia, they were not allowed to cross the 20th parallel (the leper-line) without a special permit. In South Australia certain towns could be declared off-limits to Aborigines. Across the Northern Territory, Western Country, and Queensland, Aborigines could not own property, which was in the hands of the welfare director. There were numerous restrictions on how Aborigines could handle money. In Queensland, large sums had to be put into trusts. A local protector could authorize the use of sums up to £20; larger amounts had to be authorized by the director. While most of Australia did not have a minimum wage, in Queensland labor was mandatory on settlements and missions. As such, Aborigines earned wages that were some 24–65 percent of the minimum wage. In the Northern Territory and Queensland, Aborigines could not marry without the permission of the director. Except in New South Wales and Victoria, all children were under the legal control of the directors, Native Welfare officers, and Aborigine boards. Aborigines could not vote for the state government in Queensland and Western Australia.[12]

Noonuccal helped the council in its successful campaign to have Aborigines counted in the national census via a monumental 1967 national referendum. However, it was clear to her and many others that this victory was only one stop on the long road to indigenous liberation. In April 1969 she energized Aboriginal delegates—including those of the Black Power "generation"—at FCAATSI's annual conference with a widely publicized speech, "Political Rights for Aborigines": "When you leave this conference and go back to your rat holes—the rat holes you call homes, that you have inherited from the Australian society, unite your people, and bring them out fighting!"[13]

FCAATSI's push for indigenous rights included building relationships with other movements across the Global South. In 1969 it argued that its policies on Aborigines needed to move toward land autonomy, as in neighboring Melanesia. The council distributed a memorandum on the international rights of Aborigines to "the indigenous members of the Legislative Council of Papua-New Guinea, Māori Council of New Zealand, suitable authorities in Nauru, Fiji and Western Samoa, the organization of African States, the ILO," and the United Nations for comment.[14]

Through her art and activism, Noonuccal played a critical role in expanding this international dimension. In September 1965 Dudley Randall reviewed her book of poetry *We Are Going* in the *Negro Digest*. According to Randall, the picture of Noonuccal on the back of the book suggested that she was "an attractive young matron of Philadelphia or

Atlanta," but her use of words like "corroboree" showed that she was Australian. He felt that Negro Americans would sympathize with the book; her poems like "The Protectors" referenced the sexual abuse of dark girls by White men. She also mentioned Little Rock in a reference to racial segregation in Australia. However, he unflatteringly found that her "Aboriginal Charter of Rights" read like a rhetorical "political statement" as opposed to poetry.[15] Despite this lukewarm reception, the review certainly helped to expose Noonuccal to an African American audience.

Noonuccal's internationalism was shared by her longtime comrade Faith Bandler, who was born in 1918. Bandler's father, Wacvie Mussingkon, was kidnapped in 1883 from Vanuatu's Ambrym Island. He was sold as a slave in Mackay, Queensland. In 1897 he escaped from the sugar plantation where he worked for no pay. He would later meet Bandler's mother, who was of Indian and Scottish descent.[16]

Bandler's political education emerged from her father's stories about being blackbirded. Her family engaged African and African American print media and politics; her mother subscribed to the NAACP's *Crisis*. Bandler possessed an awareness of the Atlantic slave trade and her family sang "Negro spirituals" in the evenings. Her brothers played Paul Robeson's records and sang his songs. Bandler and her siblings experienced racism and segregation, but "never really took any of the White kids' cheek"; in one incident, after being called *n——ggers* by classmates, they half-cooked a bandicoot and made some of the offenders eat it after school. However, while Bandler understood herself as a Black South Sea Islander who identified with African Diasporic freedom struggles, her consciousness about Australian Aboriginal struggle was limited.[17]

This significantly changed during World War II, when she joined the Australian Women's Land Army. She picked cherries as an agricultural laborer and recalls that a fence divided the orchard she worked in; on one side were the Land Army women and the other were all less-paid Aboriginal laborers. She emerged from the war with more questions about Aboriginal politics.[18]

In 1960 Bandler met Paul and Eslanda Robeson during their tour of Australia. Having spent time in Aotearoa, the Robesons expressed concern at its mistreatment of the Māori. Bandler organized for them a film screening of the movie *Manslaughter*, which detailed atrocities inflicted on Aboriginal peoples. This enraged Paul, who denounced the conditions affecting Black Australia for the duration of the trip. The Robesons met with several of their "darker brothers and sisters." At one meeting, Eslanda's talk about "the Negro problem throughout the world" spanned Africa, the Congo, African Americans, and the rights of the Australian Aboriginals. Paul left the country embittered, remarking, "I intend to return to Australia. I shall make films and give concerts. The proceeds shall benefit the aboriginal population languishing in poverty. I already did that in Africa, and now I want to repeat it once more in Australia."[19]

Black London and Black Power

In 1973 Bandler traveled to London to participate in an event sponsored by ABJAB, a London-based expatriate group that campaigned for Aboriginal civil and land rights. According to ASIO, while there she sought a meeting with Trinidad and Tobago's Althea Lecointe-Jones, who led London's Black Panther Party.[20] Only a few short years before, Noonuccal had attended the World Council of Churches' 1969 Consultation on Racism in London's Notting Hill. Noonuccal felt that the meeting was a "revolutionary step." It focused on the freedom struggles of Latin America, Southern Africa, African Americans, Latinos in the United States, the Māoris, and Aborigines. While there she met political luminaries like Oliver Tambo of South Africa's African National Congress, and Nathan Hare, Black Power activist and founder of the *Black Scholar*. The consultation passed a number of critical resolutions, concluding that force could be used to combat racism in situations where nonviolent strategies had failed.[21]

After the talks, Noonuccal remained in London to investigate racial conditions there. She described several "Black raves in England"— African Americans, Pakistanis, Indians, West Indians, and Africans. With racism getting worse in the United Kingdom, Noonuccal argued, England's "Black man" was "gearing himself for a violent situation." In Birmingham and Notting Hill, Blacks outnumbered Whites. As they also dominated the "medical, transport and food fields," she felt that they could bring London to a standstill.[22]

Noonuccal declared that there was "an underground movement of Black Powerists in London" working to free Black people. Since peaceful means had failed, they were preparing to take over the White world "through violent revolution." Learning from past revolutions and guerilla struggles such as Vietnam's, Black Power activists were teaching men, women, and children "the art of revolution." Ten-year-olds were being trained how to kill policemen. Noonuccal reported that Black Power agents were traveling to Africa, England, and the United States, setting up "institutes of Black Power studies." At the Caribbean (Bermuda) Black Power conference, Black people were being called to arms. "The young black people in England, America and Africa," she declared, "have begun to walk away from Martin Luther King and are joining the revolutionaries." She predicted that in a decade, White America would join forces with Russia, while China would ally itself with the Black Powerists of the world. Australia would be asked to align with White America. Australia had ten years to figure it out—"instant evolution" or "bloody revolution."[23]

While in London, Noonuccal wrote an essay titled "White Racism and White Violence." Intercepted by ASIO after it was given to a member of the CPA,[24] the essay poignantly historicized White violence in Australia. Noonuccal argued that unless White Australians addressed the realities of racism, Australian White society would cease to exist. Racism was linked to the British invasion of the continent and the first killings of Australian Aborigines, whom Whites refused to recognize as human beings. The attempts at the genocide of Aborigines included murder, poison, and the rape of children and women. Noonuccal framed this violence in the context of the Black Diaspora: "Wherever White men invaded and stole the land from the Blacks the White man's violence took a terrible toll on the indigenous people all over the world." White society wrote the Aboriginal community off as a dying race. This, she argued, was followed by an era called "the soothing of the dying pillow," when White violence was transformed into Christian missionary work aimed at allowing them to die out "as humanly as possible." White Australians had "turned from one form of violence to another."[25]

Noonuccal asserted that Aborigines were destined to become slaves of White Australians because of Australia's racist policies that separated Black families, denied Black communities the right to express their own culture and languages, forbade them to vote or drink certified liquor but allowed them to consume methylated spirits, to work without pay, and to be driven from their tribal lands. This brutal system had successfully brainwashed Aborigines to think that they were subhuman and inferior. In addition, White violence was perpetuated through the misguided theory of White supremacy. This allowed White Australians to think that they, the criminals, were somehow the victims. Noonuccal continued,

> Racism is a complex state of mind. Racists believe that schools must be segregated, not to keep Blacks separate but to preserve the "superior" child. Police are given excessive power in the Aboriginal missions and reserves and fringe settlements, not to deny basic constitutional rights to second-class citizen Black people but to "stop crimes in the neighborhood." Blacks are not denied jobs because of their skin color but because they are not qualified. Housing integration is not opposed because White people don't want to live next door to "boongs" but because Black people "lower property value."[26]

London was politically transformative for Noonuccal. Prior to her trip, she had expressed only tacit support of Black Power. However, witnessing the movement's local and international dimensions significantly informed her own national politics. Australia, she argued, needed to take heed of the London experience. Healthy racial cooperation was possible in the Pacific, but those who silenced the truth through "whisper campaigns" would have to "accept responsibility for a violent bloody revolution."[27]

Upon her return to Australia, Noonuccal's views on Black Power were widely publicized. In September she informed Sydney's *Sun* that White "do-gooders" would "be far better off helping the poverty-stricken people of their own race." Whites who worked for Aboriginal advancement did so because it was an easy way to earn high salaries, and they did so at the expense of Aboriginals. Arguing against immediate integration, she argued that Aboriginals needed to first be given financial resources to develop independent satellite towns away from White communities. Aborigines *needed power*.[28]

Noonuccal stated that she was "an advocate of Black Power," and that "Black revolt was inevitable." Australia had done nothing to help Aboriginals, and a revolution was needed for a radical improvement in social and economic equality in Australia. Any violence in the situation would come from the White population.[29] For Noonuccal, what needed to be done *for* Aborigines needed to be done *by* Aborigines. "No man can walk straight without pride of race. To get their pride back, the Black man [would] have to search the gutters where the White man threw it down years ago."[30]

Beginning to disavow racial coalition politics, Noonuccal left FCAATSI in 1970 and helped found the National Tribal Council, an Aboriginal and Islanders organization that operated under the motto, "We stand for self-reliance." Its manifesto called for full economic, legal, and social equality for Aboriginals and Islanders. It aimed to operate on its own resources, and while accepting advice from Whites, limited voting power to Aborigines and Islanders. It raised funds to obtain a building for a recreation center, to host Black studies courses in history and culture for urbanized Aborigines, to open a preschool center, and to establish a contracting company. The Queensland branch organized activities that focused on financing, housing, health, education, economics, legal aid, social, and sporting activities.[31]

The aims of the Tribal Council spoke to Australia's emerging Black Power generation, such as Noonuccal's son Denis Walker (who became its Queensland secretary), and activist Sam Watson. Already stimulated by discussions about segregation in Australia, the United States, and South Africa, and the activism of Malcolm X and Martin Luther King, Watson gravitated toward Brisbane's Black political leadership. This included Noonuccal and Pastor Don Brady, who worked with First Nations groups and Black communities in the United States. Watson was moved by Noonuccal's political work as well as her positionality as a "single parent who did not take sh——t from anybody." Brady and Noonuccal "brought back their observations on how indigenous and colonized communities in other parts of the world were able to deal with the challenges that confronted them. The most significant factor that emerged was that Indigenous communities were forming their own Elders Councils."[32]

In January 1970 the Tribal Council led a demonstration in Brisbane against the Queensland Aborigines Act. Brady spat on and burned a copy of the act.[33] In September 1971 it organized a major protest in which clashes with police broke out. According to Watson, "two centuries of hate, anger, and frustration [were] meted out on the police that day." Walker and Watson formed the Black Panther Party in the aftermath of the protest. They imported the literature of Huey P. Newton, Eldridge Cleaver, Angela Davis, and George Jackson, released a version of the US Black Panther Party's 10/10 program based on the needs of the Aboriginal community, and established police patrol, legal aid, community news, and health service programs. The party was publicly framed around its advocacy for armed self-defense against state violence. Its membership would come to include Paul Cole, Gary Foley, Sue Chilly, Carol Buchanon, Gary Williams, Billy Craigie, and jazz/blues singer Marlene Cummins. Cummins has publicly raised issues of sexual abuse within the party.[34]

In a 1972 interview with *Honi Soit*, the newspaper of the University of Sydney's Student Representative Council, Walker stated that it had been necessary to form the Black Panther Party from the ranks of grassroots Aboriginals, as the Tribal Council was becoming a "bourgeois elitist type organization." Having studied US-based groups like the Nation of Islam and the Weathermen, he felt that the Panthers had laid out the clearest revolutionary ideology. For Walker, Black Power called for an anti-capitalist revolution and Black self-determination. He drew on Papua New Guinea as an example in which if independence was not anti-capitalist, then "the bulk of Niugini people [would] be struggling against Black capitalism and Black exploitation as much as they were struggling against White imperialism."[35]

Noonuccal was aware of the significance of her cross-generational and gendered relationship with Australia's Black Power movement. Years before, she had convinced Black Power activist Patricia Korowa to join FCAATSI and then Victoria's AAL.[36] In October 1972 Noonuccal spoke on this complicated relationship during a 1972 tour of Aotearoa. In Victoria she told an audience that "the central issue in the struggle for civil rights was undoubtedly land rights," which was the only way in which a policy of self-determination could be marked. Aboriginals wanted a separate society, as the White man's education or sciences were of no use to Aboriginal peoples. She called for "a conference between all the indigenous people of the Pacific":

> We all face common problems and a common enemy and we could produce a . . . charter of rights for the indigenous people of the Pacific. If the

church groups are not prepared to finance such a venture I am prepared to go to Russia or China for backing, perhaps not Russia, but certainly China. . . . They'll back us.

For Noonuccal, it appeared as if "the Whites of the United States, South Africa and other parts of the world" flocked to Australia because they believed that the Black man there "knew his place." They were "dead scared" of the "Blackman in their own country" and so they were coming to a place where they thought he would be always under control. But she doubted they would be right and reiterated her belief about a racial power shift in ten years. "The Aborigine will be a force to be reckoned with," she reasoned, referencing Australia's Black Panther Party. The party was doing work in urban cities and also establishing contacts with rural communities. Still, the Panthers needed "an older negotiator to work with them, to speak for them." She did so at times, but even she was not always considered radical and was sometimes seen as being "too kind to the White man. . . . The Panthers feel that the only good White man is a dead one." This made them "as racist as the Whites," but perhaps she was just too optimistic. The Panthers asserted that White society was greedy, violent, and untrustworthy. While she agreed (quite frankly, she had repeated similar notions over her decades of organizing), she felt that "before you bring a revolution you must know what you are going to do after the revolution." Since only 1 percent of the country was Aboriginal, she felt that the Panthers might be "committing suicide," but their job was to stay alive.[37]

Noonuccal Visits the United States

As Noonuccal began to ease away from national politics in the mid-1970s, she continued to play an advisory role as an elder activist and advocate for indigenous culture. In 1972 she bought property on Minjerribah, which today is a forty-five-minute ferry ride from Brisbane. On her land, Moongalba (sitting-down place), she established the Noonuccal-Nughie Education and Cultural Centre, where she hosted local and international visitors. In 1978 South Africa's Cornelius Marivate spent an unforgettable day there, during a trip to speak at Brisbane's Moral Re-Armament Conference. Marivate lectured in Tsonga languages at the University of South Africa. A radiant photograph of him and Noonuccal at Stradbroke suggest that they had a rich exchange. He wrote to her daughter-in-law Katrina Smith, thanking her for giving him the opportunity to meet and listen to Noonuccal and see where she lived. Marivate traveled back to South Africa with her poetry collection *My People*, which, "a constant inspiration," had been given to him by Charles Perkins in Canberra.[38]

She continued to travel in these years, including to writers' conferences across Oceania. Between 1978 and 1979, Noonuccal visited the United States. In the fall of 1978, she was a poet-in-residence at Bloomsburg State College, Pennsylvania. Her trip was initially sponsored by an invitation from Bloomsburg assistant professor of English Margaret Lauer and organizations like the Fulbright Program and the Australian-American Educational Program.[39] In January 1978 she shared Lauer's invitation with Australia's Council for the Arts, informing the council that her poetry was being used in Black studies courses in the United States, and that the country's Black and Brown communities made it an important destination for her to do her work.[40] She hoped to take and distribute materials on Aboriginal history, culture, art, and literature. This included *The Art of Black Australia*, a catalogue that they had used in Nigeria at FESTAC. Aiming to educate Americans about Australia's "forceful and talented Black culture," she sought help from the journal *Meanjin* for donations.[41]

Noonuccal wrote to Lauer about her itinerary, stressing that she wanted to visit American Indian reservations, Los Angeles (where her son Vivian lived), and possibly pass through Hawai'i. To assist Lauer, she passed on the contact information for Gordon Braithwaite of the National Endowment for the Arts (NEA), Herbert Shore in La Jolla, California, Sylvia Wynter of Stanford's African and Afro-American Studies Program, and Sherley Williams of UC-San Diego's Department of Literature.[42]

Lauer informed Noonuccal that Bloomsburg was prepared to give her an honorarium of $1,000 for her residency. She referenced the possibility of Noonuccal making visits to neighboring institutions, such as Bucknell, Lockhaven, and Pennsylvania State University. She suggested that she do readings at Washington, DC's Library of Congress and the Shakespeare Folger Library. She was also trying to coordinate her trip to coincide with the annual Modern Languages Association (MLA) conference. Lauer referenced Noonuccal's request to visit Black and urban colleges; she knew "two people" at community colleges in New York who had "many Black and Third World students." She urged Noonuccal to respond. Noticeably, she did not mention any historically Black colleges or universities in the region, such as Howard, Morgan State, and Lincoln Universities. Referring to a conversation that she had with Jennifer Keefe of the Council for the International Exchange of Scholars, Lauer noted that there was "some woman historian" who was having a conference on Africa in Baltimore. Keefe thought that Noonuccal might be interested to present as a Third World participant, but Lauer thought she might be too busy. She knew that Noonuccal wanted "to see some Chicanos and Indians" and she would inquire about such via her son who lived in Albuquerque.[43]

As early as March 1978, Lauer had informed Bloomsburg administrators and Keefe that Noonuccal wanted to visit some predominantly Black colleges and "minority groups" in the Southwest. Between April and June, Lauer wrote to Noonuccal, stating that she needed to do more work to address her interest in visiting HBCUs, but Cheyney University was nearby. She planned to write to a former colleague who taught at a "Black school," Bronx Community College, "in the midst of a Black and Puerto Rican section." Here she thought that Noonuccal would have the chance to meet Black writers from New York, such as African American playwright Adrienne Kennedy, who had been at Bloomsburg recently. Lauer had recently met two Black women who were "very interested" in Noonuccal's trip; they were professors at her alma mater, the University of Michigan. She offered to write to Robert Hayden, who was also at Michigan—they had never met, but their kids had attended the same nursery school. She also offered to write to a few Black women poets. Unabashedly she admitted, "The only one I have actually met is Sonia Sanchez," whom she did not know "really well, but perhaps well enough"—and thought she could write to her. She had also talked to some women in the Third World women's group at the MLA meeting in Chicago and would get back to them. She turned the conversation back to New Mexico with the phrase "Now, Indians."[44]

Noonuccal's arrival at Bloomsburg, located about a hundred miles from Philadelphia, was highly anticipated. Bloomsburg's *College News-*

letter lauded one of her performances, referring to her as "not only an Aboriginal poet," but "perhaps the most articulate spokesperson for her entire race." While on campus, she made presentations, met with the International Students Club and the Third World Cultural Society, and gave signings of *We Are Going*. Her official itinerary included a week in Washington, DC, a weekend trip to Philadelphia for a poetry festival, and visits to Penn State University, Lock Haven State College, and Mansfield State College.[45]

Still, all was not well. Noonuccal's final itinerary did not adequately address her firm anticipation that she would visit Black and Brown educational organizations, women, political groups, communities, artists, and activists. In fact, her official application for travel grants specifically stated that she would work with "Black and Third World students at urban colleges in New York."[46]

Take, for instance, her trip to Washington, DC, which, organized by Keefe's Council for International Exchange, spanned the last week in October. Noonuccal's schedule included a film screening and reading with Myra Sklarew's poetry class at American University's Department of Literature, a joint poetry reading with Anne Darr at Georgetown University's Department of English, and a poetry reading with Reed Whittemore at the University of Maryland's English Department. These were all White poets. She conducted interviews with the National Public Radio's "Voices in the Wind," a taped reading for the Library of Congress, a late-night live reading on Radio Pacifica (WPFW, FM 89.3), and a taped interview with Poet Laureate of Maryland Grace Cavalieri's "Poet and the Poem" Radio Pacifica series. Noonuccal had dinners with the Council for International Exchange and Fulbright administrators, and attended a reception organized by geophysicist Albert Crary and his wife. However, aside from a Black Women Poets meeting with Zora Martin-Felton and the Smithsonian's Anacostia Neighborhood Museum (which Noonuccal really enjoyed), and an impromptu "pass through" at Howard, her itinerary was devoid of critical engagement with Washington, DC's vibrant Black heritage.[47]

Conspicuously absent from the array of colleges that Noonuccal formally visited in the Washington, DC, area were Howard, Morgan State, and Federal City College. Were these schools intentionally *not* included? It would have been hard to ignore the glowing cultural and political visibility of Howard. The week before her arrival in "Chocolate City," Howard students and faculty participated in a massive demonstration at the White House against the visit of Rhodesian prime minister Ian Smith. This protest included a performance by Sweet Honey in the Rock. Days later, the university held its weeklong homecoming festivities. Featuring an Ashford & Simpson concert, the "Mecca" held its parade and football game at RFK Stadium on October 21, three days before Noonuccal reached the "Diamond District." On October 23, Howard's Afro-American Studies Department and its Institute for the Arts and the Humanities sponsored a talk on Black liberation by Communist Party activist Harry Haywood. On Friday, October 27, C. L. R. James, Drake Koka of South Africa's Black Allied Workers, and Anne Sheperd Turner (one of the Wilmington Ten) spoke at Howard's School of Social Work Auditorium.[48]

Noonuccal would have been enthralled by Howard's student newspaper, the *Hilltop*. She would have seen its October 27 interview with June Jordan, known that Carole Singelton was directing Langston Hughes's play *Mulatto* at Howard's Ira Aldridge Theatre, read that Henrietta Edmonds had become chairperson of Howard's Drama Department, noticed that Haile Gerima was premiering a new film, and noted how Florida Agricultural and Mechanical University's American football team had stretched its winning streak to fifteen games. She would likely have been disappointed to learn that Professor James Garrett had been denied tenure by Howard, an action that the *Hilltop* felt was similar to the termination of progressive professors Frances Welsing and Acklyn Lynch.[49]

Noonuccal was disturbed by this void, and she was not the only one. In December 1978 Dave Warren of the US Department of the Interior's Institute of American Indian Arts wrote to Braithwaite, who was deputy to the chairman for minority affairs at the NEA. Warren described Noonuccal as Australia's leading Aboriginal poet, who was "internationally recognized as an interpreter of her people's culture." He praised her work in establishing museums and cultural centers in Australia and her programs at Moongalba as a collective effort to introduce Black and White urban children "to the heritage of the Aboriginal peoples."[50]

Warren was concerned that her itinerary had not been fully developed. He felt that it "would be our loss" if a cultural leader of Noonuccal's stature were to return to Australia having visited only Bloomsburg and nearby institutions in Pennsylvania. It would have been "especially tragic" if she were not able to experience America's "rich cultural diversity" and interact with "so-called minority" artists. Her trip was an opportunity to establish a distinctive and consistent exchange with Australian peoples. As part of this effort, the Institute of American Indian Arts (IAIA) in Santa Fe, New Mexico, the School of Communications at Texas Southern University (TSU, a Houston-based HBCU), UC-Berkeley's African American Studies Program, and the University of Southern California's Center for Technology, the Arts, and Cultural Transformation (TACT) sought to arrange for her to visit their respective institutions, give presentations, and screen *Shadow Sister*, a biographical documentary of Noonuccal and Moongalba.[51]

Warren proposed that she spend three to five days in New Mexico with the students and faculty at the IAIA and indigenous communities from the surrounding pueblos. In Houston, Berkeley, and Los Angeles, he said, she could commune with Black, Latinx, and Asian American communities on- and off-campus. Such efforts would deepen understanding between all parties. He sought and was awarded a grant from the NEA to facilitate such a trip. Distributed by Helen Redbird-Salem via the Native American Council of Regents, these funds extended Noonuccal's stay into the spring of 1979.[52]

Warren was supported by Herbert Shore, who at the time directed TACT, an interdisciplinary consortium of various programs. At the suggestion of Braithwaite, Shore wrote to the Religious Communities for the Arts for funds. Signed "Chivambo" (as in the Mozambique Liberation Front's Eduardo Chivambo Mondlane), his letter included a copy of Noonuccal's résumé and an article about her work in the journal *World Literature Written in English*. Shore had visited Noonuccal at Moongalba, where he observed her work with urban Aboriginal and White children in a push to "preserve, maintain, and develop Aboriginal culture in a changing (and sometimes hostile) world."[53]

Describing her as a warm, sensitive, and dynamic leader, Shore found that Noonuccal's visit to the United States had not been "a richly rewarding one." Noonuccal wanted to meet artists and cultural leaders "among the Native American, Black, Hispanic, and Asian-American communities, but for some reason, those responsible for her itinerary were not in a position to provide these opportunities." She spent all her time at Bloomsburg, but did have "a rewarding but all-too-brief visit to Washington, DC and Howard University." In DC she was given a reception by the Australian embassy, conducted a television interview, and recorded the piece for the Library of Congress. No further arrangements had been made for her. He also stressed that funds be provided for her to accept the offers for visits made by TSU, IAIA, and Berkeley's African American Studies Program.[54]

Noonuccal's trip to the West Coast was financially sponsored through Grant Spradling and the Religious Communities for the Arts. Before leaving Bloomsburg, she graciously thanked Lauer for arranging her visit. She also asked that "all tapes, recordings, and materials" that she had left at the college be "dispersed and used" on a nonprofit basis, authorizing their reproduction on an educational basis. In a memo to Bloomsburg's vice president, she pushed for the establishment of an exchange program that could be centered around Aborigine, Australian, American Indian, and African American students.[55]

In New Mexico she visited Acoma Pueblo, a federally recognized tribal entity some sixty miles west of Albuquerque. She also spoke at Santa Fe's IAIA, which she visited on January 27, 1979. She brought back with her the IAIA's book *One with the Earth* and a photograph of the 1978 Longest Walk, the 3,000-mile trek from Alcatraz, California, to Washington, DC, by thousands of indigenous and allied communities to bring national attention to the issues of Native peoples in the United States. The picture included Muskogee Creek elder and medicine man Philip Deere, who was also a spiritual leader in the American Indian Movement (AIM).[56]

From January 29 to February 2, 1979, Noonuccal visited TSU in Houston, Texas. She had a full week of events—a KTSU radio interview with a student, lectures and film screenings in classes on fine arts, daily living, mass communications, urban communications, and film criticism, a luncheon with faculty and students, meetings with the school's president and Fulbright director, and the keynote speech for the university's First International Student Poetry Forum.[57]

TSU used Noonuccal's visit to launch its First International Student Poetry Forum, which, under the theme "Dreams, Illusions, and Reality," featured four other community poets. Sponsored by TSU's School of Communications, the forum was held at the university's Student Life Center. Houston's *Informer and Texas Freeman* advertised the event, noting that Noonuccal was a leading exponent of Aboriginal culture. Noonuccal helped to design the event's flyer, which included a drawing of her carpet snake totem. The flyer stated that she was the most celebrated poet of Australia, and one of its most polemic civil rights artists. It described how poetry, stories, and paintings were mediums from which Noonuccal shared "sacred truths" with the world. It ended with, "Behold, the raisin in the sun." Scribbled on a copy of the flyer was a note that Noonuccal considered her poems to be political propaganda. This was likely written by TSU's School of Communications dean Carlton W. Molette II or his wife, Barbara Molette, who also attended the event. Dean Molette was also hoping to get her to visit HBCUs Dillard University (New Orleans) and Huston Tillotson (Austin).[58]

The Molettes were icons in Black theatre, and co-wrote more than twenty plays, books, and short stories. Highly enthused by her visit, they gave Noonuccal copies of their plays and books *Booji*, *The Escape*, *Noah's Ark*, and *Dr. B. S. Black*. Dean Molette wrote to Noonuccal while she was in Los Angeles, thanking her for her positive impact upon students, faculty, and administration and for her thought-provoking poetry. This was not an "empty thanks"; he provided her with a $500 honorarium. He hoped that her visit marked the beginning of an ongoing association between TSU and Australian Aborigines. He immediately wrote to H. C. Coombs at the Australian National University, describing Noonuccal's "indelible impression" on TSU and about establishing a student and faculty exchange program between TSU and Australian Aborigines. Molette also passed on materials that Noonuccal wanted to place in the school's library to TSU president Granville Sawyer.[59]

In Berkeley, California, she read poetry and screened *Shadow Sister*. This included a presentation at Berkeley's Pacific Film Archive in January 1979, where she made "a great impression" on students and the general audience. She carried back with her a syllabus for an African American studies course on major Black authors by Berkeley professor Erskine Peters.[60]

She also traveled to Oakland, California, where she was awarded an International Award for her role in *Shadow Sister* by the Black Filmmakers Hall of Fame, during its sixth annual Oscar Micheaux ceremony,

Figure 3.2. Oodgeroo Noonuccal (Kath Walker) with students at Texas Southern University, 1979. Box 45, Papers of Oodgeroo Noonuccal, Fryer Library, University of Queensland, Australia.

held at Oakland's Paramount Theatre of the Arts. She was presented the award by UC-Berkeley professor of African American studies Albert Johnson. The organization also invited her to participate in a lecture at Oakland's Laney College during Black History Month. Along with actor Paul Winfeld, she talked about the state of art in their respective fields.[61]

On March 4, 1979, Noonuccal screened *Shadow Sister* and gave a poetry reading at Los Angeles' Inner City Cultural Center. Featuring a carpet snake, the flyer described her as a "famous Black Australian poet from the Aboriginal Tribe."[62] Artist C. Bernard Jackson had founded the Cultural Center in the aftermath of the 1965 Watts uprisings. In April 1979 he wrote to Noonuccal at Moongalba, asking her to stay in touch because he was anxious "to be kept abreast of the situation in which Black people find themselves in Australia." He also purchased a copy of the film.[63]

At the Inner City screening, Noonuccal met actress and director Revalyn Gold (Pamela Jones). Gold was part of the "first wave" of LA Rebellion, the legendary collective of African Diasporic filmmakers who attended UCLA.[64] Gold's long list of acting credits has included roles in *Cornbread, Earl, and Me* (1975), *Sister Act 2* (1993), and *Deep Cover* (1992). At the time of meeting Noonuccal, Gold had recently produced, scripted, and directed *Forward Ever* (1978), a three-part documentary about Pan-Africanism, the All-Africa People's Revolutionary Party (AAPRP), and African Liberation Day in Washington, DC. She had also completed *One*, a film about a contemporary African American dancer who falls during a performance and is transplanted to Africa, where she is supported by other African women. According to Gold, "The same women are repeated in different places in history, culture, time, and space. We're all one person in a way."[65]

This is perhaps how she viewed her connection with Noonuccal. The two women discussed "Black world organizing and unity." Gold gave Noonuccal her Los Angeles contact information and logistics for the AAPRP's Washington, DC, office (1226 Euclid Avenue, NW). Referring to herself as Chido, she also gave Noonuccal the address of Edmond Boston (Turwanire KT Mandla) and the AAPRP branch in Inglewood, California.[66]

Noonuccal also gave talks and read poetry at a number of schools. While in California, she visited San Diego's Torey Pines High School, where students wrote and sent letters to Moongalba, expressing respect for Aboriginal people and admiration for her beautiful poetry. They wished she could have stayed longer and enjoyed watching *Shadow Sister*. With love, one Pia Lundqvist wrote that Noonuccal had helped her to realize "the many different peoples who [had] been exploited, killed, degraded, and captured by the White man."[67]

Noonuccal's concluding report to the Fulbright Committee thanked the program for its support of her trip, which she divided into two parts—her residency at Bloomsburg and her subsequent travels. She stated that, as an Aborigine, she was glad to meet "minorities whose history was so familiar." As a woman, she found it gratifying to see many women in places of leadership, in contrast to Australia. She was excited by her reception of the filmmaker's award as well as the standing ovations that the film received from White and Black audiences. She hoped that these audiences had learned much about the "oldest Australians." She also screened the film at the Canadian Association for Commonwealth Literature and Language Studies conference in Montreal. She described the reading with other Black women poets as a "wonderful experience."[68]

She credited Shore for organizing the second part of her trip and thanked Berkeley's Johnson and TSU's Dean Carlton for their kindness. Over the duration of her trip, she gave sixteen interviews, twenty-five film screenings, nineteen poetry recitals, and eighteen lectures to primarily creative writing and communication classes. Her major highlights included the gala presentation of the film award, her meeting of famous Black actors, and the Laney State College lecture with Winfeld. She found it important to visit Native American villages and the Bureau of Indian Affairs; she was sorry that she ran out of time while giving readings and lectures there. She also hoped that her discussions with TSU regarding an exchange program with Aboriginal and Island students would become a reality.[69]

However, in her report to the Australian-American Educational Foundation, she noted a "deficiency in the preparation" of her itinerary, which she attributed to her personal arrangements. She had found herself "in the difficult situation of staying with Lauer," who was also largely responsible for the trip but had an "ulterior motive" for Noonuccal's visit. She felt that Lauer had "academic advancement in mind and was very jealous" of her "working with others at Bloomsburg."[70]

Noonuccal brought back numerous materials—photographs, flyers, and books—that are testimony to the diverse array of African American communities that she engaged with. This included a letter from Ruwa Chiri announcing the release of *Afrika Must Unite*, the bi-monthly publication of Chicago's United Afrikans for One Motherland International (UFOMI), a copy of *Mahogany* magazine, and DC-based poet Ambrosia Shepherd's *Ambrosia's Black Rap in Rhyme*.[71]

Upon her return to Australia, one press release announced that she had "caused a sensation" in the United States as Americans knew "virtually nothing about Aborigines." Noonuccal gained much from her trip. She had a "tremendous experience" and "even found that an old dog could learn new tricks." She hoped that "many more Blacks both in the United States and Australia" got the opportunity "to see how the other lives."[72] She continued to be an advocate for Aboriginal culture at arts festivals and writers' conferences across Malaysia, Fiji, New Zealand, China, and also Papua New Guinea, which is the subject of our next chapter.

4

Nilaidat

Black Power in Papua New Guinea

On July 1, 1970, in the late-night hours of one of many "anti-colonialist hate sessions," twelve students at the University of Papua New Guinea (UPNG) formed the Niugini Black Power Group (NBPG). Emerging from a core of Melanesian nationalists known as the Apostles, the NBPG's vociferous vision of Black Power broadly engaged the freedom struggles of Papua New Guinea, Oceania, the Africana world, and the Global South. It denounced Australian colonialism, police repression, White power, and segregation in Papua New Guinea. It challenged the environmental exploitation of the mineral resources of the semiautonomous region of Bougainville, condemned Indonesian imperialism in West Papua, defended Aboriginal sovereignty in Australia, and supported ethnic secessionist movements across the colony. The NBPG also engaged the ideas of Negritude, pan-Africanism, anti-apartheid, Black liberation theology, civil rights, and global expressions of Black Power.[1]

The group used literature, theatre, poetry, visual art, activism, debates, and demonstrations in its calls for Black self-determination. In doing so, it helped to pioneer a Black Arts movement in Papua New Guinea. This movement engaged questions of Melanesian identity, race, decolonization, ethnicity, and gender, and produced a tremendous canon of indigenous art. As it helped to transform UPNG into a far-reaching beacon of Melanesian anti-colonialism, the group helped to transform the term "Melanesia"—once a negative colonial imposition—into a powerful identifier of Black internationalism in Oceania.

The NBPG frequently expressed its political ideas, activities, and art through *Nilaidat* (Our Voice), UPNG's fortnightly student newspaper. Launched in 1968, *Nilaidat* attuned itself to Papua New Guinea's emerging Black cultural revolution.[2] In 1971 the newspaper announced the NBPG's forthcoming magazine, *Niugini Black Power*. The magazine aimed "to focus on the contemporary voices of the Black people in search of Niugini identity." Its main contributors were the key architects of the NBPG—Martin Buluna, Leo Hannett, Arthur Jawodimbari, John Kaputin, and John Kasaipwalova.[3]

In May 1971 *Nilaidat* published an intriguing interview with Hannett, a leading spokesperson for the group. Conducted by Australian journalist Jean Gollan and titled "Niugini Black Power," it was headlined by a sprawling photograph of two bare-chested Papua New Guinean men with raised Black Power salutes, one of whom had donned a long-linked chain around his neck. The interview began with quotes from Frantz Fanon's *Black Skin, White Masks*. According to Gollan, misinformed notions of Black Power had framed the movement around notions of violence, "ghetto bred racialism, tear gas, and murder." However, while the NBPG was forced to operate under the pressure of these popular notions, its ideas were based more on a "Fanon-inspired African Negritude" movement and more pro-Black than it was anti-White.[4]

Six months in, the group had garnered wide campus support. According to Hannett, its driving philosophy was to "redeem the identity" and pride "of the Black man." Black Power was "essential to nation building" in Papua New Guinea, where colonialism had forced Niuginians to condemn their indigenous ways of knowing. As such, the first stage in the NBPG's step-by-step program for liberation was to psychologically "grapple with the minds" of Niuginians who had been enslaved by a "colonial inferiority complex."[5]

Hannett stated that the NBPG was influenced "but not enslaved by" the ideology of Black Power in the United States and the philosophy of "African Negritude." It had localized the concepts of Black struggle to reflect its own aspirations, as Black people across the world suffered from "the same sort of treatment from the ruling White races." As such, the NBPG stood "in solidarity with all Black people," who, as an "exploited race," needed to exert themselves as a "world-wide ethnic group to make any impact."[6]

Gollan asked whether the situation in Papua New Guinea would ever be like that of the United States, where violence seemed to be the only way for Black people to assert themselves. Hannett hesitated to predict such a thing, as Black Power did not aspire to be violent. However, as long as "the White man in his ethnocentric prejudice" refused to deal

Figure 4.1. Leo Hannett, n.d. Douglas Oliver
Collection, University of Hawaiʻi at Mānoa Digital
Image Collections. Photograph by Douglas Oliver.

with Black people as equals, then Black people needed to use whatever means necessary to liberate themselves. Still, Black Power was not simply anti-White, nor really directed toward White society at all. Rather, it was focused on building Black self-awareness. But, he argued—supposedly referencing Malcolm X—"Black Power is a thing that the White man can't initiate or propagate and therefore won't tolerate for Black consumption." Later that year, he toured Australia and spoke at Monash University's Niugini Forum. In September, his interview was published in the university's student newspaper, *Lot's Wife*.[7]

In August 1971 Hannett and Kasaipwalova spoke about Black Power at a Students and Politics Seminar at the Lae Institute of Technology, some two hundred miles north of Port Moresby. Just the month before, Kasaipwalova had clashed with anthropologist Margaret Mead at a forum where he allegedly stated that multiethnic Black unity in Papua New Guinea would occur once White people were "seen as the enemy."

His long and well-received speech at Lae stressed that Black Power was needed in Papua New Guinea, where the "White power structure" had to be destroyed. He spoke to his student audience about the death of East New Britain's district commissioner, Jack Emanuel, who was murdered by four men in a "payback killing." The commissioner had worked against the interests of Papuans and used Black police to fight against their own people. As such, while Kasaipwalova pitied Emanuel as a human being, since he was "a White man who [terrorized] native people," Papuans needed to "rejoice at his death."[8]

Hannett's speech, "Niugini Black Power," is a classic Black Power manifesto. Stridently masculinist in its interpretation of Black Power, it forcibly described the origins, objectives, and philosophy of the group. It also reflected critical engagement with global Black Power discourses, anti-colonialism, pan-Africanism, African Diasporic literatures, and Black liberation theology. It would later be published in three variant versions, which is reflected in the following close read.

According to Hannett, the obvious task of the NBPG was to "redeem ourselves from our oppressors first of all" and in doing so "redeem our oppressors also to the totality of their humanity." Liberally quoting Paulo Freire's *Pedagogy of the Oppressed*, he saw this as the "great humanistic and historical task of the oppressed—to liberate themselves and their oppressors as well." While the NBPG did not have a rigid organization, its members shared a commitment to the philosophy of Black Power. Addressing the group's small numbers, he remarked that it took "a man of mettle to risk one's name and be counted among the freaks, the ungrateful, the communist and other titles" given to those who were breaking out of the "morality of the colonialists." Still, the group's initial "twelve Apostles" had doubled in number.[9]

Hannett addressed those who agreed with the group's aims but thought that the term "Black Power" was "both dangerous and irrelevant" in Niugini. To them, Black Power connoted violence, looting, and hatred of Whites, and reflected an alien experience of the United States. Some argued that it was ridiculous to fight for Black Power in Niugini, where the population was majority Black. Hannett insisted, however, that the term "Black Power" was "vitally important" for the movement and was as "relevant to Niugini as a betel nut." This was a reference to the popular practice of chewing the nut for its stimulating properties. The phrase "Black Power" gave the philosophy of self-determination political "bite," just as "ginger, pepper, and limestuff" did when chewing the betel.[10]

The NBPG was also adamant in the use of the word "Black" because the crux of the issue was that Niuginians were not proud of being Black. Furthermore, Blackness represented more than phenotype. It served as a reference to their rich and racially distinct identity, culture, and social and religious values. The group insisted on using the word "Power." However, it sought more than Kwame Nkrumah's "political kingdom"—it also sought to cultivate national awareness and cultural identity. According to Hannett, Nkrumah's famous quote, "Seek ye first the political kingdom and the rest shall be given to you," was not a truism and "totally misleading."[11] He elaborated:

> It would be naïve and simplistic and downright dangerous for any Niuginian to think that just the handing over of the outward symbols of political control of our country at independence will make us ipso facto total masters of ourselves politically, socially, economically and religiously. By exchanging the White political actors with Black ones and letting them play the same game within unchanged political machinery . . . would only bring about quantitative change but no qualitative change whatsoever. A guillotine is always a guillotine no matter what color is the person who controls it. Similarly, an oppressive system is always an oppressive system unless there is first of all a radical transformation in the whole thinking of the controlling agent which would necessitate to bring about a complete overhauling of the whole political machinery.[12]

Niuginians needed to be leery when colonialists used words like "preparation" for independence, because this meant the training of Black elites to continue to run a "colonial autocracy" for the benefit of Australia.[13]

"Niugini Black Power" argued that those in Papua New Guinea did not need to be politically astute to recognize that their Black political leaders had successfully formulated laws that consolidated White political and economic dominance. This included the 1970 Public Order Bill, which suppressed free speech, and the Bougainville Mining Ordinance, which grossly supported the exploitation of the region's copper resources. But, argued Hannett, such was life—"where once we had

White exploiters, now we have democratically elected Black slave traders in the House of Assembly." Furthermore, the opponents of Black Power failed to realize that there was "dominative White Power in all sectors of Niugini life." He chastised racist employment policies, foreign capital investments, and rent breaks for expatriate officers—Papua New Guinea had used to be a "White man's grave" but had become "the White man's paradise and the Black man's hell." Hannett also pushed back against calls by the Returned and Services League of Australia (RSL) for an ordinance to increase the police force. Such laws had historically been used to oppress Niuginians, like the "White Woman Protection Ordinance" and curfews that extended into the 1950s.[14]

Hannett decried every time that a "Malcolm X Niuginian" was forced to meet with those persons who accepted false gifts from racist institutions like the Australian government, the RSL, and the Planters Association. This was the same act by which the "old men" of Niugini had once sold their lands for a song—beads, axes, and sticks of tobacco. Now, Black men in the House of Assembly were being bought off with "a few bottles of beer, promises of trips to New York, and portfolios."[15]

Hannett's paper included a statement that the NBPG gave to a United Nations mission to Papua New Guinea that interviewed UPNG students on March 4, 1971, and found "many political, economic, and social problems." The principal secretary of the mission was Dahomey's Maxime-Leopold Zollner, who, if we recall, was a vocal advocate of West Papua's independence from Indonesian colonialism. According to the document, the Black man in Niugini was a colonized being, deprived of economic and political power. White power had an invidious stranglehold on Black Niuginians, who needed to fight against White colonialism. It called for an all-Black assembly by 1972, for foreign investment to be registered in as opposed to outside Papua New Guinea, and a conditional temporary quasi-citizenship for all non-indigenous people in the country. The statement also called for self-government, for the people's control of all of Niugini's mineral resources, and for universal education *not* based on the English language for qualifying standards. It also satirically called for the UN to enforce a "Black Niugini policy towards foreigners" to match Australia's "Whites-only" immigration policies, and to avoid racial problems, establish a homogeneous Black society.[16]

The NBPG emerged as the UN's Afro-Asian bloc was pressuring Australia to set dates for independence in New Guinea. According to Merze Tate, this bloc felt that the colony was "becoming synonymous with conditions in Rhodesia, Southwest Africa, and Portuguese Mozambique and Angola." For Tate, Australia did not want Papua New Guinea to become a seventh state because of pushback from "technically advanced and color conscious" Australians. This would have meant "unlimited migration into Australia of a Brown, primitive people constitutionally eligible" to vote. Educated Niuginans would not tolerate "second class citizenship," which "would justify the suspicions of the Afro-Asian Bloc," White liberals, and "most Negroes" in America that Australia was "a Pacific South Africa."[17]

Niugini Black Power called for self-respect, self-definition, and self-determination. It was essentially a "philosophy of liberation"—the "only alternative for the Black man in Niugini if he was to survive as a person worthy of respect." The NBPG stood in solidarity with liberation struggles of oppressed groups of any race, sex, color, or creed. Black Power advocated the redemption of the oppressed and the removal of obstacles that hindered Black people from achieving the "full flowering" of their personality. Citing Kwame Ture and Charles Hamilton's *Black Power*, Hannett argued that Niugini's "basic need was to reclaim its history and identity" from cultural terrorism and the "depredation of self-justifying White guilt."[18]

Hannett argued that cultural terrorism had "fossilized" Black people to a "vegetative state of a thing" and an "exotic specimen of the human race," which was now displayed in the Highlands city of Mount Hagen for the "vulgar gaze" of tourists and the "financial enrichment" of the White expatriates. But Niuginians were "not the wards of the White race," the White man's burden, or a "child race." It was pathetic to see Niuginians accept "emasculating titles" such as "boi," "manki masta," or "natives," while Whites were referred to as "masta," "missis," "Taubada" (big White man), and "Sinabada" (big White woman). Every time a Niuginian in a "condescending, frog perspective" said "yesa masta" or "yesa missis," he was allowing the White man to depersonalize him or "castrate his manliness." Hannett felt it a pity to see Niuginian tribal leaders who rightfully held their heads high in the village, but melted in "total submissiveness, filial obedience," and deep obeisance when in front of insignificant White men. Younger men and women once said of their leaders, "When the old men speak let no more words be said." However, authority had now been unquestionably given to any White man, young or old. This total reversal of loyalty, which was once based on seniority, achievement, and leadership, was now based on the myth of White supremacy. This was best expressed in Tok Pisin—"Masta I tok; tok I dai" (The master has spoken, all speech must die).[19]

Hannett argued that every time Niuginians were placed in Western education systems, they learned languages that were biased against their culture. He chastised Niuginians who attacked their indigenous concepts like tribalism, animism, and polygamy. Tribal identities were the bricks upon which national consciousness could be built. In animism lay "the only hope" of remaining human and sane, for it held no dichotomies between the spiritual and material, and humans were one with the natural "cosmic reality." But, he asked, "what did Christianity have to offer the Black man?" He answered, "Nothing but self-condemnation, split personality, and hypocrisy." A "force of cultural invasion" and colonialism, Christianity had meant the same wherever lands had been conquered "under the banner of the cross" by those who claimed "to be repositories of divine injunction to conquer, civilize, and Christianize." This included the Pilgrim settlers of the *Mayflower*, who viewed America as a savage land whose riches were there for the Christian suiters to "sow spirituals and reap temporals." It was then little wonder that expatriate exploiters thought it was their "divine mission" to exploit Papua New Guinea.[20]

Black Power sought redress against these issues and called for Black self-criticism and self-awareness. The process of Freire's conscientization would create proud Black people whose world was dominated by "generally ethnocentric minority groups whose weird practice of the cannibalism of racism" had "been eating out" their very souls. Black people needed to liberate themselves because freedom was never given—it needed to be "wrenched from the oppressors." The NBPG's essential message was, "Black man, know thyself and act accordingly." Still, the group did not have a blueprint for nation building. As a small organization, it chose to carry out collective education in the form of forums, programs of conscientization, public debates, and the production of literature. As redeemed Niuginians, they would be able to build a nation formed on their values and aspirations.[21] The NBPG would do its part to help drive a stunning Black Arts movement that emerged from but extended far beyond the campus.

Black Power's Apostles

The NBPG emerged from a student group known as the Apostles. In 1976 Taban Lo Liyong informed the First Independent Papua New Guinea Writers' Conference that these Apostles gave Port Moresby "its taste of Black Power." A former student of Howard University and chair of UPNG's Literature Department (1975–1977), Liyong remarked that the group was "awake to the fight for national independence." They "talked straight and back," and "led integration of eating and drinking places." There was at least one Black woman among them, and one member had conducted a marriage of two members.[22]

The Apostles were allied with a political body of students from the slightly older Administrative College, the Bullybeefers, who were known for "discussing politics whilst eating bully beef off tin cans." It was from the ranks of both these groups that the country's leading political and economic leaders, writers, nationalists, and civil servants emerged. This included Bullybeefer Michael Samore, Papua New Guinea's first prime minister. According to Liyong, the radicalism of the Bullybeef Club (largely politicians) was "matched by the over-activism of the Apostles" (primarily artists). During the path to political independence, the protest literature of the Apostles denounced colonial rule and the "antics of Europeans in Papua New Guinea." This included verbal lashings of a "kiap or two," diatribes against the churches and airport attendants, and calls for cultural rediscovery.[23] Liyong's take speaks to a tradition of transnational student activism that marked the Administrative College, Lae's Institute of Technology, and UPNG.

Hannett's own experiences demonstrate this. Born in 1941, he hailed from the autonomous northeastern province of Bougainville and studied at Catholic seminaries in Rabaul and Madang. During his time at Madang, he read and was enthralled by the works of James Baldwin, Tom Mboya, and Martin Luther King Jr. His autobiographical essay "Disillusionment with the Priesthood," published in *Black Writing from New Guinea* (1973), explained his political development. In Rabaul he became more conscious of the wide gap in the standard of living between the priests and pupils. For example, the students once slaughtered a cow for a feast. They were given the head and scraps, while the priests enjoyed the meat. But what mattered most was his realization that "the priests themselves were not free from racial prejudices." Rabaul had two cinemas, one for natives and one for Europeans. The priests would sometimes take "light-skinned students to the European one—the Gilbertese, some Papuans and one or two Tolais. Solomon Islanders were told that we were too Black!" In addition, they also had two masses–one for Europeans and one for Niuginians.[24]

Hannett was also moved by the 1962 Hahalis Welfare Society movement, which occurred on Bougainville's Buka Island. Encouraged by the society, some eighty villagers from Hahalis refused to pay a £2 head tax to the colonial state, choosing instead to use their collective resources to benefit their community. The administration denounced the group as being a cargo cult and sent a seventy-member police patrol to arrest them. Some hundred villagers resisted. The police claimed that two thousand villagers walked into the police camp, and after the men "pushed the women onto the police batons," they began to use these same batons against the entire crowd. One hundred and twenty villagers were sentenced to six months on charges of riotous behavior. According to Albert Maori Kiki, the *South Pacific Post* referred to the province as "Little Katanga," in reference to the Congo. Those arrested were dragged onto a boat handcuffed.[25]

Hannett was "emotionally connected" to the issue as one of its leaders, Francis Hagai, was a former schoolmate of his. After leaving Rabaul, Hannett went to Madang, where his political awareness extended beyond issues at the village level to involve concerns of a national and international nature. The building of a copper mine in Bougainville was one such issue. He formed a student group with his *wantoks* John Momis and Ignatius Kilage to discuss these issues. The priests denounced their influence on "the growing restlessness" of other students, while they continued to "bless the status quo."[26]

A UN visiting mission to Papua New Guinea helped Hannett and his cohorts to think more about New Guinea's political future. The delegation, led by Liberia's Nathaniel Eastman, visited the seminary on March 23, 1965, and had a "lively exchange" with the students about the UN's views on self-determination for Papua New Guinea. The students called for Australia to educate Niuginians in an effort to develop true national identity, and to give students a sense of world politics via international travel. They also protested against wage discrimination, as expatriates were paid more than indigenous workers.[27]

Eastman informed the students that they were the country's elites, and he defended Papua New Guinea's right to self-determination. He knew that racial segregation was openly practiced and abused in the territory. He later informed the UN that companies like Burns Philp discriminated in their stores and paid "woefully low" wages. Managers of several large companies "admitted that they could pay higher wages but explained that the expatriate farmers were against it." Meanwhile, the Australian administration "lowered the salaries of local public service employees." The education system did not "meet the needs of the population" and UPNG should have been developed years earlier. There was also unjustified discrimination in primary schools. Non-indigenous pupils could all attend the primary schools reserved for them, but hundreds of indigenous students were refused admission to "T" primary schools due to inadequate space or a shortage of teachers. The territory needed to give immediate effect to all UN resolutions that related to decolonization. Yet some people in the territory seemed reluctant to get rid of foreign domination, mistakenly believing that the withdrawal of the Australian administration would entail a loss of support from Australia.[28]

At the UN Trusteeship Council's meeting in June 1965, Eastman explained how Burns Philp "was extracting the life-blood of the people of Papua and New Guinea." It had large plantations, hotels, and government-subsidized ships and it controlled imports, most exports, and the loan business. This amounted to a complete monopoly of Papua and New Guinea's economy. Its plantation laborers worked under deplorable conditions, and were partly paid in cash and high-priced goods from company stores. Burns Philp charged excessively high shipping rates, owing to the lack of free competition, and unfairly controlled the prices of imported goods. Eastman had been told in Rabaul of a group of indigenous people who had planned to establish a cement block factory but had been refused a bank loan because the factory would have competed with one owned by Burns Philp.[29]

Hannett and other students established the magazine *Dialogue* to communicate with students from other tertiary institutions, such as the

Papuan Medical College and the Teachers Training College. Edited by Hannett, the first issue focused on "brotherhood" and was well received by the church. Switching tone, the second edition addressed inequities in a timber lease deal in Bougainville. Hannett's article "Now Is the Moment of Truth" informed indigenous people that "White men were human after all," and not "demigods or sacred cows." He stated that, according to the UN Charter, the administration needed to protect the rights of Niuginians. But the church, the administration, and the planters were birds of a feather. The students printed and distributed a thousand copies of the issue across the country and in Australia. One priest ordered them to burn their remaining five hundred copies. The group was severely chastised and Hannett was strongly encouraged to resign from the seminary. He did not do so.[30]

According to Momis, Hannett was a visionary who had a remarkable ability to bridge the gap between Western-educated and village-educated leaders. As students they were influenced by anti-colonial movements in Africa, the radical theology and social justice efforts of leaders of the Catholic Church in Latin America, and the civil rights movement in the United States. They were also moved by the unfair conditions of plantation labor in Papua New Guinea, including at the church's own farms.[31]

Hannett brought these experiences to UPNG as a student in 1966. In 1968 he wrote a response to the assassination of Martin Luther King Jr. in *Nilaidat*. Hannett cited King's 1963 "Letter from a Birmingham Jail," hailing King as "a martyr of the hypocrisy of American democracy." Stressing that King's life and death were of relevance to Papua New Guinea, he asked, "Is it sufficient for me now to lie snugly on my bed of sanctimonious bombastic complacency and watch sadistically while the dignity of my neighbors is slowly sapped dry by inhuman living conditions, exploitation, and all sorts of injustice? . . . We too in New Guinea have a dream." This was to see their land grow into a free nation based on equal rights. This meant that tribalisms, disunity, racism, and discrimination needed to be stamped out.[32]

In July 1968 he responded to the assassination of US senator Robert Kennedy in *Nilaidat*. He called for students to "speak a language of self-confidence" and cement alliances with "the voiceless masses at home, in the plantation, and in the town slums where the indigenous people" were being taught the language of hatred, racism, and disunity.

This, he argued, UPNG's Student Representative Council (SRC) could do via organized social action.[33]

Hannett became president of the university's Politics Club, which, in 1968, protested a visit to Papua New Guinea by Johan Maree, South Africa's high commissioner to Australia. Students and faculty challenged the commissioner during his trip to campus. Hannett "struck the first spark" by asking questions about South Africa's imprisonment of African National Congress leader Inkosi Luthuli. UPNG creative writing professor Ulli Beier's pressuring of Maree set off a chain of "mass vocal outbursts and enthusiastic clapping" in the meeting.[34]

Politics Club members followed Maree as he left campus to catch a departing flight. Led by *Nilaidat* editor Leo Morgan, students hurried to the airport by all means available—the university bus, motorbikes, cars, an "exhausted" airport shuttle bus, and the back of a truck. Surrounding and rocking Maree's car at the airport, they greeted him with boos and placards reading, "No Apartheid," "Go Home Racialist," "Leave Africa Alone," "Black Power," and "Racialists Go to Hell." Maree, in "typical 007 style," photographed the chanting, shouting, and fist-raising students, who were also singing African American freedom songs. Despite being blocked from the tarmac by airport security, the students continued to protest as the plane departed. As fate would have it, the Australian minister for external territories, Charles Barnes, arrived at the airport during the affair. The demonstrators turned the heat on him.[35]

Nilaidat published a satirical play about the incident, with characters including Mr. Big, Mr. Boer, Mr. Dusky (Hannett?), Mr. Colorless (Beier?), and the Mob. Defended by Big, Boer was questioned by Dusky and Colorless. "Why does the government gaol writers, why does apartheid oppress, and what about Black Power?"[36]

In contrast to *Nilaidat*, Papua New Guinea's daily newspaper *South Pacific Post* chided the protest. It claimed that the students were practicing "apartheid in reverse," and that Black Power had no more moral justification than did "White Power." When it refused to print a letter that supported the students, written by a "Mr. Hide," *Nilaidat* promptly did so. Hide called for the *Post* to consider more deeply the global connections between "apartheid, segregation, and racial discrimination." The horrors of the 1960 Sharpeville massacre were publicly remembered, but as an "Englishman," Hide remained shamed by the 1959 racial attacks on

West Indians in London's Notting Hill. But in refusing to understand the significance of Black Power, the *Post* was denying racism's universalism. How could the paper question the use of Black Power placards in a demonstration against apartheid? When a spokesman of nonviolence like Martin Luther King Jr. was gunned down in the streets, how could the *Post* not understand that Black Power brought hope to thousands of Blacks across America?[37]

Nilaidat closely covered West Papua's stand against Indonesia. In May 1969 the paper published a special edition on the political, historical, economic, and social implications of the issue. It printed reports from the UN and West Papuan spokespersons Marcus Kaisiepo and Nicolaas Jouwe. The paper detailed how, between 1965 and 1968, Indonesia's military bombarded West Papua with napalm, burned the houses of dissidents, and killed and tortured adults and children. One report by Kaisiepo claimed that more than fifty thousand innocent men, women, and children had been killed in West Papua.[38]

Nilaidat questioned Indonesia's motives surrounding the Act of Free Choice. It found the country's actions to be "depressingly reminiscent of Italy's enforced subjugation" of Ethiopia in 1936. UPNG students held a daylong forum about the matter. It used the event to gather supplies for children of West Papuan refugees who had fled into Papua New Guinea.[39]

That same month, Hannett led a Politics Club march of over five hundred students in protest against Indonesia, the support that it received from Australia, and the UN's refusal to deal with Indonesia's violations. He penned an open letter to Papua New Guinea's religious leaders, titled "Lumine Gentium." The document stated that churchgoers who did not express moral support for West Papua were committing "clerical sin," and "eclipsing the Sun of Justice from shining in the world through their lack of courage, complacency, and ineptitude in bearing witness to Christian principles." The protestors marched to the Australian Government House, where they sang songs like "We Shall Overcome." Meanwhile, Hannett presented a petition to the Australian administration.[40]

In response, a journalist accused him of being a "front man for a White student," suggesting that a Black person was not capable of organizing the demonstration. Even a White UPNG student found this notion to be outrageous—Hannett was "nobody's stooge." *Nilaidat* sharply rebuked the "front man" accusation: "A native can't write anything in-tellectual, he must always have been influenced by Whites. If he ever writes anything radical it must be communist-inspired or [American] Negro-inspired. . . . If he ever writes anything thoughtful it must have been thought out by others."[41]

It was at this moment in 1969 that the Apostles first gave serious thought to forming the NBPG. They opted against doing so, as they felt that this would have been tantamount to them giving in to their emotions. The group would not hold its first public act until August 1970, when it organized a forum against a "deplorable" Public Order Bill aimed at controlling demonstrations and extending police powers. The forum was held in Hohola, Port Moresby, where they were denounced as "too emotional" and anti-White by White and Black participants.[42]

The Australian Broadcast Company interviewed John Kasaipwalova at the forum. Describing himself as a Black nationalist, the young poet from the Trobriand Islands stated that the Bill was aimed at "us, at the present Black people in New Guinea." But the NBPG's Black Power movement was "a reaction against colonial oppression." The nature of oppression in Niugini was that the White population held most of the power and White culture had virtually destroyed Black identity. The NBPG refused "to sit back and let the police abuse" citizens. According to the journalist, Ian MacIntosh, observers in Papua New Guinea were not surprised by Black Power's emergence. In fact, he reckoned that the passing of the Public Order Bill reflected the administration's anticipation of Black Power.[43]

The Australian Security Intelligence Organization (ASIO) documented the activities of the NBPG. Australian officials claimed that, in January 1970, Kasaipwalova had tried to establish an anti-colonial Black Power movement in the Trobriands. In a controversy over school bus fees, he called on his community to form an action group to challenge the White power structure, as they had succumbed to the fear of the White man for too long. Australian officials were aware that in that same month, he and John Kaputin had participated in a Tertiary Students Conference.[44]

Kasaipwalova's paper at Lae, "Problems of Unity in Papua New Guinea," denounced colonial exploitation of Papua New Guinea. He argued that Black people had no identity and were very dependent on the

White man's definitions of themselves. Formal education had become propaganda machinery for perpetuating White supremacy. Hence, resentment of colonialism needed to be creatively converted to break the colonial mentality that had been instilled in Black people. Black people's inferiority complex was "not an accident of history"—it was a "dialectical product of an aggressive system of" conscious and unconscious White colonial behavior. Those who resented this cultural tyranny were branded troublemakers and communists. *Nilaidat* printed this speech in June 1970.[45]

ASIO opened a file on Kasaipwalova in 1969, when he was studying veterinary science at the University of Queensland. In a situation curiously well documented by ASIO, he lost his scholarship while attempting to study law instead. In August 1969 he was arrested after organizing a student demonstration in Brisbane around the issue of Bougainville. Weeks later, he returned to Papua New Guinea and visited East New Britain, where he observed a lesson at a high school in the Gazelle Peninsula. He was ejected from the school's premises for "causing a disturbance." ASIO reported that he had instructed the community there, the Tolai, to arm themselves with guns and take a violent stand against the Australian administration. Kasaipwalova allegedly supported Bertrand Russell's revolutionary and socialist movement.[46]

The organization noted that the twenty-one-year-old Kasaipwalova operated a book stall at UPNG—the Kabitan Book Service, which opened in the summer of 1970—where he sold left-wing literature and books on Black Power. These were apparently obtained from the Revolutionary Socialist Alliance's Red and Black Bookstore in Brisbane, Australia. ASIO documented his travels to Australia that September to speak at a seminar at the University of Sydney. It noted that his fare was paid by Bernard Narokobi, who was studying in Sydney and serving as the national officer for Papua New Guinea students within the National Union of Australian University Students.[47]

Kasaipwalova was a poet. His 1971 "Reluctant Flame" called for the fires of Niugini nationalism to fight against the chill of colonialism, and to take fuel from Black uprisings in South Africa, Vietnam, and the United States. A self-described Black nationalist, he felt that the writer's challenge was to "capture and express the people's consciousness" and break the "colonial mentality" of Black people. He had a knack for political performance. In October 1970 he was acquitted of stealing a thirty-two-cent tube of adhesive from a Port Moresby store. Pleading not guilty, he said that he had only stolen the tube so that he could raise issues of social injustice in the Supreme Court.[48]

Kasaipwalova also understood the political power of culture. In a 1970 interview in *New Guinea Writing*, poet Kumalau Tawali claimed that there was no need for Black Power in Papua New Guinea, because the world had enough problems already. Totally disagreeing with the movement, he called for reconstruction of Papua New Guinean culture instead. This bewildered Kasaipwalova, as Tawali's widely cited poem "Bush Kanaka Speaks" lamented the White man's "lack of bones," and could have been considered a work of Black Power. Kasaipwalova found the notion of cultural reconstruction to be a narcissistic dream that implied that Papua New Guinean culture was static and fixed in time. But Black Power called for a radical redefinition of values based on contemporary realities. To cry for the "milk of cultural reconstruction," argued Kasaipwalova, was to ask for "life from a corpse"; but Black people wanted to live and be free.[49]

In May 1972 Kasaipwalova chastised the editor of *Nilaidat* for describing him ambiguously as "John K." He took the opportunity to demonstrate how in the Trobriand culture, individuals were named differently than the ways of *dimdims* (White persons). While it was European custom to give someone the surname of their father, Trobriand surnames belonged to "a body of particular names with historical and social meanings" that belonged to clans. His full surname was Kasaipwalovaposovalu, which dated back some five generations to an ancestor named Posovalu, whose controversial chieftaincy defied hierarchical orders. When his rule was challenged by other chiefs, clan members talked of his pending destruction, saying, "Sena kasai la pwalova Posovalu" (Posovalu's steering is very hard). But Posovalu and his village survived, and Kasaipwalovaposovalu became his clan's name. This, he argued, demonstrated how in one's name usually lay one's clan history and was often a "psychological asset" from which one created identity and history. In contrast, he was baptized by Christian missionaries as John. As such, for the editor to print "John" in full and reduce his "real name" to "K" was to mark the beginnings of his colonial whitewashing process, which he found to be offensive.[50]

The NBPG involved itself in these kinds of political and cultural debates across Oceania. John Waiko and Tawali were among those who traveled to Sydney University to participate in Papua/New Guinea week in September 1969. While traveling across the Pacific, NBPG members faced the immigration restrictions that affected all Niuginians. For Martin Buluna to travel to the Second South Pacific Seminar at Fiji's University of the South Pacific in 1971, he had to apply for a "Permit for a Native to Leave the Territory." The five foot two, twenty-four-year-old from Samarai, Milne Bay, was given a month's permit.[51]

Leo Hannett, John Waiko, Leo Morgan, John Kasaipwalova, Robbie Namaliu, and Buluna all participated in the 1970 Waigani Seminar on Politics in Melanesia. Buluna's paper discussed how Niugini students were rejecting colonialism internationally and domestically. There was no longer any place for the "White man to impose his image" on Papua New Guinea, and his obstinance would only antagonize and alienate students. This attitude could lead to violent upheavals instigated by students. Using Brazil's Archbishop Helder Camara's references to racialism, his paper described the legacy of racist ideas in the colony, referencing how official medical handbooks for colonialists in the country condemned Niuginians as "disease-carriers," and how literature by UPNG students was regarded as having been written by Whites. He drew on Ture and Hamilton's *Black Power* to describe how White Power structures used domestic colonialism and "indirect rule" to make the political decisions that affected Black lives. But *Nilaidat* was exposing these ideas and students would no longer accept these dynamics.[52]

Hannett's paper, "The Church and Nationalism," was a seething critique of the Christian church's support of colonialism. He referenced his article from his seminary days, when he stated that it was not a sin to critique White society, because White men were "not demigods." After that, the colonial administration called for an investigation into his supposed communist or American influences. Now Hannett thanked the seminary for the lessons he learned there about colonialism.[53]

He then compared racist statements made by the church and planters in Niugini about the lack of native intelligence. An official handbook of Niugini of the 1930s asserted that the "function of a White man in a tropical country" was not to labor with his hands but to direct and control native labor from an office desk. According to Hannett, these injustices often produced "negative nationalism"—revolutionary reactions against colonial evils. This, he argued, was a necessary precondition for true nationalism. Australia's repressive tactics against Black protest had unintentionally produced nationalist movements such as the Mataungan Association of the Gazelle Peninsula and the Napidakoe Navitu Association in Bougainville. The leaders of these groups welcomed the opportunity to become martyrs, particularly if this led to arrests or imprisonment, as upon release they would become leaders. However, he felt that these leaders might emerge from their cells with martyrdom and savior complexes, becoming too possessive of their powers. He cited Nkrumah and Jomo Kenyatta as examples of this process. He also referenced Mboya's charge that missionaries had easily complied with colonial regimes, as in Africa the missionaries, colonialists, and White settlers all preached the same message to African people: Be patient, believe in God, and one day you will advance. He ended his paper with King's quote from *Why We Can't Wait*: "In the midst of blatant injustices inflicted upon the Negro, I have watched White churchmen stand on the sideline and mouth pious irrelevancies and sanctimonious trivialities." He also referenced Malcolm X's calls for the civil rights movement to wake people up to their human rights.[54]

The NBPG's activism extended far beyond the campus, and a number of its leaders furthered nationalist movements in their home communities. After completing his studies at UPNG in 1972, Kasaipwalova returned to the Trobriands. Melbourne's *Age* described the "prominent Black Power advocate" as one of the country's best-known poets. Kasaipwalova had established an organization on the island of Kiriwina, one similar to Kaputin's nationalist Mataungan Association in the Gazelle. Australian officials sent six extra police to the area in anticipation of an uprising.[55]

In 1974 the Papua New Guinea Security Intelligence Organization (PNGSIO) reported on an anti-government meeting in Port Moresby. The main speakers included Narokobi, Kaputin, Hannett, and Leo Kavaua, governor of the Papuan Black Power Movement (distinct from the NBPG). Days later a six-hundred-person protest was held, supported by Bougainville's Momis. According to PNGSIO, in his "well-calculated rabble-rousing speech," Kaputin stated that the House of Assembly would be burned if the crowd called for it. PNGSIO argued that these protests could not be seen as "legitimate political activity." Their calls were to "overthrow the Government" through "violence, sabotage, arson, racial incitement, and strikes." These statements could not be dismissed as spontaneous rhetoric but constituted "a threat to national security" and may have been seditious. It considered Kaputin one of the "most politically aware and expressive" leaders of the Mataungan movement.[56]

The militant Mataungan Association emerged in 1969 in East New Britain's Gazelle among the Tolai, in protest against the formation of a multiracial Gazelle Peninsula Local Government Council. Through demonstrations, mass meetings, and violent clashes, association members found themselves arrested. Nigerian lawyer Ikenna Nwokolo, who taught law at UPNG, defended the group in court. In 1970 the association's Oscar Tammur and Damien Kereku submitted a petition to the Trusteeship Council of the UN denouncing comments allegedly made by a southern African superintendent about killing indigenous people in Rabaul. The petition demanded that the council take steps to remove all police officers from South Africa and Rhodesia, as Australia's colonial administration had installed them to "train our people to deal and kill our own men, women, and children" due to their experience "in dealing with Black people."[57]

Hannett was very much involved in Bougainville's own fight for environmental justice. In 1969 the building of a major copper mine displaced the Bougainville community of Rorovana. It was owned by Conzinc Riotinto Australia, an international company based in southern Africa. Twenty-five unarmed women wrestled with the riot squad police in protest and were beaten with batons and tear-gassed in response. Hannett was a spokesperson for Bougainville. In 1969 he visited Melbourne's Aborigines Advancement League during a "lightning tour of Australia" to talk about Bougainville, which was "of great interest to Aborigines." He informed the *Tribune*, "We don't want to be strangers in our own land." The mine expected to make $200 million annually but would pay $38,000 a year in compensation. On Australian TV, he added, "The White man has done us injustice and, in years to come, this could lead to race violence, even guerilla warfare."[58]

A Melanesian Black Arts Movement

The NBPG expressed its Melanesian nationalism through art and literature. Its core leadership studied literature with UPNG professors

Prithvindra Chakravarti and the aforementioned Ulli Beier. Beier, of German-Jewish descent, was based in UPNG's English Department. He had previously taught at Nigeria's University of Ibadan, and in 1957 had founded *Black Orpheus*, the influential journal of African and African American literature. He attended the First Congress of Black Writers and Artists in Paris (1956), co-founded the Mbari Artists and Writers Club (1961), and was part of a crucial network of leading African artists from the Anglophone and Francophone worlds. Arriving in Boroko in 1967, Beier and his wife, Georgina, had an intriguing impact on UPNG's Black Arts movement, Ulli through writing and Georgina via visual art.

Ulli's courses were based on his extensive experiences with Africana artists. His students read Chinua Achebe, Wole Soyinka, Léopold Senghor, and *Présence Africaine*. They collectively produced a vibrant body of visual art, plays, memoirs, novels, poetry, and short stories in English, indigenous languages, and Tok Pisin. They also produced literary journals, magazines, and books like *Kovave: A Magazine of New Guinea Literature, Modern Images from Niugini, Voices of Independence: New Black Writing from Papua New Guinea, Black Writing from New Guinea, Papua New Guinea Writing*, and *Papua Pocket Poets Series*, which reached audiences in Oceania and beyond. This collective also published in journals across Oceania, like *Mana*.

UPNG's first literary magazine, *Kovave*, ran from November 1969 until 1975. Its editors included artists such as Hannett, Elton Brash, Vincent Eri, Jo Gray, and Robbie Namaliu, future prime minister of Papua New Guinea. In 1968 Beier informed Bernth Lindfors of *Research in African Literatures* at the University of Texas–Austin that *Kovave* was being printed in Hong Kong. This was due to the inefficiency of printers in Australia, which was the reason why *Papua Pocket Poets* had been inconsistently published. However, he sent him seven copies of the latter. He promised to mail Lindfors a copy of *Kovave* as it came out, forewarning that the magazine was not going to be "good for some time." He lamented, "The Australians have been here for eighty years, and no Papuan has ever produced a book." He was thus pleased that he had helped produce the first, Albert Maori Kiki's *Ten Thousand Years in a Lifetime*.[59]

Ten Thousand Years fascinatingly details the rich cultural history of Papua New Guinea but also White supremacy, segregation, racial wage discrimination, and Australian colonialism. Kiki describes how compensation for European civil servants included homes, while indigenous workers lived in shacks. Niuginians suffered "daily insults of discrimination and segregation" in Moresby, including racially segregated cinemas, bus services, and bathrooms labeled Gentlemen (White men), Ladies (White women), Tatau (Papuan men), and Hahin (Papuan women). Kiki recalls how, upon his return from Fiji, he started challenging segregation in stores that discriminated against Niuginians. This included the Burns Philp supermarket, which served drinks to Europeans in glasses but served indigenous customers in plastic cups. Still, what made Niuginians dislike Europeans the most was their attitude to indigenous women. White men would "have native women and despise them at the same time." One magazine in 1967 described Papua New Guinea as socially repugnant. Yet there was no prostitution before White men arrived.[60]

In 1969 Ulli was asked by the university's vice chancellor to establish a program for an Institute for New Guinea Culture. Meanwhile, Georgina worked with several artists via a workshop. This was significant, as the Arts Council of Papua and New Guinea had catered only to expatriates. The Beiers traveled back and forth between Papua New Guinea, Nigeria, and Europe. Ulli's global contacts helped him to facilitate a cultural exchange between Africa and Papua New Guinea. This included Mike Josselson, director of the London-based anti-Marxist Congress of Cultural Freedom, with whom Beier had worked for several years while in Africa. In 1950 Josselson had established the congress at the behest of the Central Intelligence Agency (CIA). The congress, like its CIA-funded counterpart in the United States, the American Society of African Culture, was connected to a broad network of artists from across the Africana world. Its relationships with artists from Papua New Guinea were facilitated by the Beiers, who communicated regularly with Josselson and his wife, Diana.[61]

In December 1968 the Josselsons arranged to have five pieces of Niuginian art displayed at the International School of Geneva. These were works from artists like Sokuro and Tiabe, who worked with Georgina and were convalescents in Laloki Hospital, Port Moresby. She described them as "primitive tribesmen from remote mountain areas of New Guinea." Diana felt that pieces showing "tribal motives would have more exotic appeal there." Hence, she asked for no more pieces from

Tiabe, who Georgina described as having no "intimate experience" with or romanticism of the White man's "cruel and violent" machine world. As such, his pictures were akin to modern visions of machine torture. Georgina felt that the traditional artist talent of Papua New Guinea was being unfortunately channeled into a "debased form of tourist art," which was also bought by suburban White colonials in New Guinea.[62] Over the years, the Beiers continued to send Oceanic art to the Josselsons; in one 1969 case seven pieces of Papua New Guinean art were sold at Geneva's Centre Genevois de Gravure Contemporaine at a 33 percent commission.[63]

The Beiers left for Nigeria in 1971. In 1974 the emerging Somare government asked Beier to return and form an Institute of Papua New Guinea Studies. Josselson helped him to do so. After a trip to Europe, Georgina wrote to Mike and Diana, telling them that they had arrived back in Papua New Guinea with much enthusiasm, as its government was doing well and possessed a great deal of political "common sense, justice, and wisdom." On a personal level, they were doing wonderful. While neither of their jobs had been confirmed, they had bought two homes—Georgina could not bear to live in Australian-built "fiber huts." One afternoon while they were not at home, a government official pushed underneath their door two checks totaling $57,000 in US dollars. This envelope-free stash came with a note reading, "Start the Institute of New Guinea Studies and pay yourself." Georgina wrote to friends abroad, "Action first, bureaucracy second." The Beiers also planned to buy a house in Australia. In 1974 Josselson sent him African sculptures from Geneva, Switzerland. In April 1974 Georgina wrote to Mike, happy to have received the "parcel of goodies." They moved into their house on May 1 and found that the Somare government continued to "amaze with their courage and incorruptibility, a relief after Nigeria."[64]

In 1974 Ulli wrote to Josselson, expressing how much they loved New Guinea. It was "much more relaxing than Nigeria," despite some uncertainty. They enjoyed their "rambling large house." Meanwhile, while the institute was developing, it was hard to find employable New Guineans, as most took highly paid government positions. Furthermore, he added, "the best do not want a job at all: they want to go right back to their village and organize self-help movements."[65] Indeed, we have already seen how that dynamic played out.

While the Beiers clearly had an impact on New Guinea's Black Arts movement, Black Power's critiques of White privilege, patriarchy, White power, and surveillance were inherent in this experience. In addition, Ulli has been memorialized as an initiator of Black cultural production at UPNG, but this has unfortunately obscured the impact of Black and Brown scholars like Chakravarti, who were also a part of this movement. This includes a body of scholars from Uganda's Makerere University, Kenya's Henry Olela, Ghana's Kwasi Nyamekye, Taban Lo Liyong, and Ikenna Nwokolo. Beier himself was clear about this; he notes how Nwokolo became a political role model for UPNG students like Hannett, Namaliu, and Kasaipwalova, and that he and his West Indian wife, Elaine—who opened a driving school and African fabric store in Port Moresby—changed the political and social landscape in Papua New Guinea.[66]

Still, it would be tragic not to include Oceanic scholars like Epeli Hau'ofa in this conversation. Hau'ofa, who was born and raised in Papua New Guinea in 1939 to Tongan missionaries, studied anthropology at Canada's McGill University. He did five months of fieldwork in Trinidad, where he devoured the novels of V. S. Naipaul; Naipaul's humor influenced the way that he would write. Hau'ofa grew up being *Papuan*; he returned to teach at UPNG in 1968 as a senior tutor in anthropology. While he wanted to be a writer, he was "afraid" to approach Ulli Beier, who was "a big, impressive man who walked around wearing . . . Nigerian robes." But the Beiers' work influenced his later efforts as founder of USP's Oceania Center. Hau'ofa was fascinated by UPNG's Melanesian cultural environment. He recalls that at UPNG professors knew that they were "dealing with young people who were going to be leaders of the country."[67]

In the aftermath of independence, activists of the NBPG went in many differing directions—some joined the government, some formed nationalist movements within Papua New Guinea, and others continued to produce their art. Their activism also reflects the broader politicization of students across Papua New Guinea on Black Diasporic issues. For example, students at the Institute of Technology demonstrated against

Nigeria's civil war in Biafra (1968) and the oppression of Aboriginal communities in Australia (1972).[68] Black Power in Papua New Guinea was a statement of Melanesian transnationalism. The next chapter shows how this "version" of Black internationalism would attract activists from across Oceania and the Global South.

5

Melanesia's Way

In 1976 students at the University of Papua New Guinea (UPNG) led a public protest against Indonesian imperialism in East Timor. When demonstrators trampled on a replica of an Indonesian flag, Indonesian foreign minister Adam Malik lambasted them as being immature. In a 1976 article in *Yagl-Ambu: Papua New Guinea Journal of the Social Sciences and Humanities*, UPNG teaching fellow Utula Samana challenged this perception. He described how East Timorese nationalists in the then Portuguese colony began to agitate for political independence after a 1974 military coup in Portugal. The most effective of these was the Revolutionary Front for an Independent East Timor (Fretilin) under the leadership of Xavier do Amaral and radical journalist José Ramos-Horta, who, exiled to Mozambique, built concrete relationships with the Frente de Libertação de Moçambique (FRELIMO). Indonesia invaded East Timor, claiming it as it had once done with West Papua. This invasion of some six warships, hundreds of paratroopers and marines, dozens of planes, and twenty thousand Javanese "volunteers," was denounced in Papua New Guinea. The Women's Action Group (WAG) organized a two-hundred-person demonstration that included philosopher Bernard Narokobi. UPNG students followed suit and marched to the Indonesian embassy, where they condemned Indonesian aggression in both East Timor and West Papua. Well into the 1990s, as chair of the United Nations Special Committee on Decolonization and Papua New Guinea's permanent representative to the UN, Samana continued to support East Timor's sovereignty.[1]

This kind of Black activism led detractors to describe UPNG as a "Mau Mau factory," a reference to the militant uprisings of Kenya's Land and Freedom Army.[2] While Western media outlets like *Time* magazine framed Papua New Guinea as a Stone Age civilization, from the perspective of indigenous communities across Oceania, UPNG was an influential nexus of Black modernity.[3] Papua New Guinea reflected the future—rather than just an ancient past—of the Black Pacific in terms of its radical political, cultural, and scholarly discourses on decolonization and Black internationalism in Oceania. Papua New Guinea was a critical site for appropriate technology and sustainable development. For example, Bermuda's Pauulu Kamarakafego worked in its Office of Village Development. In 1978 he gave appropriate technology workshops on designing low-cost coastal village houses using bamboo and cement. In 1979, in collaboration with the National Housing Commission, he built such a house at the National Capital Botanical Gardens for public inspection.[4]

This chapter shows how throughout the 1970s, UPNG's political meetings, cultural festivals, and academic conferences drew leaders from across Oceania and the Global South. Scholars, students, revolutionaries, and political leaders enthusiastically attended these berths, which ranged from grassroots gatherings, annual Waigani Seminars, and UNESCO meetings. For example, in 1970 Ali Mazrui of Uganda's Makarere University gave a lecture at UPNG for its Council on New Guinea Affairs Seminar on Constitutional Development. In the lecture, published as "An African's New Guinea," Mazrui argued that while traveling in Oceania he was learning not only a lot about Papua New Guinea, but much about Africa as well. Papua New Guinea was "Africa in a state of condensed concentration," and both a miniature and exaggeration of Africa politically, ethnically, and culturally. But what troubled Mazrui was that Australia was depriving Papua New Guinea of "the infrastructure of nationhood"—the worst crime of imperialism.[5]

Power, Panthers, and the Pacific

In April 1972 Australia's Roberta (Bobbi) Sykes wrote to the Niugini Black Power Group's (NBPG) John Kasaipwalova, who at the time was president of UPNG's Student Representative Council. Sykes, a leading Black Power activist, was critically involved in Australia's Canberra Tent Embassy protests. At the time, she was coordinating a Moratorium for Black Rights in Australia, Ningla'na (We are hungry for our land). With Aboriginal communities facing near genocide, national agitation had granted little results. In contrast to UPNG's production of Black scholars, there were only two Black Australian university graduates. As such,

Sykes believed that international embarrassment of Australia's government was the only peaceful means left to try. The use of violence by some 200,000 indigenous people against 12 million White Australians seemed unrealistic and suicidal, but some individuals were desperately considering such acts. Signing her letter with "In the struggle for a better world," Sykes sought any assistance or support.[6]

The Papua New Guinea Security Intelligence Organization (PNGSIO) reported that her letter generated a lot of attention at UPNG. Placed on the university's notice board, some interesting notes were scribbled on it: "Tell Russia to come build naval bases," "To Hell with Russians, they are Whites," "Bloody Irresponsible," and "GET GUNS FROM RUSSIA."[7]

The May issue of *Nilaidat* published an extensive interview with Sykes, in which she discussed the Aboriginal Tent Embassy, Australia's Black Panther Party, Black Power, and questions of Aboriginal land rights. The issue also included an article by UPNG economics professor Vern Harvey, "Aboriginal Fight for Rights," as well as photographs of Sykes, Paul Cole, and Faith Bandler.[8]

Peter Playpool, vice president of the SRC and NBPG supporter, informed journalist Ian MacIntosh that many UPNG students supported the Aboriginal struggle. They were aware of the situation because Papua New Guinea was a colony of Australia. Papua New Guinea's director of intelligence nervously reported that the SRC met to discuss the letter. It agreed to invite Sykes to give talks at UPNG and other educational institutions and pay her expenses if necessary. The director urgently reached out to his Australian counterparts for information regarding the matter.[9]

After touring Aotearoa with Māori leaders, Sykes spent a week in Papua New Guinea by invitation of the SRC in July 1972. According to the Australian Security Intelligence Organization (ASIO), she gave talks at Lae's Institute of Technology, UPNG, and Rabaul's Mataungan Association. She urged about two hundred people at Lae to rally against "Australian apartheid." Sykes discussed how Aboriginals lived dreadfully, often in rubbish heaps and "dried creek beds" amidst the slums of Sydney. Across Australia, Aboriginal peoples faced discrimination, high infant mortality rates, and police brutality. Students there had already decided to telegram the Australian government in support of National

Aboriginal Day. They collected funds for the event and staged a demonstration that coincided with Australia's Moratorium.[10]

According to ASIO, UPNG student Peter Kavo played a prominent role in the Lae demonstration. Considered "quite a radical personality," he was also working with the Australian Union of Students to set up a branch in Papua New Guinea. In 1974 foreign minister Albert Maori Kiki denied him and Aisa Apau a passport to travel to China with an Aboriginal delegation.[11]

At UPNG, Sykes addressed students during a lunchtime forum. She asked them to join the Moratorium, as "Black nations near Australia [needed] to agitate on behalf of Aboriginals." Kasaipwalova also spoke, urging White Australians in Papua New Guinea to join in and "cry in the streets" if they were truly serious about creating a multiracial society.[12]

PNGSIO placed tabs on Makeu Opa, who was also associated with Sykes while she was there. Opa studied economics at UPNG. Closely affiliated with the NBPG, Leo Hannett, and Kasaipwalova, he was also a supporter of the Mataungan Association. ASIO believed that after the killing of the British district commissioner in East New Britain, he wrote on the UPNG billboard, "Rabaul DC killed. One down, 17 to go." Over the summer, he talked to high school students about Black Power, sold Aboriginal land badges on campus, and disseminated "anti-ASIO" sentiments to students.[13]

Sykes's activities were closely monitored by ASIO's Operation Whip 52, which targeted the Moratorium. She was subjected to travel restrictions to the country. Upon Papua New Guinea's independence in 1975, Sykes, along with Denis Walker and members of FCAATSI, remained on Papua New Guinea's immigration stop list.[14]

The Black Moratorium was held in several cities throughout Australia, Papua New Guinea, and Aotearoa on July 14, National Aboriginal Day. It brought thousands of demonstrators to the streets and reflected the internationalist relationships between Niugini, Aboriginal, and Polynesian Black Power activists. In Sydney, Black speakers like Marjorie Timbery, Gary Foley, Kevin Gilbert, and Sykes electrified crowds of three thousand to five thousand at Redfern Park. Clashes broke out with the police, and leaders like activist Bob Bellear and Will 'Ilolahia, chairman of New Zealand's Polynesian Panthers, were also arrested.[15]

The twenty-one-year-old Aotearoan-born Tongan 'Ilolahia co-founded the Polynesian Panther Party (PPP) in 1971. He had been invited to participate in the Moratorium after meeting Sykes in New Zealand. During his time in Australia, he informed the *Tribune* that the party's message was Polynesian unity: "Racists try to rule us by divide and rule—by turning Māori against Islander." He described racism's economic, social, and immigrational effects on Polynesian communities in Aotearoa. Despite being only 12 percent of New Zealand's population, Polynesians formed 67 percent of prisoners in maximum security. "A lot of crap is talked overseas about New Zealand multi-racism, about how there is no racial disharmony in New Zealand. But . . . we suffer racism and exploitation every day and night." The party had established a number of community programs, a prison chapter, food cooperative, advisory and information center, homework classes, a tenant's aid brigade, newspapers, a Police Investigation Group (PIG), political education, demonstrations, cultural programs, anti-police work, and legal aid.[16]

For 'Ilolahia, Black Power meant "the power of self-determination." He was in Australia as an "active sign of solidarity, in accordance with the Panther program of inter-communalism." The Panthers had also held demonstrations after the murder of George Jackson. 'Ilolahia's first remembered encounter with overt racism occurred when he was ten years old and sent to school in London. A Trinidadian friend, George Washington, was subjected to racist insults and treatment, while 'Ilolahia was "romanticized" by the British as "the South Sea Islander with the ukulele." However, upon his return to New Zealand he received similar racist treatment in school. After reading Bobby Seale's *Seize the Time*, he realized that *he* was Washington. 'Ilolahia came to politics through the street gangs and a group called the Niggs, which pressed back against the war in Vietnam—it was "wrong that Polynesians should be fighting a White man's war against our Vietnamese brothers." Moved by the Black Panther Party's stance against racism, police violence, and community engagement, they adapted its program for Aotearoa.[17]

The party's January 1974 Platform and Program declared that it would continue to exist until Polynesian and other oppressed peoples had the "power to control and determine their own destiny," and until there was an end to the capitalist robbery of their wealth and labor. The party demanded a stop to unjust trials, imprisonment, and police harassment of Polynesian people, arguing that all incarcerated Polynesians were political prisoners. Inspired by the radical intellectual thought of Huey P. Newton, the party's Intercommunal Program supported "struggles of other oppressed people throughout the world," as the local struggle was part of the global fight against racism, exploitation, injustice, and oppression.[18]

In May and April 1973, Australian Black Panther Cheryl Buchanan visited UPNG to gather support for Aboriginal land rights. She showed a film about Sykes to some one hundred students at UPNG and was seen working with Namibian UPNG lecturer Zedekia Josef Ngavirue (who was a member of SWAPO) and UPNG's Opa. Her speech accused Australia of trying to wipe out Aboriginal peoples.[19] While at UPNG, she ran into Patrick Te Hemara of Aotearoa's Black Power group Ngā Tamatoa; both were going to attend a Land Rights Conference in Darwin, Australia. According to PNGSIO, the five feet seven, light brown, mini-Afro-wearing Te Hemara spent nine days there at UPNG's Waigani Seminar on foreign investment, international law, and national development; he gave a talk titled "White Racism: The New Zealand Experience."[20]

Launched in 1967, UPNG's annual Waigani Seminars addressed Melanesia and questions of economics, development, culture, education, history, land tenure, politics, literature, feminism, Pacific literature, Pacific brotherhood, and urbanization. Participants from across the Global South enthusiastically attended and organized at these open seminars. Through the mid-1970s, the list of notable attendees from outside Papua New Guinea included the New Hebrides National Party's Walter Lini and Barak Sope, Samoa's Albert Wendt, Brazil's Paulo Freire, and Trinidad's Lloyd Best.[21]

Black Pacific Festivals

In the aftermath of the Fifth Waigani Seminar on Development in Rural Melanesia, UPNG held its First Niugini Arts Festival in 1971. Ulli Beier informed the journal *Cultural Events in Africa* that four African plays were performed. UPNG's Drama Society presented Ghanaian writer Christina Aidoo's *Dilemma of a Ghost*; Goroka's Teachers College presented Wole Soyinka's *Brother Jero and the Swamp Dwellers*; and Madang Teachers College staged Obotunde Ijimere's *Everyman*.[22]

Throughout the 1970s, UPNG hosted a number of other Black writers' conferences and arts festivals. These affairs attracted artists from across Oceania and the broader Africana world. In 1973 the Third Niugini Arts Festival featured a week of poetry, plays, music, dramatizations, and film screenings that took place on UPNG's campus, and public places such as the Koki Market, Elba Beach, and Boroko's Tabari Place. Largely focused on art and culture in Papua New Guinea, the festival included contributions from the Global South because "there was much to be gained on both sides from such a shared experience." The Melanesian Action Group showed radical independent films on and off campus. These included Jorge Sanjinés's *Blood of the Condor* (Bolivia, 1969), Pedro Chaskel's *Venceremos* (Chile, 1971), Fernando E. Solanas's *La Hora de los Hornos* (Argentina, 1968), Cuba's *And We Became Teachers*, Jose Massip's *Maudina Boe* (about Amilcar Cabral and Guinea-Bissau's PAIGC), Santiago Álvarez's *79 Primaveras* (based on the life of Ho Chi Minh), and the radical filmmaking Dziga Vertov Group's 1970 *Wind from the East* (1970). The festival also featured films from Australia (*Come Out Fighting, Who Discovered Australia*) and Papua New Guinea (*My Brother Wantora, Niugini, Alatau War Canoes, West New Britain Mask Film, Tidikawa and Friends, Bugla Yungga,* and *Mataungan Association*).²³

Oodgeroo Noonuccal participated in the festival. At Koki Market she read poetry with PNG artists Apisai Enos, Jack Lahui, and Allan Natachee, over flute music from the Sepek and Highlands. She also lectured in a few English classes at UPNG. Dancers from Australia's Yirrkala also participated and toured the country's cultural centers. According to festival organizer Dorothy Nagrath, the combined presence of Noonuccal and the dancers helped to draw "record crowds." While there, Noonuccal penned the poem "Papua New Guinea," writing, "Oh my Rainbow Serpent, you knew before I knew that I would be at home in this silent land." She asked the Rainbow Serpent to twine itself around her silent cousins and reveal to them their hidden Opal.²⁴

Port Moresby hosted the First Independent Papua New Guinea Writers' Conference in 1976. This phenomenal cultural berth was coordinated by Liyong, chair of UPNG's Department of Literature. His organizing committee included UPNG's Elton Brash, poet Kama Kerpi, John Kaniku, Ulli Beier, and Arthur Jawodimbari of the Creative Arts Center. At the time, Liyong had published four books of poetry, including *Frantz Fanon's Uneven Ribs* (1971), one novel, and two short story collections.[25]

He had also compiled a booklet of over two hundred pages entitled *The Literature of Developed Nations: Negritude*, which he used to teach his classes on myth, language, and literature. The text described Negritude as the "most potent cultural and political philosophy" in "Africa, the West Indies, and amongst the Negroes of North and South America." Negritude was also the "cultural aim of nationalism amongst the Black people." *Literature of Developed Nations* argued that although the "colored" and indigenous peoples of Asia, Oceania, and Australia did not profess Negritude, they were also "moved to create in response to the experiences which called into being the philosophy of *Negritude*"—colonialism. It continued, "European colonization of the colored peoples of the world across Africa, the Americas, the Middle East, Asia, and the South Pacific" had resulted in the "promotion of European values and civilization and the desecration of the cultural and philosophical shrines of the colonized." Motivated by capitalism, "the European made the colored man a tool in the chain of economic production, for the colonizer's benefit." But the "alienation of the colonized man" from his cultural, political, and economic traditions in the midst of "blatant racial arrogance, stirred a revolt in the heart of the colored man, prompting him to fight for political freedom." He rejected the colonizer's values and simultaneously reinstituted the cultural values belonging to his tradition. It is from this context, it argued, that one could "talk of Other Manifestations of *Négritude* Spirit in India, Papua New Guinea, and amongst the Aboriginals in Australia, and Māoris in New Zealand."[26]

Literature of Developed Nations was divided into sections on Negritude's essence, rationale, future, and other manifestations in Asia and Oceania. It utilized extensive quotes, poetry, prose, and passages from the scholars of Negritude, and numerous Africana artists and political leaders—problematically, largely men. This included Léopold Senghor, Aimé Césaire, Kwame Nkrumah, Cheikh Anta Diop, Abiola Irele, Bloke Modisane, Léon Damas, Oladele Taiwo, Edward Wilmot Blyden, Chinua Achebe, Soyinka, Jean-Paul Sartre, Es'kia Mphahlele, Jacques Rabemananjara, Okot p'Bitek, D. T. Niane, and V. S. Naipaul. Liyong critiqued and expounded on the work of these writers. The books spanned themes such as race, slavery, revolt, the Haitian Revolution, the Second

Congress of Negro Writers and Artists (Rome, 1959), African philosophy, African origins of Egyptian society, Marxism, and the African personality. It also related Julius Nyerere's philosophy of Ujamaa to Papua New Guinea's philosophy of collective brotherhood, *Wantok*.

Liyong asserted that "other manifestations of the *Negritude* spirit" spanned Oceania. This included the work of award-winning Māori writer Witi Ihimaera, who wrote of New Zealand's "two cultural maps"—Māori and Pakeha; Liyong hoped that his students would also learn some Māori words via this section. *Literature of Developed Nations* noted Australian Aboriginal novelist Colin Johnson's efforts to recreate the belief of Noongar Dreamtime. John Waiko's literature emphasized the need for education in Papua New Guinea to be grounded in local cultural knowledges. Hannett's "main criticism of the Church was, and still is their attitude to [his] people." It asserted Apisai Enos's advocacy of "socializing Niuginians to *live in Niugini*—rather than in Africa, Europe, or Australia." However, Liyong charged, the "Melanesian Way of Life" had not yet been conceptualized. *Literature of Developed Nations* sought to address this issue. It included group assignments such as "Construct an ideology for 'The Melanesian Way of Life.'" Clearly, then, this course was not just about Negritude, but also about having students think about a "Melanesian Way."[27]

Liyong's striking press release for the Writers' Conference reflected his pedagogy, scholarship, and complicated positionality as a Black Diasporic scholar of Negritude who was based in Oceania. His call for a Melanesian Way was framed in the context of the aforementioned radical Bullybeefs and über-radical Apostles who emerged from the Administrative College and UPNG, respectively. During the road to independence, the Apostles—with their swords sharpened and drawn—recognized Bullybeefer Michael Samore as their political leader. But independence had invoked a "sheathing of the swords." The Bullybeefs, now leaders in the post-independence state, expressed a realism that seemed conservative to the "young, radical, Apostles," who, marred by doubts surrounding the reconstruction of the state, were left in disarray. He wrote, "Chief Ulli Beier was here when the writing started: he started it all. He had been in Africa when the writing mania had infected a lot of Africans." Armed with that background, he reproduced Africa's successes in Papua New Guinea. While the impact of African writers on Papua New Guinean literature was clear, the country's writers had to "abandon their crutches and begin walking in a Papua New Guinea way."[28]

This dynamic was reflected politically by the government of Papua New Guinea's attraction to Tanzania's Ujamaa system as a model for development. Liyong was glad that this period had passed, as "indigenous solutions [had] to be evolved to solve indigenous problems." He argued that Ujamaa could not be the "Papua New Guinean or Melanesian way of life." He called for a reunion of the Bulls, Apostles, and their disciples to embark on this journey, referencing these artists as only someone intimately familiar with the canon could do. He described Bernard Narokobi's *Foundations for Nationhood* as a brave expression of Papua New Guinean unity. He linked the historical perspective of Vincent Eri, which addressed the indigenous writer's response to Christianity, the traditional religion of Kama Kerpi's *Voices from the Ridge*, and the religious zeal of Leo Hannett, who moved from "disenchantment to disenchantment."[29]

Liyong argued that protest literature alone could not sustain Papua New Guinea, which needed its writers to critique the postcolonial state. As the "unofficial ombudsmen of the nation," these seers with visions of the future needed to stay "mad enough to go on writing," particularly with the persistence of Tabari Place's "Kungfu man" and the "Cowboy troubadour" (references to Kung Fu and Western films). Liyong criticized the public education system for teaching this canon of indigenous plays, novels, and poetry as "aids to learning English grammar" but not literature. As for works published in *Kovave*, *Papua New Guinea Writing*, and *Papua Pocket Poets*, he asked, when would the eras of trial pieces end and major works begin? He called for conference participants to form a Writers Union to both protect their rights and stimulate the growth of Papua New Guinean written culture.[30]

The conference drew a lineup of leading artists from across Papua New Guinea, Melanesia, Africa, and Oceania. Opened by Sir Albert Maori Kiki, it featured keynote addresses, panels, symposiums, and workshops by primarily men. Speakers included Australia's Oodgeroo Noonuccal, Nigerian writers Kole Omotoso and Adeola James, Samoa's Albert Wendt, Singapore's Edwin Thumboo, Ugandan poets Theo Luzuka and Okot p'Bitek, and Māori writers Patricia Grace and Hone

Tuwhare. Papua New Guinea was represented by Henginike Riyong, Moses Sasakila, Moi Avei, James Mopis, Harvey Kail, Apisai Enos, Elton Brash, Arthur Jawodimbari, John Kasaipwalova, Allan Natachee, Kama Kerpi, Bernard Narokobi, Vincent Eri, and Taloti Kaniku. Kumalau Tawali, Leo Hannett, and John Waiko were panelists at a symposium chaired by Ulli Beier, "The Political and Social Responsibilities of the Writer."[31]

Noonuccal delivered the conference's keynote address, in which she expressed admiration for Papua New Guinea's sovereignty: "As someone who comes from a country where racism, apathy, and ignorance is subtly and openly practiced on its indigenous peoples, I cannot help but envy your independence." She hoped to learn more about Papua New Guinea's history, culture, and dreams, continuing, "The Aborigines of Australia are looking towards the people of Papua New Guinea with hope for their own future independence." She argued that her "brothers and sisters" there were more fortunate than those in Australia, because their culture was still intact. Meanwhile, Aborigines had been "scattered to the four winds" and were "broken remnants of a once proud race of people." She remarked that the indigenous countries were struggling for their rightful place in the world in spite of an "overwhelming White backlash." Still, "the Black races" had to "eventually emerge as the builders and the rulers" in their own countries. There was a movement of great pride among the Black races, and Papua New Guinea had a critical role to play in the "Black literary world of emerging authors, poets, and playwrights." Noonuccal asked, "Is it too much to hope that before long, the Black artists of the Pacific, will meet yearly to celebrate in a Black Pacific Festival of Arts?" This, she argued, was not only essential to the "Black peoples of the Pacific and the world but was also essential to those Whites whose culture and customs [upheld] colonialism, racism, paternalism, ignorance, and apathy." Black people needed to be not only teachers, but also "the protectors of our customs and cultures" and to practice their "rights to be Black, free and vocal."[32]

Noonuccal's call for a Black Pacific Festival of Arts was not an abstract charge. She had clearly built community in Papua New Guinea. She returned to Australia with a copy of *The Literature of Developed Nations*, signed by Liyong, "For *Our* Kath with *Our* Love." She also carried back a copy of Beier's *Artist in Society*. Published by his institute, the pamphlet included lectures for a UPNG foundations course that comparatively analyzed Igbo sign writer artists of Nigeria's urban subcultures, Trobriand artist Vaosi's political wood carvings that depicted Kasaipwalova's trial, and Chicago-based Black muralists such as Bill Walker's Organization of Black American Culture (OBAC).[33] In contrast to Papua New Guinea, which welcomed and drove the forging of a Black Pacific, Australia was a racialized contested space that was antagonistic toward Black internationalism.

Only months before, in March 1976, Noonuccal participated in Australia's Adelaide Festival of Arts, which held a session on race, literature, and language as part of its Writers' Week. Chaired by Beier, this included James Baldwin, Japan's Inoue Hisashi, Māori poet Hone Tuwhare, Wole Soyinka, Henginike Riyong, and indigenous Australians Jack Davis, Kevin Gilbert, Lazarus Lamilami, Margaret Tucker, and Noonuccal. Baldwin also gave a lecture, an exhibition on the Aborigine in Australian fiction was displayed, and Beier's institute, the Aboriginal Arts Board, and UPNG were acknowledged in the program.[34]

Poet and playwright Henginike Riyong was touring Adelaide at the time. As he told interviewer John Beston at the festival, he was born in Papua New Guinea's Highlands in 1953. After completing high school at the age of fifteen, he attended UPNG in 1969–1970. *Kovave* published his autobiography, *My Life*, in 1970, which unflatteringly presented his upbringing in a Lutheran school. The mission called for *Kovave* to withdraw the story, resulting in an apology from the journal. Disenchanted, Riyong left school and returned to his village. Eventually he took up writing again, and in 1975 founded the Raun Raun Traveling Theater with Greg Murphy. He told Beston that he used village stories to create plays, and folk opera and dance to create dance dramas. The plays were always written in Tok Pisin (New Melanesian), which was understood across the country. "Papuaniugini" was his first audience, followed by Pacific Islanders across Micronesia, Polynesia, and Melanesia, groups who had something in common. He called for more travel to occur between artists from these groups. He was also interested in the idea of creating "a group of Black writers from various countries" who would intentionally study one another's creolized languages, as, for example, Papua New Guineans could not always understand the unique figurative expressions used by Nigerian writers. He hoped to spend a year in

Nigeria or Fiji to do so. He was drawn first to Pacific Island and African books, but his literary influences included Amos Tutuola, Ngũgĩ wa Thiong'o, Duro Ladipo, Wendt, Soyinka, Achebe, and Baldwin. In his book of poems *Nema Namba*, he wrote about indigenous cosmological systems, such as the chief mountain deity Nokondi and spirits such as the *korovas*.[35]

But all was not well. In the aftermath of the Adelaide festival, Noonuccal told the Aboriginal Arts Board that there needed to be provisions made "for Aborigines to meet, without interruption, the overseas indigenous artists." It was difficult to talk much with these writers, especially Soyinka and Riyong, because "the Whites crowded them so." This was done both shockingly and rudely. Riyong gave a copy of *Nema Namba* to Noonuccal. Signed, "To my awaiting sister," it perhaps hinted at this issue. She did try to plan a private meeting between the Black artists and Aborigines, but it was hopeless—White people and the media made it impossible, even though these overseas visitors very much wanted to speak with her. By the middle of the jumbling week, everyone was exhausted by the "madness of it all." The festival seemed to turn into "a political field for Women's libbers and crazy students sprouting jumbled up lines" full of curse words that they called poetry. Either way, she felt that guidelines on behalf of the Black writers badly needed to be drawn up and submitted to the conference organizers.[36]

Black Diasporic writers in Papua New Guinea formed lasting relationships that helped to forge a cultural Black Pacific. For example, in 1978 Papua New Guinean poet Tawali wrote to Noonuccal, and reminded her of the challenge and invitation that she had given to him at the 1976 Independent Writers' Conference, which was to make it to the Adelaide Arts Festival. He had been in Brisbane, and met her son Denis, but was unable to make it to Adelaide. Still, he hoped to make it to Moongalba, to learn of her wisdom, as he had been told by Katharina Smith that she "was creating something that [he] was searching for too."[37]

UNESCO, Cultural Identity, and Oceania

These discussions around a "Melanesian Way" occurred during a broader moment of academic, activist, research-oriented, and grassroots regional discussions around a "Pacific Way." Such uneven conversations were centered around questions of decolonization, indigenous cultures, and historic relationships between Polynesia, Melanesia, Australasia, and Micronesia. This reflected a definitive theme of Black internationalism in Oceania: How did communities racialized as being Black in Oceania build intentional relationships with other racialized and ethnic groups? Papua New Guinea was a site for these debates.

In 1977 the United Nations Educational, Scientific and Cultural Organization's (UNESCO) second session of the Advisory Committee for the Study of Oceanic Cultures met in Port Moresby. Chaired by Samoa's Wendt, this meeting had roots in UNESCO's 1970 General Conference meeting, which pledged to embark on studies of Oceanic cultures. A 1971 meeting of experts at the University of the South Pacific (USP) in Suva, Fiji, recommended that the project should "first serve the Oceanic peoples," who were to be "research collaborators" and cultural guardians as opposed to "passive objects of research." A subsequent 1974 meeting in Canberra, Australia, revealed that "there was growing dissatisfaction among Pacific Islanders" about the project because it was being controlled by non-Pacific Islanders and that "most of the proposals financed by the project were those recommended by foreign academics to benefit themselves and [their] institutions." At the first meeting, only seven of twenty-one committee members were Pacific Islanders, and at the 1971 meeting, four of ten. This prompted UNESCO to form another advisory committee, which had thirteen Pacific Islanders on a team of eighteen members; it met in Nukualofa, Tonga, in 1975 at the Advisory Committee's inaugural meeting. These indigenous members hailed from New Zealand, Australia, Papua New Guinea, Fiji, the Solomon Islands, Micronesia, Tonga, Western Samoa, and Hawai'i. They included Moi Avei (chairman of Papua New Guinea's National Council of Arts), John Haugie (Papua New Guinea's director of cultural affairs), Hugh Paia (permanent secretary of education, Solomon Islands), and Rangitukua Moeka'a (director of education, Cook Islands). It was decided that the secretariat would be located at USP because of its regional makeup and satellite structure.[38]

Wendt was selected as secretary of the committee, and his leadership was a tremendous intervention on the proceedings. He submitted a version of his now popular essay, "Towards a New Oceania," to the Tonga meeting, which expressed his critiques of and recommendations to the committee. He grounded his perspective in his positionality as someone who "belonged to and was rooted in the fertile portion of Oceania," which nourished his spirit, defined him and fed his imagination. Wendt affirmatively rejected colonialism, and the "detached/objective analysis" of "sociologists and all the other 'ologists'" who had plagued Oceania since "she captivated the imagination of the Papalagi in his quest for El Dorado, a Southern Continent, and the Noble Savage in a tropical Eden." He called instead for the "rediscovery of the dead," noting the diversity of Oceania and the educational and architectural wounds of colonialism, where a frightening type of *papalagi* (White) architecture was invading Oceania—super-stainless, super-plastic, super-hygienic, and super-soulless. He brilliantly used poetry to describe his radical imagination (Wendt's "Inside Us the Dark"), the need to conceptually return to the source of Oceania (Tawali's "The River Flows Back"), racism as the world's most evil or *aitu* (Kasaipwalova's "Reluctant Flame"), colonialism (Albert Leomala's "Kros"), the "wasted years of carrying the White man's cargo" (Eri's "Crocodile"), and the way forward (Mildred Sope's "Motherland"). He decried the "whitefication" of the colonized by colonial education systems (Ruperake Petaia's "Kidnapped"), which had transformed many in the region into Uncle Toms and V. S. Naipaul's "mimic men." He drew on Fiji's 1972 South Pacific Festival of Arts as a cultural awakening, which was also reflected in the work of a collective of established and emerging writers from all across Oceania through publications such as *Kovave* and the South Pacific Creative Arts Society's *Mana*. The ties of these writers "transcended barriers of culture, race, petty nationalism and politics." Their writing was "expressing a revolt against the hypocritical/exploitative aspects of [Oceania's] traditional/commercial/and religious hierarchies, colonialism and neocolonialism and degrading values." Wendt's intentionality in engaging poetry from across Oceania was a powerful political statement of unity, for despite the "glib tributes paid to a Pacific Way, there [was] much racial discrimination between" ethnic groups within Oceania.[39]

Wendt found UNESCO and other UN agencies to be just as guilty of condescending paternalism and tokenism as Oceania's "former colonial bosses." He found it unacceptable that "right from the start it was assumed that there were no Pacific Islanders capable of deciding the fate of their own cultures." Pacific Islanders needed to be given full control of

Figure 5.1. Albert Wendt and Polynesian Panther Will 'Ilolahia, ca. 1971. Photograph by John Miller.

the project and needed to determine the aims, methods of implementation, partners within Oceania, and sources of outside help. They would do the work themselves.[40]

The Tonga meeting produced a position paper, which affirmed that the assertion of cultural identity was critical in the fight for independence and nation-building efforts of "developing" countries. Papua New Guinea was an example of this dynamic. Cultural assertion was a "major feature of present liberation movements and the continuing struggle against colonialism, racism, and apartheid." In Oceania as elsewhere, this meant safeguarding its authentic cultural heritage against external threats of acculturation and deculturation and making this heritage available to artists and thinkers who could create works that reflected "the aspirations and characteristics of their own people" to help build the nation. The paper argued that a heightened sense of cultural identity would help the dispersed island nations of Oceania to "rediscover their common heritage and cut across the artificial frontiers imposed by a colonial past. The identification of common pan-Oceanic cultural features [would] help to counteract some of the less welcome features of industrial civilization."[41]

Figure 5.2. Albert Wendt visiting the Polynesian
Panthers' office in Three Lamps/Ponsonby,
New Zealand, ca. 1971. Photograph by John Miller.

Wendt still had reservations about the committee. Polynesia was
heavily represented, but only one member was from Micronesia. Furthermore, while Melanesia contained over three-quarters of Oceania's
total population, it was inadequately represented, and there were no
delegates from New Hebrides. There were no Māoris or Aborigines on
the committee, despite their being the foci of study in New Zealand
and Australia, respectively. He argued that a more equitable representation needed to be established, with the inclusion of at least one person
from each neglected area. Furthermore, he decried the lack of response
from the committee members and their failure to publicize the program,
which had hindered the implementation of some proposals.[42]

That being said, by 1976, Wendt was able to secure fifty-seven proposals from USP Center directors across Tonga, the Gilberts, the Cook Islands, Niue, New Hebrides, the Solomon Islands, and Western Samoa. To publicize the project, they used USP's satellite communication linkup; Wendt also traveled to various university centers to "discuss the project with government/museum personnel, schools, collectors of oral traditions," and others interested in cultural development. This included interviews on local radio stations. However, these proposals were created with the intention of a January 1977 meeting, and, anticipating financial support, were now jeopardized because the meeting did not occur until five months later. These delays had "damaged markedly" Wendt's credibility. He added, "Our meetings should be held to suit our project plans and schedules, not the delays at UNESCO headquarters." In fact, delay-related scheduling conflicts meant that one of the group's "most conscientious Committee members," Walter Lini of New Hebrides, could not attend the 1977 meeting.[43]

Lini was president of the New Hebrides National Party, which was embroiled in a bitter fight against British and French colonialism. He was invited to join the committee in October 1976. Even though he could not attend the second session in Papua New Guinea, he continued to cooperate with the project and give feedback on the final report.[44]

The committee approved three major projects for 1976: a workshop on the "Techniques of Recording Oral Tradition, Music, Dance, and Material Culture" in the Solomon Islands (Honiara and Malaita); a regional visual arts workshop in Tonga; and a workshop on Fijian oral traditions at Suva's Fiji Museum. These workshops were largely successful in terms of training Pacific Islanders. However, the Solomon Islands meeting reiterated a warning from the Tonga meeting in 1975 that Wendt felt could continue to adversely future workshops. The official report did not display the "deep dissatisfaction among some participants concerning" the foreign domination of the meeting. Participants felt "that the tutors should have been mainly Pacific islanders, and that they should have been given control of planning and running the Workshop." Needless to say, Wendt agreed. Furthermore, these workshops needed "to promote cross-cultural understanding and friendship between participants and tutors, disseminate knowledge about the cultures of the participants," and promote regionalism.[45]

The issue at the Solomon Islands workshop was centered on the erratic behavior of a tutor, who "identified as a White citizen of Papua New Guinea" and refused to give any advice or direction. This emphasized the division between Melanesian participants and White advisors. It was reiterated that future workshops needed to be run by indigenous advisors, while White "experts" needed to be brought in to help only with consultation. Furthermore, "knowledgeable elders of the communities" needed to be involved to "give their views on traditional culture" and research methodologies. This was in contrast to Tonga's visual arts workshop, which was run by prominent Māori artists Kātarina Mataira and Paratene Matchitt.[46]

Wendt had received feedback on only a few proposed projects, which were an oral traditions project and cultural festival in the Solomon Islands, a Māori creative writing workshop in Cook Islands, a craft workshop in Fiji, and a project on oral traditions in New Hebrides. However, he laid out a number of critical areas for the program. This included an urgent need to investigate the "cultural problems and needs" of the American territories and Francophone Oceania. It was important to continue recording oral traditions, but it was also necessary to publish already collected stories, legends, and songs to build bodies of written literature. The development of literature in indigenous languages was critical. Workshops needed to be local and based in indigenous languages; until then, most of the workshops had been confined to those who spoke English. Multipurpose centers needed to be established, Pacific Islanders needed to be urgently trained in museum work, and project funds needed to be evenly distributed across the region.[47]

The Advisory Committee for the Study of Oceanic Cultures held its second session at Papua New Guinea's National Museum and Art Gallery in Waigani. Papua New Guinean prime minister Michael Samore opened the meeting. He spoke about the importance of traditional culture in forming national identity, and the need for the work of scholars to be appreciated in the public sphere. The meeting recommended increasing the representation of Melanesia and Micronesia on the committee. It argued that "imposed artificial frontier lines" had made communication with Micronesia, US Trust Territories, French Polynesia, and New Caledonia difficult, and "strong efforts" needed to be made to keep close contact with these countries. Communication needed to be facilitated with USP's satellite communication network. Broadly speaking, the aims included training workshops, definition of authentic Oceanic cultures, appropriate methodologies for studying oral traditions, the creation of multipurpose cultural centers, the repatriation of artifacts from colonial metropoles, an inventory of Oceanic material cultures, and a study of the impact of tourism on cultural development. The meeting recognized the "danger of linguistic genocide" and the need to teach in Oceanic vernaculars. Madeleine Bissonnet of the World Health Organization suggested the need to examine traditional Oceanic medicines.[48]

Recommendations also included the future inclusion of Australian Aboriginal culture within the scope of the Oceanic cultural project, inclusion of a specialist from New Hebrides, the establishment of artist exchanges and artist-in-residence programs, studies of culture and the physical environment—particularly where natural habitats were under pressure, a ten-year plan for the study of oral traditions to foster cultural unity across Oceania, and the development of film, TV, and radio programs in indigenous vernaculars.[49]

Five working papers were closely examined, spanning issues related to the cultures, languages, and oral traditions of Oceania. This included an extensive paper written by Ulli Beier, who was an observer at the session. In the paper, titled "Proposal for Cultural Exchange Programs between Africa and the Pacific," Beier called for cultural independence in Oceania, which was a more difficult process than political independence.[50] New nations had to battle against centuries of colonial culture, whose deep roots caused people to mistakenly "regard them as an integral part of their tradition." Newly independent countries inherited colonial educational systems that had values embedded within them that could not be abandoned but only modified. Thus, they needed to produce their own "philosophers, ideologies, and spiritual leaders" in the process of developing education systems that did not promote the values of the former colonial power. Beier lamented that while Papua New Guinea promoted national culture through arts and theatre, Christian missions still forbade the playing of "bamboo flutes" and traditional dancing, which they described as "sinful." Furthermore, while it was commendable that Australia had funded the cultural development of Papua New Guinea over the prior five years, it was "worrying that a newly independent country should look almost exclusively to the ex-colonial power for support in developing its cultural programs."[51]

Colonialism had tragically resulted in the isolation of colonies from the rest of the world. This included the creation of monopoly companies, and infrastructures designed to benefit the extraction of raw materials by these industries. This had relevance for Oceania and Africa.[52] In the aftermath of independence, university and government staff were recruited from the former colonial countries, and there was little exchange of staff between the Global South. As such, while in Nigeria organizations like the British Council, Germany's Goethe Institute, and the Italian Cultural Institute were active, *Présence Africaine*, "Africa's only really cultural agency, operated in Paris long before it functioned in Dakar, Senegal." It still had not been able to "open permanent offices in Accra, Lagos, Dar-Es-Salaam, or Port Moresby." Beier argued that in order for "the artist from the Third World [to be set] free," he or she needed wide exposure to the art of other Third World countries. Beier argued that "the Black American cultural revival of the 1960s" and its focus on Africa demonstrated what could be gained from a new orientation.[53]

For the "new nations" of the Third World to produce a "genuine cultural renaissance," it would be necessary for them to "decolonize their cultures" and put the culture of the colonizers "back in its place." Senghor and Alioune Diop had long since "shown the way," and had been at the forefront of Black cultural revival since they organized Dakar's 1966 First World Black Arts Festival. Nigeria's 1977 World Black and African Festival of Arts and Culture (FESTAC) had given its Papua New Guinean delegation the opportunity to see themselves as fully fledged members of the Third World.[54]

However, such mammoth events were not enough in and of themselves. Their cost and complexity created several issues, such as bitter quarrels between the country's artists and the organizing officials of the festival, and public criticism of lavish government spending.[55] Moderate and consistent cultural exchange programs were needed. The governments of Senegal and Nigeria had given financial support to the Institute of Papua New Guinea Studies. This was "evidence of a new awareness, of a new desire to forge cultural links between Africa and the Pacific." Beier himself had organized successful programs between Ife's Institute of African Studies and the institute.[56]

Beier proposed a number of programs that UNESCO could support to facilitate cultural relationships between Africa and Oceania, although he sought more input from scholars of these regions. These included exchanges of information, the hosting of book, photographic, and art exhibitions, film festivals and film libraries, exchanges of theatre companies, music groups, staff, and university students, and the creation of a translation program. The proposal's strength lay not only in its content, but also in its intimate references to leading cultural artists of the Black world.

It called on UNESCO to create an office of cultural information on Africa, Africa America, the Pacific, India, and Southeast Asia. This clearinghouse could publish a cultural news sheet, *Cultural News from Africa and the Pacific*, that would inform readers about new books, literature, and films emerging from the regions and African and Pacific universities. It could publish and share bibliographies, discographies, film catalogues, lists of booksellers and publishers, radio station programs, and lists of literary and cultural magazines.[57]

Beier listed the names of bibliographies and offered to donate a hundred copies of the institute's *Writing from Papua New Guinea*. He suggested that UNESCO commission an ethnomusicologist to compile discographies of African and Pacific music. Universities that wanted to establish courses in African or Pacific literature often did not know where to look, while publishers of Pacific writing did not know where to sell their books. Publishers of Papua New Guinea writing were unaware of the existence of African bookshops and had not explored the possibility of promoting this literature through African American bookshops. Writers from Papua New Guinea faced the danger of compromising their work to get published by Australian presses. However, several African American presses and those in Africa (like Benin's Ethiope Press) were specifically designed to give expression to the "Black experience"; he added a list of Black bookstores and Black publishing houses.[58]

For Beier, radio stations in Africa and the Pacific could inform each other about their cultural programs, and archive, catalogue, and share their tapes and programs. African literature was relatively well known in Papua New Guinea; Beier had introduced his course on contemporary African literature at UPNG in 1967. While Liyong chaired its Department of Literature, writers like Soyinka and Achebe had briefly visited

Papua New Guinea. Achebe was being read in some secondary schools and Soyinka's plays had been performed. UPNG also produced two theses on Soyinka's work.[59]

In contrast, Pacific writing was not well known in Africa. Beier's institute had arranged a book exhibition of Papua New Guinea writing for Ahmadu Bello University in Zaria, Nigeria. He suggested that UNESCO organize a continent-wide traveling exhibition of Pacific literature via African bookshops. The same could occur in the United States, with a focus on historically Black colleges and universities and Black cultural centers. This exhibition could have a decisive impact on the future of Pacific literature, "as a large reading public for Oceanic writers [existed] potentially in Africa and among African Americans." He also called for annual book fairs to take place in New York and Lagos.[60] Film festivals needed to be prioritized. In Papua New Guinea numerous films about Australian Aboriginals and African cultures were known, but the films of Sembene Ousmane and Ola Balogun needed to be shown. Collaborative small art exhibitions could be held via organizations such as Ife's Institute of African Studies and the Institute of Papua New Guinea Studies.[61]

Beier also called for a print exhibition from Papua New Guinea to tour Africa. Similarly, Oshogbo printmakers, India's Mumtaz (who had already exhibited successfully in Papua New Guinea, Nigeria, and Fiji), Jeff Donaldson's AfriCOBRA, and artists such as Sudan's Ibrahim el Salahi, Kenya's Rebecca Njau, Nigeria's Yinka Shonibare and Samuel Ojo, Mozambique's Malangatana Ngwenya, Senegal's Ahmadu Ba, and South Africa's Dumile Feni could tour Oceania.[62] Tours of textile exhibits could include tie dying from the Yoruba, the Senufo, Sierra Leone, and the Ivory Coast, Hausa embroidered gowns, Ashanti Adinkra, and silk woven Kente. From Oceania, traveling exhibits could include mounted bark cloths of Fiji and Tonga. He also suggested photographic exhibitions.[63]

Pacific theatre groups would benefit by tours from African and African American theatre companies, such as Arthur Hall and Philadelphia's Afro-American Dance Ensemble, the national companies of Senegal or Sierra Leone, Ghana's Efua Sutherland, and Nigeria's Ola Rotimi. Beier felt that Barbara Ann Teer's Harlem-based National Black Theatre "could cause a veritable revolution in theatre" in Oceania. Nigeria's

Duro Ladipo's grassroots theatre could demonstrate "how vital, forceful theatre could be created on a non-academic level," and how to fuse "dance, poetry, drama, music and the visual arts." It would also be "exciting" to have Soyinka present his own plays in Oceania. In addition, Australian Aboriginal directors Bob Maza and Brian Syron and Papua New Guinea's Kambau Namaleu could have contributed to the theatre life of African countries.[64]

The proposal called for student, artist, musician, and faculty exchanges between universities in Africa and Oceania through scholarships and residencies. It argued, for example, that if "Papua New Guineans are to learn how to develop a theatre that can be taken out into the villages, that relies on a minimum of props and technology and that is immediately relevant to local audiences," then they would greatly benefit by "going to Nigeria to work with some of the travelling companies like Duro Ladipo and Hubert Ogunde, or from going to the United States to study" with African American street theatres. As Georgina Beier pointed out in her own proposal to the committee, some university art schools in Africa continued European traditions. As such, artists going to Africa from the Pacific may have found it more beneficial to go to workshops or to live with practicing artists. Ulli argued that nothing could be gained if the same colonial ideas were being promoted by Black people rather than by White people. Nigeria's Segun Olusola had visited UPNG in 1974, and had built a great rapport with UPNG's student theatre group, which put on a production of Jawodimbari's *The Sun*. Beier attached a paper entitled "The Black American Cultural Revolution" for discussion. He suggested that African American Bill Walker, who started the Chicago mural movement, could be "given an opportunity to stimulate a similar movement in the Pacific," as "his impact on Port Moresby, Suva and Redfern could be explosive, not just artistically, but also socially."[65]

The proposal also discussed comparative studies between Africa and Oceania, which Beier felt had received some considerable attention. African literature and history were being taught at UPNG. Eri's *Crocodile* was being taught at the University of Nigeria. It was important that Oceanic writers be invited to future African writers' conferences. After FESTAC, Beier argued, Papua New Guinea was "clearly an accepted member of Third and the Black World"; it was almost inevitable that its literature would be taught in the African literature departments of African universities. This process could be codified by a conference of university teachers interested in literature, oral traditions, art, music, history, and sociology and perhaps span the relevance of African studies in the Pacific; the relevance of Pacific studies in Africa; establishing closer links between African and Pacific universities; and a "research scheme to trace African origins of some Pacific groups." Beier's proposal concluded with a list of individuals who had shown interest in decolonization of culture and cultural exchanges, who could help administer these projects, such as historian Adu Boahen, ethnomusicologist Kwabena Nketia (University of Ghana), Rowland Ibiodun, Ibrahim el Salahi (Khartoum Technical Institute), Okot p'Bitek (University of Kenya), Charles Hunt (Fiji Museum), Nora Vagi Brash of Papua New Guinea's National Theatre Company, Liyong, Wendt, Jawodimbari, and Noonuccal. Beier argued that as his institute had promoted cultural exchanges between Oceania and "Africa to a greater extent than any other Institution," he hoped that it would play a responsible part in the project. At the end, the session's final report advised the advisory committee to adopt Beier's working paper, that UNESCO extend its Cultural Exchange Program to include the scheme, that UNESCO and the Institute of Papua New Guinea Studies seek funds from African and Oceanic governments for the project, and that UNESCO sponsor a similar exchange between Oceania and Southeast Asia.[66]

This chapter has shown the centrality of Papua New Guinea's significance in building a Black Pacific. It attracted activists, artists, and scholars to its shores to discuss issues of race, decolonization, and identity in Oceania. The next chapter shows how Papua New Guinea and Black Australia represented Oceania at FESTAC, Nigeria.

6

Black Pacific Festivals

FESTAC, Nigeria, and Oceania

The Second World Black and African Festival of Arts and Culture (FES-TAC) was held in Lagos, Nigeria, in 1977. Scholar Jonathan Fenderson describes FESTAC as "the largest, most elaborate, and, perhaps, most anticipated international arts festival ever to take place on the African continent." The festival survived a slew of controversies, logistical challenges, and contradictions, and, in the end, for over twenty-nine consecutive days hosted some sixteen thousand participants from forty-seven countries via events, exhibitions, and a colloquium.[1] FESTAC's International Festival Committee (IFC) organized the Black world into sixteen geographical zones to prepare for the talks. This included an Australasian zone, whose joint delegation from Papua New Guinea and Australia brought to and took back from Nigeria their own plethora of promises and problems. The delegation included Arthur Jawodimbari, Nora Vagi Brash, and Oodgeroo Noonuccal. For the newly independent nation of Papua New Guinea, the time at FESTAC was a global declaration that it defined itself as a Black nation. For Australia's Black delegation, their presence there reflected a call for support in their ongoing fight for self-determination and land rights.

Australia, Papua New Guinea, and FESTAC

In January 1974 Chief Anthony Enahoro, FESTAC chairman and Nigerian federal commissioner for information and labor, visited Australia. He was there to formally invite the Australian Aboriginal and Islander community to participate in the festival, which at the time was scheduled for 1975. Also present were IFC international coordinator Frank Pilgrim, Aboriginal artist John Moriarty, and C. J. McGuigan, project officer for the Aboriginal Arts Board of Australia's Department of Aboriginal

Affairs (DAA). The group discussed Black Australia's possible contribution to the gathering. Pilgrim outlined how FESTAC was largely being organized via Nigeria and other Black governments. However, the IFC would directly deal with Black Australia, just as it did with other Black communities that were part of other nation-states, such as the African American and British-based delegations. Australia was invited to be part of a zone comprised of Aotearoa, India, and Papua New Guinea. They discussed voting in a zone vice-president who would travel to Lagos every six months to attend IFC meetings.[2]

Visual artist Moriarty was the first recognized indigenous football (soccer) player to represent Australia internationally. He was born circa 1938 to a Yanyuwa mother and an Irish father. Australia's racist discourses defined him as a "half-caste," and at the age of four he was placed in a church home. He became one of the "Stolen Generation"—thousands of Aboriginal children who were forcibly separated from their families and placed in government or church homes to "assimilate" them into White culture. The traumatic impact of this experience on Aboriginal communities lingers.[3]

According to McGuigan, it was felt that Black Australia could contribute to FESTAC in exhibits about Africa and the origin of man, and in the areas of crafts, visual arts, musical instruments, science and technology, drama, film, dance, music, and books, and in seminars on Black civilization and education. The group discussed the possibility of the Australian and New Zealand governments acting on behalf of Aboriginal and Māori communities, respectively. However, it was decided that Aboriginal communities would themselves determine Australia's contribution to FESTAC. Therefore, there needed to be a structure in which an Aboriginal committee or person could deal directly with Nigeria or the DAA. They felt that it would be of "great value" if Blacks in Australia worked directly with Niuginians and Māoris, which would develop further links with Black communities across Oceania.[4]

The Australian Coordinating Committee then set about organizing a delegation of some one hundred Aboriginal and Torres Strait Islanders to the festival. Jack Davis and Black Panther Sam Watson attended an April 1974 meeting in Brisbane, as part of the Aboriginal Publications Foundation. Davis, a celebrated Aboriginal poet from Perth, was part of the 1970 Black Australian delegation to Atlanta's Congress of African

Peoples. He suggested that there needed to be a sense of urgency in publicizing the Nigeria trip to the Aboriginal community. He also insisted that Aboriginal people (perhaps as opposed to other Black groups in Australia) needed to be given first priority.[5]

In May 1974 representatives from Papua New Guinea and Australia traveled to Lagos for the IFC's fourth meeting. Among them was Moses Sasakila, Papua New Guinean minister of sports, recreation and culture. At this meeting, Enahoro welcomed Sasakila into the fold as FESTAC vice president for the Australasian zone. The gathering included Bermuda's Earl Cameron, who headed the United Kingdom and Ireland zone, Ossie Davis of the North American zone, *Présence Africaine*'s Alioune Diop, and Ethiopia's Tsegaye Gabre-Medhin. Here some "serious reservations" emerged about having a queen of the festival, as this might turn into a "beauty-queen contest." It was decided that FESTAC should pay tribute to Africana women instead.[6]

Papua New Guinea's presence at FESTAC was part of a national project to codify the state as a Black Melanesian country. According to Sasakila, the meeting in Nigeria was the first time that the Australasian zone members had been able to collectively meet. He informed the body that the countries in his zone had varying levels of development and identities. Papua New Guinea had achieved self-governance only about five months before the meeting, in December 1973. Sasakila stressed that his government fully supported the association with FESTAC's "other Black and African nations and communities." It was also sending a team of traditional dancers to a South Pacific arts festival in Townsville, Australia, which would help their preparations. Guam's upcoming 1975 Pacific Games would be a good place to publicize FESTAC, since "almost all countries in the Pacific, which of course, are inhabited by our Black Brothers, participate in these games."[7]

Upon his return home, Sasakila informed *Papua New Guinea Writing* about his trip. He discussed the layout of the festival's zones and its inclusion of Black nations and liberation movements from across the world. Papua New Guinea and Black countries across the globe shared similar aims about cultural preservation. Africa was ahead of Papua New Guinea in terms of the production of novels, poetry, drama, and short stories. As such, he reasoned, participation in such international festivals would greatly benefit the country culturally. FESTAC was their opportunity to show the world Papua New Guinea's rich culture, to build networks with other nations, and to observe the process of cultural development that these countries used.[8]

Jawodimbari accompanied Sasakila to Lagos. Sponsored by the National Cultural Council, he also discussed his trip in *Papua New Guinea Writing*. For Jawodimbari, one of the aims of the festival was to reassert and revive the spirit of Black people. For centuries, Black countries had been victimized by White civilization and Western culture, which included drugs and alcohol. Black countries had also been isolated from each other for so long, and FESTAC was a time for them to come together physically, spiritually, mentally, and experientially to decide the future steps of their race. These countries now realized that they had been kept apart by Western propaganda and institutions. Jawodimbari hoped that musicians, painters, writers, and wood carvers would be able to go. He reasoned that after the festival, Papua New Guinea would be globally known, not as a "primitive and impossible country but as a dynamic versatile young nation." The country had "nothing to be ashamed of." In fact, it had a treasure that many Western countries lacked—cultural heritage.[9]

Jawodimbari's interview also included a picture of him in Nigeria, seated next to a Liberian delegate. This was not his first time in Nigeria. The twenty-five-year-old playwright, dramatist, poet, and short story writer hailed from Konji village in Papua New Guinea's Northern District. He completed his studies at UPNG in English literature in 1972. Having also studied political science, by 1974 he had written eight plays in English, his third language.[10]

In 1974 he became a lecturer in drama at Papua New Guinea's Center for Creative Arts. Supported by the National Cultural Council, the center was formed in 1972. Encompassing the visual and performing arts, it housed artists-in-residence with accommodations, an allowance, equipment, and materials. Traditional painters, carvers, musicians, and dancers came and worked alongside students. It hosted artists like well-known welder Ruki Fame and visual artist Jakupa.[11]

Jawodimbari used theatre "as a medium of expression, liberation and education." In early 1974 he embarked upon a global tour to study elite and popular theatre across Asia, Africa, and America, including African American–directed theatre programs; the trip was sponsored by Papua

New Guinea's Department of Education and UPNG. Interviewed by Jack Lahui in *Papua New Guinea Writing*, Jawodimbari argued that popular theatre was based on the lives of ordinary people and had an audience of commonplace citizens. Popular theatre tended to be mobile, as in Africa. Audiences paid small fees and might not feel compelled to return. In contrast, elite theatre was based on major historical occurrences or sensational events. Audiences felt compelled to go because of huge fees for front seats and bookings placed well in advance. The audience was drawn from "the upper class of an affluent society, who can afford it, and who always want to be entertained," as in Broadway.[12]

Jawodimbari traveled across Japan, Nigeria, Ghana, and the United States. In Nigeria, audiences had a sense of who he was because Ulli Beier had shared PNG art and modern writing there. He spent most of his time at the University of Ife Theater. He traveled with legendary dramatist Duro Ladipo for weeks, and saw his plays *Ede*, *Moremi*, *Oliweri*, and *Oba Koso*, which was based on King Shango. He found Ladipo's production to be of such high quality that even those who did not understand Yoruba could respond to his messages. He also witnessed the Ogumola Mobile Theater, which was run by eight women. In eastern Nigeria he stayed with Obi Egbuna, novelist and founder of the British Black Panther Party, and watched Egbuna's play *The Minister's Daughter*.[13]

In Ghana he was based at the University of Ghana, Legon. He spent time with Mawere Opoku and the Ghana Dance Ensemble. Here he met pan-Africanist playwright, director, and dramatist Efua Sutherland, who produced and performed plays at the village level. Founder of Ghana Drama Studio and the Ghana Experimental Theatre, Efua was married to African American pan-Africanist Bill Sutherland.[14]

From Ghana, he traveled to the United States. He "stayed with African Americans in Harlem" and watched the play *Revival*, produced by Barbara Ann Teer's National Black Theatre. He also saw *River Niger* and *A Raisin in the Sun* on Broadway. He then traveled to Tokyo, Japan.[15]

In his travels, Jawodimbari "integrated" easily with Africans and African Americans. He found Ghanaians to be phenotypically darker than himself, and he was surprised when a young kid called him "a White man." In Harlem, he was perceived to be African American until he spoke. These experiences influenced how he developed Papua New

Guinea's National Theatre Company. He decided to continue to focus on indigenous forms of music, dance, legends, folklore, and non-Western stage designs.[16]

In August 1974 Jawodimbari traveled to the tenth annual National Playwrights Conference in Waterford, Connecticut. He had met the artistic director of the conference, Lloyd Richards, while giving a lunchtime talk at Australia's 1974 National Playwrights Conference. He was invited to the talks because he was a pioneer playwright in Papua New Guinea, and the only one of his cohorts who still wrote. Interviewed in Waterford, he described Papua New Guineans as being "Black." He detailed his company's travels to villages by bus. When they performed in "a dusty place," they spread out a canvas to make a performance area and used a portable generator to create light for the plays. Villagers brought mats and sat on the ground.[17]

Jawodimbari, Sasakila, PNG's national sports secretariat Siump Kavana, and PNG director of cultural affairs Haugie attended a September 1974 meeting of the Australasian zone committee in Darwin, Australia. They were joined by Australian Black Power and Aboriginal Tent Embassy activist Chicka Dixon, Lance Bennett, and Barbara Spencer of the Aboriginal Theatre Foundation, Moriarty, and Wandjuk Marika. They discussed sending a delegation to Kaduna, Nigeria, for an IFC meeting that following October. It was also decided that Bennett and the Aboriginal Theatre Foundation were responsible for organizing a "tribal dance group."[18]

The committee had been unable to get much information from the Australian High Commission in Lagos about current plans for FESTAC. As such, it sought to travel to Kaduna to find out more about the nature of the venues for art exhibitions, live performances, video screening, transport, food, and the level of technical support services. The committee members were also "unhappy about the composition" of the Australasian zone, and they pushed for the inclusion of other countries from Oceania. In particular, they recommended that Fiji be included to replace Aotearoa.[19]

Whereas Papua New Guinea sought to send a group of 50 (dancers, officials, researchers, and a traditional dancing troupe), Australia planned to send 150 people (traditional dancers, choir, urban performers, artists, and officials). The group agreed to travel together via the same chartered flight. It was also discussed that nominations needed to be held to make sure that women were represented on the Organizing Committee.[20]

In October 1974 McGuigan invited Noonuccal to join the IFC. Indeed, nine months after its first meeting, women remained absent on the nine-member committee, and Noonuccal's "inclusion" was an "attempt to overcome that fault." McGuigan sent her a cache of materials from the previous gatherings. There was much work to do, and no plans had been made for the exhibit on literature and the Black civilization seminar. He asked her to join the delegation to Nigeria in November and to bring as much information as possible that she had about Aboriginal cultural activities in Brisbane.[21]

The Aboriginal Theatre Foundation of Darwin was responsible for organizing rural dancers, the Aboriginal Arts Board collected an exhibition of arts and crafts, and Aboriginal theatre director Brian Syron was commissioned to compile a Black Urban Theatre production. Funds for the trip had reached $320,000, which came from the International Committee of the Australian Council ($224,000), the Department of Foreign Affairs, and the Aboriginal Arts Board. The committee decided to send three people to Kaduna—Moriarty, McGuigan, and Noonuccal, who would represent Aboriginal women and participate in the festival.[22]

Noonuccal accepted the invitation. She attended an October 29 committee meeting and traveled to Kaduna from November 12 to 19, 1974, for the IFC's fifth planning meeting. Members of the Australasian zone engaged with organizers from across the Black world. Representatives presented reports about their preparations. The Australasia zone was represented by Haugie and Sasakila, and Noonuccal, Jawodimbari, Moriarty, and McGuigan were listed as advisors. Noonuccal had the opportunity to meet delegates such as Bermuda's Cameron, Guyana's Lynette Dolphin, and Brazil's George Alakija, a professor of Candomblé. She was one of five women of a group of twenty-seven.[23]

While in Nigeria, Noonuccal photographed the stadium grounds, numbers of Nigerians beautifully dressed in traditional garments, and herself in the country. As described previously, her plane was hijacked in Dubai on her return journey to Australia. In addition to her poem "Yussef," Noonuccal wrote at least two other pieces in response to the hijacking. This included the poem "Commonplace," which she wrote on board the plane. It read, "the rat-tat-tat of rifles bombards my sleep . . . pointed revolver sharpens my senses."[24]

She was freed in Tunisia, and her time there was short but intense. She was interviewed in Tunis by local newspapers such as *L'Action*.[25] Understandably, the hijacking remained heavy on her mind. That December she wrote "Flight into Tunis," a short story about the experience. In the piece she states how her flight from Beirut had stopped in Dubai. While Moriarty and McGuigan left the flight to stretch their legs, she stayed on board to get some sleep. After being awakened, she found herself "looking down the barrel of an automatic revolver, held in the hand of a very tall, handsome black man." She stood up and immediately asked, "Is this a high jack?"[26]

The hijacker's interpreter asked her whether she was Pakistani or Indian. Her response was that she was "an Aboriginal Australian and proud of it." She proceeded to "lecture" him and told him that "he should be working towards the success of the 2nd World Black Festival of Arts" in Nigeria. She found their actions "stupid and not in the best interest of the Arab cause," to which she had always been sympathetic. "To hell with wars, time to end them all."[27]

Apparently, the New South Wales Jewish Board of Deputies took issue with what it considered to be her refusal to publicly denounce the hijackers. The board released a pamphlet titled "Poet Who Wrote during Hijack." Noonuccal's written response in June 1975 speaks volumes about her Black internationalism and support of Palestinian freedom struggles. She stated that she had been told that Yussef was once "a brilliant young doctor." Because the Arab people were "fighting for their stolen land, which the Jewish people stole from them," Yussef was "destroying lives instead of saving them." For her, this was an "utter waste of valuable lives through ugly hatred between races." She was sick of "useless killings," which included the death of the German banker during the hijacking. Surely, she argued, "Jews and Arabs [were] also sick of the hatred and wars and useless killings." Still, she could not "oblige the Jews by hating the Arabs any more than [she] could oblige the Arabs by hating the Jews. Hanging Yussef [would solve] nothing either. He would die still hating the Jews." She further argued, "Those who desire Yussef's death by hanging are also murderers. . . . Violence begets violence as your pamphlet proves." She abhorred the persecution of Jews, and concluded, "May the Arabs and Jews reach a peaceful solution. . . . Australia has always welcomed the Jews into this country and I sincerely hope they will also welcome the Arabs for as long as Australia stands."[28]

The timing of this correspondence is interesting. In May, Samir Cheikh and Ada Salim (Eddie Zananiri), representatives of the General Union of Palestinian Students, visited New South Wales. According to Australia's Special Branch, Jewish youth staged demonstrations against their visit, while pro-Palestinian protests supported the two men. Tensions ran high as the two conducted interviews and talks across Australia. At Macquarie University clashes briefly broke out.[29]

The Australasian zone committee met in Australia that December 1974. This included Merle Jackomos of the National Council of Aboriginal and Island Women, who participated in a number of these meetings. The Kaduna delegation showed slides of Nigeria. It reiterated that Papua New Guinea and Australia needed to collaboratively "enter something worthwhile in the Festival" to avoid being "swamped by the bigger African countries." Jawodimbari informed the group that the number of delegates from its National Theatre Company had been cut from twenty to thirteen performers. He also reported that they had successfully convinced the IFC to invite other countries from Oceania, including Fiji, Nauru, Western Samoa, Tonga, West Papua, Solomon Islands, Cook Islands, New Hebrides, New Caledonia, Gilbert and Ellis Islands, and the "Orang Asli," the indigenous people of Malaysia.[30]

Noonuccal attended the FESTAC committee meeting in January 1975. Still emotionally dealing with the hijacking, she scribbled notes on the side of a report about needing to speak to BOAC staff in Dubai. This meeting also brought some clarification regarding FESTAC's Tribute to Black Women. Roberta Sykes was recruited to address this issue. Noonuccal would also contribute more to the literature exhibit.[31] The committee also met in March 1975 and was joined by Bernard Narokobi. It was noted that Jawodimbari had become assistant director of the Creative Art Center.[32]

In May 1975, issues remained with the makeup of the Australian delegation, which included thirty-five traditional dancers, sixteen members of urban theaters, and fifteen Torres Strait Islanders. No other Black women were slated to represent the country. Noonuccal was listed as an administrator, and she wrote a note next to her name, "no cost; as paper is being prepared free of cost. If woman selected is alive, she's to go as a group organizer." Some five months removed from her hijacking ordeal, this was obviously an expression of her humor.[33]

In June 1975 the IFC held its sixth meeting in Lagos. The Australasian zone's representatives included Trevor Buzzacott, Sasakila, Moriarty, and Jawodimbari. They visited the National Theatre and took photographs of its internal structure. They also noted that the colloquium was FESTAC's most important component. The delegation was invited to visit Kenya, Senegal, Ghana, the United Kingdom, and the Caribbean in the aftermath of the IFC meeting.[34] With 1,200 feet at its disposal, the Aboriginal Arts Board sought to create an exhibit that laid out Aboriginal origins, traditional and contemporary art, Australian Aboriginal culture and migration across Australia, maps of "tribal areas," photographs of rock engravings, a floor feature of Papunya sand painting, and wood carvings.[35]

In an interim report of November 1975, Bennett, the White Australian director of Darwin's Aboriginal Theatre Foundation, recalled that in 1974 it had been agreed that the Aboriginal delegation would include thirty-six tribal musicians, singers, and dancers, ten "tribal" artists, fifteen choir members from central Australia, thirty urban performers, and ten urban artists. It was also to include nine Torres Strait Islander musicians, singers, and dancers and ten officials. Given the extensive ethnic diversity in Australia, he felt it was important to have as widely a representative body as possible. This would be a challenge, as FESTAC would attract many groups. It was left to the foundation's "all-Aboriginal Committee" in conversation with group leaders from Western Australia, Northern Territory, and Queensland to decide. Bennett demanded details. He asked for "specific and accurate" information about the performance venue in Nigeria. This included the architect's plans for the amphitheater, audience area and capacity, lighting and sound equipment, photographs, plans, and technical lists. He hoped that Noonuccal's team could bring this data from Nigeria, but he had heard little from the committee since its return to Australia. He also pushed back against the inclusion of the Aboriginal choir, as "proficiency of the superimposed culture" seemed to be a "trifling achievement to flaunt abroad" in an event such as FESTAC.[36]

Bennett had much to say in general, including in response to the calls of tribal women leaders to have more women included in the dance tours. He agreed that this inclusion would give a more accurate reflection of public dance activity, as "tribal" women did often participate in these occasions. However, he argued that this made the achievement of representation in a group of thirty individuals even more "problematical than all-male groups." He called for more people to be added to the delegation. He also recommended that Stefan Haag be sent as the producer for the tribal dance segment.[37]

But Bennett did not know how to "quit when ahead." He felt that there had been a "total failure" to give him the information that he needed regarding the technical details for the "tribal dancers." He argued that "a professional dance" team needed to visit Lagos and make its own assessments. "The reports of amateurs, whether these be visiting Black politicians or on-the-spot White diplomats," he argued, would not do. His bigger gripe was that the Aboriginal Arts Board suggested that the "tribal section" be handled entirely by (urban) Black Aboriginals, who would be trained by an expert (who he assumed would be White) in the techniques of light, sound, and stage. He was clearly offended by this "unheralded change" from "professional to amateur production." Of course, he had discussed the issue with Syron, "a Black" who had actively "trained Blacks in theatre" and felt that it would take "two or three years" to conduct such training. Bennett himself knew of only two such Aboriginals, Syron and Bob Maza, who were committed to the urban component of FESTAC; neither, he argued, could claim to have Haag's (who was White) technical expertise or have presented a "tribal dance or song." He implored that the board "keep its ethnic options open." He asked whether the FESTAC audience would notice backstage technicians. He then offered a "parting word to the wise—the tribal people will not thank urbanites for squabbling, for infringing upon tribal people's basic human rights as to freedom of choice of supporters . . . and for generally soiling the tribal nest in a self-defeating quest to gain security of identity" and for "excluding help from Whites on racist grounds." He questionably continued, "For the oppressed to try to oppress the oppressor is a perfectly human failing. Let no one expect the tribal people, however, to be indulgent of their failing for long. . . . They can be harsh judges of the incompetence of others, regardless of such matters as race, or quests for identity."[38] Bennett's White paternalist and racist comments would cause further issues.

News of the delegation spread throughout mainstream Australian and indigenous print media. In February 1974 South Australia's *Black News* printed an ad for a meeting of a South Pacific Cultural Gathering Committee in Townsville, North Queensland. This gathering was centered on cultural exchange between "all the peoples of the Southern Pacific," but was to also specifically prepare for both FESTAC and Tanzania's Sixth Pan-African Congress (6PAC).[39]

A November 1975 flyer featuring the FESTAC logo asked its readers, "Are you an Aborigine or a Torres Strait Islander? Do you dance, sing, act, paint, weave, write, or play a traditional musical instrument? Would you like to travel to Nigeria next year to take part in a Festival of Arts and Culture?" Aboriginal and Torres Strait Islanders who were interested in traveling to Lagos were encouraged to consider FESTAC's areas of interest, like painting, jewelry making, and a photographic exhibition on the "Black Race." Interested parties were to contact the Nigeria Coordinating Committee.[40]

The Black delegation from Australia was clear about the political significance of their trip. Right before their departure, Melbourne's *Age* ran an article, "Blacks Will Carry Protest to Africa," claiming that delegation members would "attempt to embarrass" the Australian government at FESTAC. It argued that members of the group sought to use the festival "to highlight Australia's treatment of Blacks" and to garner the support of Black delegates in their freedom struggles. It quoted a member of Sydney's Aboriginal and Islander Dance Group: "Third world pressure is the only hope Australian Aborigines have of improving their lot. . . . We will do everything to spread the word about Australia and get as much support against Australia as possible. . . . International embarrassment is what Australia needs."[41]

The Aboriginal and Islander Dance Group was slated to present a piece of modern dance based on "traditional Aboriginal themes." It was a modern dance group formed by African American Carole Johnson in 1975. The delegation included Johnson and dancers Lillian Crombie, Michael Leslie, Richard Talonga, and Filipino dance teacher and choreographer Lucy Jumawan. According to Johnson, they were going to perform her choreographed dance *The Embassy*, which was a "recreation of emotions and moods" during the Aboriginal Tent Embassy, which was "a turning point when Aboriginal people felt they could stand on their own." According to Johnson, the group used music of contemporary Aboriginal composers like Uluru's Bob Randall and songs like the Country Outcasts' "Nullabor Prayer."[42]

FESTAC, 1977

At the end of the day, Papua New Guinea and Australia were the only countries in Oceania that sent delegations to FESTAC. In 1976 Taloti Kaniku—founder of Theatre New Guinea and chairman of the Papua New Guinea Union of Writers and Artists—wrote to Wole Soyinka, who was then in Ghana, about FESTAC. He informed Soyinka how Taban Lo Liyong had forged the union at the First Independent Papua New Guinea Writers' Conference that year. In its infancy, the union was seeking financial aid from the Union of African Writers, of which Soyinka was secretary. This was also due to the lack of support from the Papua New Guinea National Cultural Council. The union published *Kanaka*, but its annual membership fee was too small to keep it going. He also hoped to meet Soyinka in Lagos for FESTAC, as he was part of a proposed delegation that included Kambau Namaleu and Sally Anne Bagita, who was going to assist him in an exhibition that included magazines, books, poems, posters, fifteen pieces of art, radio plays, films, photographs, and other cultural activities. Yet all of this was contingent on the council's financial support.[43]

The Papua New Guinea group was comprised of Ralph Wari (executive officer to the National Cultural Council), Nora Brash (lecturer in drama at the National Arts School), Nell Pajen (actress with the National Theatre Company), Russell Soaba (writer and research fellow with the Institute of PNG Studies), Rasonga Kaiku (anthropology student at UPNG), Saio Avefa (drama student with Goroka's Raun Raun Traveling Theatre), Arnold Watiem (villager who was active in traditional dances and carving), Taloti Kaniku (tutor in literature at UPNG), Jack Lahui (who headed the Ministry of Education's Literature Bureau), and writer Sally Anne Bagita. Nigeria provided them with free tickets to travel. Gilbert Kose, Jawodimbari, and Waitea Magnolias, PNG minister for culture, were sponsored by Papua New Guinea's government to attend the festival. Magnolias officially represented Papua New Guinea. Apisai Enos, who was in the United States, was sponsored by the Institute of PNG Studies to travel to Africa. He delivered six papers on PNG culture.[44]

Brash's 1976 satirical play *Which Way Big Man* critiqued Papua New Guinea's transition from colonialism to independence, and made "fun of corrupt politicians, people wheeling and dealing at the expense of other people, and actions contradicting traditional values." Her working relationships with male artists like Jawodimbari and John Kasaipwalova were cordial, "but at that time the gender relationships were nothing much to desire." She considered a number of Oceania icons to be her role models, such as Albert Wendt, Kirpal Singh, Chinua Achebe, Marjorie Crocombe, Ulli and Georgina Beier, Noonuccal, and Soaba.[45]

Her time in Nigeria was a "highlight for young budding artists of the newly independent" Papua New Guinea. At the time, she was trying to establish herself through the National Theatre Company via her plays, poetry, and puppet plays. While the entire theatre troupe did not attend, she took along and used her marionettes in an impromptu performance. In some evenings, they enjoyed sharing their traditional dances with other delegations in FESTAC Village till the early hours of the morning.[46]

Brash found FESTAC exciting, entertaining, and vibrantly enjoyable. She spent time with a number of renowned Black artists. She met Afrobeat pioneer Fela Anikulapo Kuti during a wonderful evening at his nightclub, the New Afrika Shrine. On one occasion she read her internationalist poem "Underground Scuffle" for an audience that included Stevie Wonder. "Underground Scuffle" denounced a National Front protest in Islington, Britain, which called for the British government to stop immigration and deport migrants from the country. In response, Brash's piece called for the repatriation of British individuals back to England: "Leave the Indians to pow wow, send the pahekas packing from Aotearoa, return the convicts from terra Australia, let the Abos dance in Corroboree, stop apartheid, dismiss the whites from Azania, Let Mother England sink under the weight of her offspring of the Empire repatriated." This piece prompted Wonder to send a car for Brash the next day, and the two discussed Papua New Guinea for about an hour. She also met South Africa's Miriam Makeba while the latter was rehearsing with her band in FESTAC Village. Makeba congratulated them on their independence from British colonialism and sung her song "Patapata."[47]

Brash felt that FESTAC brought home "the reality and the true meaning of the struggles of the Black people around the world." She had a number of political exchanges with young activists from Soweto; they discussed Stephen Biko and read protest poems. She recalled a moment when her friend from Soweto gave a child who was selling bottles of Coca-Cola an "earful about being enslaved to an American Consumer company." This friend bought the kid's last drink—which he had been unsuccessfully trying to sell for over three hours—and told him to go home and sleep. Her friend emptied the bottle on the ground. The child promptly went around the corner and returned with a full crate of drinks to sell. Ironically, there was a water issue that night so the FESTAC visitors had to wash down their meals with Star beer or Coca-Cola. This "little episode" plagued Brash for years, as she empathized with "the kid who was caught up in the rat race of survival." She was aware of the contradictions of the rhetorical clichés of politicians who grabbed power but "left the folks in dire straits." She came away from FESTAC "wary of the implications of what [Papua New Guinea] would go through." Their trip was supposed to last only ten days. Instead, they stayed for the entire festival. A travel mishap landed them in Addis Ababa, Ethiopia, for a week, in the wake of the Kay Shibbir—the political violence that saw Mengistu Haile Mariam rise to the leadership of the Marxist-Leninist military junta known as the Derg (Provisional Military Government of Socialist Ethiopia). They were harassed and almost beaten by Derg soldiers for being out after curfew after the death of Tafari Benti. A day later they visited Mercato, Africa's largest open-air market. Upon leaving Ethiopia, they found themselves stranded again for a week in Manila, Philippines.[48]

This did not deter the group from international travel. Months later they embarked on their second international tour to London and Bristol. According to *Papua New Guinea Writing*, the troupe showed the world that Papua New Guinea was "no longer primitive." Brash and others performed in front of crowds of thirty thousand in places like Trafalgar Square.[49]

Brash was married to Australian writer and educator Elton Brash, former vice-chancellor of UPNG. In May 1977 Elton participated in a Southern Pacific Language and Literary Studies Conference at the

University of Queensland, Brisbane. The meeting included Pacific writers like Kaniku, Noonuccal, and Liyong.[50]

Liyong also attended FESTAC, where he served as Papua New Guinea's rapporteur of the working group on Black civilization and African languages. The PNG delegation participated in reading recitals, drama, dances, and literature performances at the National Theater and National Stadium. Aboriginal and Torres Strait Islanders participated in the colloquium, reading recitals, and dances at the National Theater and Tafawa Balewa Square. They performed in both traditional and modern dance performances. The festival showed two Aboriginal films, *Lalai* and Gerald Bostock's 1976 *Here Comes the N——gger*.[51]

The IFC produced an official book, *FESTAC '77: The Black and African World*. Bursting full of photographs (including those of Aboriginal dancers) and essays, it included a map of the Black world that included Australia and Papua New Guinea. The book's final essay was written by Aboriginal activist and footballer Gordon Briscoe (Moriarty's former teammate), which detailed White Australia's assaults on Aboriginal peoples, immigration discrimination, the White Australia policy, the Queensland Act, blackbirding (the "slave trading of South Sea Islanders"), colonial systems of assimilation, and the unfortunate status of Aboriginal fringe dwellers. According to Briscoe, British imperialism's destruction of Aboriginal society was one of the "great tragedies of human existence." The ecological attacks on Aboriginal communities had eroded essential medicine men, traditional education, and their spiritual systems.[52]

Briscoe also managed the Aboriginal delegation to FESTAC, which included Aboriginal dancers, scholars, special artists, and orators. In his memoir, he writes that the Australian government employed (co-opted) him for three months to do so. He curiously remarked that he had some previous experience with Nigerians. He left for Lagos in November 1976. Briscoe also oversaw the movement of a permanent exhibit from Australia to Nigeria, which detailed the prehistory of Aboriginal Australia. It was based on the "out of Africa theory," which detailed human migration from Africa to Australia via the Indian continent and the Indonesian archipelago. It utilized archeological evidence at Lake Mungo in New South Wales that calculated this migration as being 40,000 years old and Aboriginal arrival in the region some 120,000 years ago. The display was accented with live dancing and modern paintings.[53]

For Briscoe, his time in Africa was a personal watershed moment. He had struggled with alcoholism for years. In Africa his drinking intensified. He recalled, "It became almost a daily habit because I had more time on my hands, money in my pocket and every event that I attended involved easy access to wine and spirits." Ironically, however, upon his return to Australia he was moved to "give up the grog."[54]

Noonuccal accepted the Australian committee's invitation to provide an entry in FESTAC's literature category. At the festival, she read from her poetry, which was translated into French and which she hoped would be included in an anthology on "New Black and African Writing." Her old friend Jack Davis also attended. Writing subsequently from Moongalba, Noonuccal filed a report to the Australian Council about FESTAC that was less than flattering. It argued that the delegation was "not a truly representative group." Torres Strait Islanders did not attend, and she argued that artists such as Gloria Fletcher should have been there. "Too many Aborigines attended the colloquium" (perhaps as opposed to other Black communities) and most were from Southern Australia. Having been "left out of most things," she was not able to be an effective senior advisor to the delegation. Upon arriving in Nigeria, she was told that she would have to "kill and catch" to get information, which seemed "to be the slogan for" the festival. She spent four days at her hotel before she got to work on the exhibition. She participated in the literature component and recorded a piece for the festival's archives. Unfortunately, she felt that the Aboriginal group that she traveled with was ignored. This was a "very bad thing. . . . Black public servants have got to realize that their duty is to their delegation regardless of how tired or how hungry they might be, or how late the hour."[55]

Noonuccal also felt that the traditional dancers were "out of their element." She claimed that while she had not seen any of them with "money of their own . . . some of them were usually drunk at 7 am and hostile towards their advisors." Was this also a reference to Briscoe? Only one or two had attended meetings called by the senior vice president, stating that they were "too tired to attend." In contrast, the contemporary dancers worked hard at making the trip a success and performed "exceptionally well." She was not able to see any of the papers presented at the colloquium. She reported that after hearing snippets of what was going on, she concluded that the colloquium had become a "colosseum with the African Lions devouring the foreign lambs as they were led to the slaughter."[56]

A number of articles appeared in Australian media about the delegation. The *Canberra Times* reported how "Aborigines met other Black cultures" and shared with the Black world corroboree dances and the sounds of the didgeridoo from Groote Eylandt's Nawuradjidja Wurragwagwa—one of North Australia's best players. A series of negative sensationalist articles were written in the *Bulletin*. The first, "Black Brouhaha," centered on the early return of thirty-eight Black and Aboriginal delegation members to Australia. The author claimed that "the cheap housing built by the Nigerian Government for its 200,000 Black international visitors was not acceptable to the Australians." Upon arrival in Lagos, they found that their hotel did not have suitable telephone or transport facilities. Once moved to the new Festival Village, they were dissatisfied with poor sanitary arrangements and lack of electricity. They protested the unsatisfactory lighting provided for the dance troupe and the poor audience attendance.[57]

Weeks late, Jabani Lalara, spokesperson for the rural dancers and the Aboriginal Cultural Foundation, replied to the article. He claimed that the article had mixed up the facts. It had neglected to state that the half of the Australian Aboriginal delegation that left Nigeria was the tribal group, who had kept their sacred cultures strong. Those who stayed were "urban part-Aborigines" who had lost their culture. It was rubbish to claim that they had left because of housing—despite not being ready, it was good. The primary reason that they left was that once in Africa, the "tribal people were strongly bossed around by the urban part-Aboriginal officials from Australia." These officials kept telling the tribal Aborigines to keep away from White Australians. Yet they did little to help organize their show. "All they kept doing was calling meetings to keep pouring out to us that same story of hate." But this was not their "tribal way of thinking"—such rubbish talk against Whites made them "really wild." Why did the government give jobs to people who "rubbish their own country overseas?" They were unaware that the urban part-Aborigines went to FESTAC to "try to join up with other Black countries against Australia." They thought that the urban part-Aboriginal dancers only went to Africa to dance. They returned to Australia and were disappointed to find out about the article in the *Age*. The urban dancers had lost their friendship. The festival was not anti-White. They had two White helpers with them—Bennett and Haag, who made "good friends with the Africans." The only anti-White feelings at the festival came from the "part-colored people from the towns" of Australia. The tribal people repeatedly warned the "urban part-Aboriginal big talkers to stop bossing us and trying to divide us off from Whites in our own country." But they did not desist, so they had to leave. They were "all sad to be driven away from Africa by these city big-talkers who called themselves 'Aborigines.'" But FESTAC allowed them to see "the bad name those city people give to the real Aborigines."[58]

This curious article was printed next to a lengthy piece about FESTAC written by Brian Hoad, titled "Black Wasn't Beautiful." The article was laced with divisive comments and racist overtures. It was headlined by a photograph of Johnson's dance group and a caption that read, "The Australian Aborigines' main contribution to Nigerian festival: Filipino jazz ballet danced to American Soul music. The tribal Aborigines had by then gone home." Hoad claimed that White Australian Anthony Wallis had traveled to FESTAC as a project officer for the Australia Council's Aboriginal Arts Board. After a month in Lagos, he looked "rather tired and worldly wise" after trying to "salvage something" out of the "chaos which beset the Australian delegation to FESTAC"; he surmised that if India had been part of the delegation, things might have been more organized. He was there "to control the purse strings," and was "one of three such species of mankind who accompanied some thirty-three Aborigines and part Aborigines on their voyage of discovery." The delegation also included expert boomerang thrower Stan Roach from La Perouse and two artists from Alice Springs who brought an exhibition of Aboriginal art and artifacts.[59]

Hoad claimed that at the heart of the delegation lay "part-Aborigine" Moriarty, who had surrounded himself with six other activists whose main focus at FESTAC was "Black politics." This "Black politics" group included urban Aborigines and part-Aborigines, such as Johnson's dance group. The urban group began "activating" even before it left Australia. He referenced the "Black Brouhaha" article, in which they declared that they would perform the Tent Embassy (Hoad placed the word "embassy" in quotes), an issue that was "close to the heart of Moriarty." They intended to use the trip to bring "international embarrassment" to Australia. However, claimed Hoad, this political preoccupation had a negative effect on the group's "organizational abilities." Despite the trips of Moriarty and his "advance guard of activists" to Lagos, little was prepared for the rest of the delegation. After fifty-two hours of travel, the tribal Aborigines had nowhere to stay. The Festival Village was not ready, but Wallis was able to find them accommodations in an "incomplete hotel" outside town. Meanwhile, "Moriarty and his activists" stayed in a well-established hotel in Lagos. Allegedly, on opening day, the "activist's racism passed into the realms of farce" when they announced that White Australians could not be seen driving through the streets of Lagos in the company of Black Australians. Noonuccal established a compromise in which the Whites could ride with the delegation only if they sat in the back of the bus and kept a low posture. Regardless, claimed Hoad, Nigerians were rather surprised at how pale some of the activists were anyway.[60]

Hoad continued. The opening ceremony at the National Stadium dealt another blow to the morale of the tribal people, whose "distaste for Black Power politics" was reinforced by some rather alarming crowd control methods of Nigeria's gun-waving, horse-riding, whip-wielding soldiers. The tribal delegation entered the opening parade in their travelling clothes and had "left their instruments and weapons" back in the hotel. They were not told to "dress up," while "the rest of the Black world" was dressed "in full tribal regalia." Roach "partly saved the day" by giving out boomerangs for the delegation to wave together upon entering the arena. The local papers said they looked rather "inhibited." At this moment Moriarty and the activists decided to replace the White members Bennett and Haag with England-based Nigerian actor Jumoke Debayo.[61]

His tirade endured:

At the National Theatre on the night of January 26 Australian Aboriginal culture was finally presented to an audience of 5000 by the Aboriginal/ Islander Dance Theatre of Sydney who performed a jazz ballet choreographed by a Filipino to recorded songs of Marcia Hines, a Black American.[62]

Furthermore, the activists had their public say, which "one observer" claimed was "an exercise in fantasy" that was "devoted to dreams of blowing up parliament." The group allegedly claimed that all Black and African peoples needed to master and pass on to future generations their own cultures. This included learning and daily practicing their languages, arts, historical traditions, systems of government, philosophy, religious values, technologies, and traditional medicines. This would enable them to "enter into modernity while remaining our very selves." He also claimed that a bunch of "urban, part-Aboriginal big talkers," dancing "Filipino jazz ballet to American soul music[,] drove away from Africa those tribal people whose main concern was to keep alive the unique heritage of Australian Aborigines."[63]

Noonuccal pushed back against the "damaging" and "untruthful" *Bulletin* articles. Aboriginal delegates had "involved themselves in politics," and she saw no reason for them to do otherwise. Australians seemed to suggest that politics was strictly for Whites. Wallis had played an excellent role as assistant and advisor, although "he realized that we were under pressure from some of the African delegates about the Whites in their delegation." She doubted that Lalara had actually written his article, and while the delegation was "not as united" as it could have been, the funds were well spent for the trip. Theirs was the best-attended exhibit at the festival.[64]

Noonuccal had other concerns. Australia had nothing to fear from the "so-called Black Power people there. . . . They looked more like little saw dust dolls and things to me." She firmly believed that the key to race relations lay in the Pacific itself, and felt that regional conferences should be held in Oceania, which would be economically and artistically sound. She also felt that senior advisors should go to such festivals, and "preferably *women* who know how to manage the groups." Still, she was moved by her time in Nigeria. She brought back several pieces of popular culture from Nigeria, including programs, invitations to dinners and cocktails, newsletters, and photographs of delegates.[65]

At Sydney's 1977 PEN International Congress, poet Davis gave a reading, including his "On Flying from Nigeria to Australia," a reference to his travels to FESTAC. He shared the stage with Fijian writer Satendra Nandah and South Sea Islander Faith Bandler, who gave the extempore statement at the panel on "the emergence of New Literatures Among the

Pacific Nations."[66] Davis's sharing of FESTAC speaks of its significance as a Black internationalist watershed moment for Papua New Guinea and Australia, and how artists across Oceania continued to make concerted efforts at collaboration despite political, racial, and ethnic tensions in the region.

7

Povai

Fiji, Pacific Women, and a Nuclear Free Pacific

This chapter explores Black women's internationalism in Oceania through the political and cultural activism of three Fijian women, Amelia Rokotuivuna, Vanessa Griffen, and Claire Slatter. Rokotuivuna directed Fiji's Young Women's Christian Association (YWCA) and Griffen and Slatter were students at Suva's University of the South Pacific (USP). In 1975 they organized Suva's Pacific Women's Conference (PWC), which was a political berth from which Pasifika women addressed intersecting regional issues of gender, (neo)colonialism, environmental justice, human rights, ethnicity, race, culture, and sovereignty. The meeting featured some eighty activists, artists, and scholars from across Melanesia, Micronesia, Polynesia, and the Americas. They denounced French, Australian, North American, British, and Indonesian imperialism, neocolonialism, and militarization in Oceania. A Fiji-based regional Pacific Women's Resource Center emerged out of the conference. Rokotuivuna, Griffen, and Slatter were also critical actors in the Nuclear Free and Independent Pacific (NFIP) movement. In the aftermath of Suva's 1975 Nuclear Free Pacific Conference, they established the Pacific People's Action Front (PPAF) and its newsletter *Povai*, which aimed to help coordinate the liberation struggles of political movements across Oceania.[1]

The Pacific Way

Born in 1941, Amelia Rokotuivuna became the first Fijian executive director of Suva's YWCA in 1972. A "leftist Christian," Rokotuivuna transformed the YWCA from a space of vocational training into a powerful hub of radical praxis and political pressure, particularly around issues of decolonization, ecological justice, "Third World" feminism, and anti-nuclear testing. In 1970 she helped found the Against Testing on Muroroa (ATOM) committee, which sought to raise public awareness about the impact of nuclear testing. Her other influences included the global activism of the World Council of Churches, South Africa's anti-apartheid movement, and South African YWCA activists like Brigalia Bam.[2]

Rokotuivuna traveled the world on behalf of Pacific movements. In 1971 she represented Fiji at the YWCA's World Council Meeting in Accra, Ghana. According to *Pacific Islands Monthly*, CP Air had awarded her a nine-month travel scholarship to attend in-service and administrative training courses at various Canadian YWCA centers. She spent six months in Woodstock, Ontario, as well as London. She informed the *Calgary Herald* that the YWCA operated as a "pressure group to the Government." The association had historically conducted vocational training for Fijian school leavers in "very menial jobs," such as domestics, tour guides, and office aides. However, she was taking the association in other directions, including "a more social awareness on race relations" and a push for political education. She also spent two years working in social work in London.[3]

In November 1975 she attended a WCC meeting in Nairobi, Kenya, where she informed her audience that "structures and people's attitudes were the obstacles" to change. In 1978 she gave a guest lecture entitled "Women Moving in the South Pacific" for the Mountclair-North Essex, New Jersey, branch of the YWCA. According to the *Herald-News*, she was there to speak about how women were "leading the liberation movement in the islands of Oceania."[4]

Born in Fiji, Vanessa Griffen and Claire Slatter were childhood friends. At the University of the South Pacific (USP), they took courses in politics, history, and sociology. It was here where they first began to develop a "Pacific consciousness"—a sense of seeing Fijians as being historically, culturally, and politically connected to the broader Pacific. Founded in 1968, USP did not have the reputation that the University of Papua New Guinea (UPNG) had in terms of its discourses on the Melanesian Way, and in comparison, was a conservative institution. Still, UPNG literature was visible across Oceania, and Australian literary journals published PNG writing as "Third World" expressions. The works of UPNG writers like Arthur Jawodimbari were prominently fea-

Figure 7.1. Amelia Rokotuivuna leading a workshop at the Regional Pacific YWCA Conference at Adi Cakobau School, Fiji, 1975. Seated to the left of Rokotuivuna is World YWCA president Jewel Graham. National Archives of Fiji.

tured at USP. This kind of political thought moved Griffen and Slatter, so much that in 1974 both women conducted graduate studies in Papua New Guinea. This was seen as a "radical move" in a Pacific context and was equivalent to "going to Africa." Slatter completed a master's qualifying year, and was particularly a fan of John Kasaipwalova's work. Griffen studied drama at the Papua New Guinea Creative Arts Center. While there, she toured and performed drama with Jawodimbari's theatre company.[5]

As such, while it was not UPNG, USP still functioned as a critical site for cultural and political transnationalism among students and faculty. A number of its international students were involved in anti-colonial liberation struggles across Oceania. For example, French officials expressed concern that subversive "leftist professors" were influencing New Hebridean students who studied in Fiji or Papua New Guinea. Slatter and Griffen formed lasting relationships with two such students, Grace Mera Molisa and Barak Sope of the New Hebrides National Party (NHNP).[6]

Sope studied political science and land reform at USP. In 1972 he toured Aotearoa to speak about the relationships between French nuclear testing and French colonialism in Oceania. That year he also represented New Hebrides at the Waigani Seminar. According to *Salient*, the student newspaper of Wellington's Victoria College, Waigani provided "a forum for more radical Pacific Islanders to air their views on political independence" and other matters. It prophetically described Sope as a "radical young graduate" who in years to come would "be called upon to lead the fight against British and French colonialism" in New Hebrides.[7]

Griffen and Slatter were among the students who pushed USP to become a space of radical politicization. They both wrote articles in a 1972 issue of USP's student newsletter, *UNISPAC*, which was dedicated to women's suffrage and women's liberation. Griffen's article denounced but was not a response to a sexist article, "Against Women on Campus," which claimed that women were biologically destined to be dependents and servants of men. As men were left to develop their intellectual abilities, this resulted in technology change, which then allowed women to be partly freed from their roles as servants. They were now allowed to join men at universities, but their presence there had a disastrous effect on men—they entered fields of study preserved for men, and they also distracted men from their "world-shattering studies." Griffen brilliantly pushed back against the ideas that women were intellectually inferior to men, that women "belonged in the home," and that "society was a man's world." She argued that women's liberation freed both men and women from restricting roles, and enabled children to develop freely "without preconditions, but simply as human beings."[8]

Slatter's article "Woman Power: Myth or Reality" addressed the women's liberation movement. She analyzed the growing number of educated, technically qualified women who would challenge their male counterparts in the local economy. She called for a radical change in the education system that would abolish specializations in vocational training such as "home economics," secretarial courses for girls, and industrial arts for boys.[9]

But this *UNISPAC* issue also featured Oodgeroo Noonuccal's aforementioned article on Aboriginal civil rights, where she called for "a conference between all the indigenous people of the Pacific" and the production of a "charter of rights for the indigenous people of the Pacific."

It also had a photograph of Sope, who was running for student council, and a report by Mesulame Lutumailagi, who spent some seventy days in the United States with the Asian and Pacific Student Leader Project. Lutumailagi stayed with an African American family in Little Rock, Arkansas, that had "suffered a lot" when they first moved into their White neighborhood; the White community had "fled" since then. In Houston he visited an HBCU, likely Texas Southern, where he noticed "how deep the hatred of the Blacks towards the Whites." Black students took them to have soul food in soul cafes, where they listened and danced to soul music. They also visited Tuskegee in Alabama, joined anti-apartheid and anti–Vietnam War protests at Harvard, and witnessed pushes by students at the University of Hawai'i for cultural studies. The issue also included a review of a performance of James Baldwin's play *Blues for Mister Charlie* at the Suva New Theatre, and a full-page ad to join the anti-apartheid movement.[10]

Griffen and Slatter were also radicalized on USP's campus by student movements in Australia and Aotearoa, especially on issues such as anti-apartheid in South Africa. This is the context in which they met Rokotuivuna, who provided them with practical and efficient models of successful organizers, helped to refine their political views on issues of gender, and included them in projects. In 1973 Slatter and Rokotuivuna contributed chapters to the International Development Action Group's hard-hitting booklet *Fiji: A Developing Australian Colony*, which critiqued Australian neocolonialism in Fiji. Rokotuivuna's chapter, "Development for Whom," argued that while Fiji had been an administrative colony of Britain, it had long been an economic colony of Australia through private corporations such as the Colonial Sugar Refining Company, W. R. Carpenters, and Burns Philp. Upon achieving independence in 1970, Fiji now had "all the trappings of international sovereignty but the neocolonial ties" continued. Post-independence colonial rule functioned through corporations rather than nation-states. This had serious ramifications for development in Fiji, as its "human costs" could be "mass unemployment, frustrated aspirations, and cultural disorientation." Development needed to "create or improve material conditions of life in some way related to a perceived need for identity and self-respect" and free communities from servitude to nature, ignorance, institutions, and other human beings. Development could also be dehumanizing and was supported by uncritical leaders who stood to benefit from foreign investments. If Fiji's government was serious about rural development, its policies needed to ensure that new investments went into the rural areas, and big projects needed to be designed to "function in small packages, with low level technology."[11]

Slatter's chapter focused on the impact of tourism's rapid growth in Fiji, which she argued was based on short-term economic gains and the government's lack of sensitivity and reluctance to address tourism's "long-term economic, social, political, cultural, technological, and environmental" consequences on the future of Fiji. She wrote that "tourism in its present form perpetuates the colonial relationship between the Whites and the locals; the Whites continue, even after independence, to be the 'boss,' 'Sahib,' or 'Kemuni-saka' and are regarded as superior beings." This was undesirable, and the model of tourist development needed to be rethought to ensure maximum control of the industry by locals, as opposed to token equity in multimillion-dollar projects.[12]

The International Development Action Group also built relationships with Professors Ron and Marjorie Tuainekore Tere Crocombe, who helped to facilitate USP discussions on the Pacific Way. In December 1973 Rokotuivuna and Crocombe participated in a seminar on development sponsored by the South Pacific Commission and South Pacific Social Sciences Association (SPSSA). Chaired by Ron Crocombe, the SPSSA published papers from the seminar in a 1973 special issue of its journal *Pacific Perspective*. According to editor Sinoe Tupouniua, the issue sought to help address the desire for Pacific Islanders to know more about their collective experiences. It included Crocombe's "Seeking a Pacific Way," Rokotuivuna's "Are Planners Human?," Walter Lini's "Independence by 1977 in the New Hebrides," and Francis Bugotu's "Decolonizing and Recolonizing: The Case of the Solomons." They would later publish this as the volume *The Pacific Way: Social Issues in National Development*, edited by Ron Crocombe, Tupouniua, and Slatter.[13]

Rokotuivuna posed a challenge to the seminar: "You intellectuals, graduates, planners, economists, social workers and professionals generally—what will you say when the majority asks, 'What have you done for us?'" She judged planning by "the extent to which it involved ordinary people." Fiji and Samoa's national plans analyzed growth targets, "but gave no exposition on quality of life or what the peoples of the Pacific looked for." The targets were "so many houses, so much employment, increased GNP," and it was invariably assumed that "self-respect, dignity, and caring for humanity" would result. But when "these intangible goals were not achieved, society's oppressed were blamed." Development planning should not remain in the hands of the few. The Pacific's majority—rural subsistence farmers, unskilled and semi-skilled workers and the unemployed—needed to "join the lettered few in planning."[14]

Francis Bugotu, who was the senior education officer for the Solomon Islands, described Western standards of living and education as "alien ideologies for Third World peoples." They were "a reinforcement of a world-wide design of neo-colonialism which [bound] former colonies to metropolitan countries" and aimed to first serve "Western strategic, economic and political interests, albeit at great cost to emerging nations." He saw "a clear link between being colored and being exploited colonially." Most importantly, a transformation of Solomon Islands' society and economy needed to combine "the strengths of the traditional culture with the new powers of technology," and "begin with a model built not around towns and factories, not around beer parties and big cars, but rather around human beings living in small, rural communities," with the "village as the center of activities and of the good life." This was critical, as Honiara had "now 'advanced' to the stage where Melanesians [were] starting to become oblivious to the hungry family, next door."[15]

Bugotu's presentation and article were drawn from his presentation at UPNG's 1968 Waigani Seminar. He discussed the disguised and silent "psychology of neo-colonialism," which was intentionally used by colonialists to cause "confused passivity in the minds of the colonized." In a period of decolonization, he argued, "a new spirit of colonization is usually born disguised, to excuse the existence of colonial and paternalistic attitudes." This included excuses about the "proven" cultural, political, and economic advantages of colonial systems used to justify maintaining the status quo.[16] He continued:

> The challenge for us Pacific Islanders is not to stand wide-eyed at one
> side of the arena, blankly watching our interests being manipulated and
> aspirations changed by foreigners, but to stand in the center of the ring

and be involved, with one foot firmly on the ground. The task is to find a design for a future which serves our interests, and need not necessarily be patterned on western lines, nor serve western strategic, economic or political aims.[17]

The Solomon Islander from Guadalcanal declared it essential that Pacific peoples seek a broader range of alternatives for development than the ones offered by the colonial metropoles. Pacific Islanders needed faith in their own cultures, and needed to build programs of modernization based on their own traditions, such as patterns of communal land rights and collective responsibility that could form the basis for cooperative economics; practices of decision making by consensus could be examined by political leaders to adapt to modern parliamentary procedures; the philosophy of shared responsibility for the young, the sick, and the elderly could be incorporated into modern social welfare programs; and classless and non-elitist society forms could be utilized in new educational structures. The imposition of foreign models of society and culture merely created obstacles to real progress and development in an emerging country. In these countries, the idea of development was closely linked with the wish for freedom, which was, in fact, development, regardless of material progress. The more oppressed a people of a country were during colonial domination, the greater their desire for freedom. It also appeared to be true that "the darker-skinned races of the world" seemed "to have gone through the toughest oppressive measures of colonial practice and domination." Drawing on Freire, he reasoned that "the behavior of the oppressed" was "a prescribed behavior following the guidelines of the oppressor."[18]

Bugotu wrote, "It is a big disadvantage in this world to be black. The trouble with us Solomon Islanders is that we are *too Black*" (emphasis added). Colonialism treated Solomon Islanders like brutal savages and docile children—"loveable little barefooted dears with fuzzy-wuzzy hair." Colonialism had created a "native elite" in the Solomons—the "White Melanesians of Honiara" who misinterpreted the wishes of the village dwellers and desired "high praise for the misrepresentations." This native elite in the Solomons was derived from the same process as in Africa, and they had become exploiters of their own people, imbued with European aspirations. These were global problems that Solomon Islanders faced, and they were only a small part of the colonized Global South. Black could become beautiful once Black people faced their issues and saw the hollowness of Western-style progress.[19]

The Crocombes had lived in Papua New Guinea from 1962 to 1969, when Ron was director of the Australian National University's Research Unit. They arrived in Fiji in 1969. Having spent much time around UPNG, Marjorie felt that USP lacked "a Pacific soul"; it had done little to support the development of Pacific creative arts. Marjorie, who was from the Cook Islands, thus decided to form the South Pacific Creative Arts Society (SPCAS) with Griffen and other artists in 1972.[20]

In 1973 SPCAS launched *Mana*, a monthly cultural magazine that was released as a section of *Pacific Islands Monthly*. Edited by Marjorie, *Mana* hoped to capture and transport the upsurge of formerly passive creative talent that was breaking forth across the whole Pacific through independence, self-government, and the successful first South Pacific Arts Festival. These forces had "heralded a new wave of confidence among the Islands peoples, and visions which formerly lay dormant" were now being expressed. *Mana* was created to give Pacific Islander writers and other artists a place to publish their work. It sought to publish creative writing in a number of genres: "poetry, plays, chants, short stories, and legends as well as articles and reviews on all aspects of the arts in the Pacific area—dance, music, painting, carving, crafts, tattooing, sculpture, pottery, and any other form of creative expression."[21] In a few years it was able to operate independently.

According to Marjorie, the word *mana* exists in Polynesian, Melanesian, and Micronesian languages, and essentially refers to "supernatural power associated with creativity and excellence. It is inherent in highly respected people, in sacred objects, and in spiritual forces." Hence, it was a fitting name for the magazine. In 1980 she would describe how the independence movements of Oceania sparked a new wave of Pacific writers.[22] Griffen was certainly one of these artists; between 1973 and 1975 she extensively published short stories in *Mana*. The political potential of artists of her caliber would be demonstrated in their crucial involvement in Oceania's liberation struggles.

A Nuclear Free and Independent Pacific

In April 1975 Fiji hosted the Nuclear Free Pacific (NFP) Conference. Attended by some ninety delegates from across Oceania, NFP challenged nuclear testing in the region by the United States, Australia, and France. The delegates included representatives from the NHNP, such as Sope. In April 1974 he wrote to ATOM, arguing that action against nuclear testing needed to come from the colonies of the nuclear powers. Solidarity had to exist between Micronesia, New Hebrides, Tahiti, and New Caledonia. "I have personally contacted (secretly) a movement in New Caledonia that is strongly advocating independence from France. Because the French are taping our every move—our contacts with the New Caledonians are sacred at this stage. Signed, Our struggle is one."[23]

Pasifika women such as Rokotuivuna, the NHNP's Molisa, New Caledonia's Déwé Gorodey, and Aboriginal Cheryl Buchanan played a critical role in the weeklong talks. Indigenous activists keenly highlighted the intersections between racism, colonialism, nuclear testing, and environmental injustices. Buchanan raised the question of Aboriginal land rights. They discussed Tahiti's role as a French military base and how its riot-trained troops policed France's colonies in Oceania. The United States' militarization of Micronesia for strategic purposes was related to the capture of Aboriginal lands for uranium mining. Fijian attendees spoke of the need to build a united Pacific front. Representatives of New Hebrides noted that colonialism was the main cause of nuclear testing. Delegates from Hawai'i perhaps said it best: Unless imperialism and colonialism were defeated, it would be difficult to achieve a nuclear free Pacific.[24]

But these arguments were often contested. White representatives from Australia, Canada, and Aotearoa tended to downplay the significance of race. Rokotuivuna chaired the NFP's workgroup on racism, which emphatically argued that racism was the basis of colonialism, militarism, and oppression of Oceanic peoples. The Aotearoan delegation suggested excluding Micronesia from the NFP's proposals for a People's Treaty for a nuclear-free zone, since it was a US territory. However, Pasifika solidarity held sway. Representatives from Papua New Guinea, Palau, and Solomon Islands suggested that the treaty had to demonstrably link the environmental destruction of their lands and waters to racist colonialism, in a tone and language that their "country men and women" could understand.[25] In emphasizing these issues, Pasifika people transformed the NFP into the Nuclear Free and Independent Pacific (NFIP) movement.

The NFP issued the Fiji Declaration at the end of its deliberations. The statement expressed "the rising awareness of the indigenous peoples of the Pacific and emerging independence movements in the French territories," condemned French nuclear bombing tests on Mururoa, and denounced the territorial acquisition of Micronesia by the United States for military purposes. The conference agreed that racism, colonialism, and imperialism lie at the core of the issue. Oceania's communities and their environment were exploited because Pacific Islanders were "considered insignificant in numbers and inferior." This was why nuclear bombs were first used and continued to be tested in the region "in blatant disregard of [their] expressed opposition, rather than in areas with large concentrations of White people." Conference attendants urged Pacific peoples to "assert themselves and wrest control" over their destinies. They "rejoiced over the victories of the peoples of Vietnam and Cambodia," as "these victories proved that the struggle of oppressed" was stronger than the weapons of imperialism. They created a People's Treaty and called for Pacific peoples to intensify their movements for political independence.[26]

The preamble to the treaty declared,

> We the Pacific people, want to get some things clear, we are sick and tired of being treated like dogs. You came with guns and fancy words and took our land. You were not satisfied with that so you took our languages and raped our cultures and then tell us we should be grateful. You forced your way of life on us and we want to tell you that we do not like your way of life. It stinks. You worship dead things like your concrete jungles and now you bring in your nuclear bombs and want to "practice" on us.[27]

It continued,

> We, the peoples of the Pacific, have been victimized too long. Foreign powers came into our region, took over our lands and our destinies. Political control has been gained in some areas, in others our peoples still

suffer foreign domination. Our environment continues to be despoiled by foreign powers developing nuclear weapons for a strategy of warfare detrimental to all mankind.

Our environment is further threatened by the intention of the nuclear powers to build nuclear reactors in our lands, berth nuclear-powered vessels in our ports, and dump nuclear wastes in our ocean. These foreign powers and nuclear devices are here against our will. We, the peoples of the Pacific, refuse to be subjugated to this violation of our rights. We wish to control our own destinies and protect our environment. So long as some of us do not control our destinies none of us is free. So long as our environment is radioactive, we and our children are not free to live healthy lives. We note in particular the racist roots of the world's nuclear powers and call for an immediate end to the oppression, exploitation and subordination of the indigenous peoples of the Pacific.[28]

The NFP called for "a Pacific nuclear free zone" to extend from South America to the Indian Ocean. Its treaty was widely publicized and printed in journals such as the NHNP's *New Hebridean Viewpoints*, which detailed the meeting.[29]

In the aftermath of the conference, Rokotuivuna, Slatter, and Griffen were charged with coordinating the NFP's Continuation Committee. One of their successful tasks was raising funds to send a delegation to the UN. They also distributed a bulletin about political movements across Oceania; the committee's October 1975 issue discussed the liberation struggles of New Caledonia and New Hebrides, land struggles in Australia, an anti-nuclear march in Aotearoa and Tahiti, and incidents surrounding the deportation of Bermudian Black Power advocate Pauulu Kamarakafego from New Hebrides.[30]

In December 1975 the committee circulated a proposal to establish a Pacific People's Action Front (PPAF). Both initiatives needed constant support from all of the NFP delegates if the front was to really "act as a means of coordinating Pacific wide action and struggle." This included financial matters, as the NFP had a financial deficit to address. The committee believed that much could be achieved if Oceania's liberation movements worked "in solidarity against . . . colonialism, imperialism and racism." It argued that the region needed a "permanent regional organization to continue regular communication between the peoples of the Pacific and to coordinate" strategies, action, and support for the struggles of Oceania.[31]

The proposal noted the PPAF's emergence in the context of the NFP, which was initially a response to nuclear activity in Oceania. Still, it was obvious that it was colonialism, imperialism, and racism that motivated nuclear testing in blatant disregard of the expressed wishes of the region's indigenous peoples. At the NFP, the testimonies of brothers and sisters in the US territory of Micronesia, French colonies of New Caledonia and Tahiti, and the Anglo-French condominium of New Hebrides illustrated the roots of the matter. The conference had thus committed itself to coordinated action against all manifestations of imperialism, colonialism, and racism in Oceania through a strong and unified front to wrest control of their environment and destinies.[32]

The PPAF's specific functions were to "coordinate strategies for action and support Pacific groups" that were "struggling for their rights of self-determination and independence against the forces of imperialism, colonialism, and racism." It would politicize and mobilize the people of Oceania through newsletters and newspapers and by linking with student, labor union, youth, church, and other organizations. It aimed to facilitate the exchange of news and information between different groups; provide or raise financial support; and make international representations on behalf of Oceanic movements. The front would be located in Fiji, as it was home to the NFP's Continuation Committee and where ATOM had a wide base of support. It would work with other regional centers. Hawai'i would be a locale for coordinating movements across the United States, Canada, and Hawai'i; Buchanan and Melbourne's Black Resource Center would focus on Australia, Aotearoa, and East Timor. It hoped to establish permanent staff; Gorodey had expressed her desire to come to Fiji periodically to work for the front.[33]

The PPAF produced a newspaper, *Povai*, which was first released in October 1975 with a circulation of ten thousand copies. It was described as "a weapon against the information and communication that [was being] used to separate Pacific struggles." Submissions were to be sent to Griffen, who was its editor. Named after a Tongan "war club," *Povai* was a "Pacific people's struggle paper." Featuring well-informed articles written in English and French, across its pages one could read about the liberation struggles from Oceania and the Global South. Published into the 1980s, it printed firsthand content (newsletters, statements, briefs, interviews, and photographs) submitted by these movements.[34]

In September 1976 the Australian Security Intelligence Organization (ASIO) claimed that a branch of the front had been established at UPNG, in connection with Kamarakafego's arrival in Papua New Guinea. ASIO noted its publication of a pamphlet that defended West Papua's struggle against Indonesia. The document in question was a PPAF discussion paper written by Rex Rumakiek, "West Papua Nationalism."[35]

In July 1975 Rokotuivuna spoke about the NFP conference at a WCC meeting at the University of British Columbia, Vancouver. She noted that there was a growing sense of militance and anger among Oceania's people. The colonial powers did not have any regard for the indigenous people they colonized. Exploitation was "the spirit of the day—the issue of decolonization is not important to France and US. France has no intention of decolonizing the territories—France looks at the people in Tahiti, New Caledonia, and the New Hebrides as objects." The group was "angered by the audacity of Fiji's government to permit US and French propaganda" in the country, as it paid lip service to decoloniza-tion in the region but still serviced French and US ships. France "used the Pacific as a testing ground for nuclear devices. Children [were] being born deformed," and there was "a higher incidence of leukemia" in the region. These issues would come to a head at the Pacific Women's Conference.[36]

The Pacific Women's Conference, 1975

Months after the NFP conference, Griffen, Slatter, and Rokotuivuna attended the NGO Tribune at the UN's World Conference on Women in Mexico City, where they were joined by Molisa and Gorodey. Here they realized that there was a vast gulf between Western feminists from industrialized spaces and those who approached questions from the per-spectives of the "Third World." Papua New Guinea's government sent two women to the talks and promised to sponsor the first National Con-ference of Women in Papua New Guinea that year.[37]

For Griffen, Western women (largely White) did not fully understand the global conditions of poverty, colonialism, racism, or White privi-lege. They downplayed the concerns about racism and neocolonialism raised by Black and Brown women. Rokotuivuna felt that these Western women failed to recognize the relationships of dominance between the industrialized nations and the Global South, and how these hierarchies of power influenced their ethnocentric frameworks of feminism. As such, some of the Pasifika participants did not feel heard.[38]

Yet indigenous women at the conference made a critical impact on the talks, as they stressed the perspectives of Oceanic women on colonialism and nuclear testing. They rejected Western frames of "cultural imperialism" and feminist solidarity and called for an end to violence associated with Zionism, apartheid, and neocolonialism.[39] These experiences prepared this network for the upcoming PWC.

The initial idea for the PWC was launched in 1974 at a YWCA meeting in Papua New Guinea, where Slatter and Griffen were students. They decided to hold it in 1975, which the UN had declared International Women's Year. According to Kila Amimi, national secretary of PNG's YWCA, they had also agreed to make a weekly radio statement about women's rights for the year, coupled with frequent press releases through the *Post-Courier*. Months later, a women's collective of USP students established an organizing committee and selected Slatter as its secretary. They helped to secure funds and made contact with women's groups from across Oceania to form panels. The organizing committee initially aimed to focus on women and the topics of "family and traditional culture, religion, education, the media and the law and politics." However, the conference reached far beyond "women's issues," demonstrating that Pasifika women were concerned about all issues affecting the region.[40]

The organizing committee sent out letters to a broad range of media outlets, women's groups, and organizations. In June 1975 Slatter informed the NHNP's *New Hebridean Viewpoints* that the PWC was going to be "an event of the utmost significance for the Pacific," and the first time that such women would be able to collectively express themselves. The PWC was to be a "consciousness raising experience" and aimed to reach urban and rural women. This included the "silent majority" who labored in unrecognized and traditional modes of employment.[41] As stated by Papua New Guinea's Josefa Namsu, the PWC encouraged Pacific women to think of women's liberation on their own terms and not as European women.[42]

The PWC took place from October 27 through November 2, 1975, at Suva's USP. Its key concerns were the intersecting issues of nuclear testing, environmental justice, women's rights, and Oceanic liberation struggles. Hawai'i's Lorna Omori argued that sexism, colonialism, and racism could not be separated. Tahiti's Ida Teariki-Bordes revealed how Pacific women were giving birth to children who suffered politically from colonialism and physically from the radioactive fallout. Micronesia's Salvadora Katosang stressed that they were there on behalf of many islands that had "never stopped fighting to survive." She described how between 1946 and 1958, the United States detonated ninety-three atomic and hydrogen bombs over Micronesia. In 1946 Micronesians were displaced from the Bikini Atoll to make way for nuclear testing. Three decades later, they continued to suffer from "cultural, psychological, social, and personal dilemmas." She challenged Micronesia's status as a "strategic trust" of the United States, which the latter used for weapons testing, germ warfare development, security, and military operations. Katosang felt it was imperative to replace "the oppression of colonialism, militarism, and imperialism" with a "new social system of nationalism, complete independence, and socialism."[43]

Phyllis Corowa spoke for Australia's community of South Sea Islanders. Corowa argued that they had never been compensated or recognized as an ethnic group by Australia's government. Her community was not entitled to governmental financial benefits available to Aborigines and Torres Strait Islanders.[44]

The only two speakers who were not from Oceania were Jamaican professor of history Lucille Mair and African American linguist Thais Aubry. But they critically contributed to the talks by unpacking the global dynamics of Black liberation beyond the Pacific. Mair gave the keynote address at the PWC. Her pioneering 1974 dissertation from the University of the West Indies focused on class, color, and women in Jamaica.[45] Mair had met the Pasifika women's collective at the UN Women's Conference in Mexico. Now in Fiji, she offered "greetings from the sisters of the Caribbean to the sisters of the Pacific." She felt at home in Fiji, Jamaica's "twin-sister." Amazed to see people with similar phenotypes as those in the Caribbean and similar flora like breadfruit, she wondered at what historical moment they had "shared a common ancestor."[46]

Mair was metaphorically right. Breadfruit, now a staple in the Caribbean, is indigenous to Oceania. In Tahiti its cultivation was connected to kinship networks, spirituality, gender, and planting cycles. The bark was used to make tapa cloth. It was brought to the Americas along the racist eighteenth-century routes of colonialism and slavery. In 1793 two "floating greeneries" arrived in Jamaica's Port Royal with breadfruit plants standing over seven feet tall. Two Tahitians—Maititi and Paupo—were also taken on board as gardeners. Reportedly, when they first saw St. Vincent, they cried out "O Tahiti," thinking that it was home. Both died within a year. They never saw Tahiti again.[47]

Mair felt that Pacific and Caribbean women needed to collectively address questions of colonialism, self-discovery, decolonization, and nationhood, all of which called for the "rediscovering . . . of womanhood."[48] She argued that imperialism had violated the historical integrity of colonized peoples, who could not afford to be "brainwashed into turning their backs on their history." Enslaved African mothers once toiled in the sugar fields and "boiling rooms" of the Caribbean. Jamaica's maroon leader Nanny was a symbol of national pride and positive Black womanhood. As "one of the first great guerilla fighters of the New World," Nanny needed to be rescued from historical silence. Mair felt it imperative that women of the world knew "of their proven capacity" to resist exploitation.[49] Her insistence that her Pasifika sisters find strength in the resistance efforts of other women of color across the world describes the transformative potential of Diasporas as engines of social change.

The California-based, Spanish- and Portuguese-speaking linguist Aubry skillfully discussed the political history of Africa America. She thanked Rose Catchings of the United Methodist Church's Ministry of Women for financially sponsoring her trip. Aubry referenced Eric Williams's *Capitalism and Slavery*, *Plessy v. Ferguson*, "Negro" spirituals, the NAACP, Garveyism and the UNIA, African history and liberation struggles, the civil rights movement, Kwame Ture, Black Power, Jim Crow, the Watts uprisings, political prisoners, King's assassination, and Malcolm X. She also critiqued feminism as being predominantly a White movement and often irrelevant to Black women, but recognized the unique lens in which women of color globally experienced colonialism. Aubry contextualized African American history within two periods, colonial (chattel slavery) and neocolonial (post-chattel slavery). By defining African people in America as a colonized nation, she connected the African American freedom struggle to global anti-colonial movements.[50]

While listening to other speakers, Aubry found herself saying, "I know, Lord knows I know." Yet she admitted her presumptions about imperialism in Oceania. Aubry argued that the "African in America and Africa" had probably "been experiencing European colonialism and neocolonialism longer than any other people in the world." She also suggested that African Americans had "more terms for skin color than any other people." In the context of Oceania and the African world, both positions were certainly debatable.[51]

Māori Hana Te Hemara represented Auckland's Ngā Tamatoa. Formed in 1970, Ngā Tamatoa asserted that Black Power in Aotearoa was not simply a Pacific version of the movement in the United States, but an extension of Māori movements for *mana motuhake* (self-determination).[52] Te Hemara was part of a push that called for the Māori language to be adopted by Aotearoa's public education system. At the PWC, she spoke about the challenges facing Māori women. Despite being only 10 percent of the population, 75 percent of incarcerated women were Māori. They were doubly oppressed by the racism and sexism of Pakeha society. Discriminated against in a chauvinistic and racist education system, they were slaves in Aotearoa. Women who were so "unfortunate as to marry" a racist White man paid "for it with a lifetime of suffering from a man who [was] unable to reconcile his sexual desires with his own racism." Even still, she argued, Pakeha women oppressed Māori women as much as did Pakeha men.[53]

The Māori freedom struggle was focused on a massive land rights campaign. Activist Titewhai Harawira argued that New Zealand did not honor the 1840 Treaty of Waitangi, in which the British pledged recognition of Māori ownership of land and granted the Māori the rights of British subjects. Historically, the Māori language had been banned through legislation, which aimed to erase their culture and identity. As such, Fana Kingstone reasoned, education in the Pacific seemed to be there to produce "brown-skinned pakehas"—White in mind, but Māori in body. Kingstone urged Pasifika women to continue to forge critical relationships at the international level.[54]

Lucettee Neaoutyine and Gorodey spoke on behalf of the Kanak struggle against French colonialism in New Caledonia, the "linchpin of French imperialism in the Pacific." Inspired by Kanak uprisings in 1969, Gorodey joined the Red Scarves (Foulards Rouges). In 1974 she helped to form Groupe 1878. After organizing a protest in September 1974, Gorodey was arrested and sentenced to four months of farm labor.[55]

Gorodey declared New Caledonia to be a "society of prisons, truncheons, handcuffs and chains," where colonial laws legitimized the capture of Kanak land, locked them onto reservations "to starve in peace," and allowed the police to violently arrest and kill Kanak. She understood the international implications of White violence on the health of indigenous peoples, stating, "I do not believe that a representative of the colonial law can have any consideration for me or the health of my child because he is part of that band of colonialists who have massacred" people of color across the world—the Māori, Aborigines, Polynesians, African Americans, Africans in Rhodesia, and indigenous peoples across the Americas. The law, religion, culture, the media, education, and the family were ensnared between "the bloody jaws" of the colonial capitalist system, which denied Black women human dignity. This was why, she argued, the struggle of Kanak women was inseparable from the people's "struggle for national liberation." Kanak were oppressed as a people—not as individual women or men. Groupe 1878 did not seek a neocolonial independence that retained capitalism for multinational mining companies. Nor did the Kanak seek to be "the local valets, n——gger kings or Uncle Toms" of the Western capitalists, whether they were Australian, New Zealander, French, English, or American. As such, if Pasifika women really wanted freedom, they needed to think of ending capitalism.[56]

Neaoutyine discussed the impact of colonialism, institutional racism, and myths of White supremacy on Kanaky. Colonialism had destroyed traditional structures of education for Kanak women. This had historically involved developing skill sets based on the harnessing of natural resources—mat and basket weaving, farming, and the cutting of straw to build roofs for their homes. This was not simply about "women's work"; there were male counterparts to these ecological forms of labor. The colonial assault on these skill sets reflected an attack on indigenous forms of technology and agency.[57]

Neaoutyine pressed further. Instead of producing young women who could engage the natural environment in sustainable ways, colonial education turned Kanak women into imitations of White women, "little puppets" or "cheap exotic merchandise" for "White master[s]." Good Kanak women spoke "good French," wore European clothing, and were "good Christians." The more Kanak women denied their identities, the "better educated" they became. Once assimilated, the culturally alienated Kanak mother desired to be more white than White women. She trained her children in ways that perpetuated colonial bondage and pushed her daughters into the arms of "good husbands" among lower-level Kanak civil servants.[58]

The colonial system produced three complexes in the Kanak woman. The first was racial, in which she believed in White supremacy, and was ashamed to speak her language, meet her "parents in town," or be seen with Kanak. With the second, she "denied the village," preferring instead "to be exploited by a White boss or become a prostitute in town." The third was an issue of class, with urban women with "secondary school certificates" believing they were better than housegirls.[59]

Melanesian participants at the PWC tended to contextualize gender, culture, and women's issues in the context of imperialism, colonialism, and liberation. They firmly denounced colonialism, which had destroyed traditional culture. Nicole George writes that, in contrast, Polynesian women from the Cook Islands, Samoa, and Tonga were more focused on women's roles and family. They noted that Polynesian women had benefitted from some aspects of European civilization, which had given women a sense of independence from traditional life. They also stressed that, in terms of power and culture, the experiences of Melanesian women were different from those of Polynesia.[60] For example, Teariki-Bordes argued that unlike in Melanesia, Polynesian women in Tahiti had "always considered themselves to be the equal of the men," held high positions in society, and could become chiefs.[61] Lily Poznanski of the Solomon Islands challenged this notion, as Melanesian women historically had a "powerful influence in land dealings." Her *wantok* (countrywoman) Kuria Hughes averred that the education system brainwashed girls to accept male dominance. In a traditional society, women were much more powerful than their contemporary counterparts. Women had "lost power through modernization" but still possessed more in the village than "in the town."[62] One ponders to what extent this debate was informed by European projections of Polynesia as a space where women were beautiful, free, and available to White men, unlike Melanesian women, who supposedly were ugly, enslaved to Black men, and undesirable.

Poet Mera Molisa of New Hebrides challenged the comments of some speakers that the national topics were "clouding the overall women's issues." She felt that some women from independent countries could not relate to the impact of colonialism on other areas of society. Yet women in colonial situations *needed* to prioritize their liberation struggles. Mildred Sope canvassed the struggles of women in the national liberation of New Hebrides against British and French colonialism.[63] She was a member of the Women's Wing of the NHNP, which had been formed in 1971. Led by Hilda Lini, the Women's Wing dramatically increased the involvement of women in the party's push for self-determination. The party was also extremely successful in fostering relationships with the broader Black Diaspora, including through the Pan-African movement.

In 1974 Sope was part of a delegation that attended Tanzania's Sixth Pan-African Congress (6PAC) on behalf of the NHNP. Her husband, Barak Sope, addressed the conference, calling for it to recognize the political struggles of the Black and Brown peoples of the Pacific against neocolonialism. Sope referenced nuclear testing in Tahiti, discussed the relationship between imperialism in Africa and the Pacific, and urged 6PAC to pass resolutions denouncing colonialism and nuclear testing. Interestingly, he stressed Oceania's connections to Africa, asserting that those in New Hebrides "had sailed from Africa to the Pacific with canoes and sails." He argued that their fight was the same as in Angola, Mozambique, Guinea-Bissau, Zimbabwe, Namibia, and South Africa. 6PAC was a critical moment to put their cause on the international stage. It was the first time that Sope felt that people in "America, the Caribbean and Africa" were ready to help them in their "common struggle."[64]

The PWC passed some forty-six resolutions on the topics of women and family, politics, education, health, religion, politics, and laws. These called for research to be done on the mental and physical health of women on Pacific terms; for land to be returned to Aboriginal peoples in Australia, for a royal commission to explore issues between Aborigines and the carceral state; for education systems of women to focus on self-reliance; for the descendants of Australia's South Sea Islanders to receive compensation for loss of land, culture, and identity; for women in independent nations to support those in colonized states; and for support of the Māori protest movements occurring in Wellington, New Zealand. The Treaty of the NFP also called for the establishment of a regional Pacific Women's Resource Center (PWRC) from which information and skilled individuals could be utilized throughout the Pacific, and for a Pacific Women's Association (PWA) to support this initiative.[65]

Griffen and Slatter established the PWRC in November 1976, in Fiji's YWCA building. It was led by a steering committee with balanced representation of six members from Micronesia, Melanesia, and Polynesia. Facing the constant challenge of a lack of resources, it survived until 1980. At the PWC, participants described the center as a necessity, so that "a Pacific women's perspective could be represented internationally on social, economic, legal and environmental issues, and that Pacific women, through the PWA, could offer each other continued support and solidarity." It aimed to collect and disseminate information, conduct research and training, voice the perspectives of Pasifika women, and provide support for women's activities and groups.[66]

Its first coordinator, Sue Green, was hired to survey Oceania and compile a comprehensive study of Pasifika women, labor, and unemployment. This was unsuccessful, and after traveling to Tonga, Samoa, Niue, and New Zealand, she resigned in frustration due to neglect from the executive committee and from "lack of local support" of the center, which did not represent "a mass-based organization." According to Green, delegates to the PWC were asked to submit information about women's groups in their areas but had "either lost interest in the Conference and the Center, not told other women about the Center, or had moved to other countries." She claimed that some women were "hostile to the center." However, in Fiji's Vitu Levu, she had received requests about educational material for rural women.[67]

An executive meeting sought to address these concerns. It sought to build relationships with national organizations only and prepare research kits for local researchers. Center leaders noted that it had embarked on a number of activities, such as launching an in-house library and making contacts with regional organizations. Fiji's National Council of Women had expressed some "slight antagonism" toward the PWRC, but it had received positive interest from national groups in the Solomon Islands, Papua New Guinea, New Hebrides, and in Micronesia. There was also global interest in its activities by the Asian and Pacific Center for Women and Development (APCWD), an IWY Tribune Center in New York, and New York's Women's Division of the United Methodist Church. The PWRC released a newsletter, *Women Speak Out*. The committee also realized that the PWRC needed a guiding philosophy, as opposed to simply gathering information for the sake of doing so. They also sent research officer Makereta Waqavonovono to a 1977 APCWD meeting in Iran; Crocombe went as well. The group also sent Molisa, Griffen, and Konai Helu to the 1978 UN Decade for Women's Seminar in New York.[68]

In 1981 Griffen published *Knowing and Knowing How: A Self-Help Manual on Technology for Women in the Pacific* as part of the PWRC's Pacific Women's Resource Kit. The book compiled appropriate technologies that could be used by rural or village women. It addressed the areas of energy, water and sanitation, household improvements, food, and housing. *Knowing and Knowing How* was part of a series of manuals. The second one, *Caring for Ourselves: A Health Handbook for Pacific Women*, was also edited by Griffen. In its foreword, Slatter wrote that the book aimed to demystify both modern medicine and women's bodies. An extension of the 1975 PWC, it aimed to give women "a perspective on health that sees its relationship to women's physical, social, economic, and political environment."[69]

In July 1977 Patricia Korowa was hired to be the PWRC's coordinator. Based in Melbourne, Australia, Korowa had years of international experience. She was a former Black Power leader of Victoria's branch of the Australian Aboriginal League. After inviting Black Power advocate Kamarakafego to Australia in 1970, he invited her to attend the Congress of African Peoples (CAP) in Atlanta, Georgia, as part of a Black Australian delegation. They spent time in Atlanta and Harlem with Black and Native American organizations, such as Harlem's National Black Theatre, the Nation of Islam, the Black Panther Party, Queen Mother Moore's Universal Association of Ethiopian Women, and the Shinnecock Nation. Her experiences in the United States led her to travel back to her family in New Hebrides. French colonial authorities watched her closely,

Figure 7.2. Patricia Korowa, 1966. National Archives
of Australia. Photograph by Cliff Bottomley.

noting that she had attended CAP "to emancipate the black race." For
these efforts, in 1971 the British government marked her as an undesirable immigrant.[70]

On behalf of the PWRC, in 1977 Korowa conducted a three-month
survey tour of Papua New Guinea, Solomon Islands, New Caledonia,
Australia, and New Hebrides. Her itinerary was scheduled to coincide
with national women's meetings in Papua New Guinea and the Solomon Islands. However, her trip incurred a number of "inefficient travel
arrangements," which cost the PWRC dearly. It was expected that she
would travel to the Gilberts, Tuvalu, Nauru, and the Marshall Islands.
According to the PWRC, she did not comment adequately about Western Melanesia, and produced an "inadequate" two-page report for a
three-month trip that cost some $2,400. Korowa claimed to have met
several women who were interested in the PWC and PWRC but were
"too involved in their own activities of organizing a united front of local

women's organizations." They were more concerned with "putting their own [houses] in order." She resigned immediately upon her return.[71]

Korowa had faced her own challenges on her trip. When she flew to New Hebrides, she found that she was still declared "undesirable" due to her involvement with "the Black Power Movement." Vanuatu's British resident J. S. Champion claimed that Black Power was "known to advocate racial violence" and found it unwise to allow practitioners of such doctrines to enter the country.[72]

Lini awaited Korowa at the airport. Only two years prior, clashes with the police and the NHNP had broken out when British and French administrators deported Kamarakafego from the condominium. A fence had now been built around the runway. Appalled by the deportation, Lini cried out to Korowa to "just jump the fence." Korowa felt it unwise to do so, as she was expecting a child at the time. An immigration officer told Lini that, as Korowa had attended a Black Panther conference, she would be banned from the country forever.[73]

Lini and the NHNP's Women's Wing decried this racist act. The Women's Wing itself was a coalition that represented most of the condominium's Black women. It found it striking that Champion was preventing Korowa from doing her community work on behalf of Pasifika women. It was inaccurate to "call any Black people Black Power," as Black people were only fighting for their God-given rights that "colonial imposed laws" had restricted. In a scathing letter, they demanded that British and French officials define Black and White power and describe the dangers of both. The letter reminded these colonialists that Korowa's grandparents were stolen, blackbirded, and enslaved in Queensland, Australia. Yet racist foreigners were now keeping the "true Vanuaaku woman out of her motherland." While the ban was lifted ten hours after her deportation, her supporters demanded an apology and called for Korowa to be reimbursed for her time. Lini and Rebecca Sau signed the letter, "In struggle against French and British Colonialism."[74]

Is it not striking that centuries after European male-imposed notions of undesirability onto Melanesia, colonial officials could find Korowa too "undesirable" to return to her own home? In this case, it was their imaginations of her legitimate associations with Black Power, as opposed to simply her phenotype, that marked her as such. *Yet undesirable to whom?* Sau and Lini's remark that colonialism prevented women from doing their work speaks volumes about women and Black internationalism in Oceania. Across the region, Black and Brown women visibly internationalized the local struggles of their communities. It *was* their work to build berths across Melanesia, Polynesia, Micronesia, and Australia. As artists, activists, journalists, organizers, wives, writers, sisters, teachers, mothers, and revolutionaries, they informed the Black world of the local, transnational, and regional concerns of Pasifika peoples. They carried the burdens of issues unique to women of color, but also those of their communities.

8

1878

Black Liberation in Kanaky

New Caledonia, lying some four hundred inconspicuous miles just south of Vanuatu, lives a history that is both fascinating and troubling. Lapita pottery dating suggests that humans arrived in the 7,000-square-mile Melanesian archipelago in 1350 BCE. Thousands of years of indigenous history were violently interrupted by French imperialism in the nineteenth century. Indigenous people, who are referred to as Kanak, now make up some 4 percent of its population of 112,000 people.

French traders were drawn to the archipelago's abundance of sandalwood and whales. Along with Pacific Islanders from the Loyalty Islands, the Solomon Islands, New Hebrides, and New Guinea, Kanak were blackbirded to Queensland, Australia, and Fiji. Colonialism quickly followed. Although the island was some 17,000 miles away from Paris, France "claimed" it in 1853 and founded the capital city of Nouméa in 1854. Using the island as a penal colony, it sent over 60,000 criminals and political prisoners there. These included members of the French Commune like Louise "Red Virgin" Michel and hundreds of Maghrebis who resisted French imperialism in West Africa. The building of the Panama Canal increased its geopolitical and economic significance, and by 1900, New Caledonia had become the world's leading producer of nickel. French colonialism brought French laws. An 1859 government decree instituted native reservations for Kanak, who were forced to live only on land not desired by French settlers (*caldoches*). During an 1877 drought, French ranchers were allowed to have their cattle graze on Kanak communal lands. In 1875 Kanak were banned from entering Nouméa and were pushed into the mountains and reservations. They were also forced to work in the nickel and copper mines. One company, La Société Le Nickel, employed Chinese laborers and blackbirded Melanesians. The US consul was "personally aware of several cases of

New Hebrides workers who came with a contract to work in stores or private homes and found themselves forcibly taken to nickel mines" in conditions "approaching slavery." In one case, out "of a group of thirty-four workers, twelve had died in the mines." In 1887 Melanesians totaled 42,500 people. By 1901, the population had dropped to 29,100.[1]

According to Yann Céléné Uregei, tens of thousands of Kanak were killed between 1853 and 1870. Still, the Kanak rebelled "repeatedly and violently." In 1868 several French gendarmes and their family members were killed in acts of retaliation against French violence. In 1878 High Chief Ataï of the Couli met with the French governor to address the concerns of his community. He poured out a bag of soil in front of the governor, stating, "This is what we had." Ataï then dumped out a bag of rocks, saying, "This is what you have left us." After the governor replied that they should protect their crops by building fences, Ataï responded, "When the taro eat the cattle, I'll build the fences." Ataï launched war. His initial attack was set to occur on September 24, the anniversary of France's claim to Kanaky. In a synchronized assault that spanned over forty kilometers, about forty French civilians and gendarmes and a few Melanesians were killed in one day.[2]

"They are Black, we are White," reasoned French officials. After Ataï's soldiers killed a French commander, colonial officials placed the island under further siege. Chantal Ferrarro reveals one French officer's suggestion to deal with the "Kanak question":

> One must begin by destroying this population if one is to remain in the country. The only convenient way to come to an end, is to organize hunting parties, like we do for wolves in France, with several groups of thirty men, to destroy plantations, villages, and renew such operations several times a day at the beginning of the rainy season.[3]

French commander Henri Riviere was charged with suppressing the revolt. His racism is marked in his own ink. In his 1880 *Souvenirs de la Nouvelle Caledonie*, he wrote that Kanak had flared foreheads and large, protruding lips. Their faces were either motionless or twinkled with sagacity. Cunning and cautious, they could passionately "erupt in strokes of extraordinary animation or cold ferocity." Lazy and suspicious, liars and thieves, Kanak worshipped "the devil" and danced a terrible *pilou-pilou* dance. The bodies of these unchecked souls were a "dangerous harmony, . . . supple and nervous." Riviere claimed that Kanak people "jumped like tigers" and "crawled like snakes." The Kanak had such vitality, he reasoned, "You have to kill him twice."[4]

Of the war, Riviere argued that there would always be antagonisms between "the conquering people and the conquered people." The latter needed to be "absorbed by the other or disappear." He continued,

> But these black or copper breeds, whether from America or Oceania, do not absorb themselves. They differ too much from the White Race by the mores of instinct that have never progressed, by an invincible repugnance to work, by their complete indifference to a civilization whose benefits they cannot appreciate.[5]

Riviere brutally repressed the rebellion. Kanak living in French areas were imprisoned. More were exiled to Tahiti and other islands. Some 1,200 Kanak were killed in the yearlong war, as they fought the French via guerilla struggle. Around two hundred White settlers died. "Red Virgin" Michel supported the Kanak fight "for their independence, life and freedom." However, some Maghrebi convicts fought against them in exchange for pardons. Ataï was eventually killed. His head was sent as a trophy to Paris, where the Paris Anthropological Society claimed it "a likely missing link to apes." This attack earned Riviere a promotion to serve in Saigon, where he was integral in France's capture of Tonkin (northern Vietnam). He was killed by Liu Yongfu's Black Flag Army.[6]

In 1888 the French colonial administration distributed over one hundred thousand hectares to former convicts. In 1895 every Kanak was required to pay a head tax of ten francs. These kinds of aggressions led to a Kanak uprising in 1917, lasting for months, during which the French government offered "fifty francs for a dead Kanak and twenty-five for a live prisoner." According to Susanna Ounei, France wanted to enlist Kanak to fight in World War I. Kanak Chief Noel denounced this, asserting, "Why are we going to France to defend the land of the French against the Germans, when they are stealing our land and killing our people?" He was decapitated by an Algerian deportee, and his head sent to a Paris museum.[7]

France suppressed the Kanak population with the Code de l'indigénat, a set of "native regulations" that were used before World War II. These laws enforced segregation and limited indigenous mobility outside the reservations. Kanak were denied French common law and could not enter public bars or wield traditional weapons in European residential areas. Native crimes included "witchcraft" or charlatanism, and Kanak could not hold *pilous* or traditional festivals and feasts. They faced a daily 9:00 p.m. curfew except on Wednesdays and Saturdays, risking jail or fines if they broke it. They were forced into compulsory labor on roads and forced to work for settlers via head taxes.[8]

The Code de l'indigénat allowed nearly 90 percent of the land to be confiscated and given to the *caldoches* or the administration for economic or military ends. Not until 1946 did France grant French citizenship to the Kanak and bestow on New Caledonia the original and ambiguous status of "overseas territory." These post–World War II arrangements were part of a global plan for decolonization that did not lead to independence for New Caledonia.[9] Kanak uprisings in the 1970s emerged out of this tradition of political struggle, which inspired liberation movements across Melanesia.

Nidoïsh Naisseline and Black Paris

French imperialism violently dislocated Black Diasporas across the Atlantic, Indian, and Pacific Oceans. In the process, it displaced migrant laborers, surrealists, communists, soldiers, sailors, artists, exiles, anti-colonialists, and scholars. These men, women, and children often ended up in France's harbors, rues, hostels, dancehalls, immigration lines, hospitals, barracks, jails, and parlors. An unintended consequence of colonialism, Black Paris became linked to a politicized Africana network that touched Harlem, London, Washington, DC, Montreal, Nouméa, Dakar, Antananarivo, Brussels, and Port-au-Prince.

Paris served as a matrix of Black internationalism. The city was home to Martiniquean sisters Jane and Paulette Nardal. Jane Nardal's 1928 essay "Internationalism Noir" was published in *La Dépêche Africaine*. An anti-colonial magazine co-founded and edited by Paulette, *La Dépêche Africaine* also discussed Oceania. Both women studied at the

Sorbonne. Black women like the Nardals and Suzanne Roussi Césaire pioneered the ideas of Negritude, the global Black Francophone cultural movement of the 1930s largely framed by the experiences of men like Martinique's Aimé Césaire, Senegal's Léopold Sédar Senghor, and French Guiana's Léon Damas.[10]

Paris also became a hub for Kanak nationalism, anti-colonialism, and student activism. The city beckoned Black and White New Caledonian students to its streets. These included three critical Kanaky leaders: Apollinaire Anova-Ataba, Nidoïsh Naisseline, and Jean Marie Tjibaou. Born in 1929, Catholic priest Anova-Ataba defended his second-year dissertation in social and economic sciences at the Catholic Faculty of Paris in 1965. Titled "History and Psychology of the Melanesians," this seminal text venerated Chief Ataï's 1878 uprising as a landmark of contemporary history. It also saw in the reformist Union Caledonienne (UC, formed in 1953) the possibility of building a multiethnic "Caledonian personality." This notion was similar to Negritude's African personality. According to Bernard Gasser and Hamid Mokaddem, his dissertation was to be published in 1966 by the Negritude movement's journal *Présence Africaine* as "Caledonia Yesterday, Caledonia Today, Caledonia Tomorrow." Anova-Ataba tragically died of leukemia in that year, at the age of thirty-seven. His dissertation politically influenced Naisseline, Tjibaou, and the independence movements of the 1970s.[11]

In 1976 *New Hebridean Viewpoints* printed a brief statement by Anova-Ataba that New Caledonia could be a "viable and sovereign independent state." It could not only satisfy the basic needs of its inhabitants, but also develop via economic, commercial, technical, and diplomatic agreements with its immediate neighbors. Independence would allow New Caledonia to "exploit the full value of its own riches which the stingy help from the metropoles" did not currently allow. Anova-Ataba called for a "Federation of Oceanic States," given that the administrative system of countries like the English and French condominium of New Hebrides did not at all favor its internal development. Furthermore, he argued, it had been ethnologically proven "that the people of the Pacific" were "close relatives." As such, it was likely that they would know more about the affairs of their countries than the present European colonialists. This passage was also published in *Justice*, the journal of the Union Multiraciale of New Caledonia (UMNC).[12]

Born in 1945, Nidoïsh Naisseline traveled to Paris in 1961, where he earned a baccalaureate at the Lycée Jean-Jacques Rousseau. The son of a Maré high chief, he gained an advanced degree in sociology from the Sorbonne. His research focused on "identity crisis among young Kanak communities who traveled to urban centers like Nouméa to work or study." His arrival in France was marked by the closing of the Algerian Revolution. In Black Paris, African and Caribbean friends introduced him to the writings of Frantz Fanon, including the latter's *Black Skin, White Masks* (1952), *Wretched of the Earth* (1967), and *Towards the African Revolution* (1964). In conversation with Marxist activists, he remarked that they were as likely to "lecture to natives as the colonial assimilationists were." In 1962 he joined Caledonian Students in France, led by Jean-Paul Caillard, and contributed to its bulletin *Trait d'Union*. David Chappell has meticulously demonstrated how Naisseline expressed his political thought through traditional Kanak songs, essays, and activism. This body of work reflected his study of anti-colonial ideas of Fanon, Jean-Paul Sartre, Aimé Césaire, Albert Memmi, and Amilcar Cabral. A 1966 essay challenged missionaries who tried to sever the Kanak bonds with ancestor worship, and insisted that colonialism breaks a civilization without replacing it. In another essay, titled "The Black and Language," Naisseline compared the reforms in New Caledonia to the Civil Rights movement in the United States, where African Americans had shed blood to change the society. In December 1968 Naisseline's essay "The Indigenous Student in France" drew on Kanak oral traditions and also engaged Fanon and Memmi. He argued that Kanak students went through a number of phases: attempted assimilation; disillusionment with colonialism; a rejection of the West and calls to return to a mythic past; and the decision to "live with his time" as opposed to an "imaginary future or an idealized past."[13]

To the end of his life, Naisseline kept a copy of Fanon's *Black Skins, White Masks* by his bedside. According to Chappell, Naisseline's writings never explicitly mention Fanon, but his influences are clear. Naisseline had his "first intellectual epiphanies" while reading the book's chapters "Black and Language" and "The Lived Experience of the Black." He felt that this was "exactly what was needed." Fanon's chapter "The Colonized in Question" in his *African Revolution* and its questions of "social truth" were a trigger for Naisseline. These discourses led him to raise fundamental questions of colonialism's impact on Melanesian identity. As part of unveiling this social truth, along with his group Foulards Rouges (Red Scarves), they "rediscovered the name Kanak," which at the time was still considered a racial insult. His 1966 article "Canaque Customs and Western Civilization: Face to Face?," written in the *Trait d'Union*, focused on Fanon's concept of alienation.[14]

The activism of working-class students in Paris influenced Naisseline and other New Caledonian students. They joined the May 1968 student revolt, when students organized the Action Committee for Caledonian Autonomy and the Defense of France. Naisseline was also inspired by exchanges with West Indian, Algerian, and other African students who expressed a "common interest in justice and dignity."[15]

Influenced by radical writers like Régis Dubry and Guy Debord, Naisseline and other Kanak students formed a radical study group. In 1969 they released a bulletin, *Canaque Homme Libre* (Kanak Free Man), which included Naisseline's essay "The Black Aspect of the White Problem." He stressed that Europeans in New Caledonia were "obstinately attached" to nineteenth-century Darwinian notions of civilization. Indigenous people were defined as being football players and folk dancers but were given no agency of political thought. He referenced how in 1931 Kanak were put on display in the Paris Colonial Exposition and told to strip their clothing, stop speaking French, and act as if they were eating raw meat. This group of one hundred Kanak were displayed in a cage at the Jardin d'Acclimation in Paris and described as "cannibals."[16]

Naisseline later admitted that the piece utilized an entire paragraph from *Black Skin, White Masks*:

> I just put Kanak in place of négre and some adaptations here or there. I hid behind Fanon, but it is true that what he wrote concerned us. . . . This may have contributed to my little intellectual notoriety because it was probably the first time a Kanak publicly denounced colonization so clearly and this marked the people. In reality, I had cheated; it was Fanon's words.[17]

His engagement with Fanon's *Wretched of the Earth* deepened upon his 1969 return to New Caledonia. He felt that his chapter "Concerning Violence" spoke to his subsequent political harassment and arrests by the state. Indeed, armed with the experience of May 1968 in Paris and a "consciousness of Black Power," he actively engaged himself in the Réveil Canaque (Kanak Awakening).[18]

Naisseline was arrested after joining graffiti protests with Caillard surrounding Bastille Day. In July 1969 slogans such as "Down with Colonialism," "Long Live Free Caledonia," "Whites Out, Caledonia for the Canaques," and "Now they have the lands, and we still have the Bible" were sprayed across Nouméa. These slogans also called for a boycott of the South Pacific Games in Port Moresby, arguing that they rendered invisible the struggle of Kanak communities. "Canaque athletes, follow the example of our American brothers! Down with Racism! Long live human equality!" This was likely a reference to the sport-based activism of Tommy Smith and Juan Carlos, who raised their hands in Black Power salutes at the 1968 Mexico Olympics. Donning red bandannas around their necks, Kanak athletes from Maré raised their fists in protest at the games.[19]

In August 1969 Fote Trolue, a law student and member of Foulards Rouges, was refused service in a restaurant. He and Yeiwéné Yeiwéné wrote a leaflet about the issue and called for mobilization against racism. Quoting Sartre, he stated that when the slave says "no," he begins to exist. He ended in English with the popular phrase of Black protest, "Freedom Now." The leaflet was distributed in French and two indigenous languages. Naisseline and twelve members of the Foulards Rouges were arrested in September, partly under claims that they broke an 1863 ordinance that forbade the use of Kanak languages.[20] French police claimed that the pamphlet was a "call for murder." In response, a crowd of some three hundred people rushed the police station, demanding that they release the "Chief's son." Police charged the crowd, which led to uprisings across Nouméa. Naisseline was defended by Jean-Jacques de Félice, who had previously defended members of Algeria's National Liberation Front. He had also been banned by colonial judges from entering New Caledonia.[21]

The Foulards Rouges rallied around Naisseline. They portrayed him as a second Ataï, and released drawings representing him as a crucified Kanak Christ. As hundreds of supporters came to his trial, his statement before the court clearly identified his Fanonian influences. He called for the Whites of New Caledonia to rid themselves of their "colonizer complex," asserting that he and his comrades were accused of "condemning murder and inciting racial hatred. It is true, we wanted to commit two murders: that of the myth of the superiority of the White race and that of the myth of Canaque savagery." Naisseline argued that colonialism had "dehumanized the White man by presenting him as the man to copy, creator of the only civilization and from whom come religion, morals and aesthetics." This mystified White man was "no longer a man, but an imaginary creature, a ghost that must be brought down." This, he argued, was what Trolue was calling for. "We say, Down with the mystified White man. The proof that we love the White man is that we fight with all our energy against what prevents him from being truly a man." This was also reminiscent of Césaire's *Discourse on Colonialism*: "First we must study how colonization works to decivilize the colonizer, to brutalize him in the true sense of the word, to degrade him, to awaken him to buried instincts, to covetousness, violence, race hatred, and moral relativism."[22]

According to Naisseline, the Foulards Rouges wanted to forcibly demystify colonial society's racist image of the Canaque as being a sub-man "who utters war cries when he meets his fiancée on the banks of the Coulée." In New Caledonia, insults directed against Whites were the only ones counted as racist. Canaques were defined as beasts gifted only with brute force "to run on the stadiums, unload the boats, and carry the ministers on" their shoulders when they came "to eat bougnat from the tribe." Kanak were *corps sans-tête* (headless bodies)—they lacked "intelligence, this quality being specifically reserved for the colonizers."[23]

He argued that it was difficult for Whites and Blacks to "meet in the full extent of their personality" uninfluenced by racism, which he defined on the lines of Memmi: "Racism is the general and definitive valuation of real or imaginary differences for the benefit of the accuser and the detriment of his victim in order to justify his privileges and his aggression." The Foulards Rouges were not racist, as they did not assert the superiority of the Melanesian race over other races. Applied to Nazism and colonialism, however, Memmi's definition "fit like a glove," as these advocated "the superiority of the White race over the other races," and the imposition of a White civilizing mission across the world.[24]

Furthermore, he asserted,

> Our old people, their memories full of blood, tell us of the multiple hu-
> miliations they were victims of for daring to oppose the intrusion of the
> colonial machine into our tribes. At Chépeneché, the French soldiers
> opened fire on the Canaques who persisted in refusing to obey the French
> missionaries. It is said that at the sight of this butchery the population
> fled; pregnant women were forced to give birth to their children in the
> great outdoors.[25]

This suffering included the exile and assassination of chiefs like Ataï
who challenged colonialism. However, after these heroic resistances,
Kanak "resigned themselves to accept all that came from the exploiters,"
as "disobedience to the Whites" became "synonymous with exile, imprisonment, and sometimes even death." This, he argued, was the aim of
colonialism—"to make the colonized a man who hates himself, a man
who tries to stifle his personality, as one hides a shameful disease." Quoting an anonymous African American writer, he concluded, "A people
who have had everything taken from them, including . . . the feeling of
their own worth, will do absolutely anything to find it."[26]

The emergence of the Foulards Rouges had serious political implications for Kanak who were elected to the Territorial Assembly as part
of the White-led Union Caledonienne party (UC). It helped to drive
the formation in 1970 of the first political party for Kanak autonomy,
Uregei's UMNC.[27] It also influenced the emergence of other grassroots
organizations.

A month later, Naisseline published an article in the journal *Chris-
tianisme Social*. He asserted that the 1969 uprisings were a "spontaneous
demand for dignity, an expression of unity and the beginning of a search
for 'Canaque personality,' comparable to the struggles of other peoples
in Africa, Asia, and America." He also affirmed that he drew inspiration from Césaire's Negritude poetry and the demands of the US Black
Panther Party.[28]

In March 1972 Naisseline was again arrested, this time for interven-
ing in an altercation between a shopkeeper and a colonial official at a
restaurant. Flanked by some twenty members of the Foulards Rouges,
he told the official that he had "no right to play gendarme . . . get out!

I don't care about your uniform. This is not France!" He was sentenced to six months' imprisonment for contempt of court for speaking to a uniformed official with words and phrases like "motherf——cker, bastard, land thief, I don't care your uniform is sh——t, and get the hell out of here." Naisseline denied saying such words but admitted to hearing those insults launched by others. The court claimed that as he was now a chief, his actions could encourage a "particularly dangerous anarchy, which for order and public peace would be catastrophic."[29]

By this time, the Foulards Rouges had expanded their base through community outreach and by hosting meetings at schools, cultural association halls, and bulletins spread across Nouméa and rural areas. Its leadership included Kanaky women like Déwé Gorodey and Ounei. Gorodey was struck by the arrests of Kanak activists who were her former schoolmates. Ounei had always found the racism of her schoolteachers to be problematic and had long hoped for social change; her "dreams became a reality" when Naisseline established the Foulards Rouges.[30]

While in prison, Naisseline released statements through the Foulards Rouges' militant bulletin, *Réveil Canaque*. On one occasion, he stated that people more prestigious than him such as Martin Luther King Jr., Eldridge Cleaver, and Mahatma Gandhi had "fought for their respective brothers. They knew prison and some even knew death."[31] Between 1970 and 1974, the group released thirty-eight issues of *Réveil Canaque*. Through artwork, essays, interviews, poetry, traditional songs, folklore, music, and political satire, the paper spanned themes of racism, political meetings, colonialism, spirituality, history, education, Chief Ataï, neocolonialism in Africa, language, culture, sport, gendarme violence, decolonization, Fanon, "Kanakitude," nuclear testing in Tahiti, sexuality, and tourism. It specifically discussed the political struggles of Vietnam, Sudan, Morocco, France, the United States, Tahiti, and Reunion. Its writers included Naisseline, Uregei, Gorodey, and Jimmy Ounei. *Réveil Canaque* also reviewed Cheikh Hamidou Kane's *Ambiguous Adventure*. In April 1971 it printed Cleaver's "To All Black Women from All Black Men" and his poem "To a White Girl." In 1972 it discussed Angela Davis's recent acquittal on gun charges.[32]

The final issue featured pieces about Kanak protests in 1974, police violence, and colonialism. These were written by Naisseline, Elie Poigoune,

Henri Bailly, Groupe 1878, and Gorodey, whose essay was titled "Atai's Crime Was to Be a Kanak: French Law, Where Is Your Justice?" Gorodey was referred to as president of Foulards Rogue and a founder of a newly emerged group, Groupe 1878.[33]

Déwé Gorodey, Groupe 1878, and Black Internationalism

Déwé Gorodey is regarded as the first Kanak woman to receive a college education; she earned a BA in modern literature from Paul Valéry University in Montpellier III, France. She was born in 1949, one of eleven children; her father was a tenant farmer/sharecropper. Upon her return to New Caledonia in 1974, she became a secondary school teacher, and was forced to use a curriculum based on French history and literature that was antagonistic to her majority Melanesian and Polynesian students. After six months, she left the system and "became truly involved in the liberation movement" by joining the Foulards Rouges.[34]

In August of that year Gorodey formed Groupe 1878 with Elie Poigoune, Gabriel Monteapo, and younger Kanak from Grande Terre Island around the issue of land rights. Kanak on the island had been forcibly pushed off their ancestral lands and found themselves "surrounded by barbed wires on their reserves right next to the immense properties owned" by French settlers. The group's name honored Ataï's 1878 uprising. In September 1974 they organized a demonstration against the French administration's commemoratory military marches, in which Poigoune and Monteapo were arrested.[35] The group organized a sit-in at the courtroom during their trial, along with the Foulards Rouges, the Union Jeunesse Calédonienne, and the Union Pacifiste et Anti-Raciste de Nouvelle Caledonie. They were attacked by the police and beaten with truncheons; twelve protestors were given prison sentences ranging from two to six months. Gorodey was sent to prison for four months.[36]

Ounei was among the group of thirty protestors. She remarked that this was a critical moment for these organizers, who began to engage ideas of global capitalism and liberation. They joined the growing calls for independence from France, which included groups like Uregei's UMNC. New Caledonia's right-wing forces countered this push with extensive propaganda. According to Ounei, they spread ideas that independence would mean that New Caledonians would no longer be able to get sugar and rice, which came from Australia. "They said we would be like people in Africa, who die because they are hungry," and who were hungry because they were independent.[37]

Gorodey often represented Groupe 1878 internationally. As mentioned, in 1975 she attended Fiji's Pacific Women's Conference and the Nuclear Free and Pacific conference, and the United Nations International Women's Conference in Mexico. She also traveled that year to New York, where she visited the United Methodist Board of Ministries. According to the *Pittsburgh Courier*, the board's Ministry of Women helped to send Gorodey to Mexico to detail "the story of her people's struggle for freedom from French rule." Noting her political arrests, the popular African American paper argued that Gorodey, "a shy, warm woman and unlikely looking revolutionary," was certainly "one of many women in Mexico City" who would end up as political prisoners soon after they returned home.[38] Gorodey also addressed the UN Decolonization Committee in New York as part of an NFP delegation. While in the United States, she met with activists of the American Indian Movement, Puerto Rico's Socialist Party nationalists, and Howard University professor Léon-Gontran Damas, the French Guianese co-founder of the Negritude movement.[39]

In the aftermath of the NFP, Australian activist Chris Plant, who was a member of Against Testing on Mururoa (ATOM), wrote to the New Hebrides National Party's (NHNP) Kalkot Mataskelelele about Gorodey. Writing from Fiji, he referenced her travels to the UN. Plant expressed admiration for Groupe 1878 and felt that it could learn from the NHNP's experience. As the groups held natural links against their common enemy, France, he suggested that a lot could be gained from "joining forces."[40] All of this would bear fruit.

The Black internationalist ideas of Groupe 1878 could be read in the pages of its journal, *Nouvelles 1878 Andi Ma Dhô*, particularly in its "News of the Pacific's Anti-Colonialist Struggles" section. In November 1975 the journal discussed an Aboriginal land rights conference in Cairns, Queensland, Australia. Led by Cheryl Buchanan and Lionel Lacey of the Black Resource Center, the conference brought together Aboriginal activists from several reserves such as Palm Island. Translated into French, the conference's leaflet "promised not to talk about the mess, the pig yards where we have to live, our babies murdered because racist doctors hate us blacks, our raped women, our men imprisoned for nothing." It asked, "Brothers and sisters . . . where is the earth?" The leaflet answered its own question,

> It is within you. It is around to protect you—to keep the pigs (cops) from being on our backs. It is in all of us. Don't think it isn't. The bosses in the reserves, the pigs and all the other bastards who crush us, they want to frighten us, make us believe that we are inferior to animals, belittle us all the time. They want us to believe this because it allows them to have control of our bodies, and especially the control of our lands. But you know brothers and sisters that many of us are fighting against this, fighting against the rich who control us and against their violent society. We are walking together . . . to . . . see how to get our land. It will be a great meeting on our lands in North Queensland.[41]

Nouvelles 1878 printed a report by Buchanan and Lacey from the *Black News Service* that discussed the arrests in Brisbane of Denis Walker, John Garcia, and Lacey, who were committed to educating the Aborigines of Queensland about the state's racist laws. They had attempted to raise money to build a school in the Palm Island reserve, which looked like "a concentration camp." Walker had gone to see the union president of the University of Queensland, to ask him to organize a Black festival to raise $10,000 for the construction of the school. However, they claimed, he was a police informant and recorded their entire conversation without Walker's knowledge. Lacey and Garcia were arrested as his accomplices. These men were facing fourteen years in prison for making armed threats "with the aim of extracting money." Signed, "Power to the People," the issue included Groupe 1878's petition in support of these activists, which was written at a meeting of Kanak revolutionary groups at Magenta Beach.[42]

Groupe 1878 first publicly announced its call for Kanak independence via *Nouvelles 1878*. After the protests of September 1974, the group pondered whether to build the political awareness of the Kanak on the political fringes of society or extend its actions to inform French policy on the colony. Members decided that they needed to get out of their "ghetto mindset" and decide on two positions—either work within the existing

Kanak parties (UM and UC) to form a single group or create an independence party from these groups.[43]

Initially, they opted for the first solution because the Kanak masses
formed the base of these parties and they felt it would be wise to not cut
themselves off from older generations of Kanak who were in the UC and
the UM. After conducting five months of information tours among rural
Kanak communities, they decided to form an anti-colonial revolutionary party from the ranks of the other groups. As anticipated, in 1975
Gorodey and young organizers of the Foulards Rouges and Groupe 1878
formed the Parti de Libération Kanak (PALIKA). They ran for office in
the Territorial Assembly and won two seats.[44]

Gorodey was a critical international voice of PALIKA. The NHNP's
Viewpoints frequently noted her activities and New Caledonia's independence struggle in general. For example, the paper printed a May 1976
message, written in French and English, by a group of New Hebridean
and New Caledonian students in Paris who referred to themselves as
"Free and Socialist." Signed, "Kanaks in Paris," the message described
how for the past three years these students had marched with French
workers, immigrants, and youth against the Giscard-Chirac minority government, which was responsible for "the economic pillage, the
exploitation of our peoples, the repression and terrorist aggression of
which the revolutionary militants are the victims." They denounced colonialism in New Caledonia and New Hebrides.[45]

In November 1976 *Viewpoints* detailed how students from New
Caledonia and New Hebrides occupied the student hostel Foyer in
Paris. They objected to the racist and colonialist demeanor of its White
director, a Madame Theate. They created an Administration Committee
to run the hostel. They saw the problem of the hostel as reflective of the
situation in Kalédonia—their takeover was a revolutionary step toward
national liberation.[46]

On the night of December 27, 1975, a twenty-two-year-old Kanak
named Richard Kamouda was beaten, shot, and killed by French police in
Nouméa. He and another individual were mock boxing when police arrived and attempted to arrest them. Kamouda was hit over the head with a
truncheon. When he tried to flee, a policeman shot him without warning
at point-blank range through the stomach. He died instantly.[47]

Kamouda's death triggered a wave of protests. On behalf of Groupe 1878, Plant wrote and internationally circulated reports on the affair. A little over an hour after the killing, some six hundred people marched to the residence of French secretary general Erignac. They shouted slogans such as "They've killed a Kanak brother," "Power to the Kanak People," and "Erignac—Assassin." They stayed there till about 4:00 a.m. This was followed by a group of two thousand protestors the next day. On each occasion, the demonstrators were met by police in full riot gear—helmets, visors, shields, truncheons, automatic rifles, and tear-gas grenades.[48]

Kamouda hailed from the village of Poindimié, some 320 kilometers away. French officials falsely told his family that he had been killed in a fight. The police placed barricades and roadblocks around the village, perhaps to prevent its residents from being informed about the truth by visitors. This enraged Melanesian communities across the entire island. His death's political significance was expressed at a Poindimié march with slogans such as, "The French State is responsible for this death." According to Plant, his death was "the latest symbol of France's much-resented colonial occupation of New Caledonia," which was "undoubtedly the most oppressive" in Oceania. According to Poigoune,

After 123 years of colonial rule, where are the Kanak people?—The Kanak is walking the streets of Nouméa, unemployed, drinking alcohol. He is busy playing the monkey, dancing, and singing in front of those who have stolen his land. The Kanak is in the sports fields, busily running after medals. And he is in the churches praying. The French have made the Kanak into great sportsmen and good Christians. But they have done NOTHING to prepare him for independence. We have no doctors, no architects, no economists, no engineers,—no cadres with which to run a country. The result of France's presence here is CATASTROPHIC. And yet there are still Kanaks who can say "Long live France, Long live the Motherland."[49]

The report called for local and international action, especially through the international connections that the Kanak independence movement had been able to build via the PWC, the Nuclear Free Pacific conference, and Gorodey's trip to the UN. Telegrams of support were to be sent to her. The report was sent to Australia's Black Resource Center, Fiji's Pacific People's Action Front (PPAF), Aotearoa's Third World Action Group and Ngā Tamatoa, the NHNP, Papua New Guinea's Meg Taylor, and Hawai'i's Micronesian Independence Support Committee.[50]

As demonstrators planned protests for January 1976, news of the incident spread across Oceania. In January 1976, on behalf of the NFP, Vanessa Griffen telegraphed Kalkot Mataskelekele of the NHNP about the need to organize in support of Nouméa's mass protests. Information about the demonstrations, forwarded by the PPAF, was printed in the NHNP's *Viewpoints*.[51]

In announcing the January protests, Gorodey released the following statement:

> To organize revolutionary combat is to show efficiency while avoiding as many losses as possible in our ranks, until there are in each tribe of the mainland and Loyalty Islands, action committees ready to lead a general uprising, ready to engage in armed struggle against the French colonialists. In order to kick out the French colonialists from here, in order to avenge the death of Kamouda, there must be a direct assault, not just by means of a demonstration at Nouméa, but in all corners of the Territory with well-organized groups. These who would like to organize these revolutionary groups or committees can make contact with us from now on. To kick out the colonial system, all the Kanak people must be organized and ready to take up arms.[52]

In the aftermath of the demonstrations, Gorodey and Naisseline were both arrested and charged with writing the pamphlet.[53]

In March 1976 Gorodey sent a letter to the New Hebrides National Party describing how she was being charged with "calling for murder," crime, looting, and "armed violence" because of the leaflet. At the time, Hilda Lini was editor of *Viewpoints*. She posted Gorodey's letter "to her sisters," which included the statement. Gorodey had been found guilty the day before by the attorney general.[54] The French administration claimed that her statement was a criminal call for an armed uprising that undermined "the integrity of the national territory" and could be tried by the State Security Court. Gorodey was thus liable to serve one to five years in prison. Naisseline had coauthored the leaflet, but had not yet

Figure 8.1. Hilda Lini at NHNP office, Vila, August 1976. Vanua'aku Pati Archives, National Archives of Vanuatu.

gone before the investigating judge, as he was home on Maré. But he was due to be charged, too.[55]

If the colonialists were intelligent, Gorodey argued, they would understand that it was not in their interest to imprison her and Naisseline via the State Security Court. This would allow them to influence public opinion in France and elsewhere on the issue of Kanak independence and the Kamouda affair in the context of an economic crisis, growing unemployment, and the 1977 municipal and territorial elections. However, she reasoned, it was also true that the French government had never backed down from repression, whether in Indochina, Algeria, Comoros, Djibouti, Tahiti, the West Indies, or New Caledonia.[56]

Gorodey refused to employ a lawyer for her pending trial. She wanted to politically explain herself to the "ultra-colonial court of Nouméa." She continued,

> We do not have to plead our "Defense" before such a court because we do not expect any leniency from the representatives of a law that is not ours. This court is that of the enemy and when it condemns us, we con-

sider ourselves prisoners of war. We must only use the courtroom as an offensive ground for the national liberation struggle in the same way as the street, the construction site, the office, the reserve, wherever colonialism prevails.[57]

A few days before she penned the letter, she was interrogated by an investigating judge who, for almost two hours, tried to have her state that the leaflet did not truly reflect her views, that she was "deep down" an intelligent, nonviolent pacifist who hoped for other solutions than armed struggle. The judge claimed to want to "stretch the pole," because she was going straight to the "slaughterhouse" for admitting that she encouraged her Kanak brothers to organize an armed uprising.[58]

Gorodey responded, "The slaughterhouse? I've been there with my people for a long time." She had "nothing to lose," and "it was the colonial system itself that had always incited the Kanaks to armed violence." She told the judge that there was no point in trying to change her mind—he could keep her there as long as he wanted but she would not change her position. Three times over, the judge proposed to see Gorodey "in a less professional atmosphere outside of his office" to discuss the matter. Gorodey refused, stating that they would still have a Day of Action, and would send the proceeds of sales of her statement to the Revolutionary Front for an Independent East Timor.[59]

She also informed the NHNP that PALIKA continued to do information tours every weekend in the reserves to stay in direct contact with the people. This was also to prepare for its first congress in May 1976, which was to occur on a reserve in Poindimié. PALIKA would not be formalized until after the congress. Also, the colonial authorities were intensifying their surveillance of activists amidst concerns that their international contacts and support for their struggle were becoming effective.[60]

In a separate letter, Gorodey spoke to the colonial administration's issues with their "international contacts." Earlier that month, Plant was not allowed to enter New Caledonia to meet with Kanak leaders. He was deported to Paris. When Gorodey inquired about the incident, she was told by the head of the General Intelligence Service that Plant could not enter the territory because he was "registered" in the opposition. As he had been in the country for two weeks the past December, this decision must have occurred since the uprisings.[61]

In November 1976 *Viewpoints* noted that Gorodey and Naisseline had addressed the charges in court. The paper saw the trial as an attempt to stop the movement for independence. In January 1977 Gorodey wrote to the NHNP, thanking her "Seli Hoo" brothers and sisters for welcoming her in Vanuatu in November and December 1976. On behalf of PALIKA, she appreciated their solidarity, particularly after Kamouda's assassination. This alliance was also shown by their reception of Naisseline, the NHNP's mention of French colonialism before the UN Committee on Decolonization, and Walter Lini's stance before the 1976 South Pacific Forum. Gorodey stressed that the NHNP's fight was the same as PALIKA's, and the same battle being waged against colonialism and imperialism across the world. This was also because Oceania was being held by the "claws of international capitalism" through companies like Shell and Burns Philp and capitalist powers such as France, the United States, England, Japan, and Australia. These powers used (neo) colonialism in Oceania to exploit its riches. "Born of colonized parents," she wrote, "we daily suffer a system which denies our existence as human beings." Colonialism did not offer life—it offered slow death. The struggle for national liberation was against colonial death and history, as colonialism had imposed upon them "a history of hate, bloodshed, violence and death." They were creating a history that could not coexist or work with the colonial system, which needed to disappear. The Kanak and New Hebridean brother peoples would win through the mutual solidarity and support displayed between the NHNP and PALIKA.[62]

Viewpoints continued to discuss the trial of Naisseline and Gorodey. It printed photographs of Gorodey's trip to New Hebrides that past summer. In February 1977 it featured an iconic photograph of Walter Lini, George Kalkoa, Peter Taurokoto, and Naisseline during a 1976 meeting in Vanuatu. Written in Bislama, the caption referenced how Naisseline and Gorodey were awaiting trial.[63]

In February 1977 Gorodey was sentenced to two weeks' imprisonment. Naisseline received a suspended sentence of two months and a fine. The officer who killed Kamouda was given a suspended sentence of two weeks' imprisonment. In July *Viewpoints* noted that Gorodey

Figure 8.2. Nidoïsh Naisseline and George Kalkoa, 1976. Vanua'aku Pati Archives, National Archives of Vanuatu.

was suddenly arrested and jailed for the statement. That September she released another statement about PALIKA's fight for the political, economic, and cultural independence of the Kanak people. The party was organizing around political independence and land rights, as Kanak were placed on reserves totaling 3,700 square kilometers. Meanwhile, land for White cattle ranchers amounted to 4,000 square kilometers. Nickel companies robbed the country's soil but also were destroying New Caledonia with pollution. As state repression and surveillance of the group intensified, it had become impossible to hold public meetings in Nouméa. France continued to militarize the archipelago, which contained two thousand troops and gendarmes. PALIKA aimed to focus on political education over the next year, which meant explaining to the people the links between oppression, French imperialism, and capitalism. The conservative UC was still the largest party of the Kanak, who were also influenced by the churches, which considered PALIKA "morally lost" because it did not exclude the possibility of revolutionary violence. But every time that the group staged a nonviolent protest, it faced "the violence of the police and army." While PALIKA did not advocate violence, it held that revolutionary violence might be a necessary reply to colonialist violence. The group had "no illusions on this question."[64]

One Single Front against Imperialism

Libya, New Caledonia, and Oceania

In April 1987 Libyan leader Mu'ammar Qaddafi hosted some three hundred delegates from over sixty liberation organizations from across Oceania and East Asia at a Pacific Peace Conference in Tripoli, Libya. In an eclectic address recorded by Tripoli's Television Service, Qaddafi called for these freedom fighters to form "one single front" against US, British, and French imperialism in Oceania that stretched across the Pacific and Atlantic Oceans. He linked the indigenous struggles of Vanuatu, Australia, New Zealand, New Caledonia, and Hawai'i to those of Libya, Grenada, and Nicaragua. Qaddafi argued that the peoples of Oceania, Central and Latin America, Africa, and Asia shared a common destiny—they were all targets of imperialism because they were colored, Black, poor, or small in number and landmass. But Libya, he asserted, did not fear imperialism and would courageously lead this international fighting force.[1]

Political poetry aside, these declarations were voiced not only by Qaddafi. Participants from Oceania identified with the conference's pledge to combat colonialism, racism, imperialism, and apartheid. These included New Caledonia's Yann Céléné Uregei, a leader of the United Kanak Liberation Front (FULK). FULK was a member of the Kanak Socialist Liberation Front (FLNKS), a coalition group pushing for political independence for New Caledonia. Uregei was joined by the likes of Barak Sope, secretary-general of the Vanua'aku Party, Vanuatu's foreign minister, Sela Molisa, Rex Rumakiek of the Revolutionary Provisional Government of West Papua, and Tasmania's Michael Mansell. One of FULK's representatives stayed in Libya for several months to receive technical, agricultural, and security training.[2]

This was not Uregei's first visit to Libya. In fact, he had traveled to Tripoli in 1984 along with Éloi Machoro, oft referred to as the "Che

Figure 9.1. Kanak insurgents, New Caledonia, 1984. Museum of New Zealand, Te Papa Tongarewa, Wellington, New Zealand. Photograph by Bruce Connew.

Figure 9.2. Éloi Machoro, 1985. Photograph by Bruce Connew.

Guevara" of New Caledonia. According to Melbourne's *Age*, in September 1984 seventeen FULK members received a month's training in Tripoli in "the use of firearms, explosives and protective security." Upon their return from Libya, Machoro, a former schoolteacher and mason, actively organized against the year's elections. In November 1984 he chopped open a ballot box with an axe; a photograph of him doing so became an international symbol of Kanak liberation. Along with his *machochos*, he took over the city of Thio. They closed its nickel mines, took over boats and trucks, and drove off the French military. Machoro was assassinated by French police snipers in January 1985.[3]

Uregei was born in 1932 in Lifou, New Caledonia. A schoolteacher, he studied agriculture at France's Bureau for the Development of Agricultural Production from 1959 to 1960. Upon his return to New Caledonia, he joined and became a minister of the multiethnic Caledonian Union (UC). Influenced by the radicalism of the student movement and concerned with the moderation of the UC, in 1971 he formed the Union Multiraciale of New Caledonia (UMNC) as the first all-Kanak party. By 1975, Uregei advocated complete independence from France. This was amidst firm resistance from the French government; in July 1975 Oliver Stirn, French minister for the overseas territories, publicly declared that autonomy for New Caledonia was impossible.[4]

In July 1976 *New Hebridean Viewpoints* printed a statement by UMNC's Sixth Congress, which clearly outlined the party's political views:

> Considering the policy of colonial exploitation carried out by France in its former territories which have become independent; Considering that the Kanaks are absent from their ancestral lands which have been stolen and pillaged by French colonialism; Considering the absence of Kanaks in all the spheres of activity, after 122 years of French colonization; Considering that Kanaks did not have the right to secondary education, this being reserved only for Europeans (1853–1953); Considering that from 55,000 Kanaks, only 4 per year pass university entrance examinations, whereas the smaller European population produces 200; Considering the policy of "departmentalization" imposed by the French Government contrary to the aspirations of the people; Considering the appropriation by the French Government of the country's nickel; Considering that

Kanak independence is claimed by most Kanak members of the Territorial Assembly . . . ; Considering the decolonization policies of the United Nations; Considering the accession to independence of the Comoros and soon the Afars and Issas [Djibouti] as well as the New Hebrides; [the 6th Congress of the Union Multiracial] invites the United Nations to observe and apply its policies of decolonization so that New Caledonia could rapidly gain independence like other Pacific countries.[5]

In 1977 the UMNC charged Jean-Gabriel Eriau, French high commissioner in the Pacific, with following "personal and aberrant policies in New Caledonia" after he publicly declared that those who took "separatist paths would be liable for punishment under security laws." The party argued that he did not understand the process of decolonization that had occurred in the Comoros Islands, Djibouti, and New Hebrides.[6] In 1977 the party transformed into FULK, which was more aggressive in its calls for sovereignty.

In 1979 Jean-Marie Tjibaou, vice president of the UC and former mayor of the city of Hienghène, formed the International Front (IF). The front included the Caledonian Socialist Party, the Parti de Libération Kanak (PALIKA), the Melanesian Progressive Union (UPM), FULK, and the UC. It pushed for socialism and total independence for indigenous peoples. It aimed to obtain international recognition of the Kanak people's rights to self-determination and independence, to denounce colonialism and French imperialism in Oceania, and to associate Kanak peoples with all people struggling against colonialism and imperialism.[7]

Born in 1936 on Grande Terre and heavily educated in the Catholic Church, Tjibaou traveled to France in 1968 to study at Lyon's Institut catholique and later at the prestigious École pratique des hautes études in Paris. He read missionary Maurice Leenhardt's progressive works on Melanesian culture and attended a seminar with Roger Bastide, whose research on Afro-Brazilian cultural syncretism and applied anthropology influenced his own interests in traditional Kanak culture. Tjibaou's grandmother had been shot and killed in the uprising of 1917, and this made a great impact on his political consciousness. His rise to acclaim was marked by his 1975 organization of MELANESIA 2000, a two-week cultural festival in Nouméa. Attended by several thousand people, this was a major internationalist effort to highlight the cultural and cosmological affinities across Melanesia and Oceania. Referencing ni-Vanuatu, Māori, and Papuans, Tjibaou argued that whenever Oceanians were around Westerners or Asians, they always possessed a "feeling of complicity." They shared a cultural affinity based on "a sharing of concepts used to explain the world, relationships within society, with the land, with the gods, or future." One did not find the same affinity among Westerners, and there was always the need to explain Pacific cultures to others.[8]

Financially sponsored by the colonial state, in a moment when the Kanak community was overtly making radical demands dangerous to colonial power, the merits of MELANESIA 2000 were hotly debated among Kanak. An undated letter to the Vanua'aku Party described MELANESIA 2000 as not truly "aimed at promoting Kanak culture." Rather, the letter argued, the festival represented the interests of the system and was a distraction for the Kanak, particularly at a time of rampant inflation, meagre incomes, and hollow promises of economic recovery.[9] But Tjibaou's leadership of the front is testimony to his political shrewdness and ability to incorporate varying political factions and individuals under one banner.

Uregei was instrumental in building the front's international relationships across Oceania, Africa, and the Americas.[10] In November 1978 the American embassy based in Fiji informed the US secretary of state that Uregei had submitted a letter to delegates to Nouméa's Eighteenth South Pacific Conference, addressed to the prime minister of Tuvalu. The letter noted that Uregei, on behalf of FULK, had been traveling with the Vanua'aku Party across the world to inform the United Nations and several countries about the liberation struggle of the Kanak people, who were threatened by French colonial policies of departmentalization, annexation, and violence. New Caledonia was "on its way to becoming a New Rhodesia," and French colonialism was certain to lead to a civil war, as it had in Algeria. Kanak wanted "their independence immediately."[11]

Uregei asked to be permitted to address the conference's delegates and attached to the letter a petition that he submitted to the UN's Special Committee on Decolonization in July 1978. He had traveled to the UN in New York with Vanua'aku Party leader George Kalkoa. Both men hoped to meet with Andrew Young, US ambassador to the United Nations. Palias Matane, Papua New Guinea's ambassador to the United States and the UN, approached Young's office to arrange the meeting, but their requests were denied.[12]

The petition cited the UN General Assembly's 1960 declaration that all peoples had "a right to self-determination." It stated that Kanak were the only legitimate people in New Caledonia and, created by God as a united culture, they had been the prey of French colonialism since 1853. The French stole their land by military force and invasion. Out of 200,000 people in 1927, there were only 26,000 Kanak left, who lived in harsh conditions on reserves. Colonial power scoffed at Kanak customs in an effort to eliminate their identity and oblige them to be French. France had taken the natural resources of the Kanak and given them to the Caledonian capitalists, creating the "first industrial capitalistic nickel society." In 1978 French prime minister Jacques Chirac declared that France's overseas territories would remain parts of the country, a policy that would end up in violence, as it had in French Algeria. The fundamentally capitalistic colonial state created a "French Rhodesia when the French Parliament voted a law to set up one white electorate and one black electorate." Uregei pressed the issue of Rhodesia: "The UN and France condemned the Rhodesia of Ian Smith and the colonizers and proclaimed the legitimacy of the Black people. They demanded that the independence of the Black people be an established right. In Caledonia, the Kanak people are the only legitimate people." They accepted their responsibility to lead the liberation struggle. The document also reached out to French citizens in France, asserting that as the people accepted the abolition of empire in Africa, Indochina, and Comoros, why not New Caledonia? The situation was complicated by the support of colonialism by settlers from Europe, Africa, Asia, and Oceania. But the Kanak liberation struggle would also free the country's growing exploited migrant labor class from colonialism. Still, only Kanak had the right to vote for independence. Uregei asked the UN to put its case before the Special Committee of 24 and to send a mission to New Caledonia.[13]

The government of France still considered its colonies in the Pacific geopolitically significant. Given a recent boost in the nickel industry, New Caledonia remained a critical source for the metal, which was used in the construction of missiles and tank armor. French president De Gaulle launched nuclear testing programs in Algeria, and, upon its independence, transferred these programs to Tahiti. In 1982 the South Pacific Forum took "a soft line on" its independence. The IF sought to have the UN describe New Caledonia as a colonial territory; it also demanded that France commit to independence for New Caledonia, and that the front be recognized as its sole representative. The forum took place a month after White *colons* stormed the Territorial Assembly. They were challenging the debate on reforms that would allow White-held lands to be returned to the Kanak owners.[14]

The French state and *caldoches* responded to the increasing calls for independence with violent repression. *Povai* covered these occurrences extensively. Via an agreement between the Pacific People's Action Front, the Vanua'aku Party, and the Vanuatu Pacific Community Center (VPCC), by 1981 *Povai* was printed as an insert of *Viewpoints*. In 1981 it reported that "another Kanak," Emile Kutu, "had died through colonial violence, killed by a bullet fired by a Colon." When a *colon* refused to pay one of his workers, he shot Kutu, who happened to be sharing a car with the employee. Pierre Declerq the UC's secretary general, was brutally shot and murdered that year as well. *Povai* condemned the shocking assassination of Declerq who was French, stressing that the news alarmed "the whole Pacific islands," but "most affected Melanesians," who emotionally "shared the same customs of the indigenous people of New Caledonia." As the *wantok* system was strong across Oceania, the killings of Kanak leaders were painful for all Melanesian peoples. Vanuatu's prime minister, Walter Lini, denounced the assassination, and the Vanua'aku Party released a communiqué calling for independence for New Caledonia. The VPCC called on organizations to support the movement, and the IF received messages from over twenty groups to be read at the funeral. A Ponape, Micronesia, conference called for September 24 to be an International Solidarity Day for New Caledonia; students at the University of Papua New Guinea demonstrated at the French embassy there.[15]

In January 1981 Maila Uregei, John Lao, and Yann Uregei visited Vanuatu to invite the Vanua'aku Party to attend the UMNC's Eleventh Congress. Uregei also hoped to have more young New Caledonians study and train in Vanuatu's cooperatives. He also hoped for another group to come to New Caledonia and "train [Kanaks] as an Army." The Vanua'aku Party decided to send Sela Molisa, Kai Patterson, Kalkot Mataskelele, and Sope to the congress. The French denied Molisa a visa. Sope, who was the country's most senior civil servant, found out that his visa was cancelled upon arrival in New Caledonia. He felt that Vanuatu's government had to respond with "appropriate diplomatic action."[16] Within twenty-four hours, Sope personally expelled the French ambassador.

At the time, Pauulu Kamarakafego was working in rural development in Vanuatu. He picked up Sope from Vanuatu's airport, swearing up and down what they would do to the French. Kamarakafego was livid. In reference to his deportation in 1975, Sope said, "With what they did to you, we have to expel them." The two went together to the French colonial office and had him removed.[17]

Uregei, as secretary general, opened the congress of the UMNC and the IF by saluting "the memory of . . . Robert Poararhe, Kamouda, Baptiste. . . . They left like so many other activists, but the word they taught us remained alive for ourselves and for the hearts and consciences of our future generations." The congress was "the best demonstration of the continuity of their struggle." Future generations could be told that thanks to these elders, "the good seed" had grown, the plant was "taking root more," the struggle continued, and Kanak socialist independence was coming soon. He also talked about the struggle's relationship with Vanuatu, as the Vanua'aku Party's December 1980 congress declared,

> The people of Vanuatu and the Kanak people are united strongly against . . . French colonialism [in] New Caledonia. Delegates hope and believe that the people of Vanuatu and the Kanak people will be able to reclaim the lands that the colonialists stole from our ancestors. After 70 years under the colonialism of France and England Vanuatu has finally gained its independence, but Vanuatu's independence cannot be true if Kanak independence does not happen. . . . The independence of Vanuatu is an example to show the Kanak people that they too can achieve this independence. To help New Caledonia achieve so-called independence the Kanak people must have all the support of . . . the other Melanesian islands. To help the independence of New Caledonia the Vanua'aku Pati as well as the Government of Vanuatu must take a clear position to bring it real support.[18]

The congress agreed that it was necessary for the Vanua'aku Party and the IF to work together. It felt that the strongest way to help New

Caledonia was to obtain the government's permission to broadcast on Vanuatu radio information about the Kanak struggle. It needed the government of Vanuatu and the Vanua'aku Party to defend the Kanak struggle in international bodies like the UN, the South Pacific Forum, and the Commonwealth Congress. Uregei stated that when he was last in Vanuatu, Lini had informed him that he would submit the issue of New Caledonian independence at the forum's upcoming meeting in Port Vila.[19]

In June 1982 *Povai* released a special issue on New Caledonia. It noted how a new Governing Council with a majority pro-independence body was elected by New Caledonia's Territorial Assembly. This included Tjibaou as its vice president, and Yvonne Hnnada, Nidoïsh Naisse-line, Yeiwéné, and Machoro.[20] *Povai* printed the following statement in French:

> Since ATAI in 1878, the Kanak people, like all colonized peoples of the world, have not allowed themselves to be invaded without resistance to the colonizer. The Kanak tribes rose up against French colonization. . . . September 24th is the affirmation every year of the presence of French colonialism. . . . The Kanak people are reminded of the colonialist and racist repression, even better, the military deployment, the armed presence in the heart of the tribes in operations to intimidate the population. The history of colonial repression of the Kanak people is already long enough to list. Many violent [acts of] brutality against young, old, and female activists are still remembered. . . . It is simply necessary to quote in memory, on this day of mourning, those who fell under the bullets of the assassins armed by colonialism. Thus: 1878—ATAI, 1917—NOËL, 1975—KAMOUDA, 1979—DAYE, 1981—DECLERCQ.[21]

Furthermore, it argued, September 24 celebrated "the alienation of the Kanak people's culture" and the savage repression of Kanak activists, and groups such as the Foulards Rouges, Groupe 1878, and the UC.[22]

The issue included a statement by the group Kanak Socialist Liberation (LKS), formed by Naisseline after a split in PALIKA. The LKS critiqued a cultural event of the IF on September 24. It argued that the day should not be "limited to cultural encounters between the different communities" in New Caledonia, as Kanak culture could not be fully expressed until it had freed itself from colonialism. It implied that these kinds of events would take on a problematic folkloric character. The LKS saw September 24 as a Kanak Day of Mourning, even as leftist leaders partook in it. However, it argued, only the LKS could "lift the mourning." Cultural demonstrations devoid of political content without an informed consciousness of struggle could be dangerous. Folklore only made "the masses sleep" and disoriented them at the expense of economic development. The IF's platform unconditionally combined political, economic, and cultural independence. As such, LKS wanted to participate in the event with a focus on work, the spreading of information and economic awareness, and the implementation of economic structures that would allow the Kanak people to remove colonial mentalities. Indeed, Nouméa was part of Kanaky Earth. Uregei and other writers also wrote specifically about colonialism's "folklorization" of Melanesian culture, as their communities were used to attract tourists.[23]

In 1984 the International Front pushed for "Kanak socialist independence" through armed struggle. With Tjibaou as its president, it joined FLNKS, including PALIKA, FULK, UC, and the Kanak and Exploited Women Syndicate (GFKEL). That December Tjibaou founded and was elected president of the "Provisional Government of Kanaky." Uregei became its minister of external relations and Machoro its security minister. This formation of a Provisional Government caused a major "stir" in France. France claimed that it would speed up the process of self-determination and possible independence. This position was violently rejected by French *caldoches*, who increased their physical attacks on Kanak leaders. Clashes also broke out between French police and soldiers and Kanak activists.[24]

In December 1984 two of Tjibaou's brothers and eight other unarmed Kanak were murdered by French *caldoches* in a brutal nighttime ambush in Hienghène. As their caravan was forced to stop because of a felled tree on the road, a dynamite blast hit and set the first truck on fire. The group was set upon by armed attackers, and some travelers were ruthlessly killed at point-blank range. Tjibaou's brother Louis was found dead, his body riddled with thirty bullets and shotgun pellets. In a case that was dropped by the French government after some twenty-one months, the group of some seventeen attackers was not charged. The French magistrate claimed that they acted in self-defense, despite

Figure 9.3. Kanak insurgents read inaccurate story in *Paris Match*, New Caledonia, 1984. Photograph by Bruce Connew.

Figure 9.4. Farmer-insurgents spend one week in three doing duty based at a farmhouse on the outskirts of Thio, New Caledonia, 1984. Photograph by Bruce Connew.

several witnesses who claimed otherwise, including seven survivors from that night.[25] Machoro was killed by French police snipers the following January.[26]

Uregei's 1982 essay "New Caledonia: Confrontation to Colonial Rule" foretold of this coming violence. It was published in *Politics in Melanesia*, edited by Ron Crocombe and Ahmed Ali and printed by the University of the South Pacific's Institute for Pacific Studies. "New Caledonia" argued that France used fascist tactics to suppress liberation struggles in Algeria, Africa, and Indochina, and New Caledonia was facing these same threats.[27]

The *Boston Globe* announced that France was to send a thousand more troops into the colony. London's *Guardian* compared the White settler society in New Caledonia to that of Algeria; in fact, many of its *pied-noirs* actually went to New Caledonia after the Algerian Revolution. The *Wall Street Journal* reported that "when the French think of New Caledonia, they inevitably think of Algeria."[28]

Indeed, the situation in New Caledonia had resonance for the Black Francophone world, particularly in France's colonies such as Guadeloupe, Martinique, and Reunion. In November 1984 French officials arrested Guadeloupean Luc Reinette, the thirty-four-year-old leader of the Caribbean Revolutionary Alliance, after a bombing earlier that month. Operating since at least 1982, the alliance had claimed responsibility for some fifteen bomb attacks in one week of May 1983 against "symbols of colonialism" in Guadeloupe, Martinique, and French Guiana. Guadeloupean activists linked the arrests to the "continuing disturbances" in New Caledonia. According to the radio station of Claude Makouke's Popular Union for the Liberation of Guadeloupe, the arrests were done to reassure the French "partisans of colonialism." "There will be dead and wounded and people put into prison," the radio station broadcast, "but that will not stop Guadeloupe from seizing its national independence." As passionately recalled by Maryse Condé, in 1987 French officials arrested Reinette and two other leaders of the Popular Movement for the Independence of Guadeloupe (MPGI) for terrorist acts.[29]

News reports from across the globe claimed that these acts were due to a "New Caledonian contagion." Calgary's *Herald* claimed that advocates of Guadeloupe's independence felt that rebels in New Caledonia had gained concessions from France through violence, and that they should follow suit through armed struggle. It argued that *la contagion* had allowed the island's leaders to broaden their audience among Guadeloupe's Black majority.[30]

In September 1985 the *Miami Herald* reported that France realized that anti-colonialism in New Caledonia and activism against French nuclear testing in Tahiti had created a domino effect that was impacting Guadeloupe. The conservative Parisian paper *Le Figaro* wrote, "If we lose New Caledonia, we may lose Polynesia. If we lose Polynesia, we lose Mururoa, the site of our nuclear experiments. And if we lose Mururoa, we endanger Kourou, our spaceport in Guiana . . . and then we endanger all of our overseas departments in the Caribbean threatened by separatist and Communist minorities." The *Herald* reported on Makouke's "Conference of the Last French Colonies." Held on April 5–7, in the Guadeloupe village of Anse-Bertrand, it was attended by some thirty leaders from New Caledonia, Martinique, French Guiana, Reunion, and the Comoros, who were to join a thousand other attendees in Guadeloupe. The groups signed a joint declaration that pledged independence from France. Chaired by Marc Pulvar, member of the Movement for

Figure 9.5. Jean Marie Tjibaou, Kanaky New Caledonia, December 1984. Photograph by Bruce Connew.

Independence of Martinique, the meeting declared support for the national liberation struggles against French colonialism, asserted that the right to independence and national sovereignty did not need to be negotiated, and asserted that French colonialism was a form of genocide.[31]

Makouke, a former political prisoner, had helped to organize Groupe d'Organization National pour le Guadeloupe (GONG) and was imprisoned in the aftermath of the country's May 1967 protests. According to the *Sydney Morning Herald*, Makouke repudiated terrorism but asserted that people were "entitled to use every means available to convince the colonialists to leave." His Popular Union supported two radio stations in Pointe-à-Pitre and its weekly paper had a circulation of eight thousand. Across the country's towns and villages, one could find graffiti denouncing colonialism and linking "the Guadeloupean cause to the Kanak people of New Caledonia." Kanaky also had the support of Michel Kapel and French Guiana's National Anti-Imperialist and Anti-Colonialist Party (PANGA). The *Herald* also reported that Libyan and Guadeloupe delegations had visited one another.[32]

Libya and the Pacific Peace Conference

This was the context of Qaddafi's hosting of the 1987 Pacific Peace Conference, which was both one of the strongest and one of the most complicated acts of solidarity with Oceania anti-colonial struggles made by an African head of state. Qaddafi informed the gathering that their meeting at Libya's Gulf Sidra was a "link in the chain of encounters with the world revolutionary forces," as he had previously met there with global revolutionary forces. Now, the conference brought together freedom fighters from Oceania, East Asia, and other parts of the world.[33]

Qaddafi asserted that they were there to tell the world that they had formed one single front of freedom fighters that stretched from the Pacific to the Atlantic Ocean. In response, imperial agents from Australia and New Zealand fabricated "a rabid campaign" against them. According to the law of imperialists, he argued, man was valued according to the amount of money, land, fortunes, and large populations that he owned. These materialistic criteria denied the principles of peace, freedom, and the right to life of small islands such as Vanuatu or the Solomon Islands.

Colonialists did not "recognize Grenada" because it was a small island of 100,000 people.[34] He continued,

> Look at the . . . ethics of imperialists. Their rotten criteria are that small people, the poor, the colored and the Blacks have no right to live on the earth; they should be food for imperialism to swallow. Ourselves, our islands, and our strategic regions should be for the benefit of imperialism. Why? Because we are colored, because we are black, became we are small in number, because we are poor. You in the South Pacific, in East Asia, you are not part of America, the United States, and you are not part of Britain. In what capacity does the US and Britain protest when you move from our countries to another country in the world, to any place in the world? What is this encroachment? They impose a ban on the freedom or the movement of people.[35]

Imperialism understood only the "language of confrontation and force." The imperialists wanted to swallow "us one after the other." After Grenada it was Nicaragua, Libya, and now Vanuatu, whose prospects for independence angered imperialists. They had "installed themselves as guardians of independent Vanuatu." They now wanted to transfer their confrontations to the Pacific, where they maintained that if their bombs and missiles fell on New Caledonia, Vanuatu, or the Solomons, there would be only marginal losses—the deaths of Solomon Islanders were "preferable to deaths in Belgium, France, Britain, or Germany." In other words, he stated, "the blood of Solomon Islanders is cheap, while the blood of Europeans is expensive."[36]

This was related to Angela Gilliam's concept of "killability ratio," according to which societies are considered more advanced based on their ability to kill. If peoples were portrayed as backwards or stuck in the past, then their views about the future "are dismissed as irrelevant, unimportant, and unsophisticated." They are also savagely dangerous, particularly if they use traditional weapons such as spears. On the other hand, the society that is technologically capable of killing hundreds or thousands in warfare is often deemed to be a more advanced culture.[37]

Pointing at a map of Oceania, Qaddafi found this logic to be "cause for laughter and ridicule." Why would they not conduct nuclear tests in the North Sea or Europe? Because if dropped in Oceania, he reasoned, the bombs damaged only the lives of Pacific Islanders and not those of the "Atlanticists." As such, the imperial powers experimented on Pacific peoples as "if they were mice." This was also the case in South Africa, where Blacks were not considered human beings. They killed Black people to give life to Whites. The American bombing of Japan was testimony that the imperialists "preferred Asians to die." It had since been decided that the Pacific Ocean would be sacrificed. They did not want the world to know about Oceania, "whose voices would be heard inside the UN, the Nonaligned Movement, and other Asian-African organizations." As such, they falsified statistics about their lives, and fabricated lies that served their "filthy, antilife, antipeace, antifreedom, and antipeople policies."[38]

Qaddafi reasoned that France had "no regard" for the people of New Caledonia or Martinique. They had occupied Reunion, Chad, Gabon, and the Comoros because of claims that French inhabitants lived there. "No," he asserted, "Reunion is African." Libya's international center was the meeting of the peoples of Africa, Latin America, the Pacific, and Palestine who were fighting racism, Zionism, imperialism, and fascism. The United States, with "phony arrogance," picked quarrels with Grenada and Libya and failed. France, America, Israel, Britain, NATO, and racists were all the enemies of peace and threatened Oceania and small nations. As such, Oceania had a "common destiny with the peoples of Central and Latin America, Africa, and Asia." He called for an international anti-imperialist, antiracist, antifascist, anti-reactionary, and anti-Zionist front that would allow "small states and small dispersed islands" to have collective weight. Libya did not fear imperialism. It would lead the front and build economic and revolutionary cooperation with Pacific peoples to abolish nuclear tests and to create peace.[39]

The conference attracted grassroots activists from across the world. According to Britain's Foreign and Commonwealth Office, these included the Nation of Islam's (NOI) Louis Farrakhan, the American Indian Movement, and, from Britain, members of Britain's NOI, Spartacus R of Brixton's Cultural Awareness Program, Lester Lewis (Prince Ntum ba Azah) of Hackney's Black Peoples Association, and the "Black militant" Kuba Assegai.[40]

Michael Mansell, chairperson of the Tasmanian Aboriginal Center, highlighted the "collective murder and oppression" of his people since "the coming of the White man to Australia." White men continued to "liquidate" Aborigines in ways similar to what they had done upon their arrival. Mansell stated that their treatment was worse than South African apartheid and similar to the US terrorism against indigenous peoples and their attacks on the Great Jamahiriya of Libya. His speech was followed by delegates from Hawai'i, the National Alliance for Justice, Freedom and Democracy, the Moro Islamic Liberation Front of the Philippines, and Zaini Abdullah of Sumatra's Free Aceh Movement.[41]

The thirty-five-year-old Mansell, a lawyer and former league footballer, spent two weeks in Libya; he returned a year later with a larger delegation of Aboriginal activists. While still in Tripoli, Australia's *Age* called his hotel for an interview. Mansell informed the paper that it was a "bloody sad reflection" that Australian media were concerned about his opinions only when they were being made in a foreign city. When asked whether he sought help from revolutionary groups such as the Mathaba to support the cause for Aboriginal sovereignty, Mansell's simple response was "yes." Were these groups terrorists? This was "a matter of opinion. . . . If you look at the history of Aboriginal people, our country was invaded by a bunch of terrorists from England, and the fruits of that terrorist activity are now vested in the Australian Government who refuse to give it up to Aboriginal people. So who is the terrorist?" He stated that the Mathaba had agreed to his request to recognize Australia as a country of two nations—one being Aboriginal. He supported the Palestine Liberation Organization and the Libyan people, who had expressed support for Aboriginal peoples. He denounced terrorism— "eighteen Aboriginal people had died in police custody the previous year." The Australian government had the power to stop this practice but did not. He asked, "Were they not the terrorists themselves for refusing to act?"[42]

The Pacific Peace Conference's final statement declared that "the peoples of east Asia, Australia, and the Oceanic islands, through revolutionary and progressive organizations, liberation movements, and peace movements met in the *Great Jamahiriyah*" under the banner of "The Strategy of Confrontation Against Imperialism and Neocolonialism." There, they studied the global impact of Zionism and racism on "small peoples and nations." They considered Qaddafi's speech a basis for a future action plan that could challenge this imminent threat to their existence. The statement rejected US and French imperialist agents who criticized Libya's role in Oceania. Libya aimed to usher in a new world where justice, peace, and friendship prevailed, away from imperialist use of the Pacific for military operations and nuclear experiments. The revolutionary and progressive forces in the Pacific confirmed their membership in the International Center for the Combat of Imperialism, Zionism, Racism, Reaction, and Fascism and their intent to establish an international people's front that sought the freedom of small peoples, the unity of their lands, and preservation of their heritage, culture, and identity. They also sought to free the Pacific from imperialist bases and aggressive interventions.[43]

Uregei soon announced that FULK had joined the international front that was founded in Libya "to combat colonialism, racism, imperialism, apartheid and other forms of oppression." Allegedly, Uregei informed Libya's Jamahiriyah News Agency (JANA) that France had "entered New Caledonia with rifles" and thus needed to be thrown "out with rifles." In response, the FLNKS leadership began to distance itself from Uregei amidst feelings that it would lose regional and international support if it appeared to be influenced by Qaddafi. Yeiwéné informed Agence France-Presse that Uregei did not speak for the entire group. While FLNKS accepted Libya's moral and financial support, it rejected any offers of military aid. Uregei was temporarily suspended from his position as "foreign minister" for attending the talks.[44]

The next month, Qaddafi received the secretary general of the Liberation Movement of Reunion, who presented a "tormenting picture of the dreadful danger" resulting from French nuclear tests carried out in the Pacific and Indian Oceans. He said that the masses on these islands lived in terror and were threatened with extermination due to French nuclear testing. He claimed that France had sunk one island after carrying out more than sixty nuclear tests there.[45]

As Qaddafi explored these relationships further, the Voice of America claimed that Libya had stepped up efforts to provoke "a wave of sabotage" in Oceania. Central Intelligence Agency officials reported that Tripoli was securing its contacts in Oceania, as Qaddafi attempted to solidify his leadership in the Global South by undermining US and French influence in the region. Working through Libya's People's Bureaus in Kuala Lumpur and Canberra, Qaddafi had indeed built relationships with New Caledonia's liberation struggle. The governments of Australia, France, and New Zealand spurned these linkages. Australian prime minister Bob Hawke claimed that Qaddafi had offered funds to Aboriginal communities to establish a separate nation. These officials saw these overtures as Qaddafi's "ambitious global initiative to increase Libyan ties to leftist and radical groups and guerrilla and terrorist organizations in Latin America and the Caribbean, Africa, and Western Europe." He had redoubled these efforts "since the US airstrikes on Libya in April 1986." They believed that Tripoli was trying to build a regional network in Oceania to support Libyan subversion in much the same way it had operated in the Caribbean. Qaddafi had "grandiose plans" for this network to forge a united front of "revolutionary forces" to engage in a "collective struggle" against imperialism. They felt that he sought to "cultivate indigenous radicals and identify potential surrogates to carry out violent activities" via Tripoli's Mathaba, or World Center for Resistance to Imperialism, Zionism, Racism, Reactionism, and Fascism. Founded in 1982, the center's overt purpose was to coordinate Libyan assistance to liberation groups. New Caledonia's independence appeared to be one of Tripoli's major interests in Oceania. The CIA believed that Qaddafi's campaign to "liberate" French colonies such as New Caledonia was partly in reaction to French and US military aggression in Africa, including Chad.[46]

On the cusp of an approaching South Pacific Forum meeting, pushback against the Libya meeting came swiftly. In late April, Australia's Security Committee recommended that its government "maintain a diplomatic environment" in Oceania that was "hostile to Libyan activity," and undertake a campaign to this end that included sending senior officials to talk to other governments in the region, closely monitoring Libyan activities, possible interdiction (travel restrictions and prevention of fund transfers by Libya), long-term programs to further Australian interests in the region, improving Radio Australia broadcasts across Oceania (particularly in Vanuatu) and giving greater priority to Oceania in the Special Visitors program.[47]

The Australian Security Information Organization (ASIO) assessed the risk of Libyan retaliation (such as terrorist attacks) if Australia expelled Canberra's Libyan People's Bureau or challenged Libyan intervention in Oceania via public and diplomatic measures. ASIO found that the closure of the bureau would unlikely result in a terrorist attack from Libya. There were also serious discussions about the establishment of a bureau in Vila, Vanuatu.[48]

Meanwhile, Australia's foreign minister publicly claimed that a "small number of Aboriginal activists" who were "seeking support from Libya [were] misrepresenting their race." After talks with New Zealand's prime minister, he asserted that recent statements made by "extremist Aboriginal elements in Libya were not supported by most Aborigines." He would not discuss such Libyan involvement with Aborigines, except to say that such action was very foolish. He "did not think it was wise for people to be dealing" with Libya, and Australia's Blacks who did so were not authentic voices.[49]

In May 1987 the Australian prime minister closed the Libyan Arab People's Bureau in Canberra. The supposed rationale was that Libya's increased actions in Oceania now "posed a threat to the security and stability" of the region. Libya defined this decision as being in line with the wishes of a Zionist representative who visited Australia in November 1986. In response, Libya reconsidered its commercial and economic relations with Australia. Later that month, when Australia broke off diplomatic relations with Libya, the Libyan government denounced Australia's "White supremacist approach to the South Pacific."[50]

David Russell Lange, prime minister of New Zealand, described Libya's efforts as meddling. His administration claimed that Oceania could be destabilized if Qaddafi took a stronger interest in Vanuatu or New Caledonia: "The result would be that we would have a Cuba in the South Pacific with all the destabilizing impacts that Cuba has had on its own part of the world." Lange warned Libya to "stay away from the region" following supposed comments that it would provide funds to Kanak freedom fighters.[51]

In May 1987 JANA chided the United States for leading a "fierce political and information campaign" against an alleged Libyan threat in Oceania. Denouncing US "insolence," it stated that the peoples of Oceania would distinguish between those who wanted to "rob them" and those who sought to "bolster their rights."[52]

In response, prime minister Walter Lini unapologetically expanded Vanuatu's diplomatic relationships with Libya. His Vanua'aku Party identified with Libya's anti-imperialism as part of its efforts to actively build relationships with the African Diaspora and the Global South. In March 1987 Lini informed the Melbourne Overseas Service that it was "the right of Vanuatu as a Melanesian, independent, sovereign, and nonaligned state" to decide for itself which country it would establish relations with. It felt no need to account for it to Australia or New Zealand. Furthermore, he did not see how one could call Libya a terrorist state and not the United States or France. Lini had also condemned the United States as a "sponsor of international terrorism" after it bombed Libya the previous year. In November 1986, six Ni-Vans, one West Papuan refugee, and a Kanak activist traveled to Libya for training. Reports from Vila claimed that they were being trained in journalism. Vanua'aku Party representative Grace Mera Molisa categorically denied Australian reports that members of the party had received payments from Libya and that party members and police officers were being sent to Libya for paramilitary training. She claimed that party workers were being sent for media training and knew "nothing about" other ideas.[53]

While attending the Peace Conference, the NHNP's secretary-general, Barak Sope, organized for a further eight party members to study in Libya. Political rivals claimed that these travelers were there to be "trained in the art of international terrorism." According to Sope, these men were being trained in self-defense, weapons use, and ideological studies to serve as security for the party leadership.[54]

Ezekiel Alebua, prime minister of the Solomon Islands, refuted Hawke's comments as paranoia. The real threat in Oceania, he argued, was the greed of the "major powers" in the area. On the other hand, he stated, the Solomons, Papua New Guinea, and Vanuatu were seeking to reaffirm the preservation of their cultural and political identity so as to prevent conflicts in the region.[55]

In May, Moses Werrow, spokesman for the Free Papua Movement (OPM), announced that West Papuan freedom fighters were receiving guerilla training in Libya. These fighters had come back as a "better caliber" of jungle fighters. Interestingly, exiled OPM leader Nicolaas Jouwe informed Netherlands's media that West Papuan soldiers were "being trained as terrorists" in Libya after being lured from the Netherlands with "false promises and fairy tales" by Qaddafi. In response, Werrow stated that Jouwe was no longer a spokesman for the OPM and denied his claims. "Terrorists are criminals. Guerrillas attack only military targets. We are in a guerrilla war with Indonesia. Our fighters are in Libya being trained to fight the enemy who attacks our people."[56]

Western Samoa's deputy prime minister, Tupuola Efi, pushed back against Australia, stating that the government was "guilty of gratuitous condescension toward Pacific nations over the question of the Libyan presence in the region." If Australia and New Zealand had diplomatic ties with Libya and the Soviet Union, then why were Pacific nations not granted that same level of respect? During a television interview in New Zealand, Efi stated that he could not see any problem connected with Pacific Islanders going to Libya for paramilitary training. He was concerned about Libyan methodology, but more concerned about the Pacific's dire economic problems.[57]

In August 1987 Uregei was dismissed from his position as "external affairs minister" of FLNKS for his connections with Libya, after some nineteen activists left for Libya. However, by the end of the year Yeiwéné called for Kanak to arm themselves against increasing violence. FLNKS boycotted the presidential elections of May 1988. In the rural island of Ouvea, local "struggle committees" operated in a decentralized fashion. Armed with stones, clubs, machetes, and a handful of sporting guns, a Kanak "guerilla force" raided a French military barracks, killed four gendarmes, and seized twenty-seven others as hostages. They managed to capture Philippe Legorjus, the head of France's elite anti-terrorist squad. Led by Alphonse Dianou, they took these prisoners to a hidden cave in the rugged countryside of Gossanah, demanding independence. Some three hundred soldiers were flown to Ouvea to find them. French officials portrayed Dianou as a "Libya trained religious fanatic"; he had actually studied at a Roman Catholic seminary in Fiji. While searching for the location of the group, the French tortured several villagers. Eventually the cave was found.[58]

On May 5, secret services raided the cave, killing nineteen Kanak in the attack. While France officially denied it, Le Monde reported that Dianou and several others were captured and three executed. Dianou was left to die from an untreated gunshot wound. Le Monde described a photograph taken some three hours later that showed Dianou lying on his back on a stretcher with his knee wrapped in a bloody bandage, surrounded by thirty French soldiers and nine Kanak prisoners, "lying face down with their hands tied behind their backs or folded over their heads." Dianou lay there "in the sun in the middle of the military head-quarters, without treatment, without an infusion, some three hours after the end of the assault," when he should have been in the care of doctors.[59]

FLNKS denounced the killings, stating that "neither the dead, nor the tears, nor the sufferings and humiliation will shake the determination of the Kanak people to carry on the struggle until the final liberation of our land." Tragically, it was not over. The French military had openly tor-tured residents of Gossanah while trying to find the location of the cave, in an open football field in front of a village church. One of the people tortured was the elderly father of Kanak pastor Djoubelly Wea; he died after being stripped naked in front of villages and tortured with electric shocks. After the affair, the French continued to harass Ouvea islanders under suspicion of being involved. This included Pastor Wea, who was tied to a tree and tortured. Along with thirty-two other prisoners, he was flown to Paris.[60]

According to Hilda Lini, who covered the affair as editor of *New Heb-ridean Viewpoints*, Wea was handcuffed to a chair and forced to stand up for the duration of the flight to Paris. Lini knew both Dianou and Wea while they were students in Fiji. She first met Wea at Vanuatu's 1983 Nuclear Free Pacific Conference. In 1977 Wea completed a fasci-nating ninety-one-page anti-colonial and anti-capitalist project, "An Education for Kanak Liberation," to complete his BA at Fiji's Pacific Theological College. Based on Kanak cosmology, language, and culture, the project called for Kanak education to be centered on the concept of *wâhmakhmeto*—a process of "knowing ourselves by ourselves." Citing a 1975 speech by Uregei, it argued that the Kanak were "absent in their own country."[61]

Amelia Rokotuivuna, Vanessa Griffen, and Claire Slatter also knew Wea. On September 24, 1979, Wea and Rokotuivuna co-led an anti-French demonstration on the anniversary of the French conquest of New Caledonia, at the office of the French embassy. Wea represented PALIKA among the group of some eighty to one hundred demonstra-tors. According to the US embassy in Fiji, he was a radical extremist who called "himself an evangelical pastor even though he failed to gradu-ate." Moreover, the French were having "a difficult time" in Fiji because of this "agitation by radical elements against" the "French presence in New Caledonia," including Rokotuivuna, "a well-known radical element in Fiji."[62]

At the French embassy they engaged the charge d'affaires for about two hours, after which they threw leaflets on the floor and shouted "France out of the Pacific" and other slogans. Meanwhile the French high commissioner of New Caledonia had requested from Paris an additional force of a hundred riot troops in expectations of large-scale uprisings in Nouméa. This, they found, was not the case, as only a "small crowd" of some seven hundred to eight hundred demonstrators gathered.[63]

Griffen recalls how protestors sat on the floor. Meanwhile, megaphone in hand, Rokotuivuna led the protest from the sidewalks outside the building. As she engaged passersby, Griffen noticed "the utter disparagement and disgust with which some Fijian men viewed Rokotuivuna as they passed by. They thought she was a mad woman." Of course, Rokotuivuna was not insane. However, what is maddening is that some ten years later, Dianou would be killed by the French police, and Wea, on May 4, 1989, publicly shot and killed Tjibaou and Yeiwéné at the commemoration for the slain Kanak. He himself was immediately shot by Tjibaou's bodyguard. Wea blamed Tjibaou for the death of Dianou and the torture his father endured. He also felt that Tjibaou had "sold out" the struggle, as he had signed a peace treaty with the French settlers, known as the Matignon Accords. According to Lini, "the Kanak killed their own leaders," but the role of colonialism, French violence, and White power in the matter cannot be ignored either. This tragic moment set back New Caledonia's struggle for decades.[64]

10

Blacks Must Rule Vanuatu

Since it was colonized as New Hebrides by a joint British and French administration, Vanuatu's independence struggle rested on the cusp of the Black Anglophone and Francophone worlds. In the 1970s the New Hebrides National Party (NHNP), which became the Vanua'aku Party in 1977, embraced the political currents of Black internationalism in an effort to overthrow this matrix of White internationalism. Led by Anglican minister Walter Lini, the party embraced Black liberation theology along its tumultuous path of leading Vanuatu to political sovereignty in 1980. Upon independence, the country became a radical voice of the Nuclear Free and Independent Pacific (NFIP) movement. It advocated for the liberation struggles of Oceania and the broader Black Diaspora across the world, serving as a political conduit for the Black Pacific across Oceania, Africa, Europe, and the Americas.

The Kingdom of Melanesia

In 1973 the Melanesian Council of Churches organized a two-week South Pacific Action for Development Strategy (SPADES) Conference. Chaired by the Reverend Sitiveni Ratuvili of Fiji, SPADES was held across New Hebrides, Fiji, and Samoa. The conference was attended by an array of political organizers from across Papua New Guinea, Fiji, Cook Islands, Nauru, Tonga, Tahiti, New Caledonia, and New Zealand. This included Fiji's Claire Slatter, New Hebrides's Lini, David Kalkoa, Sethy John Regenvanu, and Tanzanian rural development officer Appolinarus Macha. Macha discussed African socialism and Tanzania's Arusha Declaration, which focused on Julius Nyerere's African socialism and aim at self-reliance at the village level. He described his work in Ujamaa village development and described the Tanzanian system as "education for self-reliance."[1] These ideas critically informed the NHNP's own plans for national development and stirred the conference.

Figure 10.1. Pro-independence demonstration, Port Vila, Vanuatu, 1978. One of the banners reads, "Blacks Must Rule Vanuaaku."

Figure 10.2. Prime Minister Walter Lini with his wife, Mary Lini, 1982. Australian National University Archives. Credit Lorraine and Michael Ovington.

SPADES discussed the relationships between culture, development, and colonialism. For Macha, development could not occur without independence. The Reverend Ropati Tiatia of Western Samoa asserted, "I have an obligation to my brother. . . . I am not completely free when I know my brother is oppressed. . . . Pacific Islanders must do away with colonialism to be full men."[2]

Conference delegates voted on a communiqué that stated that "all people under colonial government in the Pacific are oppressed and exploited." (Tahiti abstained from the vote). The statement condemned French nuclear testing in Oceania as a case of human exploitation and oppression. SPADES pledged to take a "militant stand against" this exploitative action via consultations with groups such as the World Council of Churches (WCC), the Pacific Conference of Churches (PCC), and the Melanesian Council of Churches (MCC). It argued that the education systems were in the hands of "foreign imperial educators" and not

Figure 10.3. Prime Minister Walter Lini at Commonwealth Heads of Government Meeting, 1981. National Archives of Australia.

relevant to Pacific people. Its resolutions stated that "culture identifies peoples and their environment" and should not be exploited, that the tourist industry in Oceania needed to be controlled, that Pacific peoples should be given political freedom, that a Pacific Pact should be established for regional cooperation, and that "the Church [should] review its place and mission in society."[3]

According to a report written by Roxanna Coop, SPADES denounced colonialism in all its forms. Its reports on urbanization and education complained that the school system defined as failures any students who "did not make it." However, the school system itself was a failure: "The rich get richer, and the poor think they are failures. The gap between the educated elite and the uneducated people is increasing." Education systems needed to train "modern farmers" and use indigenous languages, local syllabi, and teachers with agricultural backgrounds.[4]

The March 1973 issue of the NHNP's *Viewpoints* was dedicated to the meeting. According to Lini, who edited the paper, readers would be able to decide for themselves whether the conference delegates were right. The British residency condemned "racialist statements" made at SPADES, which could "cause bad feeling between New Hebrideans and Europeans." It regretted that a conference held "under the auspices of the PCC and the WCC should have been the occasion for extremist and racialist public statements." The Presbyterian Church claimed that the statements of delegates might "provoke racial hatred," as all races needed to create a "happy future for the New Hebrides."[5]

Viewpoints stated that the purpose of the conference was to find ways that churches could take part in the development of Oceania. SPADES believed that it was thus important to create a space where Pacific people could speak freely to one another. The conference released interviews held by the NHNP's Lini and Kalkoa. Kalkoa was asked, "Our lands have been taken, how do we get them back?" He responded in Bislama, "Mi mi ting wanom mi mi save yumi mas tekom aot mone blong yumi no narafala samting" (I think, I know that we must take what is ours, there is no other way).[6]

The PCC's John Meyer described how the delegates first spent one week in Apin, Samoa, Suva, Fiji, and New Hebrides before meeting in Vila. In the rural areas of New Hebrides there was clear exploitation that "the church was sometimes in league with." Delegates from Papua New

Guinea spoke Pidgin English, which was different from Bislama. Yet they all caught the spirit of the moment and spoke against the exploitation.[7]

Months later, the NHNP sent delegates to the Presbyterian General Assembly, which "took a strong and determined stand for New Hebridean self-government." It released a statement that was to be forwarded to the South Pacific Commission, the UN, and British and French colonial administrators. The church called for both administrations and these international bodies to move the condominium toward self-determination.[8]

In 1973 the WCC's Rex Davis wrote a letter to all "Spadeworkers." He noted that Ratuvili had been appointed to the PCC's Christian Education and Communications Program. Based in the prime minister's office, Macha had become officer-in-charge of publicity and Radio Tanzania. His charge was to travel across Tanzania to report on its Ujamaa villages. Davis hoped that the SPADES Continuation Committee could begin organizing a next meeting. He expressed concern about its focus on "the formulation and spread of an ideology of self-reliance for the South Pacific at the village, district, national, and regional levels." He thought it might be too much of an anti-intellectual start, as one had to "learn from the people." To describe self-reliance to village communities whose long history had been one of self-reliance might have seemed out of place.[9]

Davis recalled that SPADES discussed organizing a group visit to East Africa. Since then, the MCC's Roger Dixon had traveled to Kenya and Tanzania to make arrangements. They aimed to travel to Tanzania in 1974 with a group largely from Papua New Guinea. In June 1974 the WCC aimed to host Familia 74 (Ujamaa Safari) in Dar es Salaam, a gathering of some four hundred attendees that would be "SPADES very much magnified." There was space for eight couples from Oceania.[10]

Ironically, this meeting overlapped with Dar es Salaam's Sixth Pan-African Congress. As noted, the NHNP sent a delegation to 6PAC. It was joined by Peter Taurakoto and Nerry Taurakoto, who traveled there under the guise of attending Familia 74. The Taurakotos traveled across Tanzania's Ujamaa villages and felt that their focus on self-reliance could be applied in Vanuatu. The meeting was closely monitored by French and British officials; the French government was expressly concerned with the party's "dangerous liaisons" with Tanzania.[11]

Davis was editor of the PCC's *Risk* magazine, which, published four times a year, was a radical space of liberation theology. Across the 1970s it featured special issues on women's liberation (1974, "Voices of the Sisters"), Ujamaa Safari (1974), and Canada's Dene Nation (1977). In 1973 it released an issue that was based on WCC's 1973 meeting, which held symposiums on Black theology, Latin American theology of liberation, and education and theology in the context of liberation struggles. Held in Geneva, it featured James Cone and Paulo Freire. At the insistence of Davis, Lini, who had just visited London, France, and Tanzania, attended the meeting as an observer/consultant.[12]

In 1976 *Risk* released the special issue "Song of the Pacific," which was published to coincide with the PCC's Third Assembly in Papua New Guinea. The theme of that assembly was "God's mission in the changing Pacific society." In a remarkable introduction, Davis contextualized Oceania's political and cultural struggles around anti-colonialism, the NFIP, decolonization in Papua New Guinea, and colonialism in New Hebrides. For Davis, the special issue was haunted by "a melancholy mixture of rage and resignation." It included "harsh words uttered against colonizers in all their manifestations: businessmen, administrators, development experts, missionaries and tourists." Still, there was also "a love song—the lyrical praise of culture and a confident hope in the cherished traditions of island peoples." Woven into this texture of sadness and laughter, passion and praise, religious sensitivity, and proud politics was a simple story of a Pacific people that needed to "be taken seriously, even if" it represented "such a small parcel of the Third World." Strikingly, Davis had been "introduced to the world of Melanesia" at PNG's 1970 Waigani Seminar. The 1973 SPADES gathering was patterned on Waigani's open dialogue style.[13]

Amelia Rokotuivuna, Vanessa Griffen, Marjorie Crocombe, and Ron Crocombe compiled the content of "Song of the Pacific." It featured the works of poets, organizers, short story writers, activists, and scholars drawn from *Pacific Perspectives* and *Mana*. The issue included contributions from Papua New Guinea's John Momis and Jack Lahui, Samoa's Albert Wendt and Eti Sa'aga, the NHNP's Donald Kalpokas and Mildred Sope, Francis Bugotu's "Decolonizing and Recolonizing," and a summary from Griffen about the 1975 NFP conference.[14]

"Song of the Pacific" argued that the Pacific needed advocates across North America (to question US involvement in Micronesia and US Trust Territories), Africa (to call for an end to nuclear tests in Oceania), France and the United Kingdom (to address the New Hebrides question), Australia and New Zealand (to speak up about the economic hegemony of those countries in Oceania), and the rest of the world. For Davis, the Holy Spirit was "the ultimate paraclete" and advocate and Christians needed to follow suit and remember their spiritual kin in the Pacific.[15]

Risk reflected the church's concrete involvement in Pacific liberation struggles. In fact, the US embassy in Fiji suggested that the PCC was leading the anti-French campaign in Oceania. Its 1976 conference passed a resolution in support of total independence for all Pacific territories. The PCC also responded favorably to a request from Djoubelly Wea on behalf of a small church in New Caledonia that it take an anti-French stand.[16]

Through its Program to Combat Racism, in 1976 the WCC funded $10,000 each to the NHNP and Australia's Federal Council for the Advancement of Aborigines and Torres Strait Islanders. The grant was made without control over the manner in which it was used and was a sign of the WCC's "commitment to the struggle" for racial justice. In September 1984 the WCC would give grants ranging between $1,500 and $10,000 and totaling some $200,000 to forty anti-racist groups across Western Europe, the United States, Canada, Japan, Australia, the Philippines, New Caledonia, and Papua New Guinea.[17]

Davis and Lini continued to communicate about next steps for SPADES, meetings in Fiji, and also the hiring of "a fulltime consultant on community (political) development for the New Hebrides." One idea was to have someone be sent to a Caribbean conference of churches. In 1976 Lini approached Brian Macdonald-Milne of the Melanesian Church of the Solomon Islands about the need to establish a research unit, preferably under the aegis of the churches, that would investigate indigenous theology via consultation with rural communities and institutions; encourage the writing of local history, preferably by local people; and explore the historic and contemporary relationships between churches, governments, and culture. Lini asked Macdonald-Milne to be a full-time researcher for the project. Macdonald-Milne wrote to Davis about the plan.[18]

Macdonald-Milne later outlined a proposal for a Pacific Research Unit or think tank to be based in "Central Melanesia" and serve the Solomon Islands, New Hebrides, Tahiti, and New Caledonia. It would initiate and coordinate research on behalf of churches, Christian councils, and governmental and nongovernmental agencies in Oceania, in collaboration with the Pacific Theological College, University of the South Pacific (USP), and the PCC. It would share its materials through books and reports to churches, governments, national Christian councils, educational institutions, the PCC, and Pasifika peoples in European, Creole, and indigenous languages. These materials would be published with the support of USP, the South Pacific Creative Arts Society, Vila's Cultural Center, the South Pacific Social Sciences Association, the Solomon Islands Cultural Association, and Lotu Pasifika Productions. In addition, it would explicitly focus on Pacific and local histories (emphasizing oral tradition), Christianity and culture, religion and politics, local languages and education, and indigenous theology with "special reference to primal world views."[19]

In 1979 the WCC and the Evangelical Community for Apostolic Action called for a yearly reflection under the theme "Your Kingdom Come," which was to occur at all levels of the church, including women's, youth, and Bible study groups. As part of this push, in March 1980 *Youth*, the newsletter of the WCC's Youth Education and Renewal unit, released a special issue on Pacific challenges, which raised pressing questions about the church and anti-colonialism in Oceania, culture, development, tourism, and the NFIP. "Colonial rule still casts a dark shadow across the Pacific Islands," read the introduction to an essay on colonial rule in New Caledonia by French anthropologist Jean Guiart. Guiart noted that European local leaders dreamed "of a White New Caledonia policy." Melanesians and Europeans had limited social contact aside from sports and music. Young Kanak talked of independence from France and had never accepted the injustices done to them. They wanted their land back, as this was "the only way to force back the crippling weight of the colonial system, which murdered their grandfathers, enslaved their fathers and left them" as "strangers in their own country." This was now marked by the impact of migrant laborers from other parts of Oceania, namely,

Wallisians, Futunans, and Tahitians, who Guiart claimed acted toward "Melanesians as if they were part of the White community."[20]

Fiji's Ratuvili contributed an essay on development in the Pacific, suggesting that development needed to consider religious, cultural, and social factors as well as economic issues. He critically focused on three models: facilitative development, aid, and advertised self-reliance. The issue included a sample of Epeli Hau'ofa's "Our Crowded Islands," which critiqued population growth and "careless environmental planning" in Tonga. He decried the disappearing of the sand from beaches, and the notion that the society was developing with the most desirable elements of Western culture: "We are losing the best in us while adopting the cheapest, the most superficial, and often dangerous aspects of other civilizations. . . . Mutton flaps from New Zealand, secondhand clothes and shoes from America, and karate films from Hong Kong" were minor examples of the "imported rubbish" that had littered the country. In contrast, Oceania possessed a cultural-spiritual base on which economic development could be built.[21]

The *Youth* issue included Lini's widely circulated essay "Should the Church Play Politics?," which emphasized that the church needed to uphold moral standards of justice. Politics affected how moral judgments had impact in societies and could create just structures to prevent exploitation. As such, he had every right to play politics in the emerging nation of New Hebrides. For Lini, Jesus was the way, the truth, and the life because he upheld justice for all. As a church minister, Lini had every right to condemn the system's social injustices.[22]

Youth also reported on church activities in New Caledonia, where youth groups were calling for national independence. The Synod of the Evangelical Church in New Caledonia and the Loyalty Islands recognized the injustices that Melanesians had "suffered and the open and hidden oppression" to which they were subjected. It agreed with the elections of that July in which independence candidates won 82.5 percent of Melanesian votes, arguing that Melanesians were the "only ethnic group" that could "legitimately claim its independence" in New Caledonia.[23]

Also, continuing under the banner of "Your Kingdom Come," in May 1980 the Melanesian Council of Churches held a conference in Papua New Guinea, which focused on God, the poor, human struggles, the kingdom, and human power. PNG's Bernard Narokobi spoke on the theme "The Kingdom and Melanesian Human Struggles." Narokobi was a major voice of Melanesian nationalism, anti-colonialism, and liberation theology. He wrote prolifically about the need for Papua New Guinea to embrace the Melanesian Way—a worldview grounded in the cultural beliefs, experiences, and cosmologies indigenous to Melanesia. Narokobi saw that the way forward for Melanesia was to look within its own precolonial experiences—not Europe, Polynesia, or Africa. After years of publicly expressing his thoughts on Melanesia in letters to newspaper editors, Narokobi eventually published these submissions as a book, titled *The Melanesian Way,* which was edited by UPNG professor of philosophy Henry Olela. Olela hailed from Kenya, and formally taught in Duke University's African American Studies Program.[24]

For Narokobi, the Bible showed that God was "on the side of the poor and oppressed." Throughout the Old Testament, Yahweh was a "warrior at work, redeeming his people from oppression." God identified with the oppressed in order to "liberate the oppressed and the oppressor." As such, he argued, God was "decisively involved in liberation struggles. He was involved in the liberation from Babylonian captivity" as he was "now involved in the liberation struggles of Asia, Latin America, Melanesia and elsewhere." Referencing Marxism, he stressed that religion should not be "an opium of the oppressed," or, borrowing from Fanon, a projection of "the wretchedness of the Earth." In the struggles for liberation, as in West Papua or East Timor, the image of Christ was a "champion of the oppressed."[25]

He wrote, "Like Mahatma Gandhi, Jesus preached non-violence. He called blessed, the peacemakers. He called blessed those who struggled against the forces of oppression. He honored those imprisoned, tortured and assassinated for the sake of God's Kingdom." The work of ancestors and prophets like Marx, Engels, Mao, King, and Gandhi had helped to bring forth a vision of a future world. The efforts of these men and others like Nyerere told of a struggle against evil for equality and justice.[26]

Narokobi's version of liberation theology included a critique of materialism and capitalism:

> History was "marked by inequality." The medieval societies were dominated by serfdom. In the courts of Versailles and Buckingham, in Egypt,

Babylon, Persia, India, America, China and other places, the lords lived with dazzling feasts and luxury. The financiers and capitalists of the twentieth century squander wealth while the peasantry and workers struggle to live. Scribes and pharisees exploit the pupils and the congregations. Ancient Greece, Rome, modern America and other societies built their power from slavery. As slaves worked hard, the beneficiaries devoted time to sport, culture and political organizations. The very structure of class society was rooted in the economic bloodstream of the societies. This inequality has not always existed in all societies. Those of us who have some knowledge, personal experience and appreciation of societies that did not record their experiences, like the Melanesian or Indian in the Americas, can tell of institutions that prevent class societies from emerging.[27]

As such, he argued, building the Kingdom of God on Earth, or in Papua New Guinea, was an invitation to "break down the barriers" of language, tribalisms, hatred, political and religious jealousies, and the oppression of colonialism, neocolonialism, and capitalism "championed by international and national corporate entities." The way was to build up the country through Melanesian cultural institutions and practices, and not a "farcical, shapeless, soulless, coco-cola culture of an illusory universe." Citing Colombia's martyred minister Camilo Torres Restrepo, he stated that a revolutionary fought against oppressive structures for the elevation of man. Still, a Melanesian Christian understood Marx, but with their "inherent Melanesianism" and augmentation "by the risen Christ," they transcended "Marxism, Leninism, Maoism, and materialism."[28]

That year, the WCC also had a major gathering in Melbourne, Australia, under the same theme of "Thy Kingdom Come." Here, the MCC released a statement on behalf of the churches of Oceania that called for global social justice. The document aimed to spread understanding of the struggles of the South Pacific. The conference was clear that "a fundamental aspect of the gospel [was] the liberation of people from oppression. While the world heard about the struggles of Latin America, South Africa, the Middle East, and Australia . . . the Church wanted to bring attention to the unknown struggles of the South Pacific." Oceania's critical concerns were nuclear testing in Tahiti, colonialism in New Hebrides, New Caledonia, and Tahiti, discriminatory immigration policies in Australia and New Zealand, and the proliferation of missionary activities that saw the Pacific as a "classroom for missions" and threatened the cultures, communities, and lives of Pasifika peoples. The conference pledged to help Pacific peoples establish the area as a nuclear free zone, assist Pacific churches in their efforts to end colonial domination, and correct the attitude of the church to the Pacific.[29]

The Nuclear Free and Independent Pacific Conference, Vanuatu, 1983

In 1980 the Vanua'aku Party achieved independence for Vanuatu. Under Walter Lini's leadership, it immediately took up the charge of building a nuclear free and independent Pacific. In March 1981 it hosted a Nuclear Free Festival, which included speeches by Hilda Lini and Sope, a statement from Vanuatu's Christian Council, and a String Band show. Hilda Lini also represented Vanuatu at Hawai'i's 1980 Nuclear Free Pacific Conference and was invited to a Nuclear Free Forum in Sydney, Australia, that same year.[30]

In 1983 Vanuatu hosted a Nuclear Free and Independent Pacific conference, primarily coordinated by the Pacific Concerns Resource Center (PCRC) and the Vanuatu Pacific Community Center (VPCC). Some thirty-four presentations were given here. Vanuatu's deputy prime minister, Regenvanu, opened the discussions. In Sope's keynote speech, he stated that he would believe the French about the supposed safety of nuclear testing only when they stopped experimenting on Mururoa and conducted tests in Paris.[31]

The conference addressed topics spanning political independence, militarization and nuclearization, and economic dependence in the Pacific. Political independence sessions addressed external colonialism by the First World (New Caledonia, Tahiti, and Micronesia), internal colonialism (American Indians, Aborigines in Australia, Māoris, Hawai'ians, Chamorros, and indigenous Canadians), and external colonialism by the Third World (East Timor and West Papua). The sessions on nuclearization and militarization addressed the hazards of nuclear testing (Guam, Japan, Western Samoa, American Indians, and Australian Aborigines), radiation and nuclear testing (Marshall Islands, Japan, Tahiti, and Aboriginal Australia), strategy and geopolitics in the Pacific and Indian Oceans (Japan, Philippines, ANZUS, El Salvador, and

Kaho'olawe/RIMPAC), and the impact of militarization (Kwajalein, Tahiti, Belau, and Diego Garcia/Mauritius).[32]

Speakers included New Caledonia's Yann Uregei of the Kanak Independent Front (IF), Aboriginal activist Shorty O'Neill, the VPCC's Rex Rumakiek, Abilio Araujo of East Timor, Tahiti's Charlie Ching, Aida Velasquez of the Philippine Federation for Environmental Concern, indigenous Canadian activist Ron Lameman, James Castro of the Chamorro Grassroots Movement, Greenpeace, the Pacific Concerns Resource Center, Guam's Association of Pacific Island Legislatures, Hope Cristobal of the Organization of People for Indigenous Rights, Hawai'i's Protect Kaho'olawe 'Ohana Fund, Moses Ramarui and Roman Bedor of Palau, Rada Gungaloo of Mauritius and Diego Garcia, Biram Stege of the Marshall Islands, and Ripeka Evans of Aotearoa's Māori Peoples Liberation Movement. Topics spanned nuclear testing in Micronesia and Marshall Islands, American bases and uranium mining in Australia, colonialism in East Timor, relationships between Indian and Pacific Ocean liberation struggles, the Frantz Fanon circle of the French West Indies, Tahitian independence, and the dumping of nuclear waste by Japan.[33]

The Frantz Fanon Circle emerged out of the International Frantz Fanon Memorial, which was held in 1982 in Fort-de-France, Martinique. The circle argued that Fanon had only very recently been recognized in Martinique, by both the colonial elite and the Europeanized intelligentsia. But since the memorial, his works had become part of the anticolonial framework of the Francophone Caribbean, and the circle spread to Guadeloupe and French Guiana. Its paper at the NFIP spanned the genocide of indigenous peoples, slavery, and colonialism in the French Caribbean. It also discussed the recent emergence of the organized anticolonial violence of Guadeloupe's Armed Liberated Group. The Frantz Fanon Circle gathered men and women who wanted to "actualize Fanon's ideas" in nationalist liberation movements across Guadeloupe, Martinique, and French Guiana, "internationalize the colonial problem," and "establish and develop contacts between all the 'damnés de la terre.'" It also discussed Fanon's time in Algeria, his representation of Algeria's National Liberation Front at Ghana's All African People's Conference, and his books *Black Skins, White Masks* and *Wretched of the Earth*.[34]

The voices of Pasifika women were amplified at the talks. One banner, written in Bislama, English, and French, read, "Mifala Olgeta

Woman Blong Vanuatu I Sapotem Nuklia Fri Mo Indipenden Pasifik"
(We women of Vanuatu support the Nuclear Free and Independent Pacific). Hilda Lini argued that one of the best ways to build the NFIP was
to work through women's organizations across Oceania, because they
were well organized, widespread, and already addressing the intersecting issues of nuclear testing and independence. She suggested that as
long as the women knew about the movement, it would spread. Bernadette Pereira of West Samoa agreed that Oceania's women's groups were
pushing these issues. Aotearoa's Evans described how her delegation
was comprised of mostly women, reflecting how the strength and spirit
(*mana*) of the Māori struggle came from women.[35]

Indeed, it was three Māori women—Hilda Halkyard, Sharon Hawke,
and Ripeka Evans—who represented Aotearoa at Fiji's 1981 South Pacific
International Conference of Students for a Nuclear and Independent Pacific; this meeting hosted students from the Marshall Islands, Guam,
Belau, Western Samoa, Vanuatu, Polynesia, West Papua, New Caledonia,
Fiji, Aotearoa, Australia, Malaysia, the Philippines, Singapore, Tonga,
Rarotonga, Kiribati, and the Solomon Islands. They held a women's
forum at the YWCA and gave presentations on the Springbok Tour
anti-apartheid protests in support of their "sisters and brothers of Azania," the struggles of the Māori, and the Treaty of Waitangi. They also
met with Aboriginal, Tahitian, and Kanak delegates and members of the
VPCC and PCRC. Sope gave the keynote speech at the talks, and Uregei
presented a paper titled "New Caledonia, the South Africa of the South
Pacific."[36]

The 1983 NFIP passed some twenty resolutions. One denounced US
imperialism in Central America, demanding that the United States "end
all military and economic assistance" to the governments of El Salvador,
Guatemala, and Honduras and end all covert operations to "overthrow
the popular Sandinista government of Nicaragua." This was a rejection
of US support of regimes in El Salvador and Guatemala that were responsible for the illegal detention, kidnapping, torture, and death of tens
of thousands of innocent civilians, and the displacement of over one
million people; US foreign policy in Central America that was principally directed against indigenous peoples and cultures, as in the Guatemalan regime's genocidal war against the Mayans; the raids carried
out by the counterrevolutionary "Somozistas" against the Miskitus of

Nicaragua; and the establishment of US military bases in Honduras for the purposes of training Salvadoran, Honduran, and counterrevolutionary Nicaraguan troops and directing invasions into El Salvador and Nicaragua. This resolution also supported El Salvador's Farabundo Martí National Liberation Front and the Guatemalan National Revolutionary Unity.[37]

Other resolutions called for support of the independence struggles of East Timor, West Papua, Tahiti, and New Caledonia; international protests against Japan's plans for nuclear dumping in the Pacific; the dismantling of US military installations in the Philippines; a global moratorium on uranium mining and support for Aboriginal Australians; an end to US military operations and nuclear testing in Palau, Micronesia, and the Marshall Islands; financial compensation for nuclear damages in the Marshall Islands; self-determination for the indigenous inhabitants of Hawai'i (the Kānaka Maoli) and the Chamorro people of Guam; and support for the indigenous peoples of Canada and their opposition to cruise missile testing. The resolutions also called on all Pacific nations to expel French ambassadors in support of Tahiti; the PCC to bring up these issues at the next WCC meeting in Vancouver; and France to immediately cease nuclear testing. Delegates also resolved to add "Independent" to the name of the people's charter, changing it from Nuclear Free Pacific to Nuclear Free and Independent Pacific.[38]

The NFIP conference was as much about culture as it was about politics. Its delegates marched to and presented petitions at the gates of the French embassy on Bastille Day. They could be seen reading Narokobi's *Melanesian Way*, singing indigenous songs like the Māori's "E Noho Ana Au" and "We Shall Overcome," planting trees, having Kava ceremonies, making Haka greetings, and listening to Vanuatu's Huarere String Band group perform songs like "Nuclear Free."[39]

West Papua's Rex Rumakiek addressed the talks. Chair of the VPCC, Rumakiek stated that the past twenty years had witnessed several independence celebrations, but none compared to the independence of Vanuatu. The birth of Vanuatu "marked the beginning of a new era" for people's liberation in Oceania. For the first time in its history of decolonization, a country approaching sovereignty opened its doors "for other Pacific islanders fighting for their freedom." He recalled the "golden words" of Walter Lini, now prime minister of Vanuatu: "Our independence would be meaningless if some of our Pacific Island brothers and sisters are not yet free." Rumakiek detailed how in August 1980 the Māori Peoples Liberation Movement, New Caledonia's International Front, the Free Papua Movement, the Revolutionary Front for an Independent East Timor, and Awo Tahitians representing independentist parties of French Polynesia, negotiated with the Vanua'aku Party and Vanuatu's cabinet to establish an information center for liberation struggles in Vanuatu. Thus, Rumakiek officially opened the VPCC in 1981. He also had the support of the Pacific People's Action Front, the Free Papua Movement, and the Community Aid Abroad of Australia. A Trustee Committee of Hilda Lini, Sope, and Molisa was formed to direct the center's activities. Hilda Lini worked closely with Rumakiek, and was also responsible for continuing *Povai*; since she was the editor of *Viewpoints*, this made perfect sense.[40]

Its initial steering committee included Vanuatu's Kai Patterson, New Caledonia's Yann Uregei and Luis Uregei, Tahiti's Charlie Ching, Aotearoa's Ripeka Evans, East Timor's Abilio Araujo, Hawai'i's Ku'umealoha Gomes, West Papua's Fred Korwa, Australia's Shorty O'Neill, and Canada's Ron Lameman. The community sought to also work with Hawai'i's Pacific Concerns Resource Center, which had emerged out of the last NFIP meeting. In December 1983 the VPCC sought to further develop and continue the publication of *Povai*.[41]

Harlem Is the Place for Me

The VPCC was only one avenue by which Vanuatu supported liberation movements in Oceania. As an independent county, it sent representatives to speak on behalf of Pasifika Black struggles and the broader Black Diaspora in international venues. In 1981 the Commonwealth Heads of Government met in Melbourne, Australia. According to the *Aboriginal Islander Message* (*AIM*), while Black leaders from Africa, the Pacific, and the Caribbean dominated the meeting, very few publicly supported Aborigines. This included Zimbabwe's Robert Mugabe and Tanzania's Nyerere. *AIM* argued that while these men performed very well in discussion of South Africa, Namibia, and the Pacific, they unfortunately accepted the Australian prime minister's false claims that he had done a lot for Blacks. Aboriginal activist Gary Foley criticized these leaders for "grand standing about the oppression of Blacks in Africa while ignoring the plight of Aborigines in Australia." The exception, *AIM* argued, was Walter Lini and other Pacific leaders, who raised the issue of the conditions of Aboriginals at the conference. Lini followed through on his pledge to Foley that he would address these issues with the Australian prime minister and other concerned parties.[42]

In 1986 Paul Bérenger of the Mauritius Militant Movement wrote to Lini regarding Vanuatu's support of New Caledonia before the UN Committee of 24. He sought support for the Chagos Archipelago/Diego Garcia along the same lines, as its Black community had been "struggling to obtain some form of moderate compensation." Bérenger hoped to bring the case to the United Kingdom and the United States.[43]

In 1986 Vanuatu opened a permanent UN mission in Harlem, New York, becoming the first nation to do so. Vanuatu was no stranger to this mecca of Black internationalism. In 1982 Ati G. Sokomanu, president of Vanuatu, had been a guest at a reception that included the Harlem Lawyers' Association, the Association of Black Women Attorneys of New York, the Bedford-Stuyvesant Lawyers' Association, and the Barristers' Wives of New York.[44]

Harlem's *Trade Winds* announced that Vanuatu had appointed Harlem-based lawyer Robert Van Lierop as its ambassador to the UN. Of Surinamese descent, Van Lierop was the chairman of Harlem's Community Planning Board #9. He also handled affairs for Cape Verde, Mozambique, and Guinea-Bissau, and had made the documentary *Aluta Continua*, based on Mozambique's independence struggle. A co-founder of the Africa Information Service, he edited and wrote the introduction for its *Return to the Source: Selected Speeches of Amilcar Cabral*. Representatives from Vanuatu approached him because of this body of work. Van Lierop indicated that the government of Vanuatu was interested in the recreational and social activities of Harlem: "The Government feels that this is where it belongs and this is where it would like to be."[45]

From 1986 to 1994, Van Lierop represented Vanuatu at international meetings of the UN, the Alliance of Small Island States, the Global Conference on the Sustainable Development of Small Island States, the Global Environment Facility, and the Climate Change Convention. He also led its delegations to Burkina Faso (1988), Nicaragua (1984), and South Pacific Forum meetings in Fiji, Western Samoa, and Micronesia

(1986–1991). On behalf of Vanuatu, he also worked significantly in support of the Kanak liberation movement. In July 1985 Uregei wrote to Van Lierop about his support of their efforts to have FLNKS establish a permanent office in New York.[46]

In September 1987 France held a referendum on independence in New Caledonia. After France refused to allow UN observers to be present, the referendum was boycotted by FLNKS. This "New Caledonia question" was raised by the United Nations' Fourth Committee at its General Assembly's 42nd session in October 1987, which discussed "the implementation of the declaration on the granting of independence to colonial countries and peoples" in terms of Namibia and New Caledonia. Representing Vanuatu, Van Lierop circulated materials demonstrating that the referendum was not a "legitimate exercise of self-determination." This clearly impacted Black delegates to the UN. NAACP representative M. Lawrence spoke before the session, and, after denouncing South African apartheid, stressed that it was immoral how indigenous New Caledonians were being "turned into a minority." He asserted that New Caledonia's recent plebiscite on independence had occurred "without regard to United Nations principles and practices." It was thus "clearly invalid," because colonized people had largely boycotted it. He called for an open one instead.[47]

Lawrence was followed by Dick Ukeiwe, a longtime conservative and French-supporting Kanak politician who was officially recorded by the UN as a representative of France. Ukeiwe remarked that he was a French citizen of Melanesian origin, and that New Caledonia was "an integral part of the French Republic in which democracy prevailed" and "ethnic groups coexisted in freedom and equality." He was a member of the conservative Rally for Caledonia in the Republic, and at the time he was president of the Congress of New Caledonia. He claimed that racism and oppression did not occur in New Caledonia, and that Kanak were not deprived of freedom. Only those who wanted to use the UN to impose a future on New Caledonia that its majority did not want would suggest otherwise. He claimed that he had not attended the UN hearing on the FLNKS petition because "the dialogue needed to take place at home" and "not in New York."[48]

Ukeiwe was taken to task by Van Lierop, who replied that such dialogue was not going on in Nouméa because its "colonized peoples did not believe that they could obtain justice there." As such, they had come to the UN to seek justice. Ukeiwe was also challenged by Ghana's Augustus Tanoh and Haiti's Yves Auguste.[49]

Days later, the African American anthropologist Angela Gilliam delivered a petition in support of New Caledonia from the International Women's Anthropology Conference. She spoke before the committee, informing it that in her recent travels to New Caledonia she had been struck by the "apartheid-like circumstances" under which Kanak lived. As in South Africa, they suffered from police harassment, racism, misrepresentations, and disenfranchisement. White settlers possessed "80 percent" of the mineral-rich land, while Kanak lived on "the reserve," some 3,733 square kilometers of barren land with scarce water. Leaders of FLNKS were restricted to villages or reserves and were attacked by the French military forces. Like the flag of South Africa's African National Congress (ANC), the FLNKS flag was not permitted to be raised in New Caledonia. According to Gilliam, there seemed to "be a direct relationship between the number of resources which existed in many a third-world country and the degree of poverty and oppression of the inhabitants."[50]

Moreover, "the people of the Pacific" maintained that their calls for self-determination needed to be seen "in the context of the struggle of a nuclear-free and independent Pacific." Women were in the forefront of New Caledonia's independence struggle, because they suffered from sexual and economic exploitation. These women also protested the torture and imprisonment of Kanak and expressed concerns about nuclear testing and the ecological devastation of the Pacific. The International Women's Anthropology Conference called for the UN to strengthen its mandate to decolonize New Caledonia and link decolonization to the NFIP.[51]

Gilliam was immediately challenged by Simon Loueckhote of the Association de Solidarité, Liberté and Sécurité, a group of Melanesians who wanted to "remain French." Loueckhote, a colleague of Ukeiwe, claimed that FLNKS was racist, extremist, violent, and anti-democratic. Kanak were "neither oppressed nor [victims] of racism," but rather a Melanesian community of full French citizens that enjoyed its respected rights.[52]

Loueckhote was followed by Sylvia Hill of the Washington, DC–based Southern Africa Support Project (SASP). Hill outlined the project's almost ten years of anti-apartheid activism and organizing around Southern Africa. She then expressed solidarity with peoples being denied the right to self-determination, in particular New Caledonia's Kanak and the Palestinian people.[53]

Ukeiwe spoke again, and with sexist intimations claimed that Gilliam "showed her irresponsibility" because she did not understand the Kanak situation. He hoped that "everyone had appreciated how ridiculous her comparison was between the situation of New Caledonia and apartheid in South Africa." "The French of Melanesian origin were free French citizens who participated democratically in the institution of the territory and did not need to be given lessons by so-called anthropologists."[54]

But Gilliam was far from alone in making the comparison between South Africa and New Caledonia. In December 1986, during the UN vote to place New Caledonia on the list of non-self-governing territories, Van Lierop had remarked, "For us in the Pacific, New Caledonia is our Namibia, New Caledonia is our Palestine, New Caledonia is our Malvinas [Falkland Islands]."[55]

Indeed, Black people who had the opportunity to hear the case of New Caledonia tended to support its struggle. For example, Jesse Jackson, on behalf of the National Rainbow Coalition, wrote to the UN's Tesfaye Tadesse in support of New Caledonia's petition to the Decolonization Committee. His statement called for support of FLNKS and self-determination of New Caledonia.[56]

In March 1987 Sela Molisa led Vanuatu's first official visit to the United States. He spoke at the Asia Program of the Wilson Center in Washington, DC. This was in the midst of some controversy; US officials had raised issues about fishing agreements made between Vanuatu and the USSR. According to Molisa, Washington was "not interested" when his government proposed official visits in 1983 and 1985, partly due to its disdain for Vanuatu's stance against nuclear testing in the region. However, since Vanuatu had now established official relations with the USSR—and had independent diplomatic dialogues with North Vietnam, Cuba, and Libya—the United States was "more willing to talk."[57]

The *Los Angeles Times* reported that, allegedly concerned about an emerging "Soviet menace" in Oceania due to such fishing deals, one US official expressed alarm that Vanuatu could become "another Grenada." Walter Lini pushed back against this assumption. Molisa declared that the real threats in the region were "residual colonialisms, nuclear testing and chronic economic troubles." An Australian diplomat agreed that it was "French reluctance to give independence to New Caledonia" that was "the greatest potential threat to regional stability." In 1986 France conducted eight nuclear tests in French Polynesia's Mururoa Atoll, totaling eighty-four underground launches since 1961. At the South Pacific Forum, thirteen nations concluded a nuclear-free zone treaty; the United States and France disagreed with the terms, while the Soviet Union signed the pact. The Reagan administration claimed that agreement with the treaty could set a precedent for similar nuclear-free zones in militarily strategic locations and spread the "nuclear allergy" across the Global South.[58]

In March 1985 Washington's *Afro American* printed an article about Molisa's UN plea in support of independence for the Kanak of New Caledonia, asserting that "the nations of our region are in agreement, colonialism has no future" in Oceania. The detailed article traversed the history of the Kanak freedom struggle and discussed racial violence impacting the country. This included the deaths of Tjibaou's brothers and the increase of French gendarmes stationed in the colony.[59]

In 1983 Lini spoke before the 38th Session of the UN General Assembly. He first recognized the independence of Saint Christopher and Nevis, a "sister small island state." In describing the liberation movements of Africa, Asia, South and Central America, the Caribbean, and Oceania, he cited Frederick Douglass: "Power concedes nothing without a demand. . . . If there is no struggle, there is no progress." He asked that these words be part of the UN's deliberations. He continued, "After so many years, it is not easy to understand why the people of Palestine cannot return home." It was also difficult to comprehend why South Africa needed more inducements to end its illegal occupation of Namibia. Lini remarked that Indonesia was a country that they had long admired, and, as a co-founder of the non-aligned movement, considered a friend. However, a true friend was not one who simply told another what they wanted to hear. As such, he challenged Indonesia's aggression toward East Timor. "What in East Timor threatened Indonesia that hundreds of thousands of innocent men, women and children had to pay with their lives, and so many more" still paying by sudden disappearances, detentions, and tortures? Where was "it written that colonialism [was] only wrong when the colonial power was a European nation?" If they accepted Indonesia's actions there, then with what authority could they challenge Israel's annexation of Jerusalem or apartheid in South Africa?[60]

Lini stated that he was brought to these conclusions through the words of Amilcar Cabral and Cape Verde and Guinea-Bissau's struggle against Portuguese colonialism: "Hide nothing from the masses of the people. Tell no lies, claim no easy victories." This was relevant also for New Caledonia, Namibia, and South Africa. New Caledonia was the world's second-largest producer of nickel, and its mineral resources were exploited in the same manner as in Africa. He referenced Vanuatu's hosting of the 1983 NFIP, remarking that "the peoples of the Pacific have always respected and been at peace with our environment. To us, our lands, our skies, and our ocean have always been a source of spiritual guidance as well as our means of sustaining life." The relationships between sovereignty and a nuclear free Pacific were clear to all except the most myopic observers.[61]

Lini decried the shooting down of the civilian aircraft Korean Airlines Flight 007 by the Soviet Union as a great human tragedy and extended condolences to the families of the victims. Still, he pressed, why were those persons who were "silent when a Libyan airliner was shot down by Israeli fighters" and when a Cuban Airlines was blown out of the sky so morally outraged now? Was not "all human life sacred, and none more sacred than another?" He continued, "The lives of East Timorese and Vietnamese are sacred. The lives of Palestinians and Lebanese are sacred. The lives of Iranians and Iraqis are sacred. The lives of Chileans and Filipinos are sacred. The lives of Cypriots and Guatemalans are sacred. The lives of Angolans and Namibians are sacred." "Why were those who [were] so willing to isolate the Soviet Union so unwilling to isolate South Africa?" He was certain that those who allied "themselves with the evil practitioners of apartheid or other forms of racism" could not complain when others moved "into the moral vacuum they themselves have created."[62]

In October 1985 Lini addressed the UN's Special Committee Against Apartheid on the International Day of Solidarity with South African Political Prisoners. He called for the ending of apartheid and expressed Vanuatu's support for the people of South Africa. His government hoped

Figure 10.4. Activists from Vanuatu, West Papua, and New Caledonia, Port Vila, Vanuatu, 2014. Photograph by Quito Swan.

to host a regional conference about apartheid in Vanuatu, and planned to name a park after Nelson Mandela. Mandela and other political prisoners would be freed, he argued, but not by their jailers. Lini understood the historical significance of this moment. He passed on a signed copy of this speech to Howard Dodson of Harlem's Schomburg Center for Research in Black Culture.[63]

In 1986 the Melanesian Spearhead Group (MSG) was established in Vanuatu in an effort to collectively address the region's geopolitical concerns. Decades later, MSG's resource-strapped efforts speak to the potential and challenges of Melanesian unity in the postcolonial era, as it relates to conflict resolution, stability, regional security, women's rights, health, democracy, migration, and environmental crisis management. Colonialism in New Caledonia and West Papua remain political powder kegs for the MSG, the region, and the wider world. In 2015 Indonesia—a regional ally of the United States—was elected as a full member of MSG, complicating not only the group's agenda, but the future of the Black Pacific.

ACKNOWLEDGMENTS

In the 1990s I was introduced to the depths of Oceania's liberation struggles through Pauulu Kamarakafego and scholars like the late Runoko Rashidi. Three books and some twenty years later, the debts that I have incurred in the process have only increased with the writing of each one. There were significant overlaps between the completion of this book and *Pauulu's Diaspora: Black Internationalism and Environmental Justice* in terms of research, archives, fellowships, interviewees, and the communities that I worked with. My sincere gratitude goes out to the individuals and institutions who fit into that category, whom I may have neglected to mention here. Portions of this work were published as "Blinded by Bandung? Illumining West Papua, Senegal, and the Black Pacific," *Radical History Review* 131 (2018): 58–81 (chapter 2); "Giving Berth: Fiji, Black Women's Internationalism, and the Pacific Women's Conference of 1975," *Journal of Civil and Human Rights* 4, no. 1 (Spring 2018): 37–63 (chapter 5); and "Towards a Black Pacific: Leo Hannett and Black Power in Papua New Guinea," in *Expanding the Boundaries of Black Intellectual History*, ed. Leslie Alexander, Brandon Byrd, and Russel Rickford (Evanston: Northwestern University Press, 2022).

I want to thank Ashley Farmer and Ibram X. Kendi for suggesting that I submit the manuscript to their Black Power book series at New York University Press. Their encouragement and advocacy urged me to actually write the manuscript that I had been researching for some time. New York University Press editor Clara Platter and her team did a wonderful job in gently nudging me to complete the book. Thanks so much also to Heather Wiggins and Ina Gravitz.

A 2014 National Endowment for the Humanities fellowship for *Pauulu's Diaspora* allowed me to conduct research for this project across Fiji, Vanuatu, Papua New Guinea, and Australia. Thanks to the archivists, curators, and librarians of the Australian Institute of Aboriginal and Torres Strait Islander Studies, Sydney's State Library of New South

Wales, the libraries of the University of Papua New Guinea and the University of the South Pacific (Fiji and Vanuatu), the National Archives of Australia (Canberra), Papua New Guinea, and Vanuatu (thanks to Anne Naupa), and the National Libraries of Australia and Papua New Guinea. Sincere thanks are due to Lea Lani Kinikini, Salesi Kauvaka, Baizum Kamarakafego, DJ K-Note, Redfern's Tent Embassy, Kimberley Graham, and Mele village. Thanks to Hilda Lini, Barak Sope, Kalkot Mataskelekele, Daniel Nato, Vanessa Griffen, Claire Slatter, John Maynard, and Kim Kruger for your activism, interviews, and counsel. While Alex Carter helped me to map out my research travels in Australia, Gerald Horne helped me to shape my research agenda across Oceania.

A number of other fellowship opportunities and awards aided in the completion of this book. These included a 2016 Harry Ransom Center Research Fellowship in the Humanities at the University of Texas–Austin, which was supported by the Dorot Foundation Postdoctoral Research Fellowship in Jewish Studies. A 2018–2019 fellowship at the Wilson Institute for International Scholars, Washington, DC, was transformative. Thanks to Natalia Ruiz Morato, Lauren Herser Risi, Brad Simpson, Ruslan Garipov, and Yinuo Wei. A 2017–2018 American Council of Learned Societies Frederick Burkhardt Fellowship at Harvard University's Radcliffe Institute for Advanced Study provided essential time to think, write, and research. Special thanks go out to all the administrators, staff, co-fellows, student research partners, colleagues, curators, archivists, and librarians of that year, including Erica R. Edwards, Steffani Jamison, Francois Hamlin, Patricia Williams, Deborah Vargas, Quincy Flowers, Jackson Gates, Oya Gursoy, the African American studies working group, and Schlesinger Library curator for race and ethnicity Kenvi Phillips.

A 2020 library fellowship at Australia's University of Queensland's Fryer Library Special Collections allowed me to research the rich Oodgeroo Noonuccal papers. Thanks to Simon Farley, Caroline Williams, and the library's staff. Thanks to staff across Howard University's Moorland Spingarn Research Center, New York's Schomburg Institute, Stuart Dawrs and the University of Hawai'i Mānoa Library, and Helen Edwards and the archives of Evergreen State College.

The manuscript was completed during a 2020–2021 residential fellowship at Pennsylvania State University's Humanities Institute. While

COVID-19 impacted on the possibilities to engage the university's African American Studies Department, I am grateful for the support given by Michael West, John Christman, Dara Walker, and Amira Rose Davis. Many of the ideas exercised in this book emerged out of my time as a professor of African Diaspora history at Howard University. Thanks to all of my former colleagues, allies, administrators, and students at Howard who supported this work and graciously took my classes on the Black Pacific. Professor of history Jean-Michel Mabeko-Tali confirmed for me New Caledonia's significance to the Black francophone world, and my discussions about Vanuatu with professor of political science Lorenzo Morris were always fruitful. Thanks to Aaron Treadwell and Markus Weise for the research conducted at the Library of Congress.

Thanks to all those who invited me to give lectures and participate in workshops, classes, meetings, and events, including the conferences of the Association for the Study of African American Life and History, the National Council of Black Studies, the American Historical Association, the Association for the Worldwide Study of the African Diaspora, the African American Intellectual History Society (AAIHS), and the American Studies Association. Thanks to Edward Onaci and Ursinus College, Ashley Farmer, Minkah Makalani, and UT–Austin's 2019 Black Power Conference, Joseph Jordan and the Sonja Hayes Stone Center for Black Culture and History, Judy Tzu-Chun Wu and the University of California's Pacific Worlds symposium, David Armitage, Kristin Oberiano, and the Harvard University Department of History's 2018 Pacific in the World Seminar, Tonija Navas and Howard University's Ralph Bunche Center, Leslie Alexander, Curtis Austin, and the AAIHS's 2017 Writing Workshop at the University of Oregon, and a 2019 Radcliffe Institute Towards a Black Pacific Exploratory Seminar.

In addition to those mentioned, a long list of comrades helped to shape and improve the project. This includes Franklin Knight, Gerald Horne, Akinyele Umoja, Michael West, Robbie Shilliam, Jessica Millward, LaShawn Harris, Richard Benson and the Nommo Writing Collective, Stefan Bradley, Akiemi Glenn, Guy Emerson Mount, Tao Leigh Goffe, Robyn Spencer, Tiffany Florvil, Todd Burroughs, Jakobi Williams, Charisse Burden-Stelly, Sheila Walker, Jared Ball, Mark Bolden, James Pope, Jonathan Fenderson, and Bradford Young. Keisha Blain continues to be an amazing friend and colleague. Russell Rickford has always taken the time to send me references to primary documents while conducting his own research in several archives—many thanks, my brother. Bermie Massive and Crew always and forever.

Thanks must also be extended to my sincere Boston-based colleagues whom I worked with during my time at the University of Massachusetts–Boston, including Azure Parker, Layla Browne-Vincent, Denise Patmon, Tara Parker, Joseph N. Cooper, Monique Cooper, Imari Paris Jeffries and King Boston, Marshall Milner, Dania Francis, Lynnell Thomas, Aminah Pilgrim, Lorna Riviera, Paul Watanabe, Cedric Woods and the Collaborative of Asian American, Native American, Latino and African American Institutes (CANALA), Marvin Gilmore, Charlie Titus and Higher Ground Boston, Charles Desmond, David Cash, Maria Ivanova, Maria John, Marisol Negrón, Patricia Krueger-Henney, Dave Hoffman of the Boston Celtics, Aisha Francis-Samuels, Clayton Samuels, Tanisha Sullivan, Charlotte Golar Richie, J. Keith Motley, Cynthia K. Orellana, Marcelo Suárez-Orozco, Jeremy Aponte, Segun Idowu, Devin Morris, Jabari Peddie and the Teachers Lounge, Malika Ali, Chris Martell, Sheena Collier and Boston While Black, Taurus Records, Ripple Café and, of course, the one and only DJ Moor Tyme. My amazing team at the William Monroe Trotter Institute for the Study of Black Culture deserves warm gratitude—Shirley Williams, Yvonne Gomes-Santos, Maria Rogers, Elisa Cabral, Deborah Dauda, Hannah Browne, Azure Parker, and Gifty Debordes-Jackson.

Seeknfind. Maryam Sabur, I could not have completed three book projects without your precious care, brilliance, and support. My true friends and allies Glenn Chambers, Louis Woods, Furqan Khaldun, Theodore Francis, Iyelli Ichile, and Kwao Magloire have endured my years of ranting about this project; it would not have been the same without your insights, prayers, and wisdom. Nick and Lorraine Swan are the greatest parents in the world. My siblings, Nique Swan, Natalie Auzenne-Swan, Tamisheka Swan, Kashima Atwood, and Jerodd Atwood, love is always there. Now, Akinwunmi, Ifasadun, Ayah, Mariama, and Kairos, let's have some *enjera*. Mojuba Elegba.

NOTES

INTRODUCTION

1 These exchanges are fascinatingly described in Robbie Shilliam, *The Black Pacific: Anti-Colonial Struggles and Oceanic Connections* (New York: Bloomsbury, 2015). Miriama Rauhihi-Ness passed away on March 15, 2021. *Give thanks*. Other studies that focus on the relationships between Black music and the Black Pacific include Shana Redmond, *Anthem: Social Movements and the Sound of Solidarity in the African Diaspora* (New York: New York University Press, 2014); and Gabriel Solis, "The Black Pacific: Music and Racialization in Papua New Guinea and Australia," *Critical Sociology* 41, no. 2 (May 2014): 297–312.

2 "World Population Prospects, 2019," United Nations Department of Economic and Social Affairs, Population Dynamics, https://population.un.org. "Aboriginal Deaths in Custody: Black Lives Matter Protests Referred to Our Count of 432 Deaths," *Guardian*, June 8, 2020, www.theguardian.com.

3 Kath Walker, "Opening Speech, Papua New Guinea Workshop," July 1, 1976, Box 17, New Guinea Material, UQFL 84, Papers of Oodgeroo Noonuccal, Fryer Library Special Collections, University of Queensland, Brisbane, Australia (hereafter cited as Papers of Oodgeroo Noonuccal).

4 For examples of full-length studies, see Yesenia Barragan, *Freedom's Captives: Slavery and Gradual Emancipation on the Colombian Black Pacific* (Cambridge: Cambridge University Press, 2021); Chris Dixon, *African Americans and the Pacific War, 1941–1945: Race, Nationality, and the Fight for Freedom* (Cambridge: Cambridge University Press, 2018); Taj Robeson Frazier, *The East Is Black: Cold War China in the Black Radical Imagination* (Durham: Duke University Press, 2014); Fred Ho and Bill Mullen, *Afro Asia: Revolutionary Political and Cultural Connections between African Americans and Asian Americans* (Durham: Duke University Press, 2008); Gerald Horne, *White Pacific: US Imperialism and Black Slavery in the South Seas after the Civil War* (Honolulu: University of Hawai'i Press, 2007); Gerald Horne, *Facing the Rising Sun: African Americans, Japan, and the Rise of Afro-Asian Solidarity* (New York: New York University Press, 2018); J. Kēhaulani Kauanui, *Hawaiian Blood: Colonialism and the Politics of Sovereignty and Indigeneity* (Durham: Duke University Press, 2008); Yuichiro Onishi, *Transpacific Antiracism: Afro-Asian Solidarity in Twentieth-Century Black America, Japan, and Okinawa* (New York: New York University Press, 2013); Vijay Prashad, *Everybody Was Kung Fu Fighting: Afro-Asian Connections and the Myth of Cultural Purity* (Boston: Beacon, 2002); Etsuko Taketani, *The Black Pacific*

Narrative: Geographic Imaginings of Race and Empire between the World Wars (Lebanon: Dartmouth College Press, 2015); Vince Schleitwiler, *Strange Fruit of the Black Pacific: Imperialism's Racial Justice and Its Fugitives* (New York: New York University Press, 2017); Nitasha Tamar Sharma, *Hawai'i Is My Haven: Race and Indigeneity in the Black Pacific* (Durham: Duke University Press, 2021); and Shilliam, *Black Pacific*. See also Alex Carter, "Afro Aboriginal Encounters: Black Arts and the Global Politics of Black Power" (PhD diss., University of Massachusetts–Amherst, 2020). Conference panels include Alex Carter, Glenn Chambers, Tao Leigh Goffe, Guy Emerson Mount, and Quito Swan, "The African World and the Black Pacific," Second International Colloquium on African Studies, University of Massachusetts–Boston, National Autonomous University of Mexico, and Boston University, March 26, 2021.

5 Ahmed Ali and R. G. Crocombe, eds., *Politics in Melanesia* (Suva: Institute of Pacific Studies of the University of the South Pacific, 1982); David Chappell, *The Kanak Awakening: The Rise of Nationalism in New Caledonia* (Honolulu: University of Hawai'i Press, 2013); Vanessa Griffen, ed., *Women Speak Out* (Suva: Pacific Women's Conference, 1976); Walter Lini, *Beyond Pandemonium: From the New Hebrides to Vanuatu* (Wellington: Asia Pacific Books, 1980); Tracey Banivanua Mar, *Decolonisation and the Pacific: Indigenous Globalisation and the Ends of Empire* (Cambridge: Cambridge University Press, 2016); John Maynard, *Fight for Liberty and Freedom: The Origins of Australian Aboriginal Activism* (Canberra: Aboriginal Studies Press, 2007); Bernard Narokobi, *The Melanesian Way* (Boroko: Institute of Papua New Guinea Studies, 1980); David Robie, *Blood on Their Banner: Nationalist Struggles in the South Pacific* (London: Zed Books, 1989); Katerina Martina Teaiwa, *Consuming Ocean Island: Stories of People and Phosphate from Banaba* (Bloomington: Indiana University Press, 2014); Howard Van Trease, *Politics of Land in Vanuatu: From Colony to Independence* (Suva: Institute of Pacific Studies, 1987); Judy Tzu-Chun Wu, *Radicals on the Road: Internationalism, Orientalism, and Feminism during the Vietnam Era* (Ithaca: Cornell University Press, 2013); Regis Tove Stella, *Imagining the Other: The Representation of the Papua New Guinean Subject* (Honolulu: University of Hawai'i Press, 2007); Quito J. Swan, *Pauulu's Diaspora: Black Internationalism and Environmental Justice* (Gainesville: University Press of Florida, 2020).

6 Francis Bugotu, "Decolonizing and Recolonizing: The Case of the Solomons," *Pacific Perspective* 2, no. 2 (1973): 77–80.

7 Joseph E. Harris, *The African Presence in Asia: Consequences of the East African Slave Trade* (Evanston: Northwestern University Press, 1971); Joseph E. Harris, "African Diaspora Studies: Some International Dimensions," *Issue: A Journal of Opinion* 24, no. 2 (1996): 6–8; Joseph E. Harris, "Expanding the Scope of African Diaspora Studies: The Middle East and India, a Research Agenda," *Radical History Review* 87 (Fall 2003): 163.

8 Harris, "Expanding the Scope," 158.

9 Ibid., 157.

10 Harriet Jackson Scarupa, "Joseph E. Harris: Forging Links on the Diaspora Trail," *New Directions* 13, no. 4, article 3 (1986): 15, http://dh.howard.edu.

11 Merze Tate, "The War Aims of World War I and World War II and Their Relation to the Darker Peoples of the World," *Journal of Negro Education* 12, no. 3 (Summer 1943): 521–32.

12 See Keisha N. Blain, *Set the World on Fire: Black Nationalist Women and the Global Struggle for Freedom* (Philadelphia: University of Pennsylvania Press, 2018); Keisha N. Blain and Tiffany Gill, eds., *To Turn the Whole World Over: Black Women and Internationalism* (Urbana: University of Illinois Press, 2019); Brent Hayes Edwards, *The Practice of Diaspora: Literature, Translation, and the Rise of Black Internationalism* (Cambridge: Harvard University Press, 2003); Tiffany Florvil, *Mobilizing Black Germany: Afro-German Women and the Making of a Transnational Movement* (Urbana: University of Illinois Press, 2020); Cheryl Higashida, *Black Internationalist Feminism: Women Writers of the Black Left, 1945–1995* (Chicago: University of Illinois Press, 2011); Sidney Lemelle and Robin Kelley, eds., *Imagining Home: Class, Culture and Nationalism in the African Diaspora* (London: Verso, 1994); Minkah Makalani, *In the Cause of Freedom: Radical Black Internationalism from Harlem to London, 1917–1939* (Chapel Hill: University of North Carolina Press, 2011); Erik McDuffie, *Sojourning for Freedom: Black Women, American Communism and the Making of Black Left Feminism* (Durham: Duke University Press, 2011); Brenda Plummer, *In Search of Power: African Americans in the Era of Decolonization, 1956–1974* (Cambridge: Cambridge University Press, 2012); Frank Guridy, *Forging Diaspora: Afro-Cubans and African Americans in a World of Empire and Jim Crow* (Chapel Hill: University of North Carolina Press, 2010); Cedric Robinson, *Black Marxism: The Making of the Black Radical Tradition* (Chapel Hill: University of North Carolina Press, 2000); Michael O. West, William G. Martin, and Fanon Che Wilkins, eds., *From Toussaint to Tupac: The Black International since the Age of Revolution* (Chapel Hill: University of North Carolina Press, 2013); and Rhonda Williams, *Concrete Demands: The Search for Black Power in the 20th Century* (New York: Routledge, 2014).

13 Lea Kinikini Kauvaka, "Berths and Anchorages: Pacific Cultural Studies from Oceania," *Contemporary Pacific* 28, no. 1 (2016): 130.

14 Blain, *Set the World on Fire*, 8; Keisha Blain, "Teaching Black Internationalism and *Americanah*," *Black Perspectives*, November 2014, www.aaihs.org.

15 Linda Tuhiwai Smith, *Decolonizing Methodologies: Research and Indigenous Peoples* (London: Zed Books, 2008).

16 Veronika Meduna, "Tracking the Lapita Expansion across the Pacific," *Our Changing World*, Radio New Zealand, August 13, 2015, www.rnz.co.nz; Stuart Bedford, Christophe Sand, and Richard Shing, *Lapita Peoples: Oceanic Ancestors* (Port Vila: Vanuatu Cultural Center, 2010); Stuart Bedford and M. Spriggs, "Northern Vanuatu as a Pacific Crossroads: The Archaeology of Discovery," *Asian Perspectives* 47, no. 1 (2008): 95–120.

17 See Epeli Hau'ofa, *We Are the Ocean* (Mānoa: University of Hawai'i Press, 2008).

18 Ibid.

19 Bilveer Singh, *Papua: Geopolitics and the Quest for Nationhood* (London: Transaction, 2011), 17.

20 Merze Tate, "Early European Discoveries in the Pacific," 1–2, 4, Box 219-10, Merze Tate Papers, Moorland Spingarn Research Center, Howard University, Washington, DC (hereafter cited as Merze Tate Papers).

21 See Serge Tcherkézoff, "A Long and Unfortunate Voyage towards the 'Invention' of the Melanesia/Polynesia Distinction, 1595–1832," *Journal of Pacific History* 38, no. 2 (September 2003): 175–96.

22 Clements Markham, *The Voyages of Pedro Fernandez de Quiros, 1595–1606* (London: Hakluyt Society, 1904), 188.

23 William Dampier, *A New Voyage round the World*, vol. 1 (London: J. Knapton, 1699), 464.

24 Tcherkézoff, "Long and Unfortunate Voyage," 188; J. R. Forster, *Observations Made during a Voyage round the World* (1778; reprint, Mānoa: University of Hawai'i Press, 1996), 228, 231, 241, 243.

25 Tcherkézoff, "Long and Unfortunate Voyage," 176–79.

26 Charles Darwin, *The Works of Charles Darwin*, vol. 1, *Diary of the Voyage of the H.M.S. Beagle* (New York: New York University Press, 1987), 314, 320.

27 Ibid., 330, 341, 347, 353–54.

28 Ibid., 356–57.

29 Tcherkézoff, "Long and Unfortunate Voyage," 185.

30 Miriam Kahn, *Tahiti beyond the Postcard: Power, Place, and Everyday Life* (Seattle: University of Washington Press, 2011), 34; Michelle Keown, *Pacific Islands Writing: The Postcolonial Literatures of Aotearoa/New Zealand and Oceania* (Oxford: Oxford University Press, 2007), 31.

31 Joseph Banks, *Journal of . . . Joseph Banks during Captain Cook's First Voyage* (London: Macmillan, 1896), 76.

32 Forster, *Observations*, 228, 243.

33 Boyle T. Somerville, "Notes on Some Islands of the New Hebrides," *Journal of the Anthropological Institute of Great Britain and Ireland* 23 (1894): 3, 7, 13.

34 Ibid., 3–4, 7.

35 "Prince William Takes Up Search for Lost Aboriginal Skull," *Times* (London), April 2, 2014.

36 Cressida Forde, "Repatriation: The Search for Yagan," n.d., Koori History Website Project, accessed August 20, 2015, www.kooriweb.org.

37 Merze Tate, "Australian Monroe Doctrine," *Political Science Quarterly* 76 (1961); Merze Tate, "New Hebrides Group: A Possession of the Crown," Box 219-9, Merze Tate Papers.

38 Meyer Eidelson, *Melbourne Dreaming: A Guide to Important Places of the Past and Present*, 2nd ed. (Canberra: Aboriginal Studies Press, 2015), 17–19; see also Mark Cocker, *Rivers of Blood, Rivers of Gold* (New York: Grove, 2001).

39 Merze Tate, "Australasian Concern over the New Hebrides," Box 219-9, Merze Tate Papers; Kim Gravelle, *Fiji Times: A History of Fiji* (Suva: Fiji Times, 1983), 109; Reid Mortensen, "Slaving in Australian Courts: Blackbirding Cases, 1869–1871," *Journal of South Pacific Law* 4 (2000): 1; Horne, *White Pacific*, 34.

40 Henry Evans Maude, *Slavers in Paradise: The Peruvian Slave Trade in Polynesia, 1862-1864* (Palo Alto: Stanford University Press, 1981), xvi, 5, 8.

41 Karin Speedy, "The Sutton Case: The First Franco-Australian Foray into Blackbirding," *Journal of Pacific History* 50, no. 3 (July 2015): 344-64.

42 "The Search of Faith Bandler," *Sun*, August 19, 1977; Horne, *White Pacific*, 43, 52; Gravelle, *Fiji Times*, 110.

43 Mortensen, "Slaving in Australian Courts," 7-8, 15-16; Tracey Banivanua-Mar, *Violence and Colonial Dialogue: The Australian-Pacific Indentured Labor Trade* (Honolulu: University of Hawai'i Press, 2007), 140-42.

44 Horne, *White Pacific*, 39, 41.

45 Tate, "Australasian Concern."

46 Sara Lightner and Anna Naupa, "The Labour Trade," unpublished paper, July 18, 2010, 4; Gravelle, *Fiji Times*, 111.

47 See Stewart Firth, "The Transformation of the Labor Trade in German New Guinea, 1899-1914," *Journal of Pacific History* 11, no. 1 (1976): 51-65; Hank Nelson, *Papua New Guinea: Black Unity or Black Chaos?* (Middlesex: Penguin, 1972), 66, 123; Matthew Craven, "Between Law and History: The Berlin Conference of 1884-1885 and the Logic of Free Trade," *London Review of International Law* 3, no. 1 (2015): 37.

48 Tate, "Australian Monroe Doctrine," 200; Walter Lini, "Address to United Nations Committee of 24," August 1976 (Suva: USP Pacific Studies Center, 1976), Pacific Collection, Library of the University of the South Pacific, Suva, Fiji (hereafter cited as Pacific Collection).

49 Government of Australia, *An Act to Apply and Extend Certain Restrictions . . .* no. 16, 1896, and *Immigration Restriction Act*, no. 17, 1901, www.legislation.gov.au; Emma Willoughby, "Our Federation Journey—A 'White Australia' in Museums Victoria Collections," 2013, https://collections.museumsvictoria.com.au.

50 Merze Tate, "Papua Act of 1905," Box 219-9, Merze Tate Papers.

51 Government of Australia, *Pacific Island Laborers Act*, no. 16, 1901.

52 Patricia Korowa, "Pacific Islanders and Australian South Sea Islanders Key Events in History," unpublished paper, January 21, 2013.

CHAPTER 1. GARVEY'S CAVEAT

1 J. M. Scanland, "South Sea Savages to Visit the World Fair," *Louisiana Review*, February 8, 1893, 6, www.newspapers.com.

2 Alexander Crummell, *Hope for Africa: A Sermon on Behalf of the Ladies' Negro Education Society* (London: Seelys, 1853), 39.

3 Alexander Crummell, *Civilization and Black Progress: Selected Writings of Alexander Crummell on the South*, ed. John R. Oldfield (Charlottesville: University of Virginia Press, 1995), 178.

4 "Is Negro Hate an Anglo-Saxon Trait," *Liberator*, July 18, 1862, 1; Martin Delany, *Martin R. Delany: A Documentary Reader*, ed. Robert S. Levine (Chapel Hill: University of North Carolina Press, 2003), 482; "Negro Progress in Jamaica," *Los Angeles Evening Express*, September 1, 1900, 8, www.newspapers.com.

5 W. E. B. Du Bois, *The Souls of Black Folk* (Chicago: McClurg, 1903), 13; Wilfred Duhaney to Jamaica High Commission, September 12, 1916, W. E. B. Du Bois to William Wolfe, October 13, 1921, W. E. B. Du Bois Papers (MS 312), Special Collections and University Archives, University of Massachusetts–Amherst Libraries (hereafter cited as Du Bois Papers); Anna Julia Cooper, *The Voice of Anna Julia Cooper* (New York: Rowman and Littlefield, 2000), 296.

6 W. E. B. Du Bois to Australia Labor Party, March 15, 1926, Du Bois Papers; W. E. B. Du Bois, "Bond of Ideals," *Chicago Daily Defender*, September 26, 1942.

7 Gary Foley, interview by author, digital recording, Melbourne, November 11, 2014; A. Goldsmith, letter, September 6, 1920, Box I:5, Carter G. Woodson Papers, Library of Congress, Washington, DC.

8 John Maynard, "In the Interests of Our People: The Influence of Garveyism on the Rise of Australian Aboriginal Political Activism," *Aboriginal History* 29 (2005): 2.

9 Ibid., 26.

10 Ibid., 27, 31–34.

11 Ibid., 19.

12 Robert Hill, ed., *Marcus Garvey Papers*, vol. 2 (Berkeley: University of California Press, 1983), 503, 505.

13 Ibid., 455; Hill, *Garvey Papers*, vol. 9, 541.

14 "Speech by Marcus Garvey," January 8, 1928, in Hill, *Garvey Papers*, vol. 7, 96.

15 "Sydney Division," *Negro World*, May 6, 1923; *New York Age*, January 13, 1923, 1; "Armstrong to British Ambassador," January 5, 1923, in Hill, *Garvey Papers*, vol. 10, 18.

16 "Australia Sends Greetings to the Fourth International," *Negro World*, August 2, 1924.

17 "Blacks of Australia Enslaved and Brutalized," *Negro World*, September 20, 1924.

18 "Race Horrors in Australia Are Unspeakably Vile," *Negro World*, September 27, 1924.

19 "The Black Remnant and the Half Castes of Australia," *Negro World*, October 17, September 26, 1925; "Dying Out," *Brisbane Courier*, March 14, 1925, 16.

20 John Maynard, "Fred Maynard and the Australian Aborigine Progressive Association: One God, One Aim, One Destiny," *Aboriginal History* 21 (1997): 17; Maynard, "In the Interests," 19.

21 *Black Man* 2, no. 1 (May–June 1936): 1; *Crisis* 23 (January 1922): 3; "Race War in Australia," *Pittsburgh Defender*, September 29, 1928.

22 Ho Chi Minh, *Ho Chi Minh on Revolution*, ed. Bernard Fall (London: Frederick Praeger, 1967), 25–26, 40.

23 H.I.M., "Native Peoples under the Union Jack," *Negro Worker* 4, no. 2 (April 1932): 10–11.

24 Aimé Césaire, *Discourse on Colonialism* (New York: Monthly Review Press, 1972), 42.

25 Jane Nardal, "Josephine Baker, the Bal Negre, and the State of Black Musical Expression in Paris," *La Revue du Monde Noir*, May 1928, https://musicalgeography .org.

26 "Negro Troops Serving on All Fronts," *Cleveland Call and Post*, July 25, 1942; "Praise New Guinea Natives Aid to Allies," *Atlanta Daily World*, March 21, 1943, www.proquest.com. For an extensive exploration of how communities in Vanuatu engaged African American soldiers, see Lamont Lindstrom, "Big Wok: The Vanuatu Cultural Centre's World War Two Ethnohistory Project," in *Working Together in Vanuatu: Research Histories, Collaborations, Projects and Reflections*, ed. John Taylor and Nick Thieberger (Canberra: Australia National University Press, 2011), 43–57, doi: 10.22459/WTV.10.2011.07.

27 Lamont Lindstrom, "The American Occupation of New Hebrides," Macmillan Brown Centre for Pacific Studies, University of Canterbury, New Zealand, Working Paper Series 5, January 1996, 7.

28 Museum of African Art, *Tribute to Africa: The Photography and the Collection of Eliot Elisofon* (Washington, DC: Museum of African Art, 1974), 6; Raoul Granqvist, *Photography and American Coloniality: Eliot Elisofon in Africa, 1942–1972* (Lansing: Michigan State University Press, 2017), xii.

29 Eliot Elisofon, "New Guinea," 53.22, and Eliot Elisofon, "The South Seas: Its People, Its Art," 58.43, Elisofon Papers, Harry Ransom Center, University of Texas–Austin (hereafter cited as Elisofon Papers).

30 Eliot Elisofon, "New Guinea Sheep Station," January 1949, 14.3, Elisofon Papers.

31 Ibid.

32 Ibid.

33 Eliot Elisofon, "Australia-Papua New Guinea," January 1949, 14.5, Elisofon Papers.

34 Ibid.

35 Ibid.

36 Eliot Elisofon, "Storied Isles of Romance in the South Seas," *Life* 38, no. 4 (January 24, 1955): 60–77.

37 Ibid.

38 Eliot Elisofon to David Touff, September 12, 1963, 58.43, Elisofon Papers.

39 *Life Magazine* to John Thorne for Dutch Stringer, June 6, 1956, 26.3, Elisofon Papers.

40 Jack Burby to Eliot Elisofon, January 24, 1956, 26.3, Elisofon Papers.

41 Ibid.

42 Eliot Elisofon, "Japan's Dazzle after Dark," *Life* 52, no. 8 (February 23, 1962): 66–73; Eliot Elisofon to *Time*, March 28, 1956, 26.3, Elisofon Papers.

43 William Robinson to Eliot Elisofon, April 14, 1956, 26.3, Elisofon Papers.

44 "Elisofon's Forthcoming Pacific Trip—Adventure Series," June 11, 1956, 26.3, Elisofon Papers.

45 Manager at Apia to Eliot Elisofon, July 19, 1956, 26.3, Elisofon Papers.

46 William Robinson to Eliot Elisofon, May 13, 1956, 26.3, Elisofon Papers.

47 Eliot Elisofon to Ray, July 25, 1956, 26.3, Elisofon Papers.

48 Eliot Elisofon to *Life*, 26.3, Elisofon Papers.

49 George Caturani to Eliot Elisofon, 26.3, Elisofon Papers.

50 "Romantic Voyage of the Varua," *Life* 42, no. 8 (February 25, 1957): 68.

51 "Essay by William A. Robinson," December 6, 1956, 26.6, Elisofon Papers.

52 Ibid.

53 Eliot Elisofon, "Harvard-New Guinea Expedition," 30.26, Elisofon Papers.

54 Ibid.

55 US Department of State, "Summary of the Current Situation in the Territories of the South Pacific," August 13, 1947, US Declassified Documents Online, https://tinyurl.com/udrfe5tj, Library of the Wilson International Center for Scholars, Washington, DC (hereafter cited as Wilson International Center).

56 National Intelligence Estimate, "Security Problems in the Pacific Islands Area," no. 49–63, September 18, 1963, US Declassified Documents Online, Wilson International Center.

57 Lindstrom, "American Occupation of New Hebrides," 3.

58 US Department of State, "Summary of the Current Situation."

59 "Minutes of Secretary Staff Meeting," October 10, 1975, Kissinger Transcripts: A Verbatim Record of US Diplomacy, 1969–1977, US Department of State, Digital National Security Archive (DNSA), https://proquest.libguides.com.

60 Margaret Mead, "Melanesia, Black Islands of the Pacific," *Courier* 7, nos. 8–9 (1954): 27.

61 Lenora Foerstel and Angela Gilliam, eds., *Confronting the Margaret Mead Legacy: Scholarship, Empire, and the South Pacific* (Philadelphia: Temple University Press, 1992), 117, 121–22, 130.

62 Ibid.

63 "Confronting the Margaret Mead Legacy, Letter of Understanding," Box VP 003, Vanua'aku Pati Archives, National Archives of Vanuatu (NAV), Port Vila, Vanuatu (hereafter cited as Vanua'aku Pati Archives).

64 Foerstel and Gilliam, *Confronting the Margaret Mead Legacy*, 159, 171–72.

65 Ibid., 159–72.

66 "The Kanak's People's Struggle," *Tok Blog SPPF* 12 (July 1985): 5–15, http://pacificpeoplespartnership.org; "The Diary," *Globe and Mail*, June 26, 1985, M:2; www.proquest.com; Pat Grogan, "Leader of Kanak Struggle Tours US," *Militant*, September 6, 1985, 16, https://themilitant.com.

67 "Out and About," *Detroit Free Press*, September 13, 1985, 40; "Lecture," *St. Louis Post-Dispatch*, September 26, 1985, 26; "Susanna Ounei," *LA Weekly*, October 10, 1985, 10; "What's Ahead," *Record*, October 17, 1985, newspapers.com; Susanna Ounei flyer, October 8, 1985, in possession of author.

68 "New Caledonians May Boycott Vote," *New York Times*, August 26, 1985, www.nytimes.com.

69 Grogan, "Leader of Kanak Struggle."

70 Ibid.; "HUSA to Sponsor New Caledonia Forum," *Hilltop*, September 6, 1965, 8, https://dh.howard.edu.

71 Audre Lorde, "Sisterhood and Survival," *Black Scholar* 17, no. 2 (March–April 1986): 7; "Solidarity," *Tribune*, September 25, 1985, http://nla.gov.au.

72 Lucille Clifton, "Atlantic Is a Sea of Bones," Poetry Center, San Francisco Arts Commission Gallery, April 2, 1987, Poetry Center Digital Archive, https://diva.sfsu.edu.

73 Lorde, "Sisterhood and Survival."

CHAPTER 2. NEGROIDS OF THE PACIFIC

1 Johnny Blades, "Deadly Unrest Breaks Out Again in West Papua," Radio New Zealand, September 23, 2019, www.rnz.co.nz; Febriana Firdaus and Kate Mayberry, "State-in-Waiting: Papua's Rebels Unite against Indonesia Rule," *Al Jazeera News*, July 5, 2019, www.aljazeera.com.

2 Provisional Government of West Papua, "Indonesian Colonialism vs the People of West Papua New Guinea," 1, West New Guinea, Box 8:313, National Association for the Advancement of Colored People Records, Library of Congress, Washington, DC (hereafter cited as NAACP Records).

3 Tate, "Early European Discoveries"; also see Stewart Firth, "The Labor Trade in German New Guinea," *Journal of Pacific History* 11, no. 1 (1976): 51–65; Nelson, *Papua New Guinea*, 66, 123; Provisional Government of West Papua, "Indonesian Colonialism," 1; C. Hartley Grattan, *The Southwest Pacific Since 1900* (Ann Arbor: University of Michigan Press, 1963), 452–53.

4 Jason Macleod, *Merdeka and the Morning Star: Civil Resistance in West Papua* (Brisbane: University of Queensland Press, 2016).

5 "Free Papua Movement," May 1, 1981, Box 8:313, NAACP Papers.

6 Grattan, *Southwest Pacific*, 452–53.

7 Ministry of Foreign Affairs, "Final Communiqué of the Asian-African Conference of Bandung," in *Asia-Africa Speaks from Bandung* (Djakarta: Republic of Indonesia, 1955), 168.

8 "A People's Preparations for Its Freedom Brought to Naught by Indonesia's Blackmail Policy," June 20, 1968, NAACP Papers; Provisional Government of West Papua, "Indonesian Colonialism," 2; *Sydney Morning Herald*, October 31, 1961, 8, newspapers.com.

9 "Fear New Guinea May Become New Congo," *Daily Defender*, November 30, 1961, 6; "Dutch-Indonesia Dispute, Papuans," *Bermuda Recorder*, January 13, 1962, 5, Bermuda National Library Digital Collection, https://bnl.contentdm.oclc.org.

10 *Chicago Defender*, April 14, 1962, 9; *Press and Sun-Bulletin*, December 19, 1961, 1; "Indonesians Told of Logical Base to Attack Guinea," *Atlanta Daily World*, January 5, 1962, 1; "Dutch-Indonesia Dispute, Papuans."

11 "New Guinea Crisis Dates Back to 1949 Dispute," *Chicago Daily Defender*, January 23, 1962, 9; "10,000 Indonesian Volunteers Sent to Infiltrate New Guinea," *Bermuda Recorder*, February 2, 1962, 4; *Age*, January 22, 1962, 5.

12 "Papuans Say Fight Faces Indonesia," *Post-Standard*, December 21, 1961, 2; "Poisoned Arrows Threat by Papuans," *Age*, January 22, 1962, 5; *Age*, May 32, 1962, 4.

13 "A People's Preparations for Its Freedom."

14 "African Calls Plight of New Guinea Natives 'A Scandal,'" *Age*, May 9, 1962, 4.

15 Charles Howard, "Africans Split on New Guinea Issue," *Afro-American*, June 9, 1962, 17.

16 Ibid.

17 *Age*, May 31, 1962, 4; "Papuans Want Same, as Most—Their Freedom," *Terre Haute Star*, July 31, 1962, 22.

18 Papuan National Committee, *Voice of the Negroids in the Pacific to the Negroids throughout the World*, 4, Box 655, Folder 5, Records of the Non-Sectarian Anti-Nazi League to Champion Human Rights, 1836–1978, Rare Book and Manuscript Library, Columbia University, New York.

19 Ibid., 5.

20 Ibid., 20.

21 Ibid., 24, 26.

22 Ibid., 28–29.

23 Ibid., 30.

24 "The Problem of West New Guinea (West Irian)," October 12, 1960, West New Guinea: General, 1961 2/61–3/61, JFKNSF-205–001, Box 205, Papers of John F. Kennedy, Presidential Papers, National Security Files, John F. Kennedy Presidential Library, Boston (hereafter cited as JFK Papers).

25 "Memorandum of Conversation," May 28, 1963, Netherlands General 1963 and Indonesia, 3/31/62–6/30/62, JFKNSF-143–007, Box 143, JFK Papers.

26 "Papuans Seek Help from Negro Brothers and Sisters," *Pittsburgh Courier*, April 14, 1962, 32, newspapers.com.

27 Ibid.; *Chicago Defender*, April 14, 1962, 9.

28 Ibid.

29 "Papuans Want Same, as Most"; *Chicago Defender*, April 14, 1962, 9; "Stone Age Habits of Papuans Slow Changeover to New Independence," *Amarillo Globe-Times*, October 5, 1962, 20.

30 "A People's Preparations for Its Freedom."

31 Ibid.

32 Jakarta to State Department, June 9, 1969, POL 19 West Irian, RG 59, National Archives at College Park, College Park, MD (hereafter cited as NACP).

33 Jakarta to State Department, April 27, 1967, NACP.

34 Jakarta to State Department, June 9, 1969, NACP.

35 Memo of Conversation, December 12, 1967, NACP.

36 Jakarta to State Department, May 10, 1968, NACP.

37 Ibid.

38 Jakarta to State Department, February 29, 1968, April 27, 1968, May 2, 1968, June 18, 1968, NACP.

39 State Department Report on Implementation of Act of Free Choice, August 9, 1968, NACP.

40 Jakarta to State Department, July 29, 1968, June 12, 1969, NACP.

41 Jakarta to State Department, April 22, 1969, NACP.

42 Conversation with Ambassador Ortiz Sans, April 25, 1969; Jakarta to State Department, August 7, 1969, November 19, 1969, NACP.

43 "Memo, Act of Free Choice," November 17, 1969, NACP; also see David Webster, *Fire and the Full Moon: Canada and Indonesia in a Decolonizing World* (Vancouver: University of British Columbia, 2010); and Matthew Jones, *Britain, the United States, Indonesia and the Creation of Malaysia* (Cambridge: Cambridge University Press, 2012).

44 "Urgent Appeal to Members of the United Nations," September 1, 1973, Box 8:313, NAACP Papers.

45 Ibid.

46 Herman Womsiwor to Roy Wilkins, April 29, 1971; National Liberation Council of West Papua, "African Papuans Being Slaughtered by Indonesian Government," Box 8:313, NAACP Papers.

47 Roy Wilkins to Kurt Waldheim, January 4, 1972; Herman Womsiwor to the NAACP, September 25, 1975; "Papua, West Guinea," *Crisis Magazine* (March 1972): 5, Box 8:313, NAACP Papers.

48 Seth Rumkorem to Roy Wilkins, December 16, 1977, Box 8:313, NAACP Papers.

49 National Liberation Council, "African Papuans Being Slaughtered."

50 "Senghor Interviewed on Africa," *Le Monde*, March 20, 1976, Foreign Broadcast Information Service Reports, Wilson Center, Washington, DC, www.readex.com (hereafter cited as FBIS Reports); "Nonaligned Nations, Liberation Fronts, Political Leaders, Meetings," July 7, 1976, Cable 1976DAKAR04287, Central Foreign Policy Files, RG 59, Electronic Cables, NACP (hereafter cited as CFPF Cables); "Senegalese President Repeats Support for West Papua New Guinea Independence," February 4, 1978, Cable 1978DAKAR01024, CFPF Cables.

51 "Senegalese Relations with South Moluccans and National Liberation Council of West Papua/New Guinea," February 4, 1976, Cable 1976DAKAR00688, CFPF Cables.

52 Wole Soyinka, "Senghor, Lessons in Power," *Research in African Literatures* 33, no. 4 (Winter 2002): 1–2.

53 Vanessa Griffen and Claire Slatter, interview by author, digital recording, Suva, November 12, 2014; "Freedom Fighters of West Papua New Guinea," *Povai* 1, no. 1 (March–April 1976): 2, September–October 1976, 8, Pacific Collection.

54 "West Papua," *Povai* 1, no. 2 (June–July 1976): 3; "West Papua New Guinea," *Povai* 1, no. 3 (September–October 1976): 8.

55 "Independence, Liberation Fronts, Foreign Policy Position, Limited War," February 24, 1976, Cable 1976DAKAR01081, CFPF Cables.

56 "Press Release—The Provisional Government of the Republic of West Papua," Box 8:313, NAACP Papers.

57 Ben Tanggahma to Mildred Roxborough, n.d., Ben Tanggahma to Roy Wilkins, February 12, 1976, Box 8:313, NAACP Papers; "Western Papua New Guinea, a Little Known Rebellion," *Le Monde*, March 17, 1976.

58 "Senegalese Relations with South Moluccans," CFPF Cables.

59 Ibid.; "West Irian Dissident Movement Seeks US Support," June 2, 1977, Cable 1977DAKAR03831, CFPF Cables.

60 "Seminar for African Alternatives," December 11, 1975, 15.6, Transcription Centre Records, Harry Ransom Center, University of Texas–Austin (hereafter cited as Transcription Centre Records).

61 Wole Soyinka, "Festac 77 and the Colloquium on Black Civilization and Black Education," 2, Folder 3, Wole Soyinka Papers, Houghton Library, Harvard University (hereafter cited as Wole Soyinka Papers).

62 "Declaration of Black Intellectuals and Scholars," 4, 187:2:34, Harold Cruse Papers, Tamiment Library and Robert F. Wagner Labor Archive, New York (hereafter cited as Harold Cruse Papers).

63 "Wole Soyinka to Jean Brierre"; Wole Soyinka to Carole Johnson, Folder 1, Wole Soyinka Papers.

64 "Declaration of Black Intellectuals and Scholars," 4.

65 Ibid.

66 Ibid.

67 Ibid.

68 Ibid.

69 Wole Soyinka to Dennis Duerden, February 23, 1976, 15.6, Transcription Centre Records.

70 Carlos Moore and Cheikh Anta Diop, "Conversations with Cheikh Anta Diop," *Présence Africaine*, Nouvelle Série, 149–150 (1989): 398, 417–18, www.jstor.org.

71 "In Western Papua New Guinea," *Le Monde*, March 17, 1976.

72 "Interview with Ben Tanggahma by Shawna Maglangbayan and Carlos Moore," *Association of African Historians Newsletter* 1, no. 9 (1976).

73 "West Papua New Guinea: Interview with Foreign Minister Ben Tanggahma," *Black Books Bulletin* 4, no. 2 (Summer 1976), by Shawna Maglangbayan and Carlos Moore, Dakar, February 16, 1976.

74 Ibid.

75 "Statement of the Revolutionary Provisional Government of West Papua New Guinea (RPG) on the Recent Splits within Our Revolutionary Ranks," November 3, 1978, Box 8:313, NAACP Papers.

76 William Blake to Mildred Roxborough, February 12, 1976; Mildred Roxborough to William Blake, March 4, 1976, Box 8:313, NAACP Papers.

77 Malcolm Gault-Williams, "Organisasi Papua Merdeka: The Free Papua Movement Lives," *Bulletin of Concerned Asian Scholars* 19, no. 4 (1987): 37, https://doi.org/10.1080/14672715.1987.10409792.

78 Information Mission of the RPG, "Statement to the Press," February 15, 1980, Box 8:313, NAACP Papers.

79 "Independence, Liberation Fronts, Foreign Policy Position."

80 "For an Independent West Papua," Box 8:313, NAACP Papers.

81 E. Mveng, "General Report," *Présence Africaine*, Nouvelle Série, 117–118 (1981): 366, www.jstor.org.

82 "President of Senegal—'West Papua Is Now an Issue for All Black Africans,'" West Papua Media, December 20, 2010, https://westpapuamedia.info.

83 Benny Wenda, interview by Deborah Dauda, Gifty Debordes-Jackson, Maria Rogers, and Quito Swan, William Monroe Trotter Institute, University of Massachusetts–Boston, November 17, 2020.

CHAPTER 3. OODGEROO NOONUCCAL

1 "Lands at Tunis Airport," Tunis Domestic Service, November 22, 1974, FBIS Reports.

2 Ibid.; Kath Walker, "Flight into Tunis," December 14, 1974, Short Stories, Box 27, Papers of Oodgeroo Noonuccal.

3 "Lands at Tunis Airport."

4 Walker, "Flight into Tunis"; Kath Walker, "Yussef (Highjacker)," November 22, 1974, Poems Unpublished, Box 27, Papers of Oodgeroo Noonuccal.

5 *Black Soldier*, Australian War Memorial, August 5, 2019, www.awm.gov.au.

6 "1936 Report of Queensland's Chief Protector of Aboriginals," 1, 9–10, Annual Report of the Director of Aboriginal and Island Affairs, C. Hartley Grattan Papers, Harry Ransom Center, University of Texas–Austin.

7 Makalani, *In the Cause of Freedom*, 85; Claude McKay, "Report on the Negro Question: Speech to the 4th Congress of the Comintern," November 1922, *International Press Correspondence* 3 (January 5, 1923): 16; Australian Security Intelligence Organization (ASIO), "FCAATSI," November 23, 1962, report, Communist Party of Australia Interest and Influence in Aboriginal Affairs, vol. 5, A6122/1528, National Archives of Australia, Canberra (hereafter cited as Communist Party and Aborigines).

8 "Fight for Aborigines Draft Program of Struggle against Slavery," *Workers Weekly*, September 21, 1931.

9 Ibid.

10 ASIO, "FCAATSI."

11 Ibid.; "Ida Lessing Faith Bandler," July 3, 1969, Faith Bandler, vol. 4, A6119/2936, National Archives of Australia, Canberra.

12 Shirley Andrews, "The Australian Aborigines," ML MSS 6222/3, Vivianne Abraham Papers, State Library of New South Wales, Australia.

13 Kath Walker, "Political Rights for Aborigines," *Smoke Signals* 8, no. 1 (June 1969): 9–11.

14 "Report of FCAATSI Conference, September 1969," Kathleen Walker, vol. 8, A6119/2768, National Archives of Australia, Canberra (hereafter cited as Kathleen Walker Records).

15 "We Are Going," *Negro Digest* 14, no. 11 (September 1965): 88–89.

16 Faith Bandler, *Wacvie* (Adelaide: Rigby Limited, 1977), iii.

17 Marilyn Lake, *Faith Bandler: Gentle Activist* (Sydney: Allen and Unwin, 2003), 20.

18 Faith Bandler and Len Fox, eds., *The Time Was Ripe: A History of the Aboriginal-Australian Fellowship* (Chippendale: Alternative Publishing Cooperative, 2008), 1–2.

19 Ann Curthoys, "Paul Robeson's Visit to Australia and Aboriginal Activism, 1960," in *Passionate Histories: Myth, Memory and Indigenous Australia*, ed. Frances Peter-Little et al. (Canberra: ANU Press and Aboriginal History Incorporated, 2010), 354, 358, 372.

20 "Faith Bandler," Faith Bandler, vol. 5, A6119/3898, National Archives of Australia, Canberra.

21 World Council of Churches, "Report on the World Council of Churches Sponsored Consultation on Racism, Held in Notting Hill, London," 1969, Kathleen Walker Records.

22 Kath Walker, "Report to the Australian Council of Churches of the WCC on Racism," 1969, Kathleen Walker Records.

23 Ibid. Full-length studies of Black activism in London include Kennetta Hammond Perry, *London Is the Place for Me: Black Britons, Citizenship and the Politics of Race* (London: Oxford University Press, 2016).

24 "Communist Party of Australia—Interest in Aborigines," August 24, 1969, vol. 20, A6122/2501, Communist Party and Aborigines.

25 Kath Walker, "White Violence and White Racism," June 1969, vol. 20, Communist Party and Aborigines.

26 Ibid.

27 Ibid.

28 "'Do-Gooders' Irk Aboriginal," *Sun*, September 17, 1969.

29 "Aboriginal Poet Sees Black Revolt as Inevitable," *Australian*, September 17, 1969, 8, Kathleen Walker Papers.

30 Ibid.

31 "Wanted, 10,000," National Tribal Council, FVF228, Box 39, Papers of Oodgeroo Noonuccal.

32 "Indigenous Activist's Long Struggle for Justice," *Green Left Weekly*, November 17, 1993.

33 "Self-Rule Call by Aborigines," *Tribune* 1640 (January 21, 1970): 1.

34 "Indigenous Activist's Long Struggle"; Black Panther Party of Australia (Brisbane Chapter) Ephemera, 1972, Fryer Library Special Collections, University of Queensland, Australia; Rachel Perkins, dir., *Black Panther Woman* (Sydney: Blackfella Films, 2014).

35 "Australia's Black Panthers," *Honi Soit*, March 16, 1972, Black Panther Party of Australia, vol. 1, A6122/2292, National Archives of Australia, Canberra.

36 Patricia Korowa, interview by author, digital recording, Sydney, November 2, 2014.

37 Kath Walker, "Aboriginal Civil Rights," *UNISPAC* 5, no 4, n.d., Box 26, Papers of Oodgeroo Noonuccal.

38 Cornelius Marivate and Kath Walker, extensive note on reverse, ca. 1970s, Photograph 14.223, Album 2, Box 14, Papers of Oodgeroo Noonuccal.

39 Australian-American Educational Foundation, award offer, August 22, 1978, Box 4, Material relating to trip to America, Papers of Oodgeroo Noonuccal.

40 Kath Walker to Battersby, January 31, 1978, Box 4, Papers of Oodgeroo Noonuccal.

41 Kath Walker to B. Edwards, August 29, 1978, Box 4, Papers of Oodgeroo Noonuccal.

42 Kath Walker to Margaret Lauer, June 1978, Box 4, Papers of Oodgeroo Noonuccal.

43 Margaret Lauer to Kath Walker, June 30, 1978, March 4, 1978, Box 4, Papers of Oodgeroo Noonuccal.

44 Margaret Lauer to Bruce Ferrer, March 27, 1978; Margaret Lauer to Kath Walker, April 1978, June 30, 1978, Box 4, Papers of Oodgeroo Noonuccal.

45 "More Than a Poet," *College Newsletter* (Bloomsburg State College) 5, no. 3 (October 11, 1978): 1; "Kath Walker Calendar," Box 4, Papers of Oodgeroo Noonuccal.

46 Kath Walker to Myer Foundation, July 19, 1978, Box 4, Papers of Oodgeroo Noonuccal.

47 "Kath Walker Readings," Box 4, Papers of Oodgeroo Noonuccal.

48 *Hilltop*, October 13, 27, 1978, http://dh.howard.edu.

49 *Hilltop*, October 10, November 3, 1978, http://dh.howard.edu.

50 Dave Warren to Gordon Braithwaite, December 12, 1978, Box 4, Papers of Oodgeroo Noonuccal.

51 Ibid.; "Australian Poet to Read Her Work," *Morning Press*, November 18, 1978.

52 Warren to Braithwaite, December 12, 1978.

53 Herbert Chivambo Shore to James Buell, January 5, 1979, Box 4, Papers of Oodgeroo Noonuccal.

54 Ibid.

55 Kath Walker to Margaret Reed-Lauer, December 5, 1978; Kathleen Walker to James Mitchell, December 5, 1978, Box 4, Papers of Oodgeroo Noonuccal.

56 Photo, "Tribal leaders who participated in the Longest Walk, 1978," Box 4, Papers of Oodgeroo Noonuccal; Institute of American Indian Arts, *One with the Earth* (Santa Fe: Institute of American Indian Arts, 1976), inscribed to Kath Walker, January 27, 1979, Box 25, Papers of Oodgeroo Noonuccal.

57 "Kath Walker Activities at Texas Southern University," Box 4, Papers of Oodgeroo Noonuccal.

58 Texas Southern University, "First International Student Poetry Forum"; "Noted Australian Poet to Lecture at TSU," *Informer and Texas Freeman*, February 3, 1979; Kathleen Walker, 10:15, Carlton W. and Barbara J. Molette Papers, Stuart A. Rose Manuscript, Archives, and Rare Book Library, Emory University, Atlanta.

59 Carlton W. Molette to Grant Spradling, Molette to Kath Walker, March 7, 1979, Molette to H. H. Coombs, March 7, 1979, Molette to Granville Sawyer, February 28, 1979, Box 4, Papers of Oodgeroo Noonuccal.

60 "Pacific Film Archive," *Berkeley Gazette*, January 19, 1979, newspapers.com; Edith Kramer to Jullianne Swenke, February 2, 1979; Erskine Peters, "Afro American Studies 156," Box 4, Papers of Oodgeroo Noonuccal.

61 Black Filmmakers Hall of Fame to Kathleen Walker, February 9, 1979, Box 4, Papers of Oodgeroo Noonuccal.

62 "Kath Walker flyer," Box 4, Papers of Oodgeroo Noonuccal.

63 C. Bernard Jackson to Kath Walker, April 22, 1979, Box 4, Papers of Oodgeroo Noonuccal.

64 Cynthia Young, *Soul Power: Culture, Radicalism, and the Making of a US Third World Left* (Durham: Duke University Press, 2006), 216.

65 Allyson Field, Jan-Christopher Horak, and Jacqueline Najuma Stewart, eds., *L.A. Rebellion: Creating a New Black Cinema* (Oakland: University of California Press, 2015), 388; Claudia Springer, "Black Women Filmmakers," *Jump Cut*, no. 29 (February 1984): 34–37.

66 "Pamela Jones," 1–2, Box 4, Papers of Oodgeroo Noonuccal.

67 Pia Lundqvist to Ms. Walker, March 13, 1979, Box 4, Papers of Oodgeroo Noonuccal.

68 Kathleen Walker, "Fulbright Report," Box 4, Papers of Oodgeroo Noonuccal.

69 Ibid.

70 Kath Walker, Australian Grantee Report Form, April 15, 1979, Box 4, Papers of Oodgeroo Noonuccal.

71 Ruwa Chiri to the International Afrikan Community, n.d., Box 4, Papers of Oodgeroo Noonuccal.

72 "Press Release," Kath Walker letter, Box 4, Papers of Oodgeroo Noonuccal.

CHAPTER 4. *NILAIDAT*

1 Leo Hannett, "The Niugini Black Power Movement," in *Tertiary Students and the Politics of Papua New Guinea* (Lae: Papua New Guinea Institute of Technology, 1971), 1, Papua New Guinea Collection, University of Papua New Guinea Library, Port Moresby (hereafter cited as PNG Collection).

2 Leo Morgan, *Nilaidat* 1, no. 1 (March 21, 1968), National Library of Australia, Canberra.

3 "Niugini Black Power," *Nilaidat*, February 1971, 7.

4 Leo Hannett, "Niugini Black Power," *Nilaidat*, May 1971, 1, Hawaiian and Pacific Collections, University of Hawai'i Mānoa, Honolulu (hereafter cited as Hawaiian and Pacific Collections).

5 Leo Hannett, "Niugini Black Power," *Lot's Wife* 11, no. 4 (September 1971): 9.

6 Ibid.

7 Ibid.

8 Ian Hicks, "Rejoice at Death, Urges NG Student," *Age*, August 25, 1971, 7; "Black Power," *Age*, August 26, 1971, 3.

9 Leo Hannett, *The Niugini Black Power*, unpublished paper (Port Moresby, 1971), 1–3, Hawaiian and Pacific Collections.

10 Ibid.; Hannett, "Niugini Black Power Movement," in *Tertiary Students*.

11 Hannett, *Niugini Black Power*, 4; Hannett, "Niugini Black Power Movement," in *Tertiary Students*, 3.

12 Hannett, *Niugini Black Power*, 4.

13 Ibid., 5.

14 Ibid., 5–7; Hannett, "Niugini Black Power Movement," in *Tertiary Students*, 6.

15 Hannett, "Niugini Black Power Movement," in *Tertiary Students*, 5–6.

16 "Report of the United Nations Visiting Mission to the Trust Territory of New Guinea, 1971," 6, 138, T/1728-FR, UN Digital Library, https://digitallibrary.un.org; Hannett, *Niugini Black Power*, 6–7; Hannett, "Niugini Black Power Movement," in *Tertiary Students*, 45–46.

17 Merze Tate, "Administration of Papua and New Guinea," 271; Merze Tate, "Australia and Self-Determination in Papua New Guinea," Box 219-9, 253, Merze Tate Papers.

18 Hannett, *Niugini Black Power*, 11.

19 Ibid., 12–15.

20 Ibid., 13.

21 Ibid., 15–16.

22 Taban Lo Liyong, "Press Release," July 1–4, 1976, Box 17, Papers of Oodgeroo Noonuccal.

23 Ibid., 1–2.

24 Alexander Mamak, Richard Bedford, Leo Hannett, and Moses Havini, *Bougainvillean Nationalism: Aspects of Unity and Discord* (Christchurch: Bougainville Special Publications, 1974), vii; "Leo Hannett Interviewed," *Tribune*, August 13, 1969, 5; Leo Hannett, "Disillusionment with the Priesthood," in *Black Writing from New Guinea* (Brisbane: University of Queensland Press, 1973).

25 "Hard Labor for Two Buka Island Leaders," *Age*, March 3, 1962, 5; Albert Maori Kiki, *Ten Thousand Years in a Lifetime* (Melbourne: Cheshire, 1968), 107.

26 Hannett, "Disillusionment with the Priesthood," 47–48.

27 "United Nations Visiting Mission to the Trust Territories of Nauru and New Guinea, 1965," 9, T/1646, UN Digital Library.

28 Hannett, "Disillusionment with the Priesthood," 48; United Nations Trusteeship Council, official records, 32nd session, May 28–June 30, 1965, New York T/SR.1245–1270, UN Digital Library.

29 UN Trusteeship Council, 32nd session, June 18, 1965, UN Digital Library.

30 Hannett, "Disillusionment with the Priesthood," 49–50.

31 John Momis, "Death of Leo Hannett: A Bougainville Leader of the Middle Way," June 25, 2018, *PNG Attitude*, www.pngattitude.com.

32 Hannett, "Dr. Martin Luther King," *Nilaidat* 1, no. 4 (May 9, 1968).

33 Leo Hannett, "Is Life Worth Living," *Nilaidat* 1, no. 6 (July 1968): 3–5; M. Maunsell Davis, "Student Hang-Ups and Student Action, Student Political Activity at the University of Papua and New Guinea," in *The Politics of Melanesia: Papers Delivered at the Fourth Waigani Seminar, May 1970*, ed. Marion W. Ward (Canberra: Research School of Pacific Studies, Australian National University, 1970), 285.

34 W. Hurrey, "The Demonstration," *Nilaidat* 1, no. 7 (July 8, 1968): 5–6.

35 Ibid.

36 "Papua New Guinea—76 Natural Nations?," *Nilaidat* 1, no. 7 (July 8, 1968): 7.

37 "Reason Demonstrated," *Nilaidat* 1, no. 7 (July 8, 1968): 19–20.

38 *Nilaidat*, May 22, 1969, 8.

39 *Nilaidat* 2, no. 2 (May 14, 1969), PNG Collection.

40 *Nilaidat*, June 6, 1969, 4; May 22, 1969, 1, 3, 8.

41 Davis, "Student Hang-Ups," 297; M. Buluna, "The Role of Students in Niugini Politics," in Ward, *Politics of Melanesia*, 309.

42 Hannett, "Niugini Black Power Movement," in *Tertiary Students*; Hannett, *Niugini Black Power*, 1.

43 ABC Radio, August 27, 1970, "Activities of Mr. John Kasaipwalova," Trobriand Islands, A452 1970/524, National Archives of Australia, Canberra.

44 "Black Power," A452 1970/524, National Archives of Australia, Canberra; "Trobriands Challenge," *Post Courier*, January 27, 1970.

45 Charles Cepulis, "Native Has No Dignity," *Post Courier*, January 27, 1970; John Kasaipwalova, "Problems of Unity in Papua New Guinea," *Nilaidat* 3, no. 1 (July 30, 1970): 7–10.

46 C. E. Barnes to D. J. Killen, March 27, 1969; "Student Unrest—John Kasaipwalova," Item 136/69, September 1969, A453 1970/524, National Archives of Australia, Canberra.

47 "John Kasaipwalova, Item 146/70: Students," 51–52, A453 1970/524, National Archives of Australia, Canberra.

48 Charles Cepulis, "Native Has Identity," interview with John Kasaipwalova, *Post Courier*, January 28, 1970, A452 1970/524, National Archives of Australia, Canberra; John Kasaipwalova, "The Reluctant Flame" (Port Moresby: Papua Pocket Poets, 1971); Ian Hicks, "Political Theft Idiotic: Judge," *Age*, October 27, 1970, 1.

49 "An Interview with Kumalau Tawali," *New Guinea Writing* 2 (December 1970): 13; John Kasaipwalova, "What Is Cultural Reconstruction?," *New Guinea Writing* 3 (March 1971): 14–16; Kumalau Tawali, "Bush Kanaka Speaks," in *Modern Poetry from Papua New Guinea*, vol. 1, ed. Nigel Krauth and Elton Brash (Port Moresby: Papua Pocket Poets, 1972).

50 John Kasaipwalovaposovalu, "Letter to the Editor," *Nilaidat*, May 1972, 5.

51 Lance Hill to Officer in Charge, September 1, 1969; Martin Ignatius Buluna, Application for a Native to Leave the Territory, June 29, 1971, Native Permit Records, National Archives of Papua New Guinea, Waigani.

52 M. Buluna, "The Role of Students in Niugini Politics," in Ward, *Politics of Melanesia*, 305, 307–9, 311.

53 Leo Hannett, "The Church and Nationalism," in Ward, *Politics of Melanesia*, 654, 657, 658, 665.

54 Ibid.

55 "Police Go to Trouble Spot Island," *Age*, November 11, 1972, 5.

56 "Papua New Guinea—Defense and Security—Intelligence Committee—Special Reports," A1838 3080/4/6/4/ PART 2, National Archives of Australia, Canberra.

57 Ulli Beier, *Decolonizing the Mind: The Impact of the University on Culture and Identity in Papua New Guinea* (Canberra: Australian National University, 2005), 137; "Petition from Mataungan Association, Rabaul, Concerning the Trust Territory of New Guinea," September 24, 1970, United Nations, T/PET.8/34, UN Digital Library, https://digitallibrary.un.org.

58 "Twenty-Five Women Fight with Police," *Post Courier*, August 4, 1969, 1; "The Natives Restless Tonight," *Aborigine Advancement League Newsletter* 24 (September 1969): 2; "Sydney," Faith Bandler, vol. 5, A6119/3898, National Archives of Australia, Canberra; Korowa, interview; "Leo Hannett Interviewed."

59 Ulli Beier to Bernth Lindfors, December 3, 1968, 26, Research in African Literatures Records, Harry Ransom Center, University of Texas–Austin.

60 Kiki, *Ten Thousand Years*, 92–94.

61 "A Center for New Guinea Culture"; Dianna Josselson to Georgina and Ulli Beier, December 11, 1968; Georgina Beier, "Five Contemporary Artists from New Guinea," 19.5, Ulli Beier, Congress for Cultural Freedom, Michael Josselson Papers, Harry Ransom Center, University of Texas–Austin (hereafter cited as Josselson Papers).

62 Dianna Josselson to Georgina and Ulli Beier, December 11, 1968.

63 Dianna Josselson to Georgina and Ulli Beier, February 5, 1969, August 21, 1969, 19.5, Josselson Papers.

64 Ulli Beier to Mike Josselson, September 8, 1971; Georgina Beier to Mike and Dianna Josselson, n.d.; Air Transport Service, 001269, February 2, 1974; Georgina Beier to Mike Josselson, April 12, 1974, Ulli Beier, 19.5, Josselson Papers.

65 Ulli Beier to Mike Josselson, June 2, 1974, 19.5, Josselson Papers.

66 Beier, *Decolonizing the Mind*, 137–38.

67 Nicholas Thomas, "We Were Still Papuans: A 2006 Interview with Epeli Hau'ofa," *Contemporary Pacific* 24, no. 1 (2012): 120–32.

68 See Ian Howie-Willis, *A Thousand Graduates: Conflict in University Development in Papua New Guinea, 1961–1976* (Canberra: Australian National University, 1980).

CHAPTER 5. MELANESIA'S WAY

1 Utula Samana, "East Timor: The Student Protest and the Flag Incident," *Yagl-Ambu* 3, no. 4 (November 1976): 214–32, PNG Collection; Jeremy Luedi, "Why East Timor Would Not Be Free without Mozambique," *Asia by Africa*, January 24, 2019, www.asiabyafrica.com; "Utula Utuoc Samana, Chairman, Special Committee on the Implementation of the Declaration on Decolonization," *World Chronicle*, issue 670, May 13, 1997, UN Audiovisual Library, www.unmultimedia.org.

2 Nelson, *Papua New Guinea*, 79.

3 See Michael Hanchard, "Afro-Modernity: Temporality, Politics and the African Diaspora," *Public Culture* 11, no. 1 (January 1999).

4 "Papua New Guinea: Out of the Stone Age," *Time*, December 17, 1973. See also Swan, *Pauulu's Diaspora*; "House Is Feature," *Papua New Guinea Post-Courier*,

September 26, 1978, 14, http://nla.gov.au; "A House for Everyman," *Papua New Guinea Post-Courier*, May 11, 1979, 15–16, http://nla.gov.au.

5 Ali Mazrui, "An African's New Guinea," *New Guinea and Australia, the Pacific and Southeast Asia* 5, no. 3 (1970): 45, 56.

6 "Bobbi Sykes to UPNG Students Association," Roberta Barkley Sykes, vol. 1, A6119/4228, National Archives of Australia, Canberra.

7 "Bobbi Sykes," May 17, 1972, Roberta Barkley Sykes, vol. 1, A6119/4228, National Archives of Australia, Canberra.

8 "Interview with Bobbi Sykes," *Nilaidat* 1, no. 1 (May 1972); Vern Harvey, "Aboriginal Fight for Rights," *Nilaidat* 1, no. 1 (May 1972).

9 Peter Playpool, interview by Ian MacIntosh, May 4, 1972; "Bobbi Sykes," May 17, 1972, A6119/4228, National Archives of Australia, Canberra.

10 "Aboriginal Seeks PNG Support," July 7, 1972, A6119/4228, National Archives of Australia, Canberra.

11 "Peter Kavo," May 7, 1983, Cheryl Rose Buchanan, vol. 1, A6119/3923, National Archives of Australia, Canberra; "Papuan China Visit Banned," *Tribune*, January 29, 1974, 11, http://nla.gov.au.

12 "Aboriginal Seeks PNG Support"; "Australians Should Cry in the Streets," May 4, 1972, A6119/4228, National Archives of Australia, Canberra.

13 "Peter Kavo," May 7, 1983; "Makeu Opa," May 16, 1973, A6119/3923, National Archives of Australia, Canberra.

14 "Entry into Papua New Guinea," September 4, 1975, Roberta Barkley Sykes, vol. 2, A6119/4229; "Operation Whip 52, Roberta Sykes," July 18, 1972, A6119/4228, National Archives of Australia, Canberra.

15 "Bobbi Sykes," *Contact*, July 11, 1972, A6119/4228, National Archives of Australia, Canberra; "Thousands Act for Black Rights," *Tribune*, July 18, 1972.

16 "Will 'Ilolahia, NZ Black Panther Speaks," *Tribune*, July 11–17, 1972.

17 Ibid.; Catherine Powers, "Brown Power," *New Zealand Herald*, July 14, 2006, www.nzherald.co.nz.

18 Polynesian Panther Party, "Platform and Program, January 1974," Hawaiian and Pacific Collections.

19 "Cheryl Rose Buchanan, Visit to Papua New Guinea," May 29, 1973, A6119/3923, National Archives of Australia, Canberra.

20 "Black Power—Patrick Te Hemara," May 9, 1973, May 16, 1973, A6119/3923, National Archives of Australia, Canberra.

21 Max Quanchi, "The Waigani Seminars and Other Talk-Fests," presented at Pacific Science Inter-Congress (11th) in conjunction with the 2nd Symposium on French Research in the Pacific, March 2–6, 2009, Tahiti, French Polynesia.

22 "Waigani Seminar," *Papua New Guinea Post-Courier*, April 30, 1971, 15, http://nla.gov.au/nla.news-article250255170; Ulli Beier to Maxine, November 25, 1971, 14.5, Transcription Centre Records.

23 Third Niugini Arts Festival 1973 program, Box 17, Papers of Oodgeroo Noonuccal.

24 Kristy Powell to Kath Walker, June 20, 1973, M. S. Grecus to Kath Walker, September 4, 1973, Box 17, Papers of Oodgeroo Noonuccal; Kath Walker, "Papua New Guinea," *Kovave* 5, no. 1 (June 1975): 5.

25 Program, First Independent Papua New Guinea Writers' Conference, July 1–4, 1976; press release, First Independent Papua New Guinea Writers' Conference, 1, Box 17, Papers of Oodgeroo Noonuccal.

26 Taban Lo Liyong, *The Literature of Developed Nations: Negritude* (Boroko: Literature Department, University of Papua New Guinea, 1976), 49, 55, 121, Box 17, Papers of Oodgeroo Noonuccal.

27 Ibid.

28 "Press Release," 1–2.

29 Ibid.

30 Ibid.

31 Program, Box 17, Papers of Oodgeroo Noonuccal.

32 Kath Walker, "Opening Speech," July 1, 1976, Box 17, Papers of Oodgeroo Noonuccal.

33 Liyong, *Literature of Developed Nations*, 47; Ulli Beier, *The Artist in Society*, Discussion Paper no. 15 (Port Moresby: Institute of Papua New Guinea, 1976).

34 Program, Adelaide Festival of Arts, Writers' Week, March 6–13, 1976, www.adelaidefestival.com.au.

35 John B. Beston, "Papuaniugini: An Interview with Henginike Riyong," 1976, Box 17, Papers of Oodgeroo Noonuccal.

36 Kath Walker to Jane Thynne, May 19, 1976, Letters from friends who are mostly literary, Box 39, Papers of Oodgeroo Noonuccal.

37 Kumalau Tawali to Kath Walker, February 16, 1978, Box 40, Papers of Oodgeroo Noonuccal.

38 Albert Wendt, Annex VII, "The Method of Work of the Advisory Committee for the Study of Oceania Cultures," 1–2, Vanua'aku Pati, Miscellaneous Unsorted Papers, 1974–1991, Box VP 014, Miscellaneous Loose Papers, 1976–1998, Vanua'aku Pati Archives, Vanuatu National Archives, Vila (hereafter cited as Vanua'aku Pati Archives).

39 Albert Wendt, "Towards a New Oceania," UNESCO Inaugural Meeting of the Advisory Committee for the Study of Oceanic Cultures, September 29, 1975, 1–11, SHC.75/CONF.616/COL.2(a), UNESCO Digital Library.

40 Ibid., 11–12.

41 Position Paper, Inaugural Meeting of the Advisory Committee for the Study of Oceanic Cultures, Nuku'alofa, Tonga, December 8–12, 1975, Box VP 014, Vanua'aku Pati Archives.

42 Wendt, Annex VII, 2.

43 Ibid., 3.

44 Marcelle Vallet to Walter Lini, October 22, 1976; Noriko Aikawa to Walter Lini, February 10, 1978, Vanua'aku Pati, Miscellaneous Unsorted Papers, 1974–1991, Box VP 014, Vanua'aku Pati Archives.

45 Wendt, Annex VII, 3–4.

46 Annex III, "UNESCO Workshop on the Techniques of Recording Oral Tradition, Solomon Islands, November–December 1976," 21, Vanua'aku Pati, Miscellaneous Unsorted Papers, 1974–1991, Box VP 014, Vanua'aku Pati Archives.

47 Wendt, Annex VII, 4.

48 Final Report, Second Session of the Advisory Committee for the Study of Oceanic Cultures, December 30, 1977, Miscellaneous Unsorted Papers, 1974–1991, Box VP 014, Vanua'aku Pati Archives.

49 Annex VI, 5–8, 11, Vanua'aku Pati, Miscellaneous Unsorted Papers, 1974–1991, Box VP 014, Vanua'aku Pati Archives.

50 Ulli Beier, "Proposal for Cultural Exchange Programs between Africa and the Pacific"; Albert Wendt, "Second Session of the Advisory Committee of the Study of Oceanic Cultures," Annex 7, 1, Vanua'aku Pati, Miscellaneous Unsorted Papers, 1974–1991, Box VP 014, Vanua'aku Pati Archives.

51 Beier, "Proposal for Cultural Exchange Programs," 1–2.

52 Ibid., 3.

53 Ibid., 4.

54 Ibid., 4–5.

55 Ibid., 5.

56 Ibid., 6.

57 Ibid., 11.

58 Ibid., 9.

59 Ibid., 10–11.

60 Ibid., 11–12.

61 Ibid., 14.

62 Ibid., 15–16.

63 Ibid., 16–17.

64 Ibid., 17.

65 Ibid., 20–22.

66 Ibid., 23–24; Final Report, Second Session.

CHAPTER 6. BLACK PACIFIC FESTIVALS

1 Jonathan Fenderson, *Building the Black Arts Movement: Hoyt Fuller and the Cultural Politics of the 1960s* (Urbana: University of Illinois Press, 2019), 109.

2 C. J. McGuigan, "Second World Black and African Festival of Arts and Culture," February 1, 1974, Box 18, Papers of Oodgeroo Noonuccal.

3 Carol Cooper, "John Moriarty," National Museum of Australia, www.nma.gov.au, accessed October 7, 2020. See also Bunjilaka Aboriginal Cultural Centre, *First Peoples*, exhibition, Melbourne Museum, https://museumsvictoria.com.au.

4 McGuigan, "Second World Black and African Festival," Notes on the Participation of the Australasian Zone, Box 18, Papers of Oodgeroo Noonuccal.

5 Nigerian Co-ordinating Committee, minutes, April 26, 1974; B. G. Dexter to Chairman, October 1974, Box 18, Papers of Oodgeroo Noonuccal.

6   John Haugie, "2nd World Black and African Festival of the Arts and Cultures Committee Meeting," September 1974; Dexter to Chairman; 2nd World Black and African Festival of Arts and Culture, "Queen of the Festival," Box 18, Papers of Oodgeroo Noonuccal.

7   Moses Sasakila, "2nd World Black and African Festival of Arts and Culture," Box 18, Papers of Oodgeroo Noonuccal.

8   Iava Parapa, "Interview with Moses Sasakila," *Papua New Guinea Writing* 15 (September 1974): 12, PNG Collection.

9   Arthur Jawodimbari, "Cultural Revival," *Papua New Guinea Writing* 15 (September 1974): 13, PNG Collection.

10 Ibid.; "Emerging Nation Playwright Buses Plays to Villagers," *Lubbock Avalanche-Journal*, August 11, 1974, 65, www.newspapers.com.

11 Air Niugini, *Paradise Magazine*, 1976.

12 "Arthur Jawodimbari," *Papua New Guinea Writing* 13 (March 1974): 12, PNG Collection.

13 Ibid.

14 Ibid.

15 Ibid.

16 Ibid.

17 "Emerging Nation Playwright."

18 "Minutes of Meeting of Australian Co-ordinating for Nigeria Festival, Darwin," September 2, 1974; Haugie, "2nd World Black and African Festival," September 2, 5, 1974, Box 18, Papers of Oodgeroo Noonuccal.

19 Dexter to Chairman.

20 C. J. McGuigan, "Minutes of Joint-Meeting of Nigerian Festival Co-ordinating Committees from Australia and Papua New Guinea, Darwin," September 2, 1974; Haugie, "2nd World Black and African Festival."

21 C. J. McGuigan to Kath Walker, October 25, 1974, Box 18, Papers of Oodgeroo Noonuccal.

22 Dexter to Chairman.

23 Nigerian Co-ordinating Committee, minutes, October 29, 1974; "Fifth Meeting of the IFC at Kaduna, November 12–19, 1974," report to the IFC, November 1974, Box 18, Papers of Oodgeroo Noonuccal.

24 Kath Walker, "Commonplace," November 1974, Box 27, Papers of Oodgeroo Noonuccal.

25 "Dix-Sept Otage Liberes," *L'Action*, November 1974, 1.

26 Walker, "Flight into Tunis."

27 Ibid.

28 Noonuccal, "Open Letter to the NSW Jewish Board of Deputies," July 23, 1975, Box 19, Papers of Oodgeroo Noonuccal.

29 "Visit to NSW by Two Representatives of the General Union of Palestinian Students," May 27, 1975, A6119/3650, Meredith Burgmann, vol. 2, National Archives of Australia, Canberra.

30 Dexter to Chairman.

31 Trevor Buzzacott, "Nigerian Coordinating Committee Meeting," March 13, 1975; Nigerian Co-ordinating Committee, minutes, January 31, 1975, Box 18, Papers of Oodgeroo Noonuccal.

32 Trevor Buzzacott, "Nigerian Coordinating Committee Meeting," March 7–8, 1975, Box 18, Papers of Oodgeroo Noonuccal.

33 "Nigerian Second Black and African Festival of the Arts," May 28, 1975, Box 18, Papers of Oodgeroo Noonuccal.

34 Australian Report, 6th IFC Meeting, July 10, 1975, Box 18, Papers of Oodgeroo Noonuccal.

35 Aboriginal Arts Board, outline of Exhibition of Aboriginal Arts and Crafts, Box 18, Papers of Oodgeroo Noonuccal.

36 Lance Bennett, "FESTAC," November 1975, Box 18, Papers of Oodgeroo Noonuccal.

37 Lance Bennett, "FESTAC," March 13, 1975, Box 18, Papers of Oodgeroo Noonuccal.

38 Lance Bennett, Fourth Interim Report, April 8, 1975, Box 18, Papers of Oodgeroo Noonuccal.

39 "Conferences," *Black News* 1, no. 9 (1974): 8, MLMSS 8885, Box 4, Folder 9, Pamela Beasley Papers, Mitchell Library, State Library of New South Wales, Sydney, Australia.

40 "Nigeria, 1975," Nigerian Material, Box 18, Papers of Oodgeroo Noonuccal.

41 David Broadbent, "Blacks Will Carry Protest to Africa," *Age*, January 12, 1977, 1, newspapers.com.

42 Nigerian Co-ordinating Committee, minutes, October 5, 1976, Box 18, Papers of Oodgeroo Noonuccal; "Tahiti Festival Will See Dances by Islanders, Aborigines," *Sydney Morning Herald*, April 6, 1977, 26.

43 Taloti Kaniku to Wole Soyinka, December 3, 1976, Folder 3, Wole Soyinka Papers.

44 "Why FESTAC Didn't Get What Was Expected," *Papua New Guinea Post-Courier*, March 28, 1977, 8, http://nla.gov.au.

45 Nora Vagi Brash, email to author, May 11, 14, 2020.

46 Ibid.

47 Ibid.

48 Ibid.

49 "No Longer Primitive," *Papua New Guinea Writing* 26 (June 1977): 12–13.

50 "Australian Conference on South Pacific Literature," *Papua New Guinea Writing* 26 (June 1977): 21.

51 FESTAC 77, General Program, 18, 20, 28–30, 32, http://alkalimat.org.

52 Gordon Briscoe, "The Aborigines," in International Festival Committee, *FESTAC '77: The Black and African World* (Lagos: African Journal Limited, 1977), 124–33.

53 Gordon Briscoe, *Racial Folly: A Twentieth Century Aboriginal Family* (Canberra: Australian National University Press, 2010), 187–88.

54 Ibid.

55 Nigerian Co-ordinating Committee, minutes, October 5, 1976, Box 18; Oodgeroo Noonuccal, "2nd World Black and African Festival," February 1977, Box 19, Papers of Oodgeroo Noonuccal.

56 Noonuccal, "2nd World Black and African Festival."

57 "Aborigines Meet Other Black Cultures," *Canberra Times*, January 27, 1977, 15, http://nla.gov.au; "Black Brouhaha," *Bulletin* 99, no. 5043 (February 5, 1977): 10.

58 Jabani Lalara, "'Tribal People Bossed Around," *Bulletin* 99, no. 5049 (March 19, 1977): 44.

59 Brian Hoad, "Black Wasn't Beautiful," *Bulletin* 99, no. 5049 (March 19, 1977): 43.

60 Ibid.

61 Ibid.

62 Ibid.

63 Ibid.

64 Noonuccal, "2nd World Black and African Festival."

65 Ibid.

66 *PEN Newsletter*, issue 21 (1978): 18–19, 35; *PEN Newsletter* (Sydney), PN 121 P459, Harry Ransom Center, University of Texas–Austin.

CHAPTER 7. *POVAI*

1 Griffen, *Women Speak Out*, 4, 139–40.

2 "A Light Shines On," *Fiji Times and Fiji Sun*, June 7, 2005, https://narseyonfiji. wordpress.com; Nicole Louise George, *Situating Women: Gender Politics and Circumstance in Fiji* (Canberra: Australian National University Press, 2012), 58; Kay Alsop, "Dropouts Drop In at Fiji," *Province*, April 1, 1972, 32; Griffen and Slatter, interview.

3 "People," *Pacific Islands Monthly* 42, no. 9 (September 1, 1971): 94, http://nla.gov .au; Marilyn Hehr, "Working with YWCA Gives Fijian Women a Lot of Satisfaction," *Calgary Herald*, March 29, 1972, 57, newspapers.com.

4 "Third World Women Seek Liberation," *Miami Herald*, November 30, 1975, 12; "Women Moving in the South Pacific," *Herald-News*, September 15, 1978, 24, newspapers.com.

5 Griffen and Slatter, interview.

6 "Snythèse Mensuelle de mai 1974," Box NH 026, New Hebrides Collection, National Archives of Vanuatu; Slatter and Griffen, interview.

7 "Barak Sope," *Salient* 35, no. 17 (July 29, 1972).

8 Vanessa Griffen, "About These Women," *UNISPAC* 5, no. 4 (1972): 15–16.

9 Claire Slatter, "Women Power: Myth or Reality," *UNISPAC* 5, no. 4 (1972): 16–17.

10 Ibid., 18.

11 Griffen and Slatter, interview; International Development Action, *Fiji: A Developing Australian Colony* (Victoria: International Development Action, 1973), 10–17.

12 International Development Action, *Fiji*, 18–25.

13 *Pacific Perspective* 2, no. 2 (1973); Sione Tupouniua, Ron Crocombe, and Claire Slatter, eds., *The Pacific Way: Social Issues in National Development* (Suva: South Pacific Social Sciences Association, 1975).

14 Anthony Haas, "Pacific Islanders Look at Plans for the Future," *Canberra Times*, December 31, 1973, 2, http://nla.gov.au.

15 Ibid.

16 Bugotu, "Decolonizing and Recolonizing," 77–80.

17 Ibid.

18 Ibid.

19 Ibid.

20 Marjorie Crocombe, "Mana and Creative Regional Cooperation," *Third Mana Annual of Creative Writing* (Suva: South Pacific Arts Creative Arts Society, 1977), 5–6, Pacific Collection.

21 "Mana," *Penn Gazette*, November 1973, 13, New Zealand, 146.4, PEN Records, Harry Ransom Center, University of Texas–Austin.

22 "Independence Movements Bred the New Wave of Pacific Writers," *Pacific Islands Monthly* 51, no. 8 (August 1, 1980): 140, http://nla.gov.au.

23 Barak Sope to ATOM, April 25, 1974, Miscellaneous Correspondence, NHNP/ Vanua'aku Pati: Miscellaneous Unsorted Papers, 1972–2001, Box VP 017, Vanua'aku Pati Archives.

24 Cheryl Buchanan, "Aboriginal Rights," *New Hebridean Viewpoints* 13 (June 1975): 20, Loose Papers, Box VP 004, Vanua'aku Pati Archives; NFP Continuation Committee, "Conference for a Nuclear Free Pacific Report," July 6, 1975, i, 5, Conference for a Nuclear Free Pacific, Pacific Collection.

25 NFP Continuation Committee, "Conference for a Nuclear Free Pacific Report," 24.

26 "A Fiji Declaration by the Conference for a Nuclear Free Pacific," April 7, 1978, NHNP/VP Nuclear Free Pacific Issues, Box VP 004, Vanua'aku Pati Archives.

27 Conference for a Nuclear Free Pacific, *The People's Treaty for a Nuclear-Free Pacific*, Miscellaneous 1971, 1974–1978, 1991–1996, Box VP 004, Vanua'aku Pati Archives.

28 Ibid.

29 NFP Continuation Committee, "Conference for a Nuclear Free Pacific Report," 21; "Nuclear Free Pacific Zone," *New Hebridean Viewpoints* 13 (June 1975): 21, Vanuatu Collection, Library of the University of the South Pacific, Emalus, Vanautu (hereafter cited as Vanuatu Collection).

30 NFP Continuation Committee, "Conference for a Nuclear Free Pacific Report," i; *NFPC Action Bulletin* 9 (October 3, 1975), Nuclear Free Pacific Issues, Box VP 004, Vanua'aku Pati Archives.

31 *NFPC Action Bulletin*, December 19, 1975, 1, Box VP 004, Vanua'aku Pati Archives.

32 Ibid., 2.

33 Ibid., 2–3.

34 Ibid., 3–5; *NFPC Action Bulletin* 9 (October 1975); *Pacific People's Action Front Manifesto*, April 1976, NHNP/VP Nuclear Free Pacific Issues, Box VP 004, Vanua'ku Pati Archives.

35 "Roosevelt Oris Nelson Brown—Pacific People's Action Front," September 27, 1976, New Hebrides—Political Personalities, A1838/338/1/3 Part 1, National Archives of Australia, Canberra; Rex Rumakiek, "West Papuan Nationalism," n.d., Box VP 003, Vanua'aku Pati Archives.

36 Nicole Strickland, "Nuclear Age Pawns," *Province*, July 21, 1975, 23.

37 George, *Situating Women*, 58–61, 71; "Women for Mexico Talks," *Papua New Guinea Post-Courier*, January 1, 1975, 3, http://nla.gov.au.

38 George, *Situating Women*, 58–61, 71.

39 Ibid.

40 Griffen and Slatter, interview; "International Women's Year," *Papua New Guinea Post-Courier*, January 2, 1975, 10, http://nla.gov.au; Griffen, *Women Speak Out*, iii-iv, 3.

41 Claire Slatter, "The South Pacific Regional Women's Conference," *New Hebridean Viewpoints* 13 (June 1975), Loose Papers, Box VP 004, Vanua'aku Pati Archives.

42 Griffen, *Women Speak Out*, 15.

43 Ibid., 24, 93, 102.

44 Ibid., 87.

45 Lucille Mair, *A Historical Study of Women in Jamaica* (Kingston: University of the West Indies Press, 2006).

46 Griffen, *Women Speak Out*, 114–15.

47 Banks, *Journal of . . . Joseph Banks*, 134–35; Jennifer Newell, *Trading Nature: Tahitians, Europeans, and Ecological Exchange* (Honolulu: University of Hawai'i Press, 2010), 151–52, 167.

48 Griffen, *Women Speak Out*, 111–12, 116.

49 Ibid., 114–15.

50 Ibid., 120–33.

51 Ibid., 120, 126.

52 Shilliam, *Black Pacific*, 43.

53 Griffen, *Women Speak Out*, 80–83.

54 Ibid., 34–35, 71, 80–83.

55 NFP Continuation Committee, "NFP Report," 1, Pacific Collection; Susanna Ounei, *For Kanak Independence: The Fight against French Rule in New Caledonia* (Auckland: New International Publications, 1985), 3.

56 Griffen, *Women Speak Out*, 48, 105–9.

57 Ibid., 40–41.

58 Ibid., 41.

59 Ibid., 42–43.

60 George, *Situating Women*, 63.

61 Griffen, *Women Speak Out*, 44–45.

62 Ibid., 37.

63 Ibid., 44, 94–95.

64 John Bani and Barak Sope, "The Struggle against Anglo-French Colonialism in the New Hebrides," Box 6, Sixth PAC Papers, Moorland Spingarn Research Center; American Embassy Tanzania to US State Department, June 1974, CFPF Cables.

65 Griffen, *Women Speak Out*, 136–40.

66 Vanessa Griffen and Makereta Waqavonovono, "The Pacific Women's Resource Center: A Reassessment," 5, 16, Vanua'aku Party, Miscellaneous Loose Papers, 1972–1996, Box VP 004, Vanua'aku Pati Archives.

67 Ibid., 2, 11.

68 Ibid., 14, 18, 21.

69 Vanessa Griffen, ed., *Knowing and Knowing How* (Suva: University of the South Pacific Center for Applied Studies in Development, 1981); Vanessa Griffen, ed., *Caring for Ourselves: A Health Handbook for Pacific Women* (Suva: Fiji Times, 1983), i.

70 "Aborigines Visit the US: Report on Trip by Five Aborigines to Congress of African People and United Nations," 1971, Australian Institute of Aboriginal and Torres Islander Studies, Canberra, Australia; "Snythèse Mensuelle," November 1970, Box NH 026, New Hebrides Collection, National Archives of Vanuatu.

71 Griffen and Waqavonovono, "Pacific Women's Resources Center," 16, 19.

72 J. S. Champion to President, Vanua'aku Party Women's Wing, October 7, 1977, Patricia/Patc Kruger, Box VP 015, Vanua'aku Pati Archives.

73 Hilda Lini, interview by author, digital recording, Ambae, Vila, Vanuatu, October 3, 12, 2014; Korowa, interview; Rebecca Sau and Hilda Lini to British Resident Commissioner, September 12, 1977, Patricia/Patc Kruger, Box VP 015, Vanua'aku Pati Archives.

74 "Rebecca Sau and Hilda Lini."

CHAPTER 8. 1878

1 Chantal Ferraro, "When Black Is Transparent: French Colonialism in New Caledonia, 1878–1914," in *Wansalawara: Soundings in Melanesian History*, ed. Robert Kiste (Mānoa: Center for Asian and Pacific Studies, University of Hawai'i, 1987), 126, 128, 140.

2 Robie, *Blood on Their Banner*, 88; Yann Uregei, "New Caledonia," in Ali and Crocombe, *Politics in Melanesia*, 199; Bronwen Douglas, "Winning and Losing? Reflections on the War of 1878–79 in New Caledonia," *Journal of Pacific History* 26, no. 2 (December 1991): 214, 217.

3 Ferraro, "When Black Is Transparent," 128.

4 Henri Riviere, *Souvenirs de la Nouvelle Caledonie* (Paris: Calmann Levy, 1880), 16–18.

5 Ibid., 284.

6 Ibid., 121; David Chappell, "A Headless Native Talks Back: Nidoïsh Naisseline and the Kanak Awakening in 1970s New Caledonia," *Contemporary Pacific* 22, no. 1

(2010): 39, www.jstor.org; Leonard Gordon, *Confrontation over Taiwan: Nineteenth Century China and the Powers* (New York: Lexington Books, 2009), 138.

7   Ferraro, "When Black Is Transparent," 122; Ounei, *For Kanak Independence*.

8   Robie, *Blood on Their Banner*, 88.

9   Isabelle Merle, *Experiences coloniales: La Nouvelle-Caledonie* (Paris: Editions Berlin, 1995), 371.

10 See Felix Germain, *Decolonizing the Republic: African and Caribbean Migrants in Postwar Paris, 1946–1974* (East Lansing: Michigan State University Press, 2019); and Tracy Whiting, *Bricktop's Paris: African American Women in Paris between the Two World Wars* (New York: State University of New York Press, 2015).

11 Chappell, "A Headless Native," 37–70.

12 Apollinaire Anova-Ataba, "The Independence of New Caledonia," *New Hebridean Viewpoints* 17 (July 1976): 22, Vanuatu Collection.

13 Chappell, "Headless Native," 45–46.

14 Chappell, *Kanak Awakening*, 144, 149.

15 Ibid., 153.

16 Angelique Chrisafis, "Paris Show Unveils Life in Human Zoo," *Guardian*, November 29, 2011, www.theguardian.com.

17 Eddy Banaré, "A Kanak Practice by Fanon: Nidoïsh Naisseline and the Red Scarves," *Francosphères* 6, no. 2 (2017): 141–62, https://doi.org/10.3828/franc.2017.12.

18 Helen Fraser, "Fighting Talk in the South Pacific," *Age*, August 10, 1984, 11.

19 Chappell, *Kanak Awakening*, 156; Pascal Hebert, Elie Poigoune, and Jean-Paul Caillard, "The Emergence of Kanak Independence," *Movements, Ideas, and Struggles*, October 10, 2017, https://mouvements.info. For a broader discussion of sports activism, see Joseph N. Cooper, Charles Macaulay, and Saturnino H. Rodriguez, "Race and Resistance: A Typology of African American Sport Activism," *International Review for the Sociology of Sport* 54, no. 2 (March 2019): 151–81. At Tahiti's 1971 Pacific Games, two Guam judo competitors gave Black Power salutes and turned their backs on the French national flag in protest against French colonialism in Tahiti. "Noble Sentiments . . . ," *Papua New Guinea Post-Courier*, September 21, 1971, 5, http://nla.gov.au.

20 Chappell, *Kanak Awakening*, 156.

21 "Des canaques conte le racisme français," *Esprit* 4, no. 2 (February 1971): 403–7.

22 Ibid.; Césaire, *Discourse on Colonialism*, 35.

23 "Des canaques conte le racisme français," 403–7.

24 Ibid.

25 Ibid.

26 Ibid.

27 Déwé Gorodey, "The Young Kanak's Struggle," *PRAXIS* 1, no. 206 (January–February 1976): 16; Marie Knuckey, "Discontent among the Islanders," *Sydney Morning Herald*, December 13, 1979, 16.

28 Chappell, "Headless Native," 52.

29 Ibid.; "L'uniforme injurié," *Esprit* 414, no. 6 (1972): 1043–45, www.jstor.org.

30 Chappell, "Headless Native," 52.

31 Ibid., 54.

32 Foulards Rouges, *Réveil Canaque*, vols. 1–38 (1970–1974).

33 *Réveil Canaque* 38 (1974).

34 Knuckey, "Discontent," 16.

35 Gorodey, "Young Kanak's Struggle," 16.

36 Ibid.; Knuckey, "Discontent."

37 Ounei, *For Kanak Independence*, 5.

38 Elaine Magalis, "Women Political Prisoners Being Increased over World," *Pittsburgh Courier*, March 12, 1977, 13.

39 Chappell, *Kanak Awakening*, 139.

40 Chris Plant to Kalkot Mataskelekele, June 20, 1975, NHNP/VP Nuclear Free Pacific Issues Including Correspondence, Miscellaneous, Box 002, Vanua'aku Pati Archives.

41 "For a Revolutionary Kanak Party," *Nouvelle 1878* 27 (1975): 2, NHNP/VP Nuclear Free Pacific Issues Including Correspondence, Box 002, Vanua'aku Pati Papers.

42 Ibid.

43 Ibid.

44 Ibid.

45 "Caledonia-New Hebrides," *New Hebridean Viewpoints* 17 (July 1976): 23, Vanautu Collection.

46 *Vanuaaku Viewpoints* 7, no. 1 (January 1977): 15, Vanuatu Collection.

47 Chris Plant, "Killing Heightens Call for Independence in New Caledonia," January 2, 1976; Chris Plant, "New Caledonia, Murder of Young Kanak by White Colonialist Police," January 1, 1976, Miscellaneous, Unsorted Papers, 1982–1992, Box VP 004, Vanua'aku Pati Archives.

48 Plant, "Killing Heightens Call for Independence"; Plant, "New Caledonia, Murder of Young Kanak."

49 Plant, "Killing Heightens Call for Independence."

50 Plant, "New Caledonia, Murder of Young Kanak," 4.

51 Vanessa Griffen to Kalkot Matas Kele, January 9, 1976, *Viewpoints* (April 1976), Vanua'aku Pati, Box VP 004, Vanua'aku Pati Archives.

52 "Letter Received from Déwé Gorodey," March 4, 1976, *New Hebridean Viewpoints* 22, no. 7 (April 16, 1976).

53 "New Caledonia . . . Kanak Leader Jailed by the French," *Vanuaaku Viewpoints* 7, no. 7 (July 1977): 27, Vanuatu Collection; "Kanak People Must Be Organized," *Tribune*, May 5, 1976, 9, http://nla.gov.au.

54 "Letter Received from Déwé Gorodey."

55 "Déwé Gorodey," March 26, 1976, Vanua'ku Pati Papers, Miscellaneous, 1980–1983, Box VP 002, Vanua'aku Pati Archives.

56 Ibid.

57 Ibid.

58 Ibid.

59 Ibid.

60 Ibid.

61 Déwé Gorodey, letter, March 22, 1976, Vanua'aku Pati Archives.

62 "New Caledonia: French Attempt to Imprison Déwé Gorodey and Nidoïsh Naisseline," *New Hebridean Viewpoints* 19 (November 1976): 15; "Gorodey Sends Greetings," *Vanuaaku Viewpoints* 7, no. 1 (January 1977), Vanuatu Collection.

63 "Over the Horizon," *New Hebridean Viewpoints* 19 (November 1976); *New Hebridean Viewpoints* 20 (December 1976); "SAPOT Wetem Man New Caledonia," *Vanuaaku Viewpoints* 7, no. 2 (February 1977), Vanuatu Collection.

64 "The News in a Nutshell," *Pacific Islands Monthly* 48, no. 4 (February 1, 1977), http://nla.gov.au; "New Caledonia . . . Kanak Leader Jailed"; "Déwé Gorodey on Kanak Struggle," *Vanuaaku Viewpoints* 7 (September 1977): 9–12, Vanuatu Collection.

CHAPTER 9. ONE SINGLE FRONT AGAINST IMPERIALISM

1   "Qaddafi Addresses Pacific Peace Forum," LD202226, Tripoli Television Service in Arabic, 2023 GMT, April 20, 1987, FBIS Reports; "Pacific Peace Conference Issues Final Statement," LD211748, Tripoli Television Service in Arabic, 1550 GMT, April 21, 1987, FBIS Reports; "Qaddafi Addresses Pacific Peace Forum," Central Intelligence Agency Brief, CIA-RDP0501559R000400420014–4, CFPF Cables.

2   "Gaddafi Gathers Pacific Clients," *Age*, April 7, 1987, 1, newspapers.com.

3   Robin Smyth, "War Fear as Kanak Hero Is Killed," *Observer*, January 13, 1985; "Gaddafi Gathers Pacific Clients"; Robie, *Blood on Their Banner*, 116–28.

4   Chappell, *Kanak Awakening*, 23; "A Stern 'Non' to Self-Rule for New Caledonians," *Pacific Islands Monthly* 46, no. 7 (1975): 9.

5   "Statement from New Caledonia," *New Hebridean Viewpoints* 17 (July 1976): 21, Vanuatu Collection.

6   "New Caledonia Kanaks Accuse Eriau," *Vanuaaku Viewpoints* 7, no. 8 (August 1977): 13, Vanuatu Collection.

7   Uregei, "New Caledonia," 128.

8   Robie, *Blood on Their Banner*, 102; Alban Bensa and Eric Wittersheim, "Nationalism and Interdependence: The Political Thought of Jean-Marie Tjibaou," *Contemporary Pacific* 10, no. 2 (Fall 1998): 374–75.

9   Undated letter, Vanua'aku Pati Papers, Box VP 002, Vanua'aku Pati Archives.

10 Uregei, "New Caledonia," 128.

11 "Letter of Yann Céléné Uregei," Vanua'aku Party, Miscellaneous Papers, 1966–1993, Box VP 018, Vanua'aku Pati Archives, 1966–1995, Vanua'aku Pati Archives.

12 Amembassy Suva to Secstate Washdc, "United Front for the Liberation of the People of Kanak," 1978SUVA02294, November 5, 1978; "New Hebrides and New Caledonia Representatives Seek Appointments with Ambassador Young," 1978USUNN04841, November 8, 1978, CFPF Cables.

13 Yann Céléné Uregei, "Petition for the Special Committee on Decolonization of the United Nations in New York," Vanua'aku Party, Miscellaneous Papers, 1966–1993, Box VP 018, Vanua'aku Pati Archives.

14 "South Pacific Forum Takes Soft Line on Independence," *Povai* 4, no. 10 (1982), in *Vanuaku Viewpoints* 11, no. 70 (September 1982), Vanuatu Collection.

15 "New Caledonia, Another Kanak Murdered," *Povai* 3, no. 3 (1981): 1; "New Caledonia, Assassination Condemned," *Povai* 3, no. 5 (1981): 1, Pacific Collection.

16 "New Caledonia," February 13, 1981, Vanua'ku Pati Papers, Miscellaneous, 1980–1983, Box VP 002, Vanua'aku Pati Archives; "New Caledonia," *Vanuaku Viewpoints* 10, no. 57 (April 9, 1981): 5, Vanuatu Collection; Barak Sope, interview by author, digital recording, Vila, Vanuatu, October 5, 2014.

17 Sope, interview.

18 "Congress of the Multiracial Union and the Kanak United Liberation Front," January 29, 1981, Vanua'ku Pati Papers, Miscellaneous, 1980–1983, Box VP 002, Vanua'aku Pati Archives.

19 Ibid.

20 Helen Hill, "Political Changes in New Caledonia," *Povai* 4, no. 10 (1982): 4, Pacific Collection.

21 *Povai* 4, no. 10 (1982): 4, Pacifica Collection.

22 Ibid.

23 "FLNKS et le 24 septembre 1982," *Povai* 4, no. 10 (1982): 4, Pacifica Collection; Uregei, "New Caledonia," 120.

24 Robie, *Blood on Their Banner*, 102; "Caledonia Rebels Cause Paris Stir," *Globe and Mail*, November 26, 1984, www.proquest.com.

25 Robie, *Blood on Their Banner*, 105–11; Robie, "Kanaks Bitter as Massacre Killers Set Free," *New Zealand Sunday Times*, December 10, 1986.

26 Robie, *Blood on Their Banner*.

27 Uregei, "New Caledonia," 131.

28 Michael Dobbs, "France to Put More Troops on New Caledonia," *Boston Globe*, January 13, 1985, 2; Jonathan Steel, "Mitterand's Island of Broken Dreams," *Guardian*, January 18, 1985, 15, www.newspapers.com; Roger Ricklefs, "New Caledonia Crisis Hits a French Raw Nerve," *Wall Street Journal*, January 22, 1985, 1, www.proquest.com.

29 John Vincour, "France Arrests a Separatist Leader in Guadeloupe," *New York Times*, November 29, 1984, A13, www.nytimes.com; Maryse Condé, "Pan-Africanism, Feminism and Culture," in Lemelle and Kelley, *Imagining Home*, 15–16.

30 "Guadeloupe Independence Movement Stirring," *Calgary Herald*, June 10, 1985, 63, www.newspapers.com.

31 Alfonso Chardy, "US Monitors Influence of Separatists in Guadeloupe," *Miami Herald*, September 9, 1985, 3A; "Declaration of General Policy, Conference of the Last French Colonies, April 5–7, 1985," New Caledonia, Box 75, Robert Van Lierop

Papers, Schomburg Institute for Research in Black Culture (hereafter cited as Van Lierop Papers).

32 Mort Rosenblum, "Caledonia Fires Tension in the French Caribbean," *Sydney Morning Herald*, May 25, 1985, 23.

33 "Qaddafi Addresses Pacific Peace Forum," FBIS Reports.

34 Ibid.

35 Ibid.

36 Ibid.

37 Angela Gilliam, "Papua New Guinea and the Geopolitics of Knowledge Production," in Foerstel and Gilliam, *Confronting the Margaret Mead Legacy*, 274.

38 "Qaddafi Addresses Pacific Peace Forum," FBIS Reports.

39 Ibid.

40 "Libya: Second International Conference Against Imperialism," April 1986, 2–3, National Archives of the UK (TNA): FO 973/455.

41 "Pacific 'Revolutionary' Forces Resume Conference," LD201044, Tripoli JANA, 0920 GMT, April 20, 1987, FBIS, Wilson Center.

42 "Heady Michael Mansell Leads for Defence of Another Australia," *Age*, April 25, 1987, 2, newspapers.com.

43 "Libya, Pacific Peace Conference Issues Final Statement," LD211748, Tripoli Television Service in Arabic, 1550 GMT, April 21, 1987, FBIS Reports.

44 "Kanak Group to Join Libyan International Force," HK281248, Hong Kong AFP, 1244 GMT, April 28, 1986; "New Caledonia Independence Movement on Libyan Ties," BK080248, Hong Kong AFP, 0202 GMT, May 8, 1987, FBIS Reports.

45 "Al-Qaddafi Receives Reunion Liberation Official," LD04/315, Tripoli, Voice a/ Greater Arab Homeland in Arabic, 1130 GMT, May 4, 1987, FBIS Reports.

46 "Revolution in South Pacific Causes US 'Panic,'" LD240903, Tripoli, JANA in Arabic, 0700 GMT, May 25, 1987, FBIS Reports; Directorate of Intelligence, "Libyan Activities in the South Pacific," May 4, 1987, CIA-RDP90TO0114R000200270001–7, Central Intelligence Agency declassified documents, www.cia.gov.

47 "Cabinet Minute, April 29, 1987," Libyan Activities in the South Pacific—Decisions 9351/SEC and 9351/SEC (Amended), A14039, National Archives of Australia, Canberra.

48 "Possible Action against Libya, April 29, 1987," A14039, National Archives of Australia, Canberra.

49 "Aboriginal Activists Warned on Libya Contact," BK020944, Melbourne Overseas Service in English, 0830 GMT, May 2, 1987, FBIS Reports.

50 "Libya, People's Bureau Closure in Canberra 'Unjustified,'" LD210757, Tripoli, JANA in Arabic, 0715 GMT, May 21, 1987; "Libyan Envoy Comments on Bureau Closure," BK200758, Melbourne Overseas Service in English, 0700 GMT, May 20, 1987, FBIS Reports.

51 "Lange Claims Libya Meddling in South Pacific," BK170655, *Auckland New Zealand Herald* in English, March 10, 1987, 8, FBIS Reports.

52 "Libya," *Middle East and South Asia Review*, May 11, 1987, 2, FBIS Reports.

53 "Melbourne on Libya's Interests, Aims in S. Pacific," BK101105, Overseas Service in English, 0803 GMT, March 10, 1987; "Vanuatu Government Adviser Interviewed on Libyan Issue," BK081143, Melbourne Overseas Service in English, 0803 GMT, May 8, 1987, FBIS Reports.

54 Sope, interview.

55 "Pacific Nations Refute Claim of 'Libyan Threat,'" LD201112, Tripoli, JANA in English, 1117 GMT, May 20, 1987, FBIS Reports.

56 "Papua New Guinea Irian Jaya Rebels Receiving Training in Libya," BK120114, Hong Kong AFP in English, 0052 GMT, May 12, 1987, FBIS Reports.

57 "Western Samoa Leader Criticizes Australian Libya Ties," UK070310, Melbourne Overseas Service in English, 0230 GMT, May 7, 1987, FBIS Reports.

58 "New Caledonian Party Fires Uregei for Libyan Links," BK210039H, English, 0015 GMT, August 21, 1987, FBIS Reports; "The Official Version of the Death of Alphonse Dianou Disputed," *Le Monde*, May 26, 1988.

59 "Official Version," *Le Monde*.

60 Mary-Louse O'Callaghan, "17 Die," *Sydney Morning Herald*, May 6, 1988, 1, 11; Helen Fraser, "The Visionary Who Dreamed of a Future for Kanaks," *Sydney Morning Herald*, June 5, 1989, 17; David Robie, "Killings Are a Blow to Peace in Pacific," *Dominion* (Wellington), May 6, 1989.

61 Lini, interview; Djoubelly Wea, "An Education for Kanak Liberation," 1977, Suva, PMB 1084, Pacific Theological College, Master of Theology and Bachelor of Divinity Theses and Projects, 1968–1993, Pacific Manuscripts Bureau, Research School of Pacific and Asian Studies, Australian National University, Canberra.

62 American Embassy to Secretary of State, Washington, DC, "French Position in the Pacific," October 1, 1979, 1979SUVA03345, CFPF Cables.

63 Ibid.

64 Vanessa Griffen, email to author, November 2020; Lini, interview.

CHAPTER 10. BLACKS MUST RULE VANUATU

1 Sitiveni Ratuvili, *SPADES, South Pacific Action for Development Strategy: A Report of the Conference on Development Held in Vila, New Hebrides in January 1973* (Suva: Pacific Conference of Churches, Christian Education and Communications Programme, 1973), 3–4, 28; Griffen and Slatter, interview.

2 Ratuvili, *SPADES*, 35–37.

3 Ibid., 3.

4 "Report of SPADES Conference," *New Hebridean Viewpoints* 9 (March 1973): 2–3, Vanuatu Collection.

5 "Statement of SPADES Meeting in British Newsletter," editorial, *New Hebridean Viewpoints* 9 (March 1973): 1, 5, Vanuatu Collection.

6 Ibid.

7 Ibid.

8 "Presbyterians for Independence 'Without Delay,'" *New Hebridean Viewpoints* 3, no. 10 (June–July 1973): 1, Pacifica Collection, USP Emalus Campus Library, Vila, Vanuatu.

9 Rex Davis to Walter Lini, June 20, 1973, NHNP World Council of Churches Correspondence, 1973–1974, Box VP 002, Vanua'aku Pati Archives.

10 Ibid.

11 "Resolutions of the New Hebrides National Party Governing Council, November 8–11, 1974," 3, Box VP 003, Vanua'aku Pati Archives; American Embassy Tanzania to US State Department, June 1974, CFPF Cables.

12 Ibid.

13 Rex Davis, "Introduction," in "Song of the Pacific," special issue, *Risk* 12, no 1 (1976), Harvard University Divinity School Library.

14 Ibid.

15 Ibid.

16 American Embassy to Secretary of State, "French Position in the Pacific."

17 World Council of Churches Program to Combat Racism, 1976; Baldwin Sjollema to Walker Lini, August 23, 1976, NHNP Miscellaneous Papers and Correspondence, 1976, Box VP 002, Vanua'aku Pati Archives; "Church Council Gives $200,000 to Black Groups," *Globe and Mail*, September 27, 1984, www.proquest.com.

18 Rex Davis to Walter Lini, March 7, 1974, Brian Macdonald-Milne to Rex Davis, August 3, 1976, NHNP Miscellaneous Papers and Correspondence, 1976, Box VP 002, Vanua'aku Pati Archives.

19 "A Proposal for a Pacific Research Unit," August 1976, NHNP Miscellaneous Papers and Correspondence, 1976, Box VP 002, Vanua'aku Pati Archives.

20 Jean Guiart, "Colonial Case-Study: New Caledonia," *Youth* 4, no. 1 (March 1980): 5–6.

21 Sitiveni Ratuvili, "Development in the Pacific," *Youth* 4, no. 1 (March 1980): 8.

22 Walter Lini, "Should the Church Play Politics?," *Youth* 4, no. 1 (March 1980): 11.

23 "Church Backs Independence," *Youth* 4, no. 1 (March 1980): 6.

24 Melanesian Institute for Pastoral and Socio-Economic Service, "Your Kingdom Come: Partnership in Mission and Development," *Point* 2 (1980): 3, PNG Collection; see also Narokobi, *The Melanesian Way*.

25 Bernard Narokobi, "The Kingdom and Melanesian Human Struggles," *Point* 2 (1980): 48, 49, 52, 57.

26 Ibid., 59–61.

27 Ibid., 62–63.

28 Ibid., 67.

29 Melanesian Institute, "Your Kingdom Come," 190–93.

30 "Vanuatu, Nuclear Free Pacific Festival," March 14, 1981; Beverley Simmons to Vanuaaku Pati, July 17, 1980, Nuclear Free Pacific Issues, Including Correspondence, Miscellaneous 1971, 1974–1978, 1991–1996, Miscellaneous Loose Papers, 1971–1996, Box VP 004, Vanua'aku Pati Archives.

31 Nā Maka o ka 'Āina, *A Nuclear Free and Independent Pacific*, DVD, 1983.

32 PCRC Steering Committee, Nuclear Free and Independent Pacific Conference, 1983, Nuclear Free Pacific Issues, Including Correspondence, Box VP 004,
Vanua'aku Pati Archives.

33 "List of Papers Presented to the NFIPC/83 Conference Held in Vanuatu, July 10–20,
1983," Nuclear Free Pacific Issues, Box VP 004, Vanua'aku Pati Archives.

34 "French West Indies," NFIPC/83 Paper No 28, Nuclear Free Pacific Issues,
Box VP 004, Vanua'aku Pati Archives.

35 'Āina, *Nuclear Free and Independent Pacific*.

36 *Māori Peoples Liberation Movement of Aotearoa Newsletter*, January, February–
March, 1982, Nuclear Free Pacific Issues, Box VP 004, Vanua'aku Pati Archives.

37 "Nuclear Free and Independent Pacific Conference," NFP/1983, Resolutions 1–20,
Box VP 004, Vanua'aku Pati Archives.

38 Ibid.

39 'Āina, *Nuclear Free and Independent Pacific*.

40 Nuclear Free and Independent Pacific Conference, "VPCC—Report," July 1983,
Box VP 004, Vanua'aku Pati Archives.

41 VPCC Interim Steering Committee Meeting, Vanuatu, December 18–22, 1983, Box
VP 004, Vanua'aku Pati Archives.

42 "The Pacific Supports Blacks," *Aboriginal Islander Message* 26 (October 1981),
Australian Institute of Aboriginal and Torres Strait Islander Studies, Canberra,
Australia.

43 Paul Bérenger to Walter Lini, July 11, 1986, Vanua'ku Pati, Miscellaneous Papers,
1978–1991, Box VP 018, Miscellaneous Loose Papers, 1966–1995, Vanua'aku Pati
Archives.

44 Bennie Wynn, "Vanuatu's UN Mission Opens in Harlem," *Harlem Third World
Trade Winds* 5, no. 2 (May–June 1986); Sid Cassese, "A Hired Voice for Vanuatu,"
Vanuatu Articles on RFVL, Box 85, Van Lierop Papers.

45 Wynn, "Vanuatu's UN Mission."

46 Robert Van Lierop to Sethy Regenvanu, January 26, 1994, Box 85; Yann Céléné
Uregei to Robert Van Leirop, July 25, 1985, New Caledonia, Box 75, Van Lierop
Papers.

47 "Summary Record of the 12th Meeting, 4th Committee," October 13, 1987,
New York, General Assembly, 42nd session, A/C.4/42/SR.12, 8.

48 Ibid., 8–9.

49 Ibid.

50 Elizabeth Youngling, Jamie Arjona, Ofira Fuchs, Agnes Sohn, and Natalye
Tate, "Rereading the Archives: Uncovering Spaces of Feminist Engagement in
IWAC," *American Anthropologist* 114, no. 3 (September 2012): 521–23; Angela
Gilliam, International Women's Anthropology Conference, to Chairman of the
4th Committee, October 5, 1987, General Assembly, 42nd session. A/C.4/42/4/
Add.3; "Summary Record of the 14th Meeting: 4th Committee," October 16,
1987, New York, General Assembly, 42nd session, A/C.4/42/SR.14, 8–9.

51 "Summary Record of the 14th Meeting," October 16, 1987, 8–9.

52 Ibid., 9–11.

53 Ibid., 11–12.

54 Ibid., 13.

55 Gilliam, "Papua New Guinea," 282.

56 Jesse Jackson to Ambassador Tesfaye Tadesse, August 12, 1987; Jesse Jackson, "Independence and Self-Determination for the Territory of New Caledonia," statement, August 12, 1987, Box 75, Van Lierop Papers.

57 "Vanuatu: Still Caught in the Net of Big-Power Politics," *Wilson Center Reports*, March 1987, 4–5, Box 85, Van Lierop Papers.

58 Robert Troth, "US, Australia, Wary of Soviet's South Pacific Role," *Los Angeles Times*, February 22, 1987, 1; "Soviets Fish for Increased Influence in the South Pacific," *Hartford Courant*, February 22, 1987, A13, www.newspapers.com.

59 Arnold de Mille, "New Caledonia Fights for Right to Determine Its Own Independence," *Washington Afro American*, March 30, 1985, Box 75, Van Lierop Papers.

60 Walter Lini, statement to the 38th session of the United Nations, 1983, Miscellaneous Loose Papers and Other Items, Box VP 016, Vanua'aku Pati Archives.

61 Ibid.

62 Ibid.

63 "Address by Walter Lini to the United Nations," October 11, 1985, United Nations, Special Committee against Apartheid, 84.7, Box 84, Van Lierop Papers.

INDEX

Page numbers in *italics* indicate illustrations.

Black people," 129; and European
colonialization, 129; journal of, 72, 199;
manifestations of spirit of, 130; and
Naisseline, 204; and Nardals, 199; and
NBPG, 9; and RPG, 63–64, 66–67; and
Senghor, 9, 64–65, 72; at University of
Papua New Guinea, 68. *See also* Black
internationalism
"Negro Progress in Jamaica" (*Evening
Express* of Los Angeles), 27
Negro Worker, 32
Negro World, 29–30, 31
Nema Namba (Riyong), 133
Ness, Tigilau, 1
Netherlands: and Indonesia's
colonialization of West Papua, 61;
Pacific colonies, 50–51, 52, 54; and
West Papuan independence, 52
New Caledonia: basic facts about, 195–98;
as becoming "French Rhodesia,"
222; and Black Francophone world,
228; compared to Algeria, 228;
compared to South Africa, 254, 259,
260; Conference of the Last French
Colonies, 229–30; elections favoring
independence, 249; European
naming, 11; as French colony, 195;
French militarization of, 215; French
referendum on independence in, 258;
IF petitions to UN for decolonization
of, 223; independence movement,
46–48, *48*, 187, 199; mineral resources,
262; NFIP resolution supporting
movement for, 255; nuclear testing in,
181, 229; pro-independence Governing
Council, 225; racism in, 195, 196–98,
203; UN debate on independence,
258–60. *See also* entries beginning
with Kanaks
"New Caledonia: Confrontation to
Colonial Rule" (Yann Uregei), 228
New Guinea: African Americans during
World War II in, 33; compared to

South Africa, 31; CPA exploitation
of peoples of, 77; divided between
Netherlands, Germany, and Britain,
51; inhabitants as characterized by
Elisofon, 36–37; Japanese during
World War II, 53; as land of Stone Age
peoples, 42, 44; police violence against
Blacks, 31
New Guinea Writing, 113
New Hebridean Viewpoints, 180, 183, 199,
209, 214–15, 219, 223, 239, 244, 256
New Hebrides: British and French
joint colonial administration in,
22, 241; European naming, 11; and
Kamarakafego, 180, 193; and nuclear
testing, 181; protests in Paris, 209; and
PWRC, 191; women of, as described by
Europeans, 15. *See also* Vanuatu
New Hebrides National Party (NHNP):
"leftist professors" in, 171; and NFP
Conference, 178; Pacific as nuclear
free zone, 180; and PALIKA, 214; at
Presbyterian General Assembly, 245; at
6PAC, 245; training in Libya, 237; and
WCC, 247; Women's Wing, 189, 193.
See also Vanua'aku Party
New South Wales, 154–55
New York Agreement (1962), 58, 62
New York Times, 47
New York World, 31
New Zealand: as European name, 11;
and Libyan actions in Oceania, 236;
Polynesians in, 126; population, 2;
racism in, 126; Treaty of Waitangi, 17,
186. *See also* Māoris
Ngavirue, Zedekia Josef, 127
Nicholls, Doug, 78
Nilaidat (Our Voice), 97, 108–11, 112, 114,
124
Niugini. *See* Papua New Guinea
Niugini Arts Festivals, 127–28
Niugini Black Power, 97–98
"Niugini Black Power" (Hannett), 100–102

in, 66; inhabitants as incapable of independence, 42, 52, 58; inhabitants as part of "Negroid race," 55, 56; "internal self-determination" versus "external self-determination," 58; Japanese occupation, 51; Koreri movement, 51; as land of Stone Age peoples, 42, 52, 58; NAACP support for, 63–64; national anthem, 55; and Netherlands, 52; and NFIP, 255; Oceania's solidarity with, 66; PNC, 52, 53–56; protests (2019), 50; "Revolutionary Provisional Government of West Papua," 71, 72; and UN, 54, 55, 58, 61–62, 63. *See also* Provisional Government of West Papua New Guinea (RPG)

"West Papua Nationalism" (Rumakiek), 182

Which Way Big Man (Nora Brash), 160

White Pacific (Horne), 3

"White Racism: The New Zealand Experience" (Te Hemara), 127

"White Racism and White Violence" (Noonuccal), 82

Whites: at Adelaide Festival of Arts, 134; attitude toward Indigenous women, 118; Blacks' fear of, 6; as bringers of civilization, 22, 27; continued domination of, through Black agents, 101–2; cultural terrorism of, 103–4; as dehumanized by colonialism, 203; education systems of, 104, 107, 111–12, 136, 243–44; as masters after independence, 174; sexual availability of Indigenous women, 31; and UNESCO study of cultures of Oceania, 135, 139; women at UN World Conference on Women in Mexico City, 182–83. *See also* Europeans

Why We Can't Wait (King), 115

Wilkins, Roy, 63

Williams, Gary, 84

Williams, John (Apostle of Polynesia), 21

Williams, Marshall, 61

Winfeld, Paul, 94

"Woman Power: Myth or Reality" (Slatter), 172

women (Indigenous): absence of prostitution before arrival of Europeans, 118; blackbirding of, *18*; and Black internationalism, 193–94; considered sexually available by Whites, 12, 14, 15, 31; education of, 187–88; and environmental justice on Bougainville, 116; European attitude toward, 118; and FESTAC, 149, 153, 155, 156–57, 167; as having disastrous effect on men, 172; and Indonesian invasion and killings in East Timor, 122; as leaders in Foulards Rouges, 205; of Melanesia as described by Europeans, 15, 189; and New Caledonian independence, 259; of New Hebrides as described by Europeans, 15–16; and nuclear free Pacific, 254; Ogumola Mobile Theater, 151; opposition to nuclear testing by, 178; PWC, 169, 183–90, 210; PWRC, 190–93; racial attributes of, as seen by Europeans, 12; rape of, during World War II, 35; services of, of Rennell Islands as sold by chief, 40; *UNISPAC*, 172–73; as warriors against colonialization, 17; white patriarchal characterizations of, 36–38, 39; Women's Wing of NHNP, 189, 193. *See also* sexualization of Indigenous women; specific individuals; specific organizations

Women's Action Group (WAG), 66, 122

Women Speak Out, 191

Womsiwor, Herman, 53, 59, 62–63

Wonder, Stevie, 160

Woodson, Carter G., 28

ABOUT THE AUTHOR

QUITO SWAN is Professor of African American and African Diaspora Studies at Indiana University Bloomington. He specializes in the histories of Black internationalism, Black Power, and the Black Pacific. This is his third book.